Adventure Therapy:

Therapeutic Applications
of
Adventure Programming

Dr. Michael A. Gass

Association for Experiential Education

KENDALL/HUNT PUBLISHING COMPANY
4050 Westmark Drive   Dubuque, Iowa 52002

This edition has been printed on recycled paper.

Printed in the United States of America
10 9 8 7 6 5 4 3

ABOUT THE ASSOCIATION FOR EXPERIENTIAL EDUCATION

The Association for Experiential Education (AEE) is a not-for-profit, international, professional organization committed to furthering experiential-based teaching and learning in a culture that is increasingly "information-rich but experience-poor." By allowing the student, client, or customer to be involved in decisions about what they need to learn, and how they might go about learning, we believe life-long learning is the result.

AEE sponsors local, regional, and international conferences, projects, seminars, and institutes, and publishes the *Journal of Experiential Education*, the *Jobs Clearinghouse*, directories of programs and services, and a wide variety of books and periodicals to support educators, trainers, practitioners, students, and advocates.

AEE's diverse membership consists of individuals and organizations with affiliations in education, recreation, outdoor adventure programming, mental health, youth service, physical education, management development training, corrections, programming for people with disabilities, and environmental education.

To receive additional information about the Association for Experiential Education, call or write to:

AEE
2885 Aurora Avenue #28
Boulder, CO USA 80303-2252
(303) 440-8844
(303) 440-9581 (fax)

ABOUT THE THERAPEUTIC ADVENTURE PROFESSIONAL GROUP (TAPG)

Therapeutic Adventure is the professional group for those AEE members who use experiential education therapeutically within the fields of health, mental health, corrections, education, and other human service fields. Our primary mission is the networking of professionals within our various fields and the sharing of information, techniques, and concerns regarding the therapeutic use of experiential education. We define therapeutic as moving toward healthy change. Additionally we seek to represent the interests of our membership to the Board and larger professional communities through: newsletters, publications, articles, workshops, and pre-conference activities.

The Therapeutic Adventure Professional Group is committed to the development and promotion of experiential education in therapeutic settings. We are also committed to the professional development of our members and the profession as a whole.

ACKNOWLEDGEMENTS

Success is a journey and not a destination.

When I began this project in 1987, I felt that I had a pretty good idea of what was happening with the use of adventure experiences with so-called "therapeutic populations." Little did I know what it meant to be entering into a writing project in an area that was undergoing an incredible level of transformation. As this project began to unfold, I quickly realized that it would be impossible (if not inappropriate) for one person to write a text of such breadth, given the rapid developments in the field.

One of the motivations for me to keep writing and editing this enormous project was the multitude of questions I kept receiving from both novice and established professionals implementing or conducting adventure therapy. I took a sabbatical leave from my position at the University of New Hampshire in 1990-91 to work on this project and for the AEE Office in Boulder, Colorado. During this time I became even more aware of the large number of professionals seeking information on such programs, often with little guidance on what "worked" and what didn't. This project is meant to provide the best of what is currently available for interested professionals.

This project has been supported by a large number of people and the greatest tragedy of this book is that I'm bound to forget some of the important people who contributed to it in its 5-year process. One of the most important people in this effort has been Timmy Comstedt. Our joint editing process served as a means to provide clarity and consistency in the text and a great deal of credit for the book's completion is due to her persistence and ability to read the book's chapters and still raise a child. Marla Riley, from the International AEE Office, has been an important source of pulling a number of logistics together and is to be commended for her efforts in working with the Publisher. Dan Garvey and Babs Baker have been Executive Directors for the AEE during the book's evolution, and Dan's friendship and impetus to begin and take on the project and Babs' encouragement to finish it were important sources of support. Tracy Webster and Christine Tsimekles have typed things into the computer for me when my fingers were unable to continue in an organized manner and I am grateful.

Foremost in creating the substance of this text are the authors. All of them have contributed their time, thoughts, and energy to place their insights down on paper in the truest spirit of service and professionalism. All of the profits generated from this text are going directly to the

Association for Experiential Education in an unrestricted manner. The influence of their work is inspiring. Nowhere in our field are the ideas and insights of such a wide range of professionals found as they are in this book. The process of choosing what would be included in the book was a very selective process and my gratitude also goes to those individuals who contributed pieces that we just weren't able to include due to space limitations.

The reviewers in the selection process provided an important vehicle to ensure that the most prominent pieces of work in the field were selected in a fair and equitable manner. These individuals included Cindy Clapp, Craig Dobkin, Brian Farragher, J. T. Fields, Jackie Gerstein, Nancy Gilliam, H. L. (Lee) Gillis, Kim Goody, Pam McPhee, Relly Nadler, Colleen O'Brien, Simon Priest, Chris Roland, Sue Rudolph, Tom Smith, Sue Tippett, and Betsy Webb. Their input provided feedback to each writer and validated the process by ensuring the level of quality found in this text.

I would also like to thank my colleagues who have contributed to my own professional growth. Craig Dobkin has greatly enhanced my ability to think in a creative and innovative manner. Ron Croce, Pam McPhee, and my other colleagues at the University of New Hampshire have provided invaluable insights into my work. Lee Gillis and Simon Priest have pushed me to write more clearly and purposefully. Rebecca Howard has been of great assistance in helping me to organize myself in a chaotic world. Emerging professionals (e.g., the Taco Salad Group) continue to confirm my belief about the progressive development of the field.

Most importantly, I would like to thank my family for all of their support. Cristina, Tony, and Amaryth provide those things that are most important to me on this earth. I hope that I always keep their love in its truest perspective.

Dr. Michael A. Gass

Note that several names, pictures, and diagrams are included throughout the text to highlight critical concepts. All names from case examples have been changed to protect client anonymity. All pictures included in the text are staff, students, or other professionals not involved in a therapeutic process.

DEDICATION

This book is dedicated to Cristina Dolcino for helping me with the faith, love, and laughter to keep my life in perspective;

to those professionals in the field who invest their creative energies into populations who need their services the most;

and to all children, for they are our most valuable resource.

FOREWORD

COOKING WITH GASS

by H. L. (Lee) Gillis, Ph.D.

Adventure therapy professionals come in a variety of flavors. I have found that they can range from the highly spiced advocates of extended-day wilderness experiences to the seasoned "inpatient" adventure therapist, one thinking of extended wilderness experiences as the only true way to bring about changes in a client population while the other believes that one-hour initiative experiences are the best thing to hit psychotherapy since sliced bread. No doubt seasoned veterans have seen arguments get hot among professionals when therapeutic adventure experiences are questioned, or when practitioners from different training backgrounds begin to discuss who is most ethically and professionally qualified to conduct adventure therapy. Even researchers can become embroiled when trying to compare the effects of programs that appear to be as different as apples and oranges, but are using the same language, citing similar sources, and making the same claims. What is called for now and is delivered in this book are the basic ingredients to help to clarify several fundamental questions from within and outside adventure therapy.

The primary questions examined throughout this book are:

- What is adventure therapy?
- Is adventure therapy a set of techniques that any therapist can add to their files and use whenever indicated?
- Is the field evolving into a process unto itself, so different from traditional psychotherapy that it may become recognized as a "fifth force" for behavior change, along with psychoanalysis, behaviorism, human existentialism, and family systems theory?
- If we are a "fifth force" of sorts, what are some of the basic ingredients of the field and what are some suggestions of ways to successfully combine them with other therapies?
- What is the information base that will provide necessary information for novices as well as advanced advocates?

Note that this book is not intended to be a cookbook; rather its strength lies in its ability to present the ingredients of the field for professionals, as well as a strong rationale to evaluate if their interventions and programs will be successful. This book establishes a common set of information that can help us to more clearly delineate what it is that we do—both to our colleagues and our critics. This book also allows programs to have a common set of readings that their staff can use in training, allowing them to understand the ingredients that help to explain how and why adventure therapy works. It assists existing programs in becoming more effective through adding strategic components that other practitioners have found to be successful. Lastly, it helps all of us to define if we are a profession of adventure therapists or psychotherapists who use adventure/challenge techniques.

I believe that most adventure therapy practitioners would agree that the use of adventure challenge components in a therapeutic program changes the flavor of psychotherapy. We are not clear, however, on whether this change is enhanced by using a metaphor to frame an adventure activity or wilderness experience. Nor do we know which activities and debriefing methods work best and with which populations. This book offers several articles for practitioners to understand how to use the "right" activity, design an appropriate metaphor, and debrief in a meaningful way. My hope is that the articles contained in this book will help to answer the many questions among new and seasoned "adventure therapists" as well as colleagues unfamiliar with these approaches.

Each of these questions points to the need for a culinary artist like Mike Gass to make sense of the table currently spread before us. He has brought together several great "cooks" who don't spoil the broth, but instead give the field of adventure therapy—its proponents and critics—much food for thought. Such a menu has the potential to energize the field and allow us to "live long and prosper."

ADVENTURE THERAPY:
THERAPEUTIC APPLICATIONS
OF ADVENTURE PROGRAMMING

Section 3—Programming of Adventure Therapy Experiences

Section 4—Processing of Adventure Therapy Experiences

Section 5—Research of Adventure Therapy Programs

Section 6—The Future of Adventure Therapy

SECTION 1

THE OVERVIEW AND THEORY OF ADVENTURE THERAPY

Craig Dobkin

1

FOUNDATIONS OF ADVENTURE THERAPY

MICHAEL A. GASS, Ph.D.

"How can dangling off a cliff be therapeutically relevant?"

"These patients need to be in a group working on their issues, not outside playing on a ropes course!"

"This client is too 'sick' to leave the hospital grounds to go climb a mountain!"

These are the kinds of statements commonly made by mental health professionals when they first encounter the approaches and concept of adventure therapy. Sometimes the most difficult part in implementing adventure therapy programs, whether they are based in the wilderness or at a mental health facility, is to present cogent arguments for the use of adventure therapy in providing and enhancing treatment. The purpose of this section of the book is to: 1) outline the interaction of experiential learning and adventure therapy, 2) provide a general rationale for using adventure experiences as therapeutic processes, and 3) introduce the three following articles that present separate but related viewpoints of the effectiveness of adventure therapy programs.

THE INTERACTION OF EXPERIENTIAL LEARNING AND ADVENTURE THERAPY

While the area of adventure therapy has developed as a discrete addition to the mental health field, many of the origins, principles, and philosophies of adventure therapy are founded in the field of experiential education. Before a rationale of adventure-based therapy is presented, a general overview of experiential learning is provided to illustrate the connection between these two disciplines.

Definition of Experiential Learning

Most experiential learning programs are founded on the belief that learning or behavior change must focus on including *direct experience* in processes of growth (AEE, 1991; Dewey, 1938). All change has some form of experience as a base for its origin, but experiential learning asks that the learner be placed as close as possible to that base of origin because this process is often more valuable for the transmission of knowledge than other forms of learning.

Given this perspective, experiential learning often requires problem solving, curiosity, and inquiry of the learner (Kraft & Sakofs, 1985). It is sometimes loosely defined as "learning by doing combined with reflection." It is an active rather than passive process, requiring the learner to be self-motivated and responsible for learning and the "teacher" to be responsible *to*, and not *for*, the learner (King, 1988).

Experiential learning is also predicated on the belief that change occurs when people are placed outside of positions of comfort (e.g., homeostasis, acquiescence) and into states of dissonance. In these states, participants are challenged by the adaptations necessary to reach equilibrium. Reaching these self-directed states necessitates change with its resultant growth and learning. Several elements inherent in this process include (Kraft & Sakofs, 1985):

1. The learner is a participant rather than a spectator in learning.
2. The learning activities require personal motivation in the form of energy, involvement, and responsibility.
3. The learning activity is real and meaningful in terms of natural consequences for the learner.
4. Reflection is a critical element of the learning process.
5. Learning must have present as well as future relevance for the learner and the society in which he/she is a member.

It is important to note that experiential education is not a product of learning but a learning process that should be implemented under appropriate circumstances.

4

Application of Experiential Learning to Adventure Therapy

Given the above definition, one can understand the application of such principles to therapy. Like experiential learning, adventure therapy focuses on placing clients in activities that challenge dysfunctional behaviors and reward functional change. Reworking the principles outlined by Kraft and Sakofs (1985), one can observe how this might occur (the adaptations are underlined):

1. The client becomes a participant rather than a spectator in therapy.
2. Therapeutic activities require client motivation in the form of energy, involvement, and responsibility.
3. Therapeutic activities are real and meaningful in terms of natural consequences for the client.
4. Reflection is a critical element of the therapeutic process.
5. Functional change must have present as well as future relevance for clients and their society.

RATIONALE FOR USING ADVENTURE EXPERIENCES AS THERAPEUTIC PROCESSES

While there is more than one accepted method of conducting adventure-based therapy (e.g., Roland, Keene, Dubois, & Lentini, 1989; Schoel, Prouty, & Radcliffe, 1988), there are several critical components that seem to serve as a foundation for most well-established adventure therapy programs. These principles provide a rationale as well as a theoretical framework for conducting adventure experiences for therapy. It is important to note that in most cases, adventure therapy is not used to replace other therapeutic interventions and practices; instead, it is used to enhance established treatment objectives and to provide a richer therapeutic environment for change so that therapy is more successful.

The rationale for using adventure experiences to enhance therapeutic assessment and treatment has been well documented (e.g., Gillis & Bonney, 1986; Kimball, 1983; Kirkpatrick, 1983; Mason, 1987). The seven areas included in this rationale that provide the basis for most adventure therapy programs in North America are:

1) **Action-centered therapy**—One advantage of using adventure experiences with clients is that it turns passive therapeutic analysis and interaction into active and multidimensional experiences. Didactic and

verbal processes, which are the central medium of interaction in most "talking" therapies, are augmented in adventure programs by concrete physical actions and experiences. Clients' behaviors are viewed from another perspective; they are asked to "walk" rather than merely "talk" their behaviors. Therapeutic interaction becomes observed and holistic, involving physical and affective as well as cognitive interaction for the purposes of examining client patterns and beliefs.

Action-centered therapies also heighten the amount of non-verbal interaction between clients (Gillis & Bonney, 1986), allowing a greater examination of how clients truly interact. Mason (1987) has also pointed out that in a therapeutic context, non-verbal communication is five times more believable than verbal communication. This adds to the increased validity of client interaction and the resulting beneficial change. This enriched perspective provides therapists with a multidimensional perspective of client interaction for generating positive change based on observed behavior.

2) **Unfamiliar environment**—As individuals enter into therapy, they often possess a strong resistance to treatment and change (e.g., homeostasis). One of the goals of adventure experiences is to take participants out of familiar environments and immerse them in situations that are new and unique.

Doing this enhances therapy because it provides an environment where clients possess few expectations or preconceived notions about their success. It creates a non-risk atmosphere for clients to explore problems rather than be overwhelmed or incapacitated by them. Both of these qualities tend to limit self-destructive behaviors (e.g., dysfunctional behavior when interacting with others) and free intellectual and emotional energies for adaptation and change.

Another benefit of an unfamiliar environment is that it is simplified and straightforward, presenting clear problems for participants to address (Walsh & Golins, 1976). This simplification often limits the side-issues or external stressors that complicate many of the problems confronting individuals.

A third benefit is that the unfamiliar environment provides an environment that is contrasting to a client's current reality state. As stated by Walsh and Golins (1976):

> Contrast is used to see generality which tends to be overlooked by human beings in a familiar environment or to gain a new perspective on the old, contrasting environment from which the learner comes. The learner's entry into a contrasting environment is the first step towards reorganizing the meaning and direction of his [sic] experience. (p. 4)

It is important to remember that what is unfamiliar for one person may not be for another. Therapists using adventure environments must ensure that the quality of unfamiliarity is met to achieve the goals of this concept.

3) **Climate of change**—Although passive and action-centered therapies are useful, they hold little motivation for clients to change when dysfunctional patterns can be maintained by clients in therapy. When properly implemented, adventure experiences introduce "eustress," or the healthy use of stress, into the client's system in a healthy and manageable yet challenging manner (Selye, 1978).

This type of stress places individuals into situations where the use of certain positive problem-solving abilities (e.g., trust, cooperation, clear and healthy communication) is necessary to reach a desired state of equilibrium. The process of striving to attain this state of equilibrium is sometimes referred to as "adaptive dissonance" (e.g., Walsh & Golins, 1976), where clients must change their behaviors to achieve states of desired attainment. The adaptive processes used to create change become healthy and functional processes for rectifying the client's dysfunctional behavior patterns.

It is also important to recognize that adventure experiences provide an inherent level of motivation based on clear consequences for inappropriate behaviors. Such consequences are not arbitrary or evaluative, but true and neutral representations of the results of client processes and behavior. From this type of feedback, clients are presented with vivid and accurate representations of positive as well as negative behaviors. A client's interpretation of these concrete and resulting behaviors provides a powerful medium for interpretation and a valuable climate for changing dysfunctional behaviors with the assistance of the therapist.

4) **Assessment capabilities**—Much of the material used for constructing change is obtained from the actions of clients as they involve themselves in adventure experiences. Kimball (1983) and Creal and Florio (1986) relate this process to the psychological theory of "projection." Based on this premise, clients project a clear representation of their behavior patterns, personalities, structure, and interpretation on to the adventure activities because of the unfamiliarity and ambiguity of the client's previous experience with the situation. As outlined by Kimball (1983):

> Like the well-known Rorschach ink blots, wilderness challenges are high in ambiguity. The client must interpret or structure the task demands as well as his/her own response to it. The challenges of the wilderness expedition offer great latitude in response. The greater the latitude and the higher the stress, the more likely the client will "project" unique and individual personality aspects into the "test" situation.

By careful observation of the client's responses to a multitude of 'diagnostic' situations—rock climbing, route-finding, water rationing—the skilled mental health counselor identifies life-long behavior patterns, dysfunctional ways of coping with stress, intellectual processes, conflicts, needs and emotional responsiveness. When properly observed, recorded, and articulated, this data can be the basis for long term therapeutic goals. (p. 7)

The material obtained from initial adventure experiences becomes extremely valuable for planning treatment interventions and strategies. It is particularly helpful in the construction of metaphors and the designing of future adventure experiences to produce therapeutic change.

5) **Small-group development/Genuine community**—The use of small-group development in adventure activities is a critical factor for behavioral change (e.g., Kerr & Gass, 1987). Activities are usually structured so that conflict will arise when stressful situations are encountered but will be resolved with positive group interaction (Walsh & Golins, 1976). Individual desires must be met, but they must be accomplished within the needs of the group. A true systemic perspective is taken as group members struggle with individual and group needs.

6) **Focus on successful rather than dysfunctional behaviors**—As stated earlier, dysfunctional clients often carry their symptoms and failures with them when they begin therapy. Entering therapy can be extremely threatening, heightening defense mechanisms and resistance to change. In unfamiliar adventure environments, clients are presented with opportunities to focus on their abilities rather than on their dysfunctions. This type of orientation diminishes initial defenses and leads to healthy change when combined with the successful completion of progressively difficult and rewarding tasks. Rather than being resistant in therapy, clients are challenged to stretch perceived limitations and discover untapped resources and strengths. Client efforts are also framed by the therapist to center on the potential to achieve self-empowerment by establishing and maintaining functional interventions.

7) **Changes in role of therapist**—Adventure activities also create several changes in the dynamics between therapists and their clients, for instance, the change from a passive role as therapist to an active role. Therapists are encouraged to actively design and frame adventure experiences around critical issues for clients, focusing on the development of specific treatment outcomes.

Adventure therapists do more than offer a variety of activities for enjoyment, they use these activities as the medium for change. Using adventure activities in this manner has obvious correlation to therapy. As

8

recommended by Gillis and Bonney (1986), adventure therapy should frame the physical involvement of such activities around specific psychological and behavioral issues, focusing on changing dysfunctional behavior patterns by using an active, directive, and problem-solving method.

Another change in client/therapist dynamics is the placement of therapists in an approachable position with clients. During shared adventure experiences, therapists have the opportunity to be involved in similar physical challenges. These dynamics, combined with the informal setting of the adventure experiences, can remove many of the barriers limiting interaction that may exist in other more "formal" therapies. While still maintaining clear and appropriate boundaries, therapists become more approachable and achieve greater interaction with clients.

CURRENT AREAS OF USE WITH ADVENTURE THERAPY

It is interesting to note that use of adventure therapy has evolved into three general areas of implementation. These areas are:

1) **Wilderness therapy**—here the therapeutic experience occurs in remote wilderness settings and tends to consist of small-group (8–15), multiple-day (e.g., 24 days), round-the-clock intervention. Unless clients "drop out" of these programs, the members of the group remain the same throughout the entire therapeutic experience. Because of the distance clients often have to travel to participate in this type of program, the therapy is limited to this one intensive experience, and follow-up contact with therapy is often limited. Outward Bound and adapted Outward Bound programs (e.g., Santa Fe Mountain Center) were the primary innovators of this type of therapeutic programming.

2) **Adventure-based therapy**—here the therapeutic experience occurs at or very close to the therapeutic facility of the client (in fact, many times clients of adventure-based therapy tend to be restricted to the grounds of the facility for insurance requirements). These programs tend to be in-patient programs where patients are in multiple-day treatment programs, and adventure therapy is only one part of the therapeutic intervention being used. Because clients are admitted and discharged at different times, these therapeutic groups can change in number and membership quite regularly. The adventure experiences that are used tend to be "contrived" (i.e., the physical structures used for conducting the adventure experience tend to be constructed by adventure programmers specifically for the adventure therapy experience. Some examples of this

include portable initiatives, low and high ropes course elements, and indoor rock-climbing walls.). While such programs possess the same origin as wilderness therapy programs with Outward Bound, their expansion can be linked to a number of programs like Project Adventure (see Schoel, Prouty, & Radcliffe, 1988).

3) **Long-term residential camping**—based on the values inherent in wilderness camping (e.g., Loughmiller, 1965), this form of outdoor programming focuses on placing adolescents or other adjudicated populations into outdoor camps (e.g., Eckerd Foundation Camps, Salesmanship Clubs) or on mobile travel units (e.g., wagon trains, sail training on clipper ships) to produce functional client change. These programs often place clients in these settings for long periods of time (e.g., one year). Clients are often responsible for providing basic life needs through their own efforts in preparing food, constructing primitive shelters for living quarters (e.g., lean-to wood or tarp shelters), and learning the skills necessary for survival in challenging environments (e.g., fire building, sail training). Much of the inherent value of such programming in these types of settings is seen to extend from the value of developing a positive peer culture, confronting the problems encountered with day-to-day living, and dealing with existing natural consequences.

These three areas represent the majority of adventure therapy programs in North America. They generally share many of the same characteristics, although, as seen later in the chapter written by Nancy Gilliam, there are some critical differences.

The following three chapters in this section of the book expand on the rationale for using adventure experiences to enhance therapy. In the first chapter, Stephen Bacon and Rocky Kimball, two of the central figures in the development of adventure therapy in the 1980s, have combined much of their recent as well as previous writings into an article focusing on the assumptions, strength, and content of wilderness therapy. Both authors draw on their knowledge and experience in working with clients in wilderness-based therapy programs. The variables inherent in wilderness therapy that they outline currently represent much of the present thinking in the field of adventure therapy.

The second article focuses on the healing to be found in wilderness. John Miles does a wonderful job of outlining specific ways that the wilderness serves as a natural medium for therapy.

The final article represents a clinical picture of the adventure therapy process. Relly Nadler has taken many of the initial foundations of adventure programming (e.g., Walsh & Golins, 1976) and integrated these concepts with much of the current thinking about the therapeutic process of change (e.g., White & Epston, 1990; O'Hanlon, 1990).

2

THE WILDERNESS CHALLENGE MODEL[1]

RICHARD O. KIMBALL, Ph.D.
STEPHEN B. BACON, Ph.D.

Introduction

Michael has a problem; he is over 15 feet off the ground. Although he is tied into a rope by a belayer above him, Michael is scared. The rock that offered so many footholds at the beginning of the climb is becoming smoother and steeper. Michael has been ascending the rock by jamming his feet into cracks and footholds.

Only one foot is wedged in now. It hurts. The foot supports all his weight; the weighted leg twitches spasmodically. His other foot skitters aimlessly and frantically over the rock face in search of purchase. His fingers, which tightly grip the chalky sandstone, begin to sweat, turning the chalk into a thin, slippery film of mud.

Michael looks up. The top of the climb is guarded by an intimidating bulge of rock. If he wants to make it to the top, he has a choice. He can either muscle over the bulge or circumvent it entirely by climbing out and onto the face.

Some choice. He imagines himself falling. Michael, a 15-year-old who is in trouble with the law and at school, begins to cry. His peers, who have either climbed the rock or are about to, cheer him on. His instructors, who have trekked with Michael in the wilds for a week, exhort him to succeed.

Michael inches up, tears streaking his dusty face. Occasionally relying on a taut rope from his belayer, Michael manages the bulge. Over the lip, unclipping the rope, he whoops triumphantly and slaps his seated belayer on the shoulder in appreciation. He turns to gaze out at the vista below him.

Blood trickles down from a small gash on a knee; he wonders when he cut it. He did not feel it. His knuckles are chaffed white by the rock;

his palms are pitted and coarse like sandpaper. He feels good. He feels complete. He feels heroic. (Golins, 1980)

This kind of dramatic experience often characterizes an emerging form of adolescent residential treatment: wilderness therapy. Where did wilderness therapy come from? What is it really? What are important factors that determine its success or failure? And what does the empirical literature have to say about its outcomes? This chapter will attempt to answer these questions.

WILDERNESS THERAPY

Wilderness therapy is primarily derived from Outward Bound, a wilderness challenge program founded by the innovative German educator Kurt Hahn. Hahn was one of the foremost pioneers of experiential education—of "learning by doing." He first put his ideas into practice at the Salem School, an institution established in the 1920s in Germany. However, Hahn's liberal and progressive thinking soon ran afoul of Adolf Hitler's administration and, after a period of imprisonment, he was deported to England in 1933.

Hahn's commitment to experiential learning and intellectual freedom was matched by an equally fervent commitment to a fairly traditional set of personal values. He defined those values as follows: "The foremost task of education is to ensure the survival of these qualities: an indefatigable spirit, tenacity in pursuit, readiness for sensible self-denial, and, above all, compassion" (Richards, 1981).

At this point, Hahn was faced with a dilemma: how could one educate children in a way that would ensure the survival of these qualities, the adoption of prosocial values, without turning his school into an indoctrination center that would destroy his students' intellectual freedom? His solution is succinctly described in one of his best known quotes: "We believe it is the sin of the soul to force the young into opinions, but we consider it culpable neglect not to impel every youngster into health-giving experiences—regardless of their inclinations" (Richards, 1981, p. 43).

Hahn proceeded to create an academic environment where students were thrust into experiences that were conducive to the natural and spontaneous emergence of prosocial values. Students were not to adopt a code of ethics "on faith" or through compulsion; rather, they would independently discover the validity and utility of such a code through experience. In searching for such situations, Hahn found that two categories of experience were particularly conducive to values formation:

wilderness training and rescue training. With some adaptation, these two types of experiences continue to dominate the curriculum of both Outward Bound and wilderness therapy programs.

In summary, the Hahnian approach to education was not only experience-centered, it was also value-centered. "Learning through doing" was not developed to facilitate primarily the mastery of academic content or intellectual skills; rather, it was oriented toward the development of character and maturity. In this sense, Hahn's ideas were perhaps better suited to a psychological model of change than an educational one.

Hahn's essential premise—that certain experiences could spontaneously call forth prosocial values—formed the basis of the Outward Bound program. Established in 1942, its original purpose was to help young British seamen to survive the rigors of sailing the North Atlantic during World War II. The Outward Bound training program not only met those goals, its effectiveness was such that it gradually captured the hearts and minds of western educators. Since 1945, Outward Bound has spread to five continents and includes 46 schools.

Outward Bound arrived in the United States in 1962. It was welcomed warmly and five Outward Bound schools were soon established. Even more significantly, literally hundreds of programs using some aspect of the Outward Bound approach came into existence in the 1960s. By the 1970s, the number of replicators was in the thousands and still climbing. By the 1980s, the adventure-based education model had become so pervasive that it was rare to find a community where there was no access to some kind of wilderness challenge program. Increasingly, schools, colleges, youth services, hospitals, recreation centers, social service agencies, and vocational programs were making them available.

Outward Bound and the independent replicators of the Outward Bound process began to work with clinical populations in the early and mid-1960s. Since Outward Bound's primary target population was adolescents, it is not surprising that wilderness therapy was first applied to troubled and/or adjudicated teens. As early as the mid-1960s, Outward Bound established relationships with and special programs for organizations such as the Job Corps, inner-city youth programs, state training schools, group homes, and residential treatment centers. In the 1970s and 1980s, this list was expanded as Outward Bound and the other wilderness challenge programs worked with a broader list of adolescent populations, including substance abusers, the developmentally disabled, rape and incest victims, sexual abuse perpetrators, psychiatric patients, at-risk teens, and so forth. At present, some wilderness therapy program has been used with almost every type of adolescent clinical population.

THE CONTENT OF WILDERNESS THERAPY PROGRAMS

There is such a wide variety of organizations and programs employing some form of wilderness therapy that it is difficult to define the process precisely. However, there are some activities and processes that do characterize the approach.

First of all, wilderness therapy is a group process; there is no such thing as "individual" wilderness therapy. The adolescents, who are commonly referred to as "students," experience the wilderness challenge program in a small-group context. The group usually ranges in size from 6 to 14 people.

The program or course curriculum usually consists of a series of challenges which incrementally increase in difficulty. The challenges tend to be designed so that mastery requires the group to persevere, to be creative, to apply skills, and to rely on each other. Often the challenges are structured so that they appear to be insurmountable or dangerous. In reality, this is only a perception; usually the tasks are quite resolvable and all of the activities are designed to be safe. The essential idea is to present challenges that are high in perceived risk but low in actual risk. An example of such a challenge is the rock climb where the novice feels tremendously exposed even though he/she is tied in firmly to a safety line. While most of the challenges are offered to the group, the program may also include some individual challenges such as a long-distance run.

As the name implies, wilderness therapy programs are almost always conducted in the wilderness. However, the need is not so much for wilderness as it is for an unfamiliar environment. Hence, wilderness therapy courses have sometimes been conducted in the "wilderness" of an unfamiliar urban environment. Similarly, while many of the challenges are adventure-oriented, such as mountaineering or sailing, students are also asked to master human service-oriented challenges such as working with developmentally delayed people or the homeless.

Wilderness therapy programs tend to spend a great deal of time helping students to understand the meaning and relevance of their wilderness experiences. To this end, they employ therapy techniques, time alone for reflection and journal writing, psycho-educational techniques, individual counseling, staff modeling, and self-disclosure. Partially because of its roots in the Outward Bound movement and partially because of adolescent development needs, wilderness therapy tends to be value-centered; that is, it tends to explicitly or implicitly move students toward prosocial values such as selflessness and the acceptance of personal responsibility.

The length of a wilderness therapy experience varies widely depending on funding availability, type of population served, identification as a primary or adjunctive treatment modality, and so forth. Some programs are only a day-long experience while other programs last for months or even a year. With the exception of one-day programs, wilderness therapy tends to offer round-the-clock programming; indeed, some adherents feel that total immersion in the wilderness milieu is necessary to achieve maximum impact.

At the conclusion of a wilderness therapy program, students tend to be strongly bonded with their group; they also have a feeling of personal empowerment and a sense that others can be trusted. Increased self-knowledge is often reported, as are alterations in one's sense of values. It is common for students to resolve to change certain aspects of their lifestyles and habit patterns. The combination of these cognitions and emotions forms a dramatic peak experience.

Wilderness therapy is an intensive, time-limited process. Although there are exceptions, follow-up to such programs is generally done by community agencies or professionals who have not been involved directly with the wilderness therapy process, except in a referring capacity. Only a few wilderness therapy programs have the ability to offer a long-term, community-based program. In the rare case where some form of follow-up is offered, it generally consists of brief (one- or two-day-long) gatherings that concentrate on re-experiencing some form of wilderness challenge.

It is increasingly common to involve other family members in a wilderness therapy program. Most frequently this involvement consists of a discussion with the parents of the child's wilderness experience, but it is not unusual to find wilderness therapy programs offering parent-skills training classes and family therapy.

In order to illustrate the points above with a concrete example, a month-long wilderness therapy program will be outlined. A typical program might include the following experiences:

1) *Precourse*: Respond to inquiries with written materials. Screen out inappropriate candidates via phone or personal interviews. Consult with referring professionals when appropriate.

2) *Day 1*: Parents bring their teens to a wilderness setting for the course beginning. After a brief, educational meeting, the parents leave and the adolescents are introduced to the purpose and rules of the program. Small groups are formed, the students undergo some warm-up and introduction activities, and equipment is issued.

3) *Days 2-7*: Students embark on a backpacking expedition into the mountains. They learn First Aid, basic cooking, camping, and orienteering skills, and they take turns at being appointed "leader for the day." Some

high-impact activities—such as rock climbing and a peak ascent—are performed. The group discusses their individual and collective responses to each activity during frequent group meetings. Each student has several individual sessions with one of the staff members.

4) *Days 8-15*: The students switch to the whitewater portion of their program and learn basic river-running skills. Group and individual therapy sessions continue. The staff members are able to custom design the activities and challenges to meet the specific needs of the students on the course. The staff tend to be less directive and less skill-oriented; the students assume more responsibility for mastering the wilderness challenges.

5) *Days 16-19*: The students spend 3 days alone in the wilderness with their journals and a small amount of food. During this period, they engage in a variety of exercises designed to promote reflection and self-knowledge. In many cases, the solo time also includes regular individual therapy with a staff member.

6) *Days 20-22*: The students return to the mountains where they are given a final challenge: travel for 3 days through demanding terrain with no assistance from the staff members. This expedition tests whether students have assimilated the lessons of teamwork, personal responsibility, problem solving, and so on.

7) *Days 23-24*: The course ends with an individual challenge—a marathon run—and a celebration to mark the completion of the program. The parents attend the course-end celebration, are briefed on the events of the past month, and receive some parent-skills training classes to ensure that they can follow up on the positive alterations in their children's behaviors.

In summary, in spite of wide variation across wilderness therapy programs, there are some important common themes. These include the use of the small-group format, the opportunity to master demanding challenges, immersion in an unfamiliar environment, a focus on understanding the meaning of the program activities, and an emphasis on creating an environment which implicitly supports prosocial values. Most often, these techniques succeed in engaging the students and generate some form of life-affirming peak experience, an experience that often results in a resolve to alter one's life choices in a positive direction.

SOCIOLOGICAL ASSUMPTIONS

Kurt Hahn was fond of saying that modern youths suffer from "the misery of unimportance." He believed that adolescents who felt that they were needed would naturally manifest motivation and responsible behavior. Conversely, the unneeded teenager would behave in a variety of inappropriate ways.

Hahn's argument that adolescents are ignored by and alienated from the modern western world seems to be even more true in 1987 than it was in Hahn's day. Adolescents find themselves at the onset of puberty facing a vast array of challenges and opportunities; however, they are frequently deficient in many of the basic life skills, such as self-confidence, self-discipline, judgment, and responsibility, which are necessary to prosocially manipulate the world around them.

Adherents of wilderness therapy believe that the western world lacks significant roles for adolescents. They have no important tasks, no significant duties. Instead of being initiated into adulthood by being given increasingly higher levels of responsibility and authority, teenagers receive a level of recognition which only barely supersedes that of young children.

Sociologist James S. Coleman (1974) of the University of Chicago contrasts that modern urban lifestyle with the essentially rural/small town lifestyle of 100 years ago. In those more simple times, children grew up with capabilities because much of their experience involved significance, meaning, purpose, and relevance. They were important to the economic survival of the family unit.

The population of 100 years ago was primarily rural and had limited access to media information. Without radios, televisions, satellite communications, and computers, the community and the family unit remained relatively unchanged from generation to generation. The home and school, in partnership, had the job of passing on the attitudes, values, and behavioral skills necessary for successful living. It was a lifestyle in which young people were significant. It was a lifestyle where young people were prepared for adulthood by a clear and concrete set of experiences, expectations, and challenges.

Adolescents often worked 10 hours a day alongside one or both parents. Young people received on-the-job training for adulthood as they watched their parents perform essential tasks, make important decisions, and exercise judgment. At an early age, children became participants, rather than merely observers, in the world of work. Milking cows, cutting fence posts, weeding fields, gathering eggs, and chopping fire wood were typical tasks performed by children. Successful performance of these tasks was essential if the family wished to function smoothly; there were significant natural consequences if the duties were neglected.

Living in an extended family offered important opportunities for inter-generational dialogue, collaboration, and tradition. Grandparents, parents, and children worked, played, were born, and even died in the presence of one another. The family nourished basic trust and effectively passed on skills, attitudes, and values from one generation to the next.

The modern society that Hahn observed had recently left the rural/small town lifestyle behind. By the end of World War II, thousands of families had moved away from the networks of the extended family and the stability of rural life. Between 1935 and 1950, incredible social changes took place. In 1935, 70% of the population lived in a rural/small town (Glenn, 1987). Between 1935 and 1950, according to the U.S. Census, 70% of Americans lived in an urban environment. Urbanization virtually eliminated the likelihood that children would work for any significant time in direct contact with their parents.

By 1986, the average American family was uprooted every 2½ years and members often knew very little about their neighbors and relatives (Glenn, 1987). Thirty percent of all children under 6 years of age lived with just one parent or no parent at all (Glenn, 1987). In the rare instances of a two-parent family, frequently both parents worked and time for meaningful dialogue and collaboration within the family unit was virtually nonexistent.

In the earlier, primarily rural lifestyle, children learned life skills every day because they were needed to help the family to function and survive. In the urban, post-World War II settings, children are not needed to ensure the day-to-day functioning of the family. They spend most of their time in passive situations—both at home and at school.

While adulthood and responsibility have been postponed, schooling has been extended. However, this schooling seems to breed dependency rather than development of life skills. Most school practices complicate the transformation from a child to an adult that ideally culminates in a consolidation of identity with a readiness for the transition to adulthood. The search for identity requires youths to develop autonomy, initiative, and industry, resulting in perceptions of competence and self-worth. Unfortunately, school is a brutally conforming and demanding institution that teaches compliance rather than development of learning skills.

Today's secondary education system is a teacher-intensive model: the teacher prepares the lessons, explains, lectures, and entertains. Too often, adolescents are taught to passively regurgitate what the teacher has given them. With diminished opportunity for meaningful direct experiences, isolated from the opportunity to collaborate and dialogue with adults at both home and school, and bombarded by the debilitating effect of the media, adolescents are denied experiences that might help them to learn the skills of independent living.

The deterioration of the institutions previously responsible for inculcating norms and values—churches, schools, and the family—has left a void that is now primarily filled by the media. By the time children enter school, they will have spent more hours watching television than they will spend in the classroom during 4 years of college (Novak, 1976). By the age of 14, the average child will have witnessed on TV the destruction of more than 12,000 people (Novak, 1976). A recent government report investigating the effects of media on youth asked:

> How many instances are there of a constructive intervention to end disagreement? What other instances of tact and decency could an avid televiewer chronicle during the same hour? How often is reconciliation dramatized? What strategies for ameliorating hate are displayed? How many times does the child viewer see behavior in loving and helpful ways? What examples of mutual respect does he [sic] view? What can be learned about law and order? How many episodes of police kindness does he [sic] see? How frequently does the glow of compassion illuminate the screen? (Siegal, 1969, p. 279)

In conclusion, youths today are born into a society that is information-rich but experience-poor, where family-unit bonds are attenuated and stressed, where schooling further isolates children from meaningful challenges and direct participation in society, and where the media often model destructive, anti-social values. It is no wonder that we now reap the fruits of this maladaptive strategy: youth violence, crime, and anomie.

Juxtaposed to these societal trends, Outward Bound and its derivative, wilderness therapy, can be seen as educational processes where adolescents are initiated into the prosocial values that form the basis of western culture. Operating from this value-centered perspective, wilderness therapy approaches adolescents not as character disorders, substance abusers, or victims, but rather, as individuals who have not had the opportunity to develop a strong set of prosocial values. Given exposure to the proper experience, they will develop self-worth, personal responsibility, and a sense of connection to society and others.

VARIABLES THAT CONTRIBUTE TO TREATMENT EFFICACY, SUCCESS, MASTERY, AND PERSONAL EMPOWERMENT

Wilderness therapy, by design, is a frontal assault on learned helplessness, dependency, and feelings of low self-worth. Through performance-based success and mastery, adolescents are able to discover previously untapped inner resources. Wilderness therapy cultivates perceptions of capability, potency, and significance. These perceptual changes are the key to behavioral, motivational, and emotional changes in troubled youths.

These outcomes are made possible through an incremental problem-solving process. Students are given skills and resources and then introduced to demanding challenges that require the utmost in individual effort and cooperation, often in a stressful context. The problems appear to be insurmountable or dangerous; however, in reality, they are structured so that success and mastery are not only possible, but probable. Success builds upon success. Small successes early in the course lay the foundation for larger successes in the later stages. Even small changes, when they occur in the crucial area of perception, have the potential to ultimately transform a student's entire personality system.

The attention of outside observers is quickly drawn to the dramatic nature of the activities which characterize wilderness adventure. Personal empowerment, however, does not automatically result from the dramatic component of the activity; rather it arises from the way such problems are structured. Walsh and Golins (1976) identified six characteristics of the problem-solving tasks.

The first is that the problems are planned, prescribed, and managed. They are designed by the staff to fit the needs and capabilities of the learner.

Second, the problems are structured incrementally so that skills development parallels the graduated difficulty of the tasks. Confidence is developed through successive achievements and accumulated skills.

Third, the problems are concrete. Success and failure stand out in bold relief. The tasks have a beginning and a clear ending.

Fourth, the problems are manageable. While they can be solved, success is not guaranteed. When a student cannot simply dismiss a problem as impossible and yet when the problem's successful resolution is uncertain, maximum motivation is achieved.

Fifth, the problems offer real consequences. Success or failure is readily apparent. Feedback to the learner is immediate. Because the outcomes are consequential, the individual and the group learn to assume responsibility for their actions and choices.

Finally, the tasks are holistic. Problem resolution requires the students to draw upon the full complement of their physical, emotional, and cognitive resources. For example, to climb a mountain one must cognitively plan the route, develop the necessary emotional commitment to attempt the challenge, and succeed at the physical task.

The intentional use of stress is central to the change process of wilderness therapy. Stress is often magnified by the students' tendencies to exaggerate the level of risk inherent in adventurous activities. Certainly rock climbing, rappelling on vertical cliffs, exploring deep caves, and traversing steep snowfields entail some genuine danger; however, these potential risks can be managed much more simply than the novice imagines. Regardless, students often feel as if they are in a genuinely life-threatening situation.

The resulting anxiety sets the stage for a potentially transformational experience. When failure-oriented adolescents summon the courage, discipline, and resolve to master a difficult challenge, they have challenged their self-definition as well. Interpreted metaphorically, either consciously or unconsciously, mastery experiences set the stage for new psychological perceptions.

The successful resolution of anxiety and the mastery of a challenge that appeared beyond one's capabilities result in an increased sense of self-worth and potency. Self-efficacy Theory (Bandura, 1977) suggests that when performance accomplishments are perceived to be of great magnitude, they tend to broadly generalize to other situations.

As described above, mastery experiences are frequently dramatic and come in sudden, triumphant moments. One should not underestimate, however, the power of the more mundane. For youths whose "reality" has always appeared hopelessly complex and perhaps out of control, the isolation and simplicity of the outdoors helps to bring them back to basics and into a more manageable world. Hiking 7-12 miles a day, accepting responsibility for the chores of daily living, and successfully managing oneself emotionally—these activities also shake up and reorganize what had previously constituted reality.

In the final analysis, wilderness therapy seeks to snap adolescents out of self-defeating attitudes and perceptions and to replace anomie, cynicism, and alienation with feelings of empowerment, perseverance, and confidence.

Community

Group process lies at the core of wilderness therapy. Because personality is formed and shaped largely through our contact and involvement with others, it can be reshaped through this same intimate contact. Wilderness therapy is living together, not just carrying out a program. Fulfilling physical needs, healing, personal growth, and even physical triumphs are experienced in relation to, and with the support of, others.

The group process frames all decisions that affect the group. It is a way of life, not just a therapeutic tool. The group decides what needs to be done and carries out their decision. Guided group discussion is used to settle problems, to give individuals feedback, and to evaluate performances. When an adolescent has a problem, it is dealt with in the immediate context and with the help of the group. All the group members are affected, and therefore all have a stake in the resolution of the problem. It is through the repeated use of this group process that adolescents develop the greatest insight into their own behavior.

The attainment of personal comfort and security in the wilderness requires a cooperative community framework and effective group dynamics. These requirements provide opportunities for the adolescent to help and to be helped. This sense of mutual dependence and trust is therapeutic for most youths. Adolescents need to feel that what they do affects others—that they matter and that their existence is significant. In the wilderness, even individuals who may never have felt important to others discover that the group depends upon them.

A small group of 8-10 youths offers an opportunity for the evolution of a genuine community. Cooking, map reading, water conservation, river crossings, camp site selection, and countless other problems demand cooperation and the use of each individual's strengths. A system of exchange eventually evolves: one person might be a good route finder, another an excellent cook, a third demonstrates leadership under adverse circumstances. The group learns to maximize one person's strength and minimize another's weakness. The adolescents learn that the power of a supportive group is greater than the sum of its individual resources. This realization establishes the therapeutic milieu.

The group develops cohesiveness as members struggle against the daily challenges of a hard hike, a climb, and the capricious nature of the weather. With the support and power of the group, individuals push back preconceived psychological barriers and discover hidden resources and new limits. Occasionally, a genuine emergency—a sprained ankle or an imminent electrical storm—may bring the group even closer. Once again, the reality of truly being needed impels adolescents into working cooperatively as a team.

Group cohesion results in an atmosphere that promotes honest emotional expression and sharing. Every night, the group members discuss the day's successes and failures and resolve problems so that the next day will go more smoothly. Group counseling sessions become extremely candid after weeks of building trust. Although the group learns that anger, frustration, fear, and anxiety are universal human feelings, acts of kindness, friendship, and compassion become the norm.

There is a strong desire in adolescents to experience family, community, and in-depth relationships. Opportunities to contribute to others are important. These opportunities are rare in modern society, but they abound in the context of wilderness adventure. The resulting sense of family fulfills a critical developmental need. With the group providing a necessary safety net, the troubled adolescent is prepared to take on the seemingly impossible tasks and emotional demands of the wilderness. Likewise, the group provides the security and supportive atmosphere for adolescents to develop insight into their behavior.

Emphasis on action

One of the primary attractions of wilderness therapy is its emphasis on concrete actions and experiences. Particularly in the 1960s, before behaviorism had become quite so popular, adolescent treatment was dominated by the psychodynamic approach and its emphasis on the verbal process. Unfortunately, this verbal process was not very effective when the participants (i.e., the adolescents) were not highly motivated. One comment which typified that period, and remains true today, was offered by Francis J. Kelly (1974), a corrections expert and an early advocate of Outward Bound-type programs for troubled youths:

> In addition, the de-emphasis on language skills present in [troubled youths'] cultural milieu together with an inferior educational experience produce adolescents who prefer a motoric rather than a conceptual expression of conflict [resolution]. Their deficiency in language skills contributed to the failure of the extant and traditional "talk therapies" in vogue during the decades of the 1950s and 1960s. During this period adolescents were committed to the youth authority, subjected to individual and group psychotherapy, primarily introspective and insight oriented, offered a modicum of vocational training (the majority for jobs which did not exist), housed for 9–10

months, and returned to the community. If it was a "good" program they were no better, unfortunately in most instances they were much worse when they arrived.... To summarize this brief background: [during this period]...there was great dissatisfaction with existing programs attempting to meet the needs of acting-out adolescent delinquents who, due to their motoric preference for conflict resolution and lack of language skills, fail to profit from the traditional, cognitively-oriented treatment approaches. (p. 2)

Conversely, wilderness therapy attempts to meet youths "on their own turf" in the world of action, rather than forcing them to use the chosen modality of adults: verbal expression. This choice leads to reduced resistance, a quickened ability to build rapport, and more genuine engagement in the program.

However, experience alone is of little value; there must be some way to structure the experience so that it is useful to adolescents. The key concept is to expose youths to a sense of order or law in the natural and the social worlds. As discussed above in the sections on sociological background, wilderness therapy is implicitly based on the assumption that a primary cause of emotional and behavioral disturbances in youth is the lack of a significant relationship with the social and the natural worlds. It is assumed that reestablishing that relationship will result in an increase in maturity and other therapeutic changes.

In wilderness therapy, reestablishing this relationship is sometimes called "letting the mountains speak for themselves." During a wilderness challenge program, the experiences are structured to facilitate a direct dialogue between the adolescent and the wilderness. Living and traveling in the outdoors provide an opportunity to learn from nonhuman forces: weather, distance, amount of food, and so on. If natural laws are transgressed, those same forces will administer the consequences. Adults, the normal source of consequences and authority, play a relatively minor role.

In addition to this direct dialogue with the wilderness, the programs are designed so that teens also experience natural social laws. Because most of the challenges and wilderness activities require sincere effort and a spirit of cooperation and interdependence, students who lack these prosocial attitudes are quickly exposed. Self-centeredness on the part of an individual has a significant impact on the group. For example, if one student is unwilling to carry his/her share of the group equipment, another student must endure a greater load. If a certain student in a canoe is unwilling to cooperate with his/her partner, that canoe will not travel in a straight line. The partner is directly affected, and all the other canoes in the group are affected indirectly because they must slow down or stop. This not only provides a graphic and concrete example of inappropriate behavior, it also motivates the peer group to offer constructive feedback. This motivational side effect is an important benefit for a group of troubled youths, most of whom are generally hesitant to criticize peer behaviors regardless of their inappropriateness.

In summary, it can be argued that many apparently self-centered, uncooperative, irresponsible, or even pathological behaviors will be minimized or eliminated if adolescents are exposed to direct feedback from the natural world and their peers. The key to this success is to implement the wilderness therapy approach in concert with the developmental process. The adult is removed from the authority role, supplanted by the wilderness and the group. The teen has no developmental need to resist the natural world; hence, prosocial behaviors are achieved with relatively little effort even from the most resistant adolescents.

Finally, there is the concept that high-impact adventure experiences have a natural appeal to youths who are in a stage of life where they are drawn to such activities because of their innate thrill. This attraction to excitement is compelling and vital; it should not be dismissed as a simple interest in being stimulated by "adrenalin rushes." Passing through a rigorous challenge can provide a profound sense of "I exist" or "I can affect the world." Such an existential affirmation can be extremely helpful to adolescents in their quest for a stable and meaningful self-image.

In summary, wilderness therapy is oriented toward action and experience as opposed to verbal processing and cognitive analysis. It can be argued that this approach has several advantages over a more traditional model. First, it is a better fit for adolescents who prefer action over expression. Second, it allows adolescents to be exposed to natural consequences in a way that is relatively unmediated by adult authority figures. Finally, it appeals to the natural adolescent attraction to exciting activities.

Wilderness environment

The wilderness environment is radically different from a typical therapeutic environment such as a residential treatment center or a clinic. This has profound implications for an adolescent's ability to respond positively to therapeutic programming. In most circumstances, the factors that make this difference are therapeutically beneficial; one could even argue that wilderness provides an ideal setting for clinical work with adolescents.

One of the first results of living in the wilderness is that life becomes simplified. Many of the elements that might distract an adolescent from therapeutic programming are removed. For example, the absence of technology instantly eliminates adolescents' opportunities to repress feelings by distracting themselves with television or music. Convenience stores, provocative advertising, and all of the "booming and buzzing" stimuli endemic to modern life are absent.

As we have noted, one of the most well-known advantages of programming in the wilderness is that of "natural consequences," the concept that consequences are administered by nature and not by adult authority figures. It is difficult for a resistant teen to discount feedback or consequences by claiming that the rules or the staff are "unfair" or inappropriate. For example, adolescents whose gear becomes soaked because they did not pay attention to the tarp-pitching lesson have a difficult time ignoring both the wetness of their sleeping bag and the fact of their responsibility for their predicament.

Being in the wilderness also facilitates the breaking down of inappropriate defenses and denial. The level of physical and social stress and the pressure to succeed at concrete tasks tend to minimize an adolescent's ability to maintain a false front. It is difficult to hide one's true feelings when one is wet or hungry and almost impossible to repress an emotion when one learns that it is necessary to hike three more miles before making camp.

Although the wilderness environment provides a great deal of pressure and intensity, it also offers a rare opportunity for individual freedom, especially the freedom to experiment with new psychological strategies or a fresh sense of identity. Of course, such opportunities are available in any novel environment, including a treatment center or clinic. However, in the wilderness, this kind of healthy identity formation is enhanced by a number of other factors.

First, the environment is so novel, the lifestyle so different, the mundane world so far away that the teen is impelled into a kind of "altered state of consciousness." This state is implicitly conducive to detaching oneself from the past and to letting go of unproductive personality strategies.

Second, as described in greater detail above, the adolescent enjoys a series of success and mastery experiences. The resulting enhancement of self-esteem is conducive to experimenting with new roles in life.

Finally, the adolescent is repeatedly exposed to positive models. Not only do the staff and peers serve in this capacity, even more significantly, the outdoor tasks tend to cast the youths themselves into a heroic role— perhaps for the first time in their lives. Memories of their accomplishments and feelings at certain moments in the wilderness allow the creation of an internalized heroic model. Clearly, the presence of this kind of internal model is the highest and most stable form of modeling.

In addition to its own innate positive effects, the wilderness environment also acts to multiply the power of other techniques—such as psychotherapy or social skills training classes—that have been developed for use in the traditional clinical milieu. A variety of factors contribute to this potentiating effect. The ability to break down defenses while in the wilderness has already been discussed in detail above; an adolescent quickly becomes available to the therapeutic process in the outdoors. In addition, the tangibility of the activities provides an opportunity to experiment with new life-skills and graphically measure success or failure. Moreover, the supportive, small-group atmosphere promotes trust, rapport building, and risk taking. Finally, the overall wilderness setting is conducive to a feeling of renewal and revitalization. In summary, a wilderness challenge program provides an enormously supportive context for the practice of extant psychological methods.

Although it is difficult to define the construct precisely, most people who have participated in wilderness therapy programs agree that there is an aesthetic, or archetypal, or even spiritual/transcendent aspect to the environment. Bacon (1983) argued that students unconsciously equate the wilderness environment with an archetype that Jungians sometimes call "Sacred Space":

> The power of archetype is such that human beings are unconsciously prepared to recognize a concrete manifestation of the archetypal pattern when they encounter it in the world. According to Jung, the archetypes are literally stamped into the human unconsciousness. They are prepared to see wilderness as Sacred Space as a bird is prepared to fly south for the winter.
>
> The usefulness to Outward Bound of wilderness as Sacred Space is that this archetype is inextricably linked with the concept of transformation and change. Seeing the wilderness as Sacred Space means that the student has implicitly accepted the possibility—or even the probability—that some kind of powerful transformation may occur. This expectation of empowerment can exist in spite of any limitations from his [sic] past because Sacred Space transformations are magical and undeserved.
>
> In reality, of course, there are some restrictions on the power of the archetypes. But there is little question that certain course experiences do invoke the presence of one or more of these primordial patterns and that the alert instructor can capitalize on their existence for the students' benefit. In so doing, he

*exposes students to much more than his own teaching abilities
or the students' own personal strengths. The students covertly
participate in age-old patterns of human development. Anyone
who has taught an Outward Bound course is aware that the
spirit of a course often seems to move beyond the capabilities
of the human beings involved in it. (pp. 53–54)*

The Outward Bound literature has periodically (e.g., Shore, 1976) discussed this "spiritual/transcendent" element in the context of comparing a wilderness challenge program to a "rite of passage." This comparison is particularly useful to wilderness therapy because of the implicit therapeutic power of a rite of passage. To understand this power, it is important to understand some of the ways in which a rite of passage differs from a therapeutic program. A therapeutic program operates in a linear manner; that is, the more of it one has, the stronger the effect. For example, the more one diets, the slimmer one becomes; the more one exercises, the stronger one becomes.

Conversely, a rite of passage is neither linear nor able to be quantified. If one experiences a true or legitimate rite of passage, then one is transformed. The length and substance of the rite is unimportant; the degree or duration of the personal transformation is not dependent on such "mundane" matters. Rather, one is elevated suddenly, and somewhat mysteriously, from one state of personhood to another. For example, in an aboriginal rite of passage, the youth becomes an "instant" adult. At the beginning of the ceremony, he is a boy, with a boy's responsibilities and privileges, and afterwards, he is a man. There is a social agreement, a contract between the boy and his community, that grants him a new station in life.

However, the primary power of the ceremony does not lie solely in its generation of a new social contract; the ceremony is greatly effective because of its enormous psychological power. Given a legitimate ceremony and an appropriate candidate, there will be a sudden, profound, positive transformation of the boy's psyche. To achieve this level of transformation so quickly and so deeply is no small psychological accomplishment. One could even argue that it surpasses the efficacy of modern methods of psychological transformation!

Of course, wilderness challenge programs cannot promise to achieve such dramatic and successful outcomes with every student. Yet there are hundreds of anecdotes describing results that approach the effectiveness and power of traditional rites of passage. It seems highly probable that the spiritual/archetypal aspects of wilderness therapy programs play a strong role in these sorts of transformations.

Transfer of learning

The novelty of the wilderness environment can facilitate growth and positive development in adolescents, but it can also be problematic in that it can interfere with the ability to transfer program learnings. The profound differences between wilderness and the home environment often inhibit generalization. This gives rise to the danger that the wilderness program will result in nothing more than a powerful peak experience—a temporary high—that has few lasting benefits.

Recognizing this potential dilemma, wilderness therapists have paid particular attention to the issues of transference and generalization. To understand these efforts, it is important to begin by reviewing one of the basic assumptions underlying wilderness therapy: the behaviors, feelings, and cognitions manifested in the wilderness are representative of the typical strategies employed by adolescents in their home environment. The microcosm of the wilderness program recapitulates the macrocosm of daily life.

This is neither a new nor a surprising concept; group and individual therapists have advanced similar arguments for decades. They suggest that "transference" in individual therapy or the clients' behaviors during group therapy represent unresolved issues from their daily life. However, it is important to reassert this point in the wilderness context because the environment and activities are so different from mundane life that certain responses emitted in the wilderness may appear specific to that environment. For example, one could propose that a student's anxiety about rock climbing signifies a simple fear of heights and not a general hesitation to take risks. Another teen's resistance to performing camp tasks might reflect a dislike of primitive living conditions and not a general lack of cooperation.

Certainly there are situations in which these kinds of responses do occur and, in such cases, the behaviors have little or no general meaning. Nevertheless, wilderness therapists believe that these responses are the exception rather than the rule. Although they occur occasionally, it is far more common to discover that the adolescent's responses fall into a pattern and that the pattern is meaningful and important.

The basic assumption described above gives rise to a similar but opposite assumption: the changes in psychosocial functioning that occur in the wilderness will automatically transfer to the home. While it is tempting to accept this assumption because of its simplicity, the experience of wilderness therapists (e.g., Bacon, 1983; Shore, 1976) suggests that it is only true in isolated cases. This difficulty in achieving "automatic transference" occurs for a variety of reasons, namely, the radical differences between the two environments, the presence of a different set of rewards and punishments for each, and so on. In summary, most wilderness therapy students need some kind of structured assistance to transfer course learnings back to their home environment.

In some instances, however, a profound transfer of the wilderness learnings seems to occur with little attention from the staff. Bacon (1983) suggests that this occurs fortuitously and idiosyncratically because some students spontaneously link their wilderness experiences with their daily life. The wilderness experiences become metaphors for challenges in their home environment.

> This is a critical point: ...in profoundly isomorphic metaphors, the student will be living two realities simultaneously.... In literal reality, he will be having an Outward Bound course experience; in psychological reality, he will be having both the course experience and the correspondent real-life experience. The mechanism of the transderivational search ties the two experiences together so tightly that one cannot be separated from the other.
>
> The concept of simultaneously living two realities is of course an ideal. In practice, the metaphor is never perfectly isomorphic with the real-life situation; even psychologically speaking, the metaphoric and real-life experiences do not perfectly merge. But there is no question that in well-formed metaphors there will be profound and meaningful links with isomorphic real-life experiences. People who have had a metaphoric experience in which the outcome has been successfully altered will have reorganized their typical life strategy. (pp. 9-10)

This theory provides an explanation for why some students achieve spontaneous and profound levels of transference; nonetheless, it does not indicate what might be done for the students who see little connection between their wilderness activities and their daily lives. For these teens, a day spent canoeing is simply that: a day paddling around on a river. And a rock climb is merely a gymnastic exercise that occurs on a cliff. The students' behaviors in these situations may actually be analogous to their life behaviors—a large potential for learning may exist—but this connection does not occur spontaneously. To gain something significant from their wilderness experiences, these adolescents need further guidance.

The most common way to work with these students is to apply the techniques of group and individual therapy. The adolescents are asked to reflect on their behaviors and understand the implications of those behaviors in terms of their daily lives. Particular attention is given to using the confrontations, feedback, and support of peers. Goal-setting and contracting techniques are also frequently employed, both for getting teens to commit to improving target behaviors while in the wilderness and for establishing expectations about what should be transferred back to the home life. In summary, the same therapeutic techniques that have been developed to help people achieve insight into the meaning and implications of their typical behaviors and psychological functioning can be used to help them discover the purpose and usefulness of their outdoor experiences.

Harmon and Templin (1978) believe that the traditional individual and group therapy techniques, approaches that emphasize verbal ability, can be complemented by the social learning model of Alfred Bandura. To this end, they suggest that transference be further facilitated by the use of the following techniques: participant modeling, performance desensitization, performance exposure, live modeling, and symbolic modeling. Using these techniques in conjunction with the psychotherapeutic techniques described above helps most students to find meaning in their wilderness experiences and contributes to their ability to transfer wilderness learnings to their daily life.

So far, we have seen that some students appear to connect spontaneously with the metaphoric nature of the wilderness activities. For those who do not, there are group and individual therapy techniques and the social learning approach to help them to recognize how their behaviors in the wilderness can be analogous to their daily life behaviors. There is another approach to facilitating transference that operates by introducing the wilderness events in a special way, a way that increases the probability that students will achieve a spontaneous metaphoric connection in the midst of their wilderness experience. This approach attempts to increase the number of adolescents who achieve transference because of their ability to make metaphoric connections.

To attain this outcome, a wilderness challenge is framed in a way that helps the adolescent to recognize the connection between it and a significant issue in their daily lives. For example, an important developmental challenge for teens is the ability to move from a childlike, self-centered stance to a position that endorses values such as compassion and interdependence. To facilitate a metaphoric experience in this area, the staff might decide to include a physically demanding day in the program, perhaps a long hike with heavy packs. Without an introduction to such a hike, it is likely that most students would view the day as an endurance test. If the students are limited to this viewpoint, it is probable that the stress implicit in the day will result in heroic endurance, interpersonal isolation, and a fragmenting of the group into subgroups of quarreling individuals.

However, such a day could be introduced differently; for example, it could be framed as a special opportunity to develop compassion for others and as a chance to find out whether this group can stick together and help each other under stress. If the staff provides an elegant introduction—one that is free from moralism and inspires the students—it is probable that the students will experience the hike as a metaphor for interdependence, healthy social functioning, and compassion. More specifically, they will make a metaphoric connection between their course experience and the developmental challenge described above: the need to achieve recognition of the values of compassion and human connectedness. Best of all, the students will have learned this lesson experientially and spontaneously; there will be little need to use therapeutic techniques to point out the analogies during the post-hike discussion.

In summary, because of the profound differences in the characteristics of the wilderness and the home environment, transference is one of the most significant issues in wilderness therapy. Transference-enhancing strategies can be divided into three types: 1) **spontaneous metaphoric transference**: the student spontaneously and independently discovers important connections between the wilderness experience and his daily life; 2) **analogous transference**: verbal therapy and social learning techniques are employed to help a student retrospectively understand the importance of his/her experiences; and 3) **structured metaphoric transference**: the staff frame the experience in such a way that the probability of the spontaneous discovery of metaphors is increased. All three of these approaches are useful, and all three are frequently employed in wilderness therapy programs. Although the heuristic metaphoric approaches are a bit more compelling, the analogous transference techniques are vitally important in work with troubled youths who are prone to miss or resist the more subtle metaphoric techniques.

The Instructor/Therapist

The wilderness therapist faces a demanding, multifaceted job. To properly care for the physical safety of the group, the adult leader must have sufficient technical wilderness skills, judgment, and personal experience. Because of the lengthy curriculum of outdoor skills, the leader must also be an effective teacher. Most importantly, as a therapist, the leader has the critical responsibility of helping youths to understand the profound implications of their course experiences.

At a time when adult-adolescent dialogue and collaboration are becoming increasingly rare, the level of personal contact between the wilderness therapist and his group of teenagers is rich with opportunity. Therapists—seen as instructors or counselors by the students—eat the same food, carry the same weight in their packs, encounter the same obstacles, and endure the same weather conditions as their younger counterparts. This closeness builds rapport, trust, and openness while minimizing a sense of a counter-therapeutic hierarchy.

By virtue of their experience and technical outdoor skills, instructors are the leaders of the group. This authority is a natural one rather than an arbitrary entitlement. The instructor is comfortable and at home in the wilderness; the students are in a foreign environment. They are off of their familiar turf. At the course outset, students do not know how to light the stoves in order to cook; they cannot read the maps; they cannot provide their own shelter; and finally, they are socially disoriented in terms of peer roles and expectations. Like newborn infants, they are dependent and experience a need for adult support.

In the early stages of the program, staff are quite directive as they teach the basic survival skills. After several days of skill development and directive leadership, the staff begin to minimize their formal leadership and to empower the group. Adolescents are often asked to serve as "leader for the day," a role with real power and responsibility. The group begins to make more and more of the important decisions. Because they are habituated to adults operating from an authoritarian stance, this paradigm shift frequently surprises and confuses troubled youths. However, as they successfully experience autonomy and independence, they begin to enjoy their newfound freedom, responsibility, and authority.

Psychologically healthy adolescents have adult role models. These people are, in some sense, their heroes. They study their heroes and strive to be like them. For troubled youths, the wilderness leader often takes on mythic proportions as hero, guide, and exemplar. By encouraging autonomy, by treating students with respect, and by listening to them, the wilderness staff become powerful modeling influences. In the idealized scenario, the wilderness counselor models qualities of effective adulthood.

In the role of therapeutic guides, staff members must act as translators between the student and the teachable moments of the course. They have a crucial responsibility for helping youths to see the daily-life implications of their wilderness experience. They help to translate the symbols and metaphors that abound.

Finally, the staff are orchestrators. The pulse, rhythm, intensity, and depth of the experience is largely engineered by the staff. Self-discovery and personal growth require the direction of a highly skilled and sensitive therapist who knows when the group is ready for stress and how much it can handle. This orchestration requires the staff to monitor and anticipate the reactions of each individual. There is only a small difference between tension that is creative and growth-oriented and tension that is defeating.

In the final analysis, the quality and effectiveness of the wilderness therapy modality are dependent on a rare hybrid of staff skills and roles. To be successful, programs must perceive their staff as therapists first and as outdoor instructors second. The means (the wilderness) must remain secondary to the ends (the therapeutic outcome). Nevertheless, because of the superordinate issue of safety, the technical proficiency of the staff cannot be compromised. The scarcity of staff with such a peculiar combination of specializations remains a significant problem in the proliferation and replication of wilderness therapy programs.

Potentialities Rather Than Pathologies

Most adolescent treatment programs have a partial or full allegiance to the perspective that adolescent misbehavior is caused by psychopathology. In other words, they believe that the patient suffers from a mental illness. Adherents of this perspective place a great emphasis on the obstacles that keep a child from succeeding in life. For example, this approach spends much therapeutic time discussing anger problems, impulse control difficulties, and emotional deficiencies. Current behavioral problems are explained by the presence of past traumas with their concomitant scars. There is a strong and ever-present focus on the negative and the problematic.

Because the psychopathology orientation has had a record of treatment successes, it has spawned dozens of fascinating theoretical paradigms. This orientation may be the most appropriate treatment approach in certain instances, but wilderness therapy has chosen to focus instead on the strengths, capabilities, and potential of the individual. Even the label given to adolescents in wilderness challenge programs, "students," emphasizes their capacities as learners. Whereas most traditional treatment programs define the teenager as sick and dependent, in the wilderness the therapeutic journey is largely one of self-discovery and autonomy.

Wilderness therapists assume that a combination of belief in the student and the opportunity to master a genuine and meaningful challenge will result in behaviors that are surprisingly healthy—behaviors that vastly exceed the expectations one might have of a "mentally ill" adolescent. Such value-forming experiences are seen as more therapeutic than analysis. Rather than using "talking therapies" to change attitudes in order to modify behavior, wilderness therapy assumes that attitudinal changes and perceptions of self-worth best follow provocative experiences that dramatically reveal psychological strengths and capabilities.

Fundamental to wilderness therapy is the development of self-efficacy or empowerment; it offers the adolescent the opportunity to do things differently and to break lifelong patterns of failure. By contrast, the mental illness model frequently identifies defects such as low self-esteem but offers few practical strategies for change.

Adventure and challenge give youths the chance to write themselves a new life-script. The activities—extended backcountry travel into remote wilderness areas, rock climbing and rappelling, mountaineering, whitewater rafting—are opportunities to challenge one's self-image. Rather than "substance abusers," "run aways," "drop-outs," or "borderlines," all students have the opportunity to re-label themselves as successful, competent, capable, and, perhaps, even heroic people. "Rise to the occasion," "Go for it," and "You can do it," become the new vocabulary and the basis for new perceptions of psychological strengths.

The danger in this approach is that too much will be asked of a truly dysfunctional student. Wilderness therapy attempts to mitigate this risk by precourse screening for severe pathology and by prescriptive programming—that is, appropriately matching the student to the length, intensity, and difficulty of the wilderness challenge. Of course, that does not entirely eliminate the possibility that some severely disturbed adolescents will slip through the screening/monitoring process and subsequently fail to gain much from the wilderness challenge. That is an acceptable risk, given the positive benefits of the nonpathological stance. In the final analysis, wilderness therapy embraces the risks, rewards, and possibilities inherent in a potential-oriented perspective.

SPECIAL OPPORTUNITIES FOR ASSESSMENT

Counselors and therapists who work with troubled youths in a wilderness program quickly come to appreciate the diagnostic opportunities inherent in the modality. Like a Rorschach test, wilderness challenges are high in ambiguity. The demands of a 3-week expedition into the wilderness are unpredictable. Everything from group dynamics to the weather is capricious and requires adaptability. Although expectations are structured and made clear, a whole universe of responses is possible. The greater the latitude of response and the higher the stress level, the more likely that students will project their personalities into the "test" situation.

Even more than in an institutional setting like a hospital or correctional institution, there seems to be no way that students can fake their way through an extended wilderness experience. Eventually, controlled behaviors and emotions give way to spontaneous reactions. Personalities and psychodynamics emerge in sharp focus.

By careful observation of the student's responses in provocative situations, the skilled mental health counselor identifies lifelong behavioral patterns, dysfunctional ways of coping with stress, intellectual processes, conflict, defense systems, and emotional responsiveness. When properly observed, recorded, and articulated, this data can become the basis for establishing long-term therapeutic goals.

Wilderness therapy presents the opportunity for another type of assessment; it allows one to determine if treatment has actually effected new behaviors and attitudes. A common concern in residential treatment is the scenario of adolescents who succeed in conforming to institutional limits but who regress to pretreatment levels of negativity when operating in the relative freedom of their home environment. The comparatively open environment of a wilderness therapy program serves as a litmus test for this type of adolescent because it requires more than mere conformity for success. Adolescents must make choices, take risks, and expose themselves to the consequences of their actions. This level of existential choice is highly similar to the freedom of the home environment. Hence, success in the wilderness is predictive of success in one's daily life.

RESEARCH

As mentioned above, there have been wilderness therapy courses offered in the United States for over 20 years. From the inception of these courses, staff, students, parents, and involved professionals have reported dramatic results: positive changes in attitudes and behaviors that last over time. Based on these reports, literally hundreds of private and public school systems, social service agencies, treatment programs, and wilderness centers included an Outward Bound component in their curriculum. As time passed, both Outward Bound and the independent organizations using Outward Bound approaches felt a need to research and substantiate anecdotal reports. The purpose of this section is to review and summarize some of those empirical studies.

Self-Confidence

Not surprisingly, the construct that has received the most examination in the adolescent wilderness therapy literature is self-confidence. A series of empirical studies have found that wilderness therapy significantly enhances the self-concept of troubled youths (Adams, 1970; Collingwood, 1972; Cytrynbaum & Ken, 1975; Gaston, 1978; Gibson, 1981; Marsh & Richards, 1985; Porter, 1975; Project Apollo, 1976; Svobodny, 1979; Walkabout, 1980; and Wright, 1982).

"Locus of Control" is a construct that is correlated with self-confidence. An internal locus of control means that these individuals believe that their choices and behaviors make a difference; they have power and control over what happens to their lives. An external locus of control refers to a belief that one's life is ruled by fate, social authorities, accidents of birth, etc., and that one's efforts and choices make little difference. Three studies—Collingwood (1972), Gaston (1978), and Wright (1982)—discovered that wilderness therapy facilitates the sense of an internal locus of control in emotionally disturbed youths.

In addition to self-esteem and locus of control, several studies have looked at other constructs related to self-concept. For example, Adams (1970) found improved ego strength and increased levels of self-reliance, and Natches and Roberts (1967) discovered that troubled youths were more assertive after a wilderness course. Both Schroeder and Lee (1967) and Freeman, Spilka, and Mason (1968) documented improvements in achievement motivation. Finally, Porter (1975) found a decrease in general anxiety levels.

Interpersonal Competence

Many child experts have argued that troubled youths have deficits in social skills and limited abilities to form close, interpersonal relationships. Several studies have examined wilderness therapy and found it to have a positive impact in this area. Gibson (1981) and Cytrynbaum and Ken (1975) found that the interpersonal competence of troubled youths was increased following an Outward Bound-type experience. Freeman, Spilka, and Mason (1968) discovered a decrease in aggression, and Natches and Roberts (1967) found an increase in participants' self-control. Porter (1975) also noted a decrease in defensiveness and a large increase in social acceptance.

Physical Fitness

Although it has been difficult to establish a linear relationship between the level of physical health and social/psychological functioning, the expression "a sound mind in a sound body" has much intuitive appeal. At a minimum, it can be argued that an improved level of physical fitness helps troubled youths to maintain better physical health. More in-depth research may someday find a clear link between fitness and social and psychological success. Two studies researched the effect of wilderness therapy on the physical fitness of troubled youths. Both of the studies— Collingwood (1972) and Wright (1982)—found increases in fitness following therapy.

Academic Achievement

Substandard academic achievement is a frequent correlate of emotional disturbance in teens. Although it is normally presented as an effect of psychological problems, it can also be a cause. Regardless of whether it is a cause, an effect, or both, authorities agree that improving academic functioning to average or above-average levels is an important goal for all therapeutic programs.

Advocates of wilderness therapy argue that it enhances academic functioning because of its strong impact on adolescent motivation. For example, when classroom instruction is complemented by emotionally-charged wilderness adventures, even resistant teens become open to writing about their experiences. To provide another example, the study of history or science can be facilitated by learning those subjects in the natural environment, especially when the lessons are complemented by problem-solving experiences and adventure. Two studies—Churchard (1980) and Marsh and Richard (1985)—have documented improvements in academic achievement after exposure to the kind of approach described above.

Recidivism

Wilderness therapy's most impressive results have been achieved with the population that is often characterized as most resistant to change: adjudicated youth. Other programs have found it difficult to document success in this area and numerous reviews (cf., Greenwood, 1985) have argued that nothing seems to work.

Outward Bound-type programs challenge this conclusion with two well-designed, well-run studies. Kelly and Baer (1968), using a random-assignment, experimental design, found that students who went to Outward Bound lapsed only half as often as the control group. William and Chun (1973) replicated this study and found even lower levels of recidivism among the teens who had attended a wilderness program. Even with a 2-year follow-up (Kelly, 1974), the wilderness therapy group continued to experience less recidivism; however, due to small sample size, the difference in recidivism between the experimental and control group was no longer statistically significant.

RESEARCH SUMMARY

Lest the results reported above seem excessively optimistic, it is important to note that in certain studies one or more of the variables under examination failed to change in a positive direction. For example, Wright (1982) found that the problem-solving abilities of the experimental group did not improve, and Collingwood (1972) did not uncover significant decreases in alienation.

On the other hand, a comprehensive review of the literature located only one study that provided contradictory evidence about the major variables discussed above. Dahaime (1982) failed to find significant improvements in the self-esteem of troubled youths following an Outward Bound-type program. However, his study suffered from small sample sizes (N=16) and thus may have lacked experimental power.

Another problem is poor experimental design. Many of the studies have small sample sizes, lack control groups, have limited follow-up, and so on. However, although they are clearly a serious drawback, these design problems are somewhat offset by the fact that there is such a regular pattern of positive findings.

This preponderance of encouraging results led three reviewers of Outward Bound and wilderness therapy literature (Burton, 1982; Gibson, 1979; and Shore, 1976) to conclude that wilderness therapy has a strong and reliable positive effect on emotionally and behaviorally disturbed adolescents.

> While many of the empirical studies are of questionable validity due to methodological shortcomings, it is clear that wilderness programs can and do result in positive changes in the self-concepts, personalities, individual behaviors, and social functioning of the program participants. Therapeutic wilderness programs are, then, a potentially powerful, albeit largely unrecognized, alternative to traditional therapeutic interventions. (Gibson, 1979, pp. 29–30)

In conclusion, Outward Bound and Outward Bound-style programs have built a record of achievement and success. Wilderness therapy is no longer an untried, undocumented, and experimental approach; rather, there is persuasive evidence that it is an effective and powerful method for treating troubled youths.

CONCLUSION

The transition from adolescence to adulthood is a difficult one. Adolescents who do not feel significant, listened to, successful, needed, or powerful are ill-equipped for the life journey ahead of them. On the other hand, adolescents who have developed a strong sense of self-worth and who believe in their potency to shape the world around them; adolescents who feel needed and significant to others; and finally, adolescents who have experienced opportunities to develop judgment and maturity—these young people will become independent, successful, and productive.

There are literally hundreds of approaches dedicated to achieving these kinds of positive outcomes with troubled youth. The wilderness challenge model differentiates itself from the remainder of the field in two primary factors. First, it is based on the Hahnian vision, a vision that sees most troubled youths as needing a reinitiation into cultural norms—an effective education in prosocial values—and not intensive psychotherapy. This social learning perspective is empowered by the experiential nature of the wilderness challenge environment which inundates adolescents with physical and social success and places them in direct dialogue with the natural world. Second, the wilderness therapy model creates an archetypal rite of passage—an opportunity to participate in an ancient method of personal transformation that has the potential to operate quickly, mysteriously, and powerfully.

The combination of these two factors results in a life-affirming peak experience. One adolescent, when asked to summarize his wilderness courses, summed up the program in the following manner:

> When this trip starts, and all through it right on up to the last day before the truck is loaded and headed towards home base, you will despise the weight of the pack, curse every rock and every dirt mound, condemn every speck of dust, spit at every dirty mud puddle, and snarl at every ridge. You will push yourself, and be pushed, both mentally and physically further than you ever imagined possible, you will endure the seemingly unendurable. And as mad as it may sound, when it's all over and you've already loaded the truck and start to roll out on the roads, you will think back over those things, all of them, and you will feel this incredible surge of power over yourself, and all of those things will add up to the most fantastic and cherished adventurous memory you will ever know. You will feel the power overcome you, and you will know without doubt that you have done something that will irrevocably remain in your mind forever. You will feel the limitation of all the things you once thought impossible for you to do slip away from your mind and you will reach the ultimate realization that there are no limits to the things you are capable of accomplishing. That will be the supreme rush. (Tommy C., age 17)

Richard Kimball earned his doctoral degree from the University of Colorado School of Education in 1978. For the next 10 years he worked in the clinical mental health system of New Mexico as the Executive Director of the Santa Fe Mountain Center. He is currently a partner in the Inventure Group, a national consulting firm specializing in career renewal, self-leadership, and executive assessment and coaching. He is also a member of the adjunct faculty at the Center for Creative Leadership where he works as a psychologist proving individual assessment and feedback.

Stephen Bacon is currently a clinical psychologist in private practice in Santa Barbara, California. He has a long history of working with Outward Bound, beginning with his work in 1980 as a residential counselor for troubled youths. From 1984 to 1987 he served as the Vice President of Research and Program Development at the Outward Bound National Office in Greenwich, Connecticut. He has written a number of critical pieces in the field, one of which includes the book The Conscious Use of Metaphor in Outward Bound.

Footnote

[1] The chapter was originally published in the book: Lyman, R. D., Prentice-Dunn, S., and Gabel, S. (1989). <u>Residential and inpatient treatment of children and adolescents</u>. Plenum Publishing Corporation.

3

WILDERNESS AS HEALING PLACE[1]

JOHN MILES, Ph.D.

For John Muir, wilderness was a restorative place, a place in which he could not only learn and grow but also restore his mental and physical well-being. He often wrote of this quality of wilderness experience. In the mountains, "cares will drop off like autumn leaves." In the "great fresh, unblighted, unredeemed wilderness" people will find hope. "The galling harness of civilization drops off, and the wounds heal ere we are aware." Muir himself seemed to have a physiological need for contact with wilderness. After he was married and responsible for the welfare of his family and their fruit ranch, he spent long periods away from wilderness. The demands of business and work took their toll, and he would seek restoration in the exploration of some wild place. He bid others to do the same:

> Go now and then for fresh life—if most of humanity must go through this town stage of development—just as divers hold their breath and come ever and anon to the surface to breathe. Go whether or not you have faith. Form parties, if you must be social, to go to the snow-flowers in winter, to the sunflowers in summer. Anyway, go up and away for life; be fleet! (Teale, 1954, p. 319)

Nearly a century has passed since Muir wrote these words, and in that time many people have followed his advice. In fact, during the latter half of the twentieth century so many people have sought the benefits of contact with nature that Muir would be amazed and chagrined. Outdoor recreation has become an industry, and even the search for "healing" in wild places has become organized and institutionalized. Now we have "therapeutic recreation" and "stress-challenge adventure" programs to assist people in following Muir's advice. Wilderness as a "healing place" has truly been recognized on a scale beyond anything that Muir imagined.

43

HOW DOES WILDERNESS
CONTRIBUTE TO HEALTH?

Wilderness experience, many claim, can allow us to build the structure of our being on a healthy foundation and also allow reconstruction and restoration of a cracked or crumbling foundation. Many programs today use wilderness for therapeutic goals of one sort or another. Undoubtedly both the experiences planned and facilitated by the program leaders and the environment itself contribute to the healing effect of wilderness experience. We are concerned here with how the wilderness environment contributes to improvement of health.

First, we should define what we mean by healing in this context. It is a broad and value-laden concept. As Webster defines it, to heal is "to make sound or whole"; it is "to cause an undesirable condition to be overcome"; "to make a person spiritually whole"; or "to restore to original integrity." Healing involves an improvement of the condition of our mind/body. We need healing when we suffer pain and a reduction of our ability to live well. When we speak of healing here, we are not referring to its usual meaning as applied to our physical selves but to a process involving physical, emotional, and even spiritual dimension. Healing usually involves all of these dimensions simultaneously. The wilderness engages the whole person and thus may be an environment ideally suited to the holistic healing that John Muir experienced and advocated to his fellows.

PSYCHOLOGICAL BENEFITS OF WILDERNESS

There have been literary allusions to the restorative and therapeutic values of nature for centuries. This is valuable testimony, but is there any "hard" evidence that wild places contribute to healing? There is, it turns out, but not as much such evidence as we believers in the powers of wilderness experience would like. Two psychologists, Stephen Kaplan and Janet Frey Talbot, recently researched what we know about the psychological benefits of wilderness. Their review of the literature led to the less-than-startling conclusion that people find experiences in natural environments highly satisfying and that they highly value the benefits which they perceive themselves to derive from experiences there (Kaplan & Talbot, 1983, p. 166). The research literature trying to document the specifically therapeutic value of wilderness experience is generally flawed methodologically. It does indicate that programs like Outward Bound "can and do result in positive changes in the self-concepts, personalities, individual behaviors and social functioning of program participants" (Gibson, 1979, pp. 13, 2, 30).

Kaplan and Talbot set up their own elaborate study of the psychological effects of wilderness experience, trying to determine how wilderness affects people and what the effects are. In summary, they identified three benefits. These seem to come progressively, beginning with an increased awareness of relationship with the physical environment and an increasingly effortless attention to one's surroundings. Sometimes people find that daily life causes them to have difficulty concentrating, to experience mental work as unusually effortful, and to be irritable in the face of noise and distraction. These may all be symptoms of "a fatigued voluntary attention mechanism that has been pushed beyond its effective limits" (Kaplan & Talbot, 1983, p. 188). Wilderness seems to free people from this condition with a functional demand on attention and an interesting environment.

> *The growing sense of enjoyment is likely to be a reflection of the decreased need to force oneself to attend. There is the discovery, in other words, that in addition to being comfortable and exciting it is also quite safe to attend to what one feels like attending to in the wilderness environment. (p. 193)*

Later in the wilderness experience a second benefit appears. People experience an increase in self-confidence and a feeling of tranquility. They come to feel that they can deal with whatever challenges the environment may offer them. This is a profoundly satisfying and even surprising experience for people who have been struggling with their "normal" world. Kaplan and Talbot suggest that these benefits are in part attributable to the realization that one cannot control the wilderness environment:

> *Although often not a conscious priority, the need for control nonetheless can be an important factor in the way an individual attempts to relate to an environment. Yet the assertion of individual control is incompatible with much of what wilderness offers and demands; rather than struggling to dominate a hostile environment, the participants come to perceive their surroundings as quite safe as long as one responds appropriately to environmental demands. Thus there is a tendency to abandon the implicit purpose of control because it is both unnecessary and impossible. (p. 194)*

By relinquishing the illusion of control over the environment, people paradoxically acquire more internal control and can relax and pay more attention to their surroundings and to their inner selves.

Finally, Kaplan and Talbot noted a third benefit which they describe as contemplation. This is made possible by a high degree of compatibility among environmental patterns, the inclinations of the individual, and the actions required to feel comfortable in the environment. The daily round of activity back home is often anything but compatible. People are bombarded with diverse information and demands and are often unable to do what their environment requires of them as well as what they desire. They may experience frustration and tension and be entirely incapable of reflection on their situation.

Wilderness is very different. Kaplan and Talbot note:

> In wilderness what is interesting to perceive tends to be what one needs to know in order to act. For many people the purposes one carries into the wilderness also fit closely with the demands that the wilderness makes: What one intends to do is also what one must do in order to survive. (p. 191)

All of this compatibility can be liberating. It can allow reflection that can lead to discovery of a different self, a self less conflicted, more integrated, and more desirable. It can lead to a new intensity of contact with nature. "They feel a sense of union with something that is lasting, that is of enormous importance, and that is larger than they are" (p. 195). Thus they tap a spiritual dimension of the human experience that generations of writers have extolled.

At the end of their decade-long research, Kaplan and Talbot had to admit that there was much to learn about the benefits of wilderness experience, but they believed they had documented and described a set of significant psychological benefits. They raised more questions than they answered, but their work should be encouraging to those who, on the basis of personal experience, literary testimony, and intuition, have been taking people into the wilderness to heal and to grow. Kaplan and Talbot conclude with the observation that "we had not expected the wilderness experience to be quite so powerful or pervasive in its impact. And we were impressed by the durability of that residue in the human makeup that still resonates so strongly to these remote, uncivilized places" (p. 201). Their work suggests that wilderness experience can contribute to the healing of people overburdened by demands of the home environment, that it calms them and improves their ability to cope with the stresses of their normal round of activity.

WILDERNESS ENHANCES SELF-WORTH

Some sociologists suggest other ways in which wilderness experience contributes to healing. They describe two conditions from which many people suffer: anomie and alienation. A person with anomie is faced with myriad possibilities in life; he/she is bombarded by stimuli and moves rapidly through a set of unrelated experiences in a condition of separation from other people. Richard Mitchell notes that such a person is "...unsupported by significant others, free to choose from meaningless alternatives, without direction or purpose, bound by no constraint, guided by no path, comforted by no faith" (1983, p. 178).

In such a condition, this person fears the outcomes of his/her actions and is plagued by an uncertainty that renders routine and normal tasks very difficult. Such a person may feel desperately in need of stability, security, and certainty.

Alienation, on the other hand, may occur when someone finds the world too predictable. Mitchell summarizes the contributing factors:

> When people can predict their own behaviors on the basis of the social order in which they are situated, when they perceive their world as constrained by social forces, bound over by rule and regulation at every turn to the extent that personal creativity and spontaneity are stifled, when they know what they will and must do in a given situation regardless of their own interests, they experience alienation. (1983, p. 179)

The effect of this condition on someone is to feel powerless and indifferent, estranged and separate from self and others. Interest in the world lessens and he/she may become depressed, lethargic, and uninvolved. The alienated person comes to believe that effort cannot bring about the outcomes desired, so why bother?

We cautiously say that these two conditions are unhealthy, or at least that they can contribute to a reduction of psychological and even physical well-being. Mitchell and others suggest that people suffering anomie and alienation need to balance their perception of their abilities with the responsibilities and possibilities available to them. They need to reduce the variability of stimuli when too much is present (anomie) and to increase it when there is too little (alienation). In a social sense, notes Mitchell, people are moved to seek competence, a sense of personal worth.

> Competence grows from the process of recognizing one's abilities and applying them meaningfully and completely.

Competence means assessing oneself as qualified, capable, fit, sufficient, adequate. Competence emerges when a person's talents, skills, and resources find useful application in meeting a commensurate challenge, problem, or difficulty. In sum, the competent individual's perceived abilities are roughly equal to their perceived responsibilities. (1983, p. 180)

Mitchell argues that certain activities provide ways for people to seek this competence and to break out of their anomie or alienation. Such activities (he explores mountaineering in considerable depth in this regard) allow people to enjoy a freedom and creativity that disrupt their emotional treadmill and open new possibilities for them. The anomie person will find a helpful measure of uncertainty. We may add to Mitchell's contention the argument that the wilderness environment in which many such activities occur contributes to the healing outcomes as well.

Central to the healing property of mountain experience, argues Mitchell, is "flow." Mihaly Csikszentmihalyi has described this "flow":

Flow refers to the holistic sensation present when we act with total involvement.... It is the state in which action follows upon action according to an internal logic which seems to need no conscious intervention on our part. We experience it as a unified flowing from one moment to the next in which we are in control of our actions, and in which there is little distinction between self and environment; between stimulus and response; or between past, present, and future. (p. 58)

This sounds remarkably similar to the "fascination" that Kaplan and Talbot earlier described, a condition in which attention flows effortlessly to whatever is being done. Mitchell, though, argues that it is the act of climbing that creates the flow experience, while Kaplan and Talbot suggest that the environment is the principle factor. The latter investigators did not study the action of mountaineering, and Mitchell studiously avoids discussion of environment as a contributing factor in flow. The question of the relative importance of action and environment in helping with problems such as anomie and alienation remains an open one.

WILDERNESS AND THE ABILITY TO LEARN

Many programs that use wilderness as a healing place seem to assume that the environment contributes to achievement of their goals

48   *ADVENTURE THERAPY*

and that certain activities do so better than others. Outward Bound schools usually use both the opportunity for flow that activities in the wilderness provide and the fascination effect of the wilderness environment. The combination of these factors may partly explain the power of the Outward Bound process.

This process is being used in many places to help young people who are in trouble, particularly delinquents. These are people who are usually unwilling to take responsibility for themselves and others; they resent the situations in which they find themselves and the necessity to work. They are often limited learners, unable or unwilling to collect new knowledge and apply it to their lives. Many lack confidence in themselves and resist the idea that anyone can be of help to them (Golins, 1978, p. 26). In acting out their resentment and frustration with their lot in life, these adolescents often find themselves in trouble with the law and in the court system. As part of their therapy, an increasing number of them are being provided an opportunity to participate in a wilderness-based adventure education program.

Golins has reviewed how such programs "...impel a delinquent to rearrange his destructive ways" (1978, p. 27). He notes how the outdoor environment contributes to this process through its "evocative" quality. The outdoors in general and the wilderness in particular are unfamiliar and captivating for most delinquent youths. It engages the participants' senses and increases receptivity to stimuli in their environment. Their chances for success seem to be increased because of their experiences. This may be because the needs and purposes of the moment (to be warm, to stay dry, to curtail hunger) are compatible with the demands of the environment, as Kaplan and Talbot observed. A person usually resistant to learning is made less so when the learning is necessary to solve basic problems of comfort and even survival.

Golins describes another way in which the outdoor environment is conducive to growth:

> The outdoors also presents itself in a very physical, straightforward way. There are mountains to climb, rivers to run, bogs to wade through. As an adolescent delinquent whose principal mode of expression is an action-oriented one and whose thinking process is mostly concrete, the possible activities in the outdoors fulfill his developmental capability. He just stands a better chance of excelling here. (1978, p. 27)

The environment may be unfamiliar, but the demand for action is familiar. Those who design the challenges of wilderness-based educational programs are very careful to present the opportunity for success. Usually the learner is presented with a progressively more difficult series of challenges, demonstrating the value of learning and the positive outcomes to be derived from applying what is learned. In the outdoors the feedback and reinforcement from successful application of something learned is immediate. Rewarded for learning, the delinquent goes on to the next challenge and the next learning experience.

Yet another way the outdoors may help delinquents is described by Golins. He notes that the "symbolic potential" of the outdoors is greater for the person who has difficulty conceptualizing and generalizing. He argues that if we subscribe to the theory that learning involves thinking about the meaning of experience, then the experiences in nature, by their power and simplicity and concreteness, are easier to generalize than learning experiences in the complex social contexts of normal life.

Consider, for instance, a young woman learning to rock climb. She must learn to depend on her belayer. She must communicate with her and must care for her in the sense that she must not knock any rocks down or otherwise endanger this person upon whom she is dependent. The problems she needs to solve are simple and straightforward. There is a beginning and end to the task at hand. The difficulties are easy to identify and define, as are the actions necessary to solve them. Tackling the rock pitch, the slanting jam crack, the "holdless" section, the climber takes the difficulties one at a time and works them out. She is in charge and, after the anxiety of the adventure recedes, feels a surge of confidence. "I did that!?" is often the comment, part surprised query, part triumphant exclamation.

From all of this the woman may generalize about problem solving, cooperation, communication, and the nature of dependency in certain social situations. The outdoor environment presents these concepts boldly so that they can hardly be missed. It places them in a pragmatic context that increases the likelihood that the learner will think about them in the larger framework of her life. "If these processes have served me here," she may reason, "then perhaps they will do so in my world in general." Golins thinks that such experiences help young people to learn to think conceptually and thereby deal more effectively with situations that have previously baffled and frustrated them.

WILDERNESS AS A METAPHOR FOR LIFE

Bacon, like Golins, has analyzed the Outward Bound process and how it works, and his thinking reveals yet another way in which wilderness contributes to healing in people who go there. Bacon's theory is that the Outward Bound experience can serve as a metaphor for the life of the participant, as a set of experiences that can clarify real-life situations and thereby help the learner contend with them. Most of the metaphorical power of the Outward Bound process, Bacon argues, comes from the conscious programming of the leader, but he also contends that an archetypal quality of the wilderness environment contributes to this power. He takes the foundation of his idea from the psychiatrist Carl Jung who suggested that there are some ways of organizing and understanding the works that are passed down in cultures and individuals from early human experience and that transcend culture to the point of being universal. Jung argued that these original patterns are produced in all of us and are a factor in how we perceive the world.

One such pattern of archetype is Sacred Space. This is a place pervaded by a sense of power, mystery, and awesomeness. Such places are not suitable for living, lacking the resources for day-to-day comfort and survival, and the seeker cannot stay there anyway for he/she has important work to do in the everyday world. If the seeker comes to the Sacred Space with full respect and a clean spirit, he/she may be empowered in a positive way. Bacon argues that wilderness is Sacred Space.

> Anyone who has spent much time in the wilderness can easily recognize the parallels between it and the archetype of Sacred Space. Wilderness is difficult to get to and difficult to travel through. One passes a series of tests in order to exist within it. It is unlike the normal world in hundreds of ways. Above all, it pervades one with a kind of religiosity or mysticism— one of the most compelling things about nature is that it seems to implicitly suggest the existence of order and meaning. (1983, p. 53)

In Bacon's view, wilderness as Sacred Space is useful to Outward Bound because implicit in this archetype is the concept of transformation and change. If Jung is correct and there is an archetype of Sacred Space within us, then when we go to such a place, especially in the context of programs like Outward Bound or Vision Quest, we accept the possibility that some kind of transformation may occur. This acceptance may not be conscious, but it is there and it makes change, growth, or healing possible.

A central principle of many psychotherapists is that a person does not change unless he/she wishes to change. Despite themselves, people cling to their problematical behaviors. Only when they become willing to change does healing become possible, as in the wilderness as Sacred

Space. A young person in trouble with the law or plagued by emotional difficulties is given the opportunity by a judge or a physician to try something new, to go into the wilderness. If they choose to go, they accept, perhaps begrudgingly or even unconsciously, the possibility of change. The outcome is certainly not a sure one, but there is the potential for something new.

> There is little question that certain course experiences do involve the presence of one or more of these primordial patterns...the students covertly participate in age-old patterns of human development. Anyone who has taught an Outward Bound course is aware that the spirit of the course often seems to move beyond the capabilities of the human beings involved. It is in this sense that one can argue that the mountains do speak for themselves. (Bacon, 1983, p. 53)

Kaplan and Talbot, without reference to Jung's archetype idea, argue that wilderness is suggestive of a larger framework, of rich possibilities not considered before:

> The wilderness experience is "real" in some rather concrete ways, as well as in a somewhat more abstract sense. It is real not because it matches one's ways of the everyday world (which of course it does not do), but because it feels real— because it matches some sort of intention of the way things ought to be, of the way things really are beneath the surface layers of culture and civilization. (1983, p. 190)

In a metaphorical way, the wilderness experience suggests the possibility of returning to the "real" world from this "other world" and finding coherence there. The wilderness traveler recognizes that daily life may not be as chaotic as previously experienced. There is, of course, no assurance that the possibility will be achieved, that the perception will be transferred back home. The transfer is possible, especially if part of the follow-up to the therapeutic wilderness experience of the "other world" fulfills the archetypal promise of Sacred Space. It is a change and holds out the possibilities of change to come. When this change helps a person to understand and cope with the world, it is a part of healing.

WILDERNESS AND PHYSICAL FITNESS

A final way in which wilderness may contribute to healing is by the physical demands that it makes upon people who travel there.

Wilderness by definition is a place without the amenities of civilization. The wilderness traveler must negotiate rough trails or travel cross-country with no trail. All the conveniences and necessities of life must be carried, usually on one's back. Physical effort is needed to satisfy basic needs, as in erecting the tent, cooking dinner, or staying warm and dry in rain or snow. The ultimate wilderness adventure, like climbing a mountain or rafting a wild and rough river, can demand considerable physical stamina and skill.

So how might the physical demands of wilderness travel contribute to healing? First, and most obviously, the demands of wilderness activity, if faced over a considerable period of time (like the 3 weeks of the standard Outward Bound course), lead to physical conditioning and stamina. A fit body can do much to enhance self-image, and a positive self-image is a boost in confidence. An increase in confidence opens new possibilities of learning and growth.

Thomas Stich (1983) notes other ways that physical activity can be helpful in dealing with psychological difficulties. When a person gains control over his/her body, as must be done in wilderness travel, there may be a corresponding gain in control in other areas. Perhaps there is also a metaphorical dimension. Traveling to a wilderness objective requires taking one step at a time, putting one foot in front of the other, pacing oneself. So it may be in daily life in a wide range of tasks. The way to the objective is not impatient rushing but steady effort. Alan Drengson has noted this quality of the physical act of wilderness walking. He calls the process "mindful walking" and points out that while one must be attentive to the physical act of walking, one can still look at the larger view and even achieve a meditative state. Meditation is an advanced state of psychological awareness and control, and wilderness walking certainly does not lead everyone automatically to that state. Some measure of the condition is often achieved, though, with beneficial effects.

Stich notes that physical exercise can cause self-expression and be an outlet for aggression and anxiety. All physical exercise provides these opportunities, including that involved in wilderness travel. Self-expression may come in many forms, as in the style in which one climbs a rock or the route one picks on a ski tour. Attacking the difficult pitch on a climb or the physically demanding long, heavy haul can be an outlet for aggression. Struggling with anxiety about bears or exposure or avalanches, pushing down the anxious upwelling while coping with the problem, then screaming with delight when the climb is done or the tricky avalanche slope passed—all provide an outlet for anxiety. The coping with anxiety is in part physical, moving beyond the threat to a position of safety. This is a concrete experience, one that cannot be denied. Back home a success (or failure) might be measured on some abstract scale, by someone sitting in judgment. The physical acting on a problem in the wilderness is real and undeniable. For a person who has often failed in society and thinks there can be no alternative, the physical, concrete experience of achievement in a wild place can be uplifting and restorative.

We can argue with confidence that wilderness has great potential to contribute to improvements in physical well-being. It cannot, of course, "cure" illness, but by its nature it can place demands on us that force us to call upon physical and emotional potential often unrealized. It can allow us to release pent-up energy and to feel our bodies, reminding ourselves that we have physical powers we may lose if we never use them. In short, the physical demands of wilderness places can perhaps motivate us to take better care of our own bodies; and such physical achievement can lead us to want more of the same and to initiate a regular physical fitness regime. In a world seemingly bent on taking the physical exertion out of every action, wilderness travel can give us a forceful reminder of what we are losing.

CONCLUSION

We have seen that wilderness environments can in many ways contribute to restoration of health. We have identified the qualities of such places that contribute to healing, as well as some of the problems where wilderness experiences can be especially helpful. Throughout our discussion we have noted that our activities in wild places are as important to healthful outcomes as the physical qualities of the places. We cannot separate the program from the place. The particular ways that being in wilderness can contribute to health can be summarized as follows:

1. In wilderness people experience increasing effortlessness in attending to their surroundings, which can be an antidote to the irritability and stress that comes with attention overload in daily life.
2. Recognition of limits regarding control of the wilderness environment can lead to reduction of the compulsion for control in other aspects of people's lives and to a more relaxed and comfortable posture generally.
3. Compatibility between environmental demands and individual inclination can contribute to personal integration and a sense of union with nature, which may lead to a sense of being at one with the universe, a highly desirable spiritual condition for many people.
4. Wilderness can be a place where people experience competence and consequently enhancement of self-worth. Thus people can be helped to cope with the contrasting conditions of alienation and anomie.
5. Wilderness is a place with high potential to captivate and stimulate, to increase one's feeling of engagement with one's surroundings. This may improve a person's ability to learn.
6. The concreteness of challenges posed by wilderness experience allow delinquents who usually fail to meet abstract challenges to enjoy success and consequent enhancement of self-image and confidence.
7. The metaphorical potential for learning in wilderness is great and may allow insight into the challenges of life back home and how they can be better managed.
8. The physical challenges of wilderness travel can enhance physical fitness and can also allow expression of frustration and anxiety, thereby reducing stress.

John Muir knew that his wilderness days restored his body, mind, and soul. He did not know how this restoration occurred, but the effect of his wilderness travels upon him was so great that he prescribed the experience to anyone with the means to go there. Today we still do not know exactly how and why nature has curative and restorative effects upon us, but as our modern lifestyle and development remove us farther from the natural world, we are consciously seeking the succor of wild places and researching the possibility that we need contact with nature to be fully functioning humans.

John C. Miles, a Professor of Environmental Studies at Western Washington University, has taught in and for wilderness for 25 years. Co-editor, with Simon Priest, of Adventure Education, *Miles continues to explore the educational dimensions of wilderness in his teaching and writing.*

Footnote

[1]The article was originally published in the 1987 Journal of Experiential Education, 10(3), 4-10.

4

THERAPEUTIC PROCESS
OF CHANGE[1]

RELDAN S. NADLER, PSY. D.

If the way out is through the door, why is it that no one will use this exit? (Confucius)

Introduction

It often happens that when people struggle in their attempts to produce desired changes to problems, they find that their solutions maintain, reinforce, or even exacerbate these issues. This is especially true when problems are difficult or maintained by a destructive pattern or cycle. In attempting to find answers to this troublesome phenomenon, Watzlawick, Weakland, and Fisch (1974) have stated that random events, followed by their unexpected, unusual, or uncommon solutions, often bring about spontaneous change when repetitious "more of the same" efforts have failed. The change process that occurs as a result of these events has many connections to the process of change observed in adventure programming. The purpose of this chapter is to identify how the use of adventure experiences in therapy brings about critical and lasting differences in clients' efforts to address their problems.

One of the cornerstones of adventure programming is the encouragement of people to do things they might not ordinarily do; to leave their safe, familiar, comfortable, and predictable world and enter into uncomfortable new territory. In doing so, unique answers or outcomes may emerge (White & Epston, 1990). Not only are adventure activities new for most clients, but so are the emotions, thoughts, and interactions that accompany these experiences. Clients may feel awkward, unfamiliar, and at risk as they move into areas that are unknown to them. The task of adventure therapists is to help clients to enter into these areas so that positive change and resulting growth can occur.

Like the pioneers and explorers of the West who went in search of riches and a new life, clients often participate in outdoor adventure courses to discover inner resources or to work on taming their own psychological "wilds" or unknowns. Many Western explorers, due to lack of water or food, encounters with unfamiliar environments, or their inability to endure and tolerate fears and apprehensions, turned back at the edge between the known and unknown. At times, they were only miles or minutes from their destination, but by not stepping over this edge into the realm of possibilities, they denied themselves success. Similarly, on adventure therapy experiences, some clients break through to the risks and successes in new territory, but others retreat or turn back to patterns of comfort and familiarity and "more of the same." Figure 1 represents the choices of this journey—to enter the world of breakthrough or that of retreat.

Breaking Through Limits to New Growth

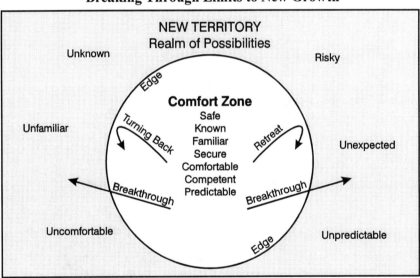

Figure 1

Although it is important to encourage breakthroughs for clients, learning what happens at the "edge" between breakthrough and retreat is crucial for the generalization and transference of experiences. It allows clients to convert their adventure experience into information on how to deal with other edges at home, work, or school. In therapeutic adventure experiences, the concepts of "edge" and "new territory" can be seen as metaphors for the emotional, cognitive, and action states that people experience in the journey between the known and the unknown.

Ideally, these states can be accepted and reframed as integral points of reference for attaining new growth, rather than being seen as foreign or dangerous. Tolerance, endurance, and adjustment of these states are necessary to allow clients to discover their own resources. In exploring the therapeutic change process of adventure programming, the process of how therapists get clients to appropriate edges becomes critical.

ADVENTURE THERAPY PROCESS

What are the aspects of an adventure therapy program that help people to break through to new territory and make the intervention so effective? Drawing from the work of Walsh and Golins (1976), Piaget (1977), and Yalom (1975), a theoretical framework containing aspects of these models helps to explain the process. This information is critical since it assists therapists in planning and continually adjusting for the facilitation of successes and the transference of the experience. The following is a brief explanation of each of the components (see Figure 2).

1. **The Client**: Clients enter experiences with a preconception of what the activities might be like. Generally, they expect to have a meaningful learning opportunity. For some clients, the anticipation of what will happen during the experience causes a sense of internal stimulation. Other clients do not experience this feeling until they are immersed in the course. The internal state that permits change to occur is referred to as...

2. **Disequilibrium**: Disequilibrium refers to an individual's awareness that the previous way of processing information no longer applies to this new experience. It is a state of internal conflict that provides motivation for an individual to make personal changes. Disequilibrium must be present for change to occur in adventure experiences. By involvement in an experience that is beyond their comfort zone, individuals are motivated to integrate new knowledge or reshape existing perceptions (e.g., through processes such as accommodation and assimilation). Clients experience the state of disequilibrium by being placed in a...

3. **Novel Setting**: Placement in an environment that is unfamiliar can help to break down individual barriers. Walsh and Golins (1976) identified the unfamiliar environments that exist in adventure experiences as unique physical and social environments. When an unfamiliar physical activity is combined with immersion in a group of virtual strangers, a heightened level

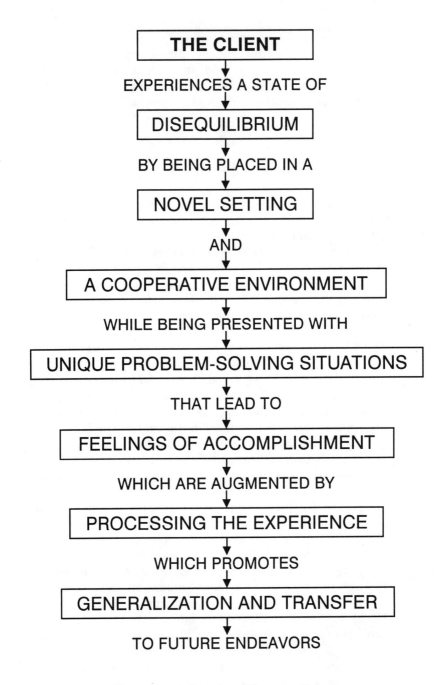

THE CLIENT

EXPERIENCES A STATE OF

DISEQUILIBRIUM

BY BEING PLACED IN A

NOVEL SETTING

AND

A COOPERATIVE ENVIRONMENT

WHILE BEING PRESENTED WITH

UNIQUE PROBLEM-SOLVING SITUATIONS

THAT LEAD TO

FEELINGS OF ACCOMPLISHMENT

WHICH ARE AUGMENTED BY

PROCESSING THE EXPERIENCE

WHICH PROMOTES

GENERALIZATION AND TRANSFER

TO FUTURE ENDEAVORS

Figure 2—Adventure Therapy Process

of arousal tends to occur. The underlying conditions of effort, trust, hope, a constructive level of anxiety, a sense of the unknown, and a perception of risk are integrated within a...

4. **Cooperative Environment**: Establishing an atmosphere that makes use of cooperative rather than competitive learning fosters opportunities for clients to develop group cohesiveness. This bonding is cultivated through a structure that focuses on shared goals and the provision of time for interpersonal and intrapersonal communication. This foundation exists while each individual and the group are continually presented with...

5. **Unique Problem-solving Situations**: New skills and problem-solving situations are introduced to clients in a sequence of increasing difficulty (Walsh & Golins, 1976). The learning opportunities are concrete and the problems can be solved when group members draw on their mental, emotional, and physical resources. Completion of such tasks leads to...

6. **Feelings of Accomplishment**: Success can lead to increased self-esteem and belief in self, improved communication skills, and more effective problem-solving skills. The meaningfulness of these success experiences is augmented by...

7. **Processing the Experience**: Clients are encouraged to reflect and, in some manner, express the thoughts and feelings that they are experiencing. Awareness of what they specifically did, thought, and felt prior to a breakthrough or retreat is emphasized. Processing is essential if there is going to be...

8. **Generalization and Transfer**: The goal of outdoor adventure experiences is to assist clients in forming their own linkages to what they are learning. This allows clients to integrate their new knowledge and desired behavior with their lifestyle during the remainder of the course and continue with these changes when they return home.

CRITICAL FACTORS OF ADVENTURE THERAPY

In the adventure therapy process, there are many critical factors that determine whether therapy will be successful. Many of these factors are shared with other, more traditional therapeutic approaches (e.g., generalization and transfer, processing). However, two components that separate adventure therapy from other approaches are the manner in which disequilibrium is achieved and novel settings.

Disequilibrium

Webster's Dictionary (1981) defines disequilibrium as a "loss or lack of equilibrium, an imbalanced state: instability; a condition of imbalance in affairs in which normally self-corrective forces are ineffective and inoperative" (p. 312). Disequilibrium is an internal conflict between cognitive processes, a psychological tension or pressure that each individual attempts to lessen. It is a moment or moments of emotional intensity, dissonance, or disorder. In attempting to reduce this tension, individuals often try a new behavior or change an attitude or belief. Disequilibrium occurs when a person is at the edge of their circle of comfort. A breakthrough or a retreat ensues, the discomfort is lessened, and homeostasis is returned. It is quite possible that adventure experiences, with their inherent physical and emotional risks, have the opportunity to create more disequilibrium than most educational or therapeutic programs. This may be one reason for the potency and effectiveness of adventure therapy programs—in reducing their disequilibrium, individuals do something different or unique and, as a result, may develop new resources and behavior patterns.

Many authors concur that this emotional state of dissonance is a precursor for change. Minuchin and Fishman (1981) write about "unbalancing" the family system. Hudson (1990) calls it "destructuring"; Perls (1969) "frustration"; Whitaker and Malone (1981) "anxiety"; Bandura (1986) "emotional arousal"; and Walsh and Golins (1976) "adaptive dissonance." Festinger (1957) labeled this state "cognitive dissonance," where inconsistency between two cognitive elements produces pressure to make these elements consonant. Prigogine and Stengers (1984) call it "chaos of fluctuations," alluding to "order out of chaos" in physics (e.g., where chaos occurs when looking under a microscope at cells the moment before the creation of a new chemical or substance).

In therapeutic adventure experiences, this creation may be a person trying out a new behavior and changing an attitude or sense of self to lessen emotional discomfort. This can lead to what O'Hanlon (1990) identified as "change the viewing" and "change the doing." Bateson (1979) would concur with this view of the change process. He argues that all information is necessarily "news of difference" and that it is the perception of difference that triggers all new responses in living systems.

In the process of confronting issues that occur during disequilibrium, clients need information to know how they had a breakthrough or what led to a retreat. This is why processing the experience is so important—individuals need to see their "news of difference" or how they changed their "viewing" or "doing." Another way of saying this is that processing can help people to move to an internal locus of control where they accept responsibility for their effort and ability, rather than attribute success to an external force like luck or chance.

Another point to highlight in Webster's definition of disequilibrium is that "normally self-corrective forces are ineffective and inoperative." This is linked to the "attempted solutions" described at the beginning of this chapter. For disequilibrium to be effective for new breakthroughs, therapists need to make sure that their clients' previous patterns of reducing disequilibrium don't work and encourage them to try something new. This is like tightrope walkers who, feeling shaky and out of balance, use a balancing pole to stabilize themselves. To take away the balancing pole or to blindfold them increases their disequilibrium but possibly their ability to change as well. Clients' self-corrective forces (e.g., patterns of behavior, belief systems, thinking, feeling, ways of getting support, breathing and posture, and metaphors or images) are often their defenses for dealing with dysfunctional situations. Encouraging people to alter or adjust these at the edge can enhance disequilibrium and allow for more breakthroughs.

Novel settings

What can therapists do to enable clients to experience more disequilibrium or dissonance, thereby promoting additional breakthroughs to new territory? Mahoney (1986) reported that the experience of novelty is the most important dynamic of therapy. Novel settings are created by having participants experience emotional states or attitudes that transport people to the edge of their circle of comfort and enhance the disequilibrium, dissonance, disorder, frustration, or anxiety they feel. When normal patterns or attempted solutions are unsuccessful at limiting this discomfort, individuals search to find new ways to ease their emotional state. Their search may lead them to restructure or reorder their cognitive map. This process is a critical initial step in bringing about appropriate therapeutic change, a unique outcome that results in breakthrough into new territory (see Figure 3).

Some examples of unique outcomes include: 1) individuals asking for help or support when they were convinced they must do everything for themselves; 2) clients sharing their "softer" feelings, like disappointment, sadness, or rejection, when before they had remained "tough"; 3) participants trying out a leadership role and getting positive feedback, when previously they had stayed in the background; 4) individuals who had always had to be in control experiencing trust and support when allowing others to take over; 5) participants leaving areas

Breakthrough to Appropriate Therapeutic Change

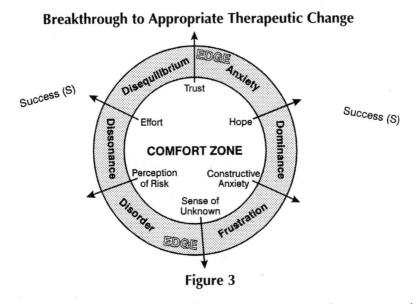

Figure 3

of comfort to achieve new goals despite their fear (e.g., the pamper pole to the trapeze bar). Outcomes like these, when processed effectively, can lead to a new sense of self, aiding in the transfer of functional change for the client's future.

The conditions for change that assist a client's adjustment in these novel settings may be overlapping or interdependent, and enhancing one or more of these conditions often determines whether the adventure therapy experience will be successful. Six of these conditions are outlined so that therapists can better understand and use them in order to accentuate disequilibrium and bring about change. These conditions are adapted from the work of Shapiro (1976) who researched the conditions that lead to "meaningful education."

1. **Hope:** This condition exists when individuals view the adventure experience as a way to eliminate their problems, heal their wounds, or fulfill their needs. There is an expectation of a positive outcome or attainment of a new goal. Many people seek out psychotherapy or new experiences because they lack hope. Adventure therapy can increase one's hope, especially when therapists take the opportunity to enhance the condition of hope.

    Some suggestions for enhancing this condition include: a) sharing stories about what other participants learned from the experience, b) asking clients to write down and share their desired goals, c) encouraging small successes until the clients achieve their desired goal, d) setting a tone of comfort and risk taking without criticism, and e) expressing hope, positive expectation, and confidence in participants.

2. **Effort**: This condition allows each client to focus on physical, emotional, and mental abilities in the therapeutic experience to provide motivation for change to occur. In adventure experiences, this can take the form of encouraging risk taking, positive interaction with others, the sharing of feelings, or heightened levels of attention. Effort can be depicted by the clichés "Go for it!" or "You only know how far you can go by going too far."

    Some suggestions to enhance effort include: a) designing activities for individuals that will increase their effort by challenging their abilities (e.g., climbing blindfolded, using only one arm, not using their voice), b) asking the participants to experiment with new roles or behaviors and to make commitments to the group about the goals on which they are going to work, c) encouraging people to push past their edges when they want to stop, d) appointing leaders, recorders, navigators, etc., for the day, e) encouraging participants to share personal histories when appropriate, f) teaching focusing or concentration exercises, and g) encouraging clients to verbally counteract their negative self-talk by saying "I can do this" or "I'll handle it."

3. **Trust**: This condition is the result of an appropriate reliance and confident dependence on others, one's self, the leader, and the experience. The more trust that exists from these four sources, the easier it is for clients to make focused efforts during tasks or endure the tension of being in disequilibrium.

    Some suggestions on how to enhance the condition of trust include: a) talking about trust in the group (e.g., ask how people know if they can trust another person or themselves), b) performing trust activities (e.g., trust falls, blind walks), c) including "go-arounds" in a group where participants share something positive about the person next to them, d) having clients finish the sentence, "It will help me trust you if you _____," e) assigning pairs activities where partners can demonstrate support for one another, f) using dyads during processing groups and changing the dyads so that everyone gets to know one another, g) having the group regularly assess levels of trust in the group and between members (e.g., encourage individuals to pick a number from 1–10 to indicate how much they trust the group), h) implementing sculpting exercises where clients make a group sculpture and stand next to people they trust the most, and (i) discussing what it takes to trust someone.

4. **Constructive Level of Anxiety**: When anxiety exists, individuals experience many of the following emotions: ambivalence, confusion, dissonance, discomfort, frustration, stress. However, when properly implemented by therapists, anxiety can be constructive and safe in assisting clients with dismantling dysfunctional behaviors and developing functional change.

Some suggestions to enhance the constructive level of anxiety include: a) increasing the sense of the unknown, b) increasing the perception of risk, c) having participants experiment with new roles, d) conducting activities differently (e.g., in the dark), e) changing the rules of activities to make them more challenging, f) withholding information or materials so that clients must rely on others, and g) assigning specific responsibilities to individuals to raise their level of anxiety.

Below are a list of common adaptations that are often used during adventure experiences to raise the level of challenge for clients. Specific therapeutic issues that often arise from implementing these adaptations are also mentioned.

(a) *Blindfold*—Clients are given a blindfold to put over their eyes during an activity. **Therapeutic issues**: Powerlessness, being out of control, relapse, trust in others or a higher power, sense of the unknown or unexpected, dependency, and use of new senses or way of knowing.

(b) *Nonverbal*—Clients are unable to speak during the activity. **Therapeutic Issues**: Powerlessness, talking too much, inability to show emotions, reliance on others, need to observe more, and communicating in a new way.

(c) *Limited Use*—Clients are unable to use one or both of their arms or legs in the activity. **Therapeutic issues**: Reliance on body versus mind, feeling like a victim, dependency, lack of teamwork, and vulnerabilities.

(d) *Partnered*—Clients are connected together at the side and must move together without any individual getting between them. They do not need to be tied or attached; just standing together can sometimes be a more appropriate therapeutic technique (e.g., with couples or families). **Therapeutic issues**: Enmeshment, compatibility, dependency, examination of how people interact, commitment, cooperation; can be used to get a non-involved client engaged when paired with a more active member.

(e) *Single Voice*—Clients can only talk through another person. Somebody else is their voice, and they can only share ideas with this person who vocalizes their idea to the whole group. This often is a good way to get a quiet person involved through the "sharing" of ideas. **Therapeutic issues**: Not being heard, being overpowered, listening, cooperating, assuming leadership role, and empowerment.

(f) *Mixed Messages/Confusion*—A client is asked to say the opposite of whatever the leader is saying in the activity. **Therapeutic issues**: Passive-aggressiveness, deflecting, oppositional, miscommunication, and family or group chaos.

(g) *Questioning*—A client is asked to make all forms of communication into a question when speaking with others. **Therapeutic issues**: Demanding or blaming others rather than soliciting, getting permission rather than acting impulsively, cooperation, teamwork, passive-aggressiveness, and indirect communication.

(h) *Destructive Statements*—Clients are instructed to make destructive statements such as "I'll never succeed at this," "That's a dumb idea," or "That will never work." The group assesses the effects of these statements on their progress. This is usually implemented for a duration of only 5-10 minutes. **Therapeutic issues**: Low self-esteem, negative self-talk, aggressiveness, fear and apprehension, power and control.

(i) *Prescribing the Symptom*—This can be used to highlight awareness of a dysfunctional pattern or symptom. **Therapeutic issues**: Pick a pattern that is symptomatic to the family or group (e.g., whining, complaining, yelling, avoiding). Pick the person with the symptom or another person to carry it out. Assess what effect it has on other members. This is another technique that generally is only used for 5-10 minutes of an activity.

5. **A Sense of the Unknown or Unpredictable**: Individuals often have a sense of awe or mystery about what they are going to experience. They often ask many questions, but answers should not be given simply to dispel their disequilibrium; clients should be encouraged to accept their feelings of uncertainty. Generally speaking, the more unknown, unfamiliar, and unpredictable the experience, the more challenge it possesses for the client.

Some suggestions for enhancing the sense of the unknown or unpredictable include: a) refraining from giving answers that allow the participant to predict and control the future, b) taking watches away from people, c) using therapeutic impediments or adversities, d) increasing the constructive level of anxiety, e) enhancing the perception of risk, f) removing the leader or therapist from activities so that participants experience full responsibility, g) varying the amount of emotional support given to clients, and h) withholding or increasing the amount of information given about activities.

6. **Perception of Risk**: This condition exists when individuals perceive the experience as a physical, emotional, and behavioral risk or danger. In most adventure programs, there is a large contrast between the perceived risk and actual risk of the activity. One of the major focuses of processing can be to help clients to understand how they can overcome their own perceived risks and how they can transfer this learning to other perceived risks that exist in their lives.

Some suggestions for enhancing the perception of risk, when appropriate, include: a) increasing the constructive level of anxiety, b) increasing the sense of the unknown and unpredictable by doing what is unexpected, c) developing behavior contracts for emotional and behavioral risks taken, d) using therapeutic adaptations, e) telling stories of what happened to other groups or participants, f) grouping people in specific order, g) withholding or increasing the amount of information given about activities, and h) emphasizing safety continuously in all activities.

CONCLUSION

When therapists know the therapeutic conditions of change and other ingredients that lead to change, they can individualize courses for each client to facilitate a large degree of growth and transference. This may mean lowering the anxiety level for one client while simultaneously enhancing the anxiety or disequilibrium for another. This challenge is often simplified by appropriately assessing participants and having a strong theoretical foundation on how to facilitate breakthroughs.

Bringing clients to their "edge" and facilitating adaptations toward prescribed outcomes can bring about a change in the client's repertoire. This new, unexpected, and visual solution can be repeated and generalized to situations at home. Adventure experiences can serve as the bridge as well as the vehicle for clients to explore new territory in all aspects of their life.

I have ascertained by full inquiry that Utopia
lies outside the bounds of the known world. — Guillaume Bude

Dr. Nadler is a licensed psychologist in private practice in Santa Barbara, California. He is also the President of Edgework Associates, a consulting firm providing adventure programs for corporations, hospitals, and families.

Footnote

[1] A portion of this chapter was also written in the book Nadler, R. S., & Luckner, J. L. (1992). Processing the adventure experience: Theory and practice. Dubuque, IA: Kendall Hunt.

SECTION 2

APPLICATIONS OF
ADVENTURE THERAPY

Colorado Outward Bound School Photo

5

PROGRAMMING APPLICATIONS OF ADVENTURE THERAPY

MICHAEL A. GASS, Ph.D.

While the processes outlined in the first section of this book provide the framework for adventure therapy, it is the programs that use these processes that demonstrate the effectiveness of adventure therapy. The manner in which adventure therapists conduct their programs is usually how the field is viewed professionally and publicly. For example, when describing a particular adventure therapy technique to other professionals unfamiliar with these approaches, I generally do not progress too far in my description until a colleague states "Oh yes, it's like that Outward Bound/Project Adventure/other experiential education program that I've heard of." Our initial conversation on theoretical principles and specific treatment issues usually does not continue until I explain how my ideas are similar to or different from my colleague's generalizations.

This situation is probably not too different from the experiences of most adventure therapy professionals. At the foundation of this conversation is a value judgment. If it is positive, I generally have an easy time explaining the treatment ideas I have in mind. If it is negative, I often find that what I offer is viewed more critically. As Martha Matthews outlines in her chapter in Section Six of this book, the manner in which programs currently conduct therapeutic experiences often represents the "best and the worst" in what is presently being accomplished by therapeutic professionals. Some programs offer valid therapeutic interventions that bring about critical treatment changes, whereas other programs have found themselves in court on charges of abuse or negligence resulting in the death of a client.

DEPTH OF ADVENTURE THERAPY PROGRAMS

As stated in the first section of this book, adventure therapy is currently being conducted in two types of treatment environments: (a) wilderness therapy settings and (b) facility-based adventure therapy settings. Another area where the programming of adventure therapy experiences differs is in the depth of the intended intervention. Several factors that determine the depth of the therapeutic adventure experience include:

1) the specific needs of the client,
2) the complexity of the client's therapeutic issue(s),
3) the background training and therapeutic expertise of the adventure therapist,
4) the length of time the adventure therapist has to work with the client,
5) the context the client came from and will return to after the adventure experience,
6) the presence of aftercare or follow-up treatment following the adventure experience,
7) the availability of adventure experience(s), and
8) the therapist's ability/limitations in using adventure experiences in his/her treatment approaches.

All programs seem to differ to some degree based on these factors. Given these qualities, a "continuum" seems to have developed that represents the depth of intervention used by therapeutic adventure programs. Using a model developed by Gillis et al. (1991), the categories portraying different degrees of intervention with adventure therapy activities are: 1) recreation, 2) enrichment, 3) adjunctive therapy, or 4) primary therapy (see Figure 1).

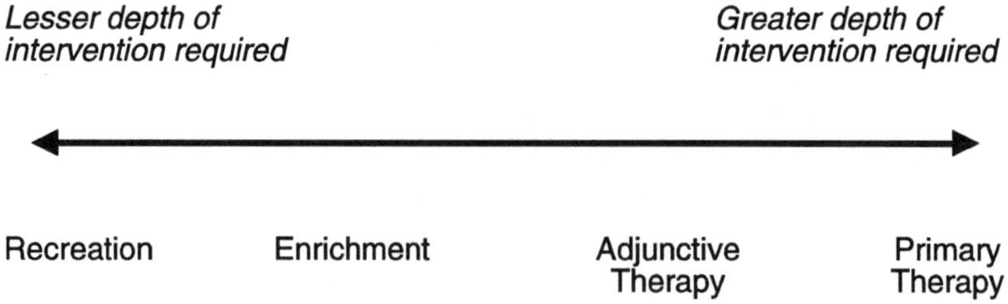

Lesser depth of intervention required   *Greater depth of intervention required*

Recreation   Enrichment   Adjunctive   Primary
                                           Therapy   Therapy

Figure 1 - Depth of Intervention Continuum

Even though this classification system was developed for looking at programs that work with families, it seems applicable to all programs using adventure experiences with therapeutic intent. It is important to note that these categories are not mutually exclusive; they represent points on a continuum rather than four separate and distinct categories. Adventure therapy programs are located on this continuum based on the eight factors identified above. A brief description of each format is presented below.

Recreation—This type of program often represents an engaging "one-shot" adventure experience that uses a single time-frame to accomplish its objective. Often because of a limited time-frame and lack of continued contact with the client population, it appears that the goal for such experiences is to have clients participate in activities so that they acquire some type of "positive" feeling. While it might be assumed that most of the clients in a program with recreational goals might be the least "clinical" of the four formats mentioned here, it can often be the most appropriate use of the adventure experience given the eight parameters presented earlier in this section. The true goal of this approach centers on the enjoyment it provides for clients, and in this way indirectly addresses treatment issues. Whatever therapeutic benefits might occur are related to the client participating in the adventure activities, which can be extremely valuable. During these experiences, steps are not usually taken to prescriptively structure activities to be related to any client issue.

Note that while the term "recreation" is the title of this category, it should not be assumed that certain professional groups (e.g., therapeutic recreation professionals) only conduct therapeutic adventure experiences in this format. The term is used to represent the value of this experience which is personally satisfying and relevant for the participant.

Enrichment—This format is characterized by adventure programs that purposely address common issues/problems that are related to client treatment. The goals of these programs often focus on using adventure experiences that possess a strong affinity for developing certain positive qualities (e.g., self-concept, trust, cooperation, decision making, problem solving). These programs tend to be longer in duration than recreational programs, and the processing techniques used in these experiences tend to be more complex, generally done to direct client attention to global issues. Much of the therapeutic benefit in these programs comes from the educational process of clients challenging themselves in the experience, reflecting on what happened, positively expanding their self-belief and the manner in which they interact with others in a group, and transferring these benefits to their lives back home.

Adjunctive therapy—This type of format differs from the first two in that it focuses on the context of the particular therapeutic issues of a client. This is not done in place of other therapeutic interventions, but in addition to the treatment interventions set forth in the primary therapeutic modality. An example of this type of intervention is illustrated in the chapter by Betsy Webb on the use of a 3-day program with survivors of violence. As pointed out in the article, this program does not stand alone as a treatment effort, but is done in conjunction with referring agencies or private therapists. Pre-course consultations are made with referring agencies and the goals derived from this information are blended into the course to make the experience more relevant for treatment. Information gathered on the course is integrated back into treatment when the client returns from the course. As stated in the article, using adventure therapy in this format can have tremendous benefits for clients (e.g., reducing length of treatment). In this type of "blending," treatment is viewed pragmatically; those interventions that are best achieved by traditional means are accomplished in this manner. Those best achieved by programs like the SVRP program (see Chapter 7) are done with adventure therapy.

Primary therapy—Whereas adjunctive adventure therapy focuses on "adding to" the therapy being conducted, primary adventure therapy "replaces" more traditional methods as the means for reaching treatment objectives. The intensity of this type of intervention can require smaller client-to-therapist ratios (e.g., 1:1) or a small group where clients share very similar problems.

Gillis et al. (1991) identified the following characteristics that define a primary adventure therapy program: 1) the goal(s) of the therapist is to make a lasting change within the context of the adventure experience, 2) there is a large amount of assessment done prior to the therapeutic adventure experience in an attempt to identify the specific context of client issues, 3) the framing done prior to participating in the adventure activity is complex, 4) specific sequencing of isomorphic activities is used in order to achieve lasting systemic change within the client, 5) processing is used by the adventure therapist to punctuate the change or to reframe inappropriate interpretations of the experience, and 6) the primary therapy takes place while participating in the activity. The authors of this concept also state that this type of format may be more of a goal than a reality at this point in the field's development.

What does all of this really look like? The following case transcript (Gillis & Gass, in press) serves as an example of an adventure experience being used as the primary therapeutic modality to produce change in a dysfunctional family. Note that this adventure experience was conducted in the fifth session of therapy in a traditional therapy office setting.

Introduction: The following illustration is an actual case example of using an adventure experience as a medium for change with an addicted at-risk youth. In working with this youth and his family, I incorporated the following framework and adventure activity. The adventure activity that was used is commonly called the "Trust Lean" or "Blade of Grass." It is probably used most often as a lead-up activity to the "Trust Fall," but with this particular case it was an appropriate activity in itself.

Therapeutic Objective: Presenting symptoms of the identified patient (IP) included substance abuse, low self-esteem, and a strong fear that his father will abandon him. The therapeutic objective of this adventure experience was to re-direct the interaction between a father ("William") and his 14-year-old son ("Billy") who had become emotionally separated in a single-parent family where the mother had left home. This "re-direction" included the following progressive steps for this activity: 1) creating a safe atmosphere for change, 2) connecting the father-son relationship in a positive manner, and 3) changing their interaction to be more functional and less dependent on Billy's acting-out behaviors, thus bringing them together.

Intervention: (Therapist speaking) "I'd like to try something with the two of you to show you what might be happening in your family and how that will affect the future for both of you. This activity is about: 1) how kids grow up to be adults, 2) how they figure out what they will be able to achieve and how to believe in those dreams, and 3) how kids test limits. Okay? Dad, here we have Billy facing away from you and looking out into his future (the son is positioned facing away from his father). Dad, you're standing back here (the father is placed behind his son) supporting him like the good father that you are.
"In this exercise, Billy is moving forward toward his future, yet we all know that sometimes, as Billy has pointed out, kids fall back and need to be re-positioned. As you know, Dad, when this happens you need to re-establish Billy's freedom as a growing teenager and your appropriate control as a parent. So this exercise is about teenagers growing up and having setbacks and parents being the best ones to help their kids get re-established and stay on the 'straight path' to their dreams.
"Before the two of you begin practicing for the times that Billy will need your support, we better make sure that the two of you are there for each other. We'll do this with some statements you'll say before Billy falls backward. They will be:
Son: 'Are you there, Dad?'
Dad: 'I'm here, Billy.'

Son: '*I'm working toward my future.*'
Dad: '*I'm here to support you.*'

"Let's just try that." (The father and son go through these series of statements. Therapist asks Billy, "When your father says that, are you always sure that he's there?" Billy replies, "No," and to help change this interaction, the therapist has the son turn around and go through the statements face to face with the father. The father is directed to continually assure the son that he will be there.)

"*Now Billy, your role here is to use your sensitivity and help your Dad in the best way you can. He wants your future dreams to come true and for you to be able to be the best person you can, but he's also frightened for you. He's so frightened sometimes that he doesn't know what he should let you do or where he should let you go. So the best thing you can do to help him in this exercise is to show him that you trust him. In this exercise, like at other times, you don't say trust, you show it. You show it here by staying straight; the straighter you are in this exercise, the more you show your Dad that you trust him and that he can trust you. So stay straight in your ankles, your knees, your back, your heart, and your head.* (The therapist anchors these statements by touching each of these areas on Billy as they are stated.) *Staying straight in each of these areas shows trust. If you really want to show your Dad that you trust him and he can trust you, you will be as straight as possible, okay?* (Son indicates that he understands and agrees).

(To Dad) "*Now there are several ways you can accomplish your role here, Dad. You're a pretty strong guy, and you can stand back about two or three feet waiting for Billy to fall, or you can stay in touch with him by starting from the very beginning of the exercise with your hands on his shoulders. Which do you think would work best?* (The father chooses to stand back and wait, which is consistent with his "hands-off" approach to interacting with Billy unless he is acting out.) *Okay, let's try it.*" The exercise is done with signals given first by Billy to his father. The son laughs uneasily at the signals and fails to lean back to his father. He describes the experience as difficult for him to lean back on his father because he doesn't know if his father is there or if his father will catch him. Dad changes position so he is touching Billy and reassuring him that he is there. The two complete the exercise quite easily with the father providing supportive assurance and staying in contact with Billy and Billy remaining completely straight in working with his father.

(Therapist says to Dad): "*I'm **very** impressed with the change in your position and how much more comfortable Billy seems to be about doing this exercise. You know the more comfortable both of you get in Billy growing, the healthier the risks he can take as a growing young adult to* be the person he wants to be. It seems that one thing we know is that if kids stand for nothing, they'll fall for anything, right? Another feature of what you did that impressed me is that it's one thing to protect Billy from falling and making mistakes, but it's another to give in and let him go too far. If he doesn't stay straight, he could hit the floor, or worse yet, destroy his mind and body on things like drugs. As with all parents, you realize that it's important for you to remember that you know what's healthy and appropriate for him." (These isomorphic statements were made in the preceding manner to match the family's belief system and to ensure their integration into the future interaction between the father and son.)

Concluding remarks: The experience was discussed further, with the therapist focusing on how the relationship of the father and son needed to be "hands on" in order to be successful. This experience, titled "Straight to your dreams" for this particular situation, served as a significant change event for this family and provided the remaining sessions with a rich source of therapeutic information and focus, including extensions to other children in the family.

This type of therapeutic adventure experience seems to fall somewhere on the continuum in Figure 1 between adjunctive therapy and primary therapy. This intervention focused on the use of prescriptive therapeutic techniques (e.g., isomorphism, punctuation, framing, reframing, anchoring, circular questioning), required a large degree of assessment to construct such a prescriptive frame, and served as a source of information for future therapeutic sessions. The therapeutic benefit of such an experience did not occur through the satisfying enjoyment inherent in the activity, the global enrichment of the trust needed to accomplish the activity, or an adjunct to a therapeutic issue that was presented earlier. The benefit arose directly from using this experience as the primary means to convey therapeutic change.

One question that arises from this discussion is "When and what professionals are properly prepared to provide such an intervention?" This **certainly** is a current issue in the field of adventure therapy. As outlined later in the final article in this section, caution is needed when using interventions that have the potential to make such a difference for clients. The concept of "cross-training" outlined in the introduction of this book is probably one of the current ways some members of the field answer this question.

The following five articles in this section of the book are meant to demonstrate the current level of programs in several areas of adventure therapy. Two additional articles (i.e., Gillis & Simpson, Wichman) in this book describe adventure therapy programs, but they are included in

Section Five of the book because they also possess statistical analyses of each program's effectiveness.

The first article in this section, written by Susan Tippet, represents a common path used by adventure therapists to create appropriate interventions for clients. In her article, she outlines the particular etiology and treatment issues of an identified client group (i.e., borderline adolescents) and then translates how, as well as why, these theoretical bases are implemented in an adventure therapy program. Her article highlights the need of programs to prescriptively apply adventure programs to specific client groups based on their needs, a common thread in all of the articles of this section. She also reinforces the need to focus treatment on specific dysfunctional issues that cause presenting symptoms, rather than on these symptoms themselves.

In the second article, Betsy Webb outlines the 3-day adjunctive therapy program for survivors of violence conducted at the Colorado Outward Bound School. While the detail provided on issues such as research is informative, what is particularly valuable in this article are the critical issues that pertain to this specific population. Adventure therapists obviously need to heed these factors, as well as others, in working with this population.

Richard Kjol and John Weber provide a narrative description of a program for juvenile sexual offenders. An important point made by these authors and others (e.g., Kimball, 1983) is that adventure-therapy interventions are not "quick cures," but are often a portion of an extended therapeutic treatment. The authors also highlight the need for obtaining a good client assessment; change is not a random event, but something that is achieved through a structured, appropriate, and workable client/therapist relationship.

One of the best examples of a program illustrating the components of both an enrichment and adjunctive program is in the third article on the "Family Challenge" program outlined by Cindy Clapp and Suzanne Rudolph. One area where adventure programs have done comparatively little exploration is in the use of adventure therapy programming in a "proactive" capacity. As the authors show, using adventure programs in this manner can prevent clients from spiraling into even further dysfunctional behavior. Adventure experiences possess a great capacity for enriching and nurturing qualities already possessed by clients. More work in this area, like the efforts by the authors of this article, would expand the therapeutic applications of adventure experiences.

The final article outlines the theoretical basis for producing functional change in clients from a systemic perspective. The integration of marriage and family therapy with adventure programming joins the best of both of these approaches. Too often individual behaviors are observed and treated out of the context that contributed to creating, maintaining, or supporting these issues. As this article outlines, treating issues within their context can: 1) provide a more appropriate means of assessment, 2) help to change dysfunctional behaviors, and 3) provide the means for creating new functional and self-reinforcing behavior for clients.

An important issue addressed in the final article, and one that possesses broad application to adventure therapy approaches, is the need for caution when using certain interventions. These experiences, with the potential to bring about such beneficial change, also possess the same potential to be damaging if used incorrectly. The Ethical Guidelines implemented by the Therapeutic Adventure Professional Group found in Section Six of this text provide an initial point for professionals to consider when using adventure experiences in therapy.

6

THERAPEUTIC WILDERNESS PROGRAMMING FOR BORDERLINE ADOLESCENTS

SUSAN TIPPET, LICSW

Abstract: A therapeutic wilderness program is presented which facilitates the accomplishment of developmental tasks and the necessary reparative work with borderline adolescents. Six key areas of programming are discussed, providing a bridge between developmental and object relations, theoretical formulations, and practice.

Introduction

Therapists employed in outpatient counseling settings encounter increasing numbers of dysfunctional, acting-out adolescents. These teenagers frequently present a multitude of problems: they do poorly in school, abuse drugs and/or alcohol, act out sexually, and are in conflict with their parents. They also may be in trouble with the law. At the base of these blatant behaviors one often finds a depressed, often suicidal youngster with few intimate friends who has a history of losses and generally inconsistent or unavailable parenting. Clinically many of them are diagnosed as possessing borderline personality disorders (Goldstein, 1983).

The treatment needs of these adolescents are extensive. As with any adolescent, they face developmental tasks: they must develop or further a sense of mastery/competence; form a positive identity; develop age-appropriate peer and adult relationships; and separate from their parents (Blos, 1968; Erickson, 1980). At the same time, these clients need reparative work because the positive resolution of earlier crucial developmental tasks has been seriously impaired (Mahler, 1979; Masterson, 1972; Mishne, 1985). These impairments often interfere with their ability to complete stage-specific developmental tasks, bringing these adolescents to the attention of mental health care workers.

Psychotherapists have traditionally focused treatment on this reparative work. Unfortunately, redoing takes time, and time is at a premium for these teenagers. Already they are behind their peers academically, socially, and emotionally, and can ill afford to postpone their developmental tasks any further. They need therapeutic programming which simultaneously provides both an arena to accomplish these age-appropriate tasks and a corrective emotional experience. Such an experience is prerequisite to positive completion of the tasks, especially that of separation/individuation, the ultimate work of this age-group.

This chapter first describes one such therapeutic wilderness program that worked successfully with these clients. Next, it presents etiology and treatment of borderline adolescents from an object relations perspective. The final section demonstrates how this clinical theory and an understanding of the developmental tasks of adolescence are specifically applied in the program.

BORDERLINE PERSONALITY DISORDER

Although it is seen as a continuum, several crucial elements distinguish borderline pathology from other disorders. The key symptom is a primary problem in the area of relationships (i.e., in the ability to be related). Deficits also exist in other ego functions, particularly in impulse control, frustration tolerance, and reality testing (specifically in regard to relationships) (Kernberg, 1976; Masterson, 1972; Mishne, 1985). Frequently these ego deficits manifest themselves in what are commonly called "acting-out behaviors," a term that ignores the fact that these behaviors represent a desperate attempt to function without the necessary skills or emotional underpinnings. Cognitive impairments also exist, although they are less obvious as these clients are often intelligent. For example, clients may be unable to plan the series of tasks necessary to reach a goal or to solve problems. The major defenses used are projection and denial, both of which are maladaptive because they distort internal and external reality. Finally, these clients suffer from an underlying depression which, although difficult to assess initially because of their bravado and acting out, quickly becomes obvious.

Borderline pathology is a serious emotional disturbance based on a developmental arrest: specifically on an inability to successfully resolve the first major separation/individuation process that occurs at approximately age two (Mahler, Pine, & Bergman, 1975). The 15- to 20-month-old toddler begins to venture out into the world and to experience him- or herself as a separate entity. The child is moving farther away from the primary caregiver(s) only to return repeatedly to make sure that the caregiver is still there. The safety and reassurance supplied furthers the child's eagerness to explore. When parents are unavailable, inconsistent, or overly involved, this process of moving out and checking in is disrupted. The emotional turmoil generated from this anxiety and the resultant anger interfere with the child's ability to maintain a clear image of the caregiver when separate from that caregiver. Object constancy is a crucial developmental achievement that provides the basis for interacting securely with the world and for forming a clear self-image or sense of identity (self-constancy).

Blos (1968) is recognized as the first clinician to describe adolescence as a second period of separation/individuation, a now commonly accepted conceptualization. Adolescence is a resurgence of the need for autonomy and for object- and self-constancy. However, the adolescent's attempts to separate bring up the intense feelings of abandonment that she or he has spent so much energy defending against. Mishne (1985) suggests that instead of moving toward autonomy, the adolescent actively tries to re-engage the parents to ward off these feelings. Drug abuse, delinquency, and defiance, although frequently seen as efforts to separate, are actually maneuvers which demand parental involvement.

TREATMENT OF THE BORDERLINE CONDITION

Freed (1980) suggests a list of treatment tasks in work with borderline states. Treatment must be reality-oriented and focused on current issues with the goal of developing problem-solving skills. To create the working alliance, the therapist must connect with a resistant client as a "real person," thus minimizing transference. The impulsive behavior that is so common with these clients must be contained to allow the underlying feelings to surface and be addressed. The therapist must supply an auxiliary ego, as the client's own ego is initially incapable of tolerating feelings or monitoring behavior. Additionally, the worker must clearly expect positive behaviors and provide avenues for them.

Masterson (1972) believes that inpatient work is especially beneficial with borderline adolescents because it provides an opportunity to create a total milieu. In an inpatient setting it is easier to provide nurturing, thereby immediately reducing the client's levels of frustration and aggression. In addition, the staff's provision of structured discipline provides control, thus lessening the client's sense of internal anarchy. The maturational lag resulting from emotional turmoil, ego deficits, and unresponsive environments is dealt with through remedial programs and the expectation of healthy behavior. When behavior is inappropriate, it is confronted, thus challenging maladaptive defenses. The depression that surfaces when acting out is contained can also be safely worked through.

It is clear that the needs of a borderline client far exceed what can be accomplished once or twice a week in outpatient individual or group sessions. Outpatient workers commonly feel that they lack access to the resources needed to adequately help these clients. At the same time, the expense, stigma, and tendency to serious regression associated with residential treatment limits the use of that modality.

TRANSLATING CLINICAL THEORY INTO WILDERNESS PROGRAMMING

Therapeutic wilderness programming provides an intensive treatment model that combines the strengths of both inpatient and outpatient settings. The trips are like short periods of residential treatment in that the client is immersed in a total milieu. However, this milieu carries a positive, competency-building connotation. Therapeutic wilderness programming provides an ego-supportive, structural encouragement for developing new skills and coping positively with continuous daily challenges. Weekly group meetings help clients to transfer what they have learned on the trips to their daily experiences. Besides providing this bridge, meetings are a time to exchange support and further the trust that is solidified on trips. Group members are also reminded weekly that they are believed in and respected; they are a group of people who not only know their weaknesses but, more importantly, have shared in successes.

Therapeutic wilderness programs are as complex as any other clinical modality. Space does not permit detailing all elements of successful therapeutic programming. However, six key areas will be discussed: developing relatedness, setting limits, designing ego-enhancing opportunities, facilitating accomplishment of developmental tasks, distinguishing challenge from stress, and supporting separation through termination.

1. Developing Relatedness

Will (1959) writes, "Fundamental to all psychotherapy is the development of a relationship which makes possible a further evaluation of the past and an increased participation in new experience" (p. 218). This is a particularly compelling statement for the borderline client for whom the core injury is in the area of object relations. These clients need a corrective experience in which negative transferences, because of their strength and counterproductive nature, are minimized. In wilderness therapy the client can develop strong connections grounded in present experiences. The connectedness between group members and leaders grows out of the members' experience of the leaders as caring adults who are truly interested in them. As one group member wrote to a leader in the group journal: "You have made much difference in my life.... You captured my interest, no one ever held my attention in my life as long as you did. The reason is obvious to me now. You cared. It was more than just a job. You really cared."

Bonding also develops among group members through shared experiences. As one member wrote in the group journal: "Rain, mud, rain, dirt, wet, cold, hungry, tired—I can't believe we made it!"

For these youngsters whose perceptions are so easily distorted, concrete tangible experiences of caring are crucial. These experiences range from leaders ensuring that the group plans include nutritious, plentiful meals and adequate clothing, to permission to say no to a threatening activity, to having people share your load when you feel as though you cannot backpack another step. When distortions occur, the other group members and leaders can side with reality, making it difficult to cling to maladaptive coping efforts.

A long-term commitment is essential to provide a corrective experience to these clients. The group, the leaders, and the agency become a surrogate family. The importance of these groups in clients' lives should not be minimized. Another group journal entry attests to the strength of feelings engendered:

> The group is everything to me, it takes a major role in my life. It means more to me than anything in the whole world (yes, even my stereo). Right now it's all I've got going for me. If it weren't for the group I would have probably gone out and done something crazy to get me killed or in a juvenile home.... The group has given me something to live for. I hope through the group I'll find other things to live for. During this trip...when we were sitting around talking out other people's problems, I began to realize that they are very similar to my own. This made me feel good, happy, sad all over, inside and out. I was torn because I never felt this before and it brought me close, very close to everyone in the group. I never thought that I could have so many good friends at once. I feel so much better and so much surer about myself. I love everyone in the group (yes, even you, Sam).

2. Setting Limits

Setting limits is often part of therapy but is especially required with borderline adolescents. Limits, besides being crucial for safety in the wilderness, define the boundaries of the relationship. A leader's refusal to set limits or to be consistent with limits is experienced by members as a repetition of the original abandonment that occurred during the initial separation/individuation period. Although this repetition experience can happen in traditional clinical settings, it is more powerful in the wilderness because of the increased similarities between the two situations.

Therapeutic wilderness leaders, like parents of the young adventurer, must create an appropriately safe, responsive environment. Winnicott's (1965) conception of the "good enough holding environment" is applicable (Davis & Wallbridge, 1981). The holding environment refers to the total milieu created by the primary caregiver, allowing the infant to make use of the caregiver's ego in developing and integrating her or his own ego. The baby needs protection from excessive impingements and overstimulation. In addition, the baby needs an environment responsive to his or her needs, both physiological and psychological. Over time, the immediacy of this response can decrease as the baby develops the ego strength to tolerate delays and to meet some of her or his own needs. An appropriate holding environment supports ego development and intrapsychic growth at all ages (Redl & Wineman, 1965).

Limits help to create such an environment in two ways. First, they are the mechanism for creating a sense of safety. Rules that prohibit violence and require wearing seat belts in the van, for example, convince group members that their safety is important to the leaders. If at any time a leader ignores an accepted safety rule, even one that is constantly protested, the ensuing chaos attests to the sense of abandonment members feel. Second, limits convey a sense of control. For these youngsters, who so continually feel out of control, the message is, "We will help you be in control." Just as in inpatient work (Masterson, 1972), acting out is immediately reduced. Kids with long histories of being out of control frequently settle down on trips, much to the amazement and sometimes frustration of their parents and probation officers.

Additionally, limits provide a place for struggle, a point of contact (Moustakas, 1959). Adolescents need to struggle in order to define themselves. Once safety has been established, they need a place for interaction, for give and take and compromise. The challenge is to provide this place without jeopardizing the integrity of the holding environment. One way to conceptualize this dilemma is to see limits as two concentric circles. The outer circle contains limits that guarantee safety. These limits are not safe to struggle around; they should not be compromised. The inner circle contains limits that are initially necessary but may be changed over time, and limits that are not safety-related. These inner-circle limits (such as "no one leaves the leaders without permission" and "cigarette butts must be pocketed") can then become the point of struggle. In this way leaders can choose their battles, maintaining a level of control which supports both their own and the group's sense of safety. It is essential that limits be legitimate, as adolescents are quick to recognize rigidity or phoniness, both of which undermine this process. Leaders must be clear on the reasons for a specific limit and be willing to stand behind it.

3. Designing Ego-enhancing Opportunities

While the corrective experience that occurs through positive relationships in a safe, nurturing, ego-supportive environment is an essential part of treatment, it is not enough in and of itself. The ego deficits that these clients display must also be directly addressed. Delays in the development of cognitive skills, impulse control, and reality testing will not automatically disappear as the emotional issues are resolved. Programming must specifically teach and reteach these skills in much the same way that a healthy young child is exposed to numerous, graduated, learning experiences that eventually result in the consolidation of a variety of strong ego skills.

The cognitive abilities most commonly underdeveloped in these clients are the skills of planning, problem solving, decision making, and negotiating. These adolescents for the most part cannot set a goal and then systematically work their way to it. They are thus largely at the mercy of whatever comes their way. Many wilderness organizations hand participants a prepackaged program. While relatively intact clients may benefit from pre-planned activities, borderline clients are deprived of vital learning experiences.

In therapeutic wilderness programming, the planning of trips is turned over to the group members as much as possible. Menu planning, for example, provides practice in decision making and negotiating. The leader must be prepared with many suggestions because initially the group will have difficulty even coming up with realistic ideas. It may take two weeks for the group to agree on meals that they want and that meet the leader's requirement of being nutritious, but at least the group will practice making decisions and working through disagreements. While giving the group as much control as possible, the leader must also initially guard against failure. Until ego strengths are developed, a group will experience inadequate food on a trip as an abandonment repetition and all potential learning will be lost.

Planning, problem solving, decision making, and negotiation are practiced repeatedly. For example, the group must decide on the type, length, and location of each trip as well as on clothing requirements. In addition to preparation, the trips themselves offer numerous learning situations: if, for example, the trail leads to a bridge over a river and the bridge has been washed out, or a couple of group members are feeling exhausted but the rest of the group wants to climb a peak as planned, the group must plan, solve problems, make decisions, and negotiate.

Post-trip processing also creates opportunities for consolidating new skills as trip experiences are generalized to apply to daily-life tasks. One group member, for example, was having difficulty following through on the steps necessary to get part-time work, all the while expressing his eagerness for a job. After a rock-climbing trip, the group spent time describing each person's climbing style. Then each person talked about how the approach to the rock face matched his or her style of relating to life in general. This group member was described as keeping his eyes on the top of the cliff and frantically scrambling. He did not take time to plan his route or series of moves, and thus made his climb more difficult. Once his style of handling problems was described, and its consequences concretely clear, this member was more willing and able to listen to alternative methods for dealing with his job difficulties.

4. Facilitating Developmental Tasks

As noted earlier, these adolescents need assistance with the normal developmental tasks of identity formation, furthering a sense of mastery and competence, developing appropriate peer and adult relationships, and separation and individuation. This latter task, addressed earlier, will be discussed further in the final section of this paper, "Supporting Separation Through Termination."

By becoming part of a group, the client immediately gains access to a positive identity. No longer are her or his identifications all negative (i.e., druggie, school drop-out, juvenile delinquent). Now, even if only tentatively at first, the client is a "wilderness group member." There are several ways to strengthen this sense of belonging and to foster positive identification. Frequently, trip pictures are put in the local newspaper with headings such as "Wilderness Group Explores Underground Passages" or "Adventure in the Water." These articles provide evidence of belonging. Numerous slides and movies of the trip are taken, and constant reviewing of the pictures creates many opportunities for reworking the trip experience. New group members are given a personal journal and a metal camping cup. It is their responsibility to designate each of these so that everyone will know whose they are. Group T-shirts and patches are also useful in solidifying a sense of membership.

These youngsters arrive at adolescence without the necessary skills to compete with their peers academically, vocationally, or avocationally, and find the usual avenues to developing a sense of mastery and competence closed to them. However, wilderness trips encompass a wide variety of opportunities for success in areas that are relatively conflict-free because of their unfamiliarity. Leaders must redefine success so that it includes not only getting to the top of the mountain but also telling a joke when someone is cranky, requesting a break when tired, offering an alternative idea when a problem seems unsolvable, fixing a meal, finding a tree for hanging the food, pulling a trick on a leader, etc.

As existing skills, talents, and personality traits are recognized and validated, group members become increasingly interested in expanding their repertoire. As they begin to feel a sense of competence, they find additional energy for learning. This process is sometimes lengthy because of the existing levels of injury and self-doubt. However, even the member who chooses not to learn a new skill watches others and learns about a new way of relating to the world. At times the entire group will decide on a difficult trip for which they must first acquire certain skills. They must then all agree to learn the skills in order to do the trip, or instead choose to plan an easier trip.

A note on control is important here. Although the leaders set the stage in a thousand ways, group members, as much as possible, should be allowed control, particularly by being permitted to say no. People cannot truly embrace life until they have the power to say no; just as the 2-year-old says no before saying yes, so these adolescents must have that option. It can be very frustrating to have a new group not get out on a trip for several months because they cannot agree on the kind of trip; however, this process is crucial. Just as effective parents provide appropriate opportunities for their children to make decisions about their lives, so must leaders.

Powerful relationships develop among group members and with the leaders through the living situation of trips which facilitates and requires interaction. Because this relating occurs without the support or interference of drugs, alcohol, or music, it can be difficult at first for some group members. However, the structure of the activities helps to reduce this discomfort. It is important for group members to learn that they can have fun in a "clean" environment. The key to positive interactions lies in the creation of safety, the meeting of basic needs, and the expectations and role modeling of the leaders. Disagreements will happen frequently but they should, because it is in their negotiation that skills are learned and connections made.

5. Distinguishing Challenges from Stress

The terms stress and challenge, although frequently used interchangeably, refer to very different processes. Stress, or excessive impingements on the holding environment, is related to a sense of jeopardy and lowers self-esteem. Challenges, on the other hand, bolster self-esteem because they are experiences which the individual or group expects to master in spite of an element of perceived risk (Lazarus & Launier, 1978).

Many wilderness programs foster physical and psychological stress (Kelly & Baer, 1968). While stress may be helpful for learning to push past self-imposed limits, it is counter-indicated for in-depth reparative work. Psychic growth requires a holding environment where anxiety is reduced. Since anxiety has been responsible for solidifying maladaptive behaviors, increasing it will only interfere in the process of true change.

The subjective experience of an activity determines whether it is defined as a stress or a challenge. Almost any activity will be experienced as a stress if it is imposed on participants. Yet the same activity can improve self-esteem if participants choose it themselves. For example, being forced to continue on a difficult rock climb is likely to undermine self-esteem even if the climb is completed. However, if participants know they can choose which climb to attempt and can come off a climb if necessary without loss of face, they will experience climbing as a challenge. Self-esteem will increase and the holding environment will be supported.

6. Supporting Separation through Termination

As separating is the core issue with borderline clients (Masterson, 1972), termination provides an opportunity to consolidate all of the work that has been done. It is a true separation that, if done correctly, can solidify the gains made and prepare the member for individuating fully from parents.

The decision to terminate must be left to each group member. Obviously premature termination is discouraged by ascertaining the underlying issues. Group members often threaten termination in order to hear how important they are to the group. They may also be acting out separation anxiety. Although it is difficult, leaders must respond to the fears underlying such threats and not themselves become rejecting out of frustration. It is usually clear whether a proposed termination is appropriate. If, for example, a member is going on to college or a full-time job or is now involved with extra-curricular activities and has made several positive friendships, it is time to move on. However, if a member suddenly claims boredom after a particularly difficult trip or is not yet functioning well outside of the group, termination is probably premature.

Once the decision has been determined to be appropriate, the group begins to prepare for the upcoming separation. Traditions or rituals marking the separation can be meaningful both to the group and to the individual leaving. For example, the leader, as the parent, buys a going-away present after soliciting ideas from members. This present is delivered on the termination trip at a time and in a manner determined by the group. Usually the group holds a "surprise party" the last night of the trip during which members share with the graduating member their sense of his or her importance to the group.

Frequently, departing members respond to the group in the group journal as well as sharing their feelings verbally. For example, a young man who joined the group at age 16, had not attended school for more than a few weeks since he was 14. During his term of membership in the group, he passed his high school equivalency exam, obtained his driver's license, and was accepted by a college. Ready to leave the group at age 19, he wrote:

> God it's hard to believe it's over; the total meaning of this probably won't hit me till tomorrow. About two and a half years ago on April 24, 1980, when I joined, I had no idea what I'd be in for. I'd do it all again if I could, but I guess you have to face endings to face beginnings. I hope in the future, someday, somehow we'll all be able to get together.... I take a piece of the group with me when I leave and leave a bit of myself behind, in the journal and in the minds of those I've had a chance to know in my time in the group. I'm ending here not because of a lack of things to say, but I'd prefer to speak them. (This ninth-grade dropout graduated from college in May, 1986.)

When played out to its fullest, one member's termination can benefit all group members. The remaining members practice for their own departure from the group as well as from home. The fears of the group that the leaders will be overwhelmed by the loss of a member or become rejecting out of anger are not substantiated, nor is the belief that the departing member will be forgotten. Leaders, like members, experience sadness as the member moves on. In the sharing of this sadness is acknowledgment of the importance of that group member. This acknowledgment validates the realness of the connection while supporting the graduate's growth onward. As a leader wrote in the group journal:

The cycles of a group—each time an old member gets ready to graduate, I look back, remembering the beginning when that person was new, so young, and so unknown. At the beginning you have no way of knowing all the struggles you'll go through together and all the special moments that you'll share; the struggles seem more frequent than the shared times, but toward the end, the hard times come less often and seem so much easier to resolve. It's as though we've found a rhythm, a way of being together that gives us structure when we disagree. It's hard to let go in the end, even though it is time to do so. Each time a member graduates it feels as though the group will never be the same and it never is. But the cycles go on, the struggles continue and someone else becomes the older member. And what of those members who have left? They continue to be important people in my life—I watch them growing from a distance now. Our time together in the group is over and yet our connection, on some deep level, remains.

CONCLUSION

Therapeutic wilderness programming has been presented as a method for attending to the present developmental tasks of borderline adolescents while simultaneously assisting in the reworking of earlier deficits. In the past, clinicians have largely focused on the latter while activities staff and wilderness leaders, where they existed, on the former. However, neither area of change can be fully accomplished without the other. From the combined insights of outdoor instructors and clinicians come truly innovative and effective methods for helping people. Tailoring wilderness programs to specific client groups is a challenging, vital process that requires continual conceptualizing. The tapestry of knowledge remains incomplete; increasing understanding is an ongoing process.

Sue Tippett, LICSW, directed a therapeutic wilderness program for adolescents for 10 years. She presents regionally and nationally on therapeutic wilderness programs and codirects Outdoor Trips for Women. She holds a master's degree from the University of Connecticut School of Social Work. Currently she consults to agencies running therapeutic wilderness programs, is an associate faculty member at Greenfield Community College's Outdoor Leadership Program, provides psychotherapy to children of homeless addicted women, and has a private practice specializing in work with adolescents, women, and families.

7

THE USE OF A THREE-DAY THERAPEUTIC WILDERNESS ADJUNCT BY THE COLORADO OUTWARD BOUND SCHOOL WITH SURVIVORS OF VIOLENCE

BETSY J. WEBB, M.S., M.S.W.

Introduction

The current rate of violent crime in the United States is increasing, particularly in the areas of sexual abuse, sexual assault, and domestic violence. A woman is more likely to be assaulted, injured, raped, or killed by a male partner than by any other type of assailant. Thirty to 46% of all children are sexually assaulted in some way before the age of 18. Violence occurs among all races and socioeconomic groups (CARE Network, 1990).

In response to these growing numbers, several adventure therapy programs have implemented programming for survivors of violence. One of these programs, the Colorado Outward Bound School (COBS), conducts 3-day therapeutic wilderness courses as an adjunct to traditional treatment. In 1990, 25 three-day courses were conducted for over 200 survivors. This program, called the "Survivors of Violence Recovery Program" (SVRP), was honored by the National Victim Center as an Exemplary Program in 1988.

The purpose of this chapter is to provide an introduction to the COBS 3-day model and to discuss issues pertinent to survivors of violence. Research into the effectiveness of the program will also be outlined. Pronouns used will be feminine as most of the survivors of violence served by the COBS are female.

ADJUNCTIVE PROGRAM MODEL

A course length of 3 days was chosen for this program after taking into consideration cost, work schedules of clients, childcare concerns, and course effectiveness. Many of the women could arrange one day off from work but were not willing to miss 2 days of employment. A longer course length would have made it difficult for clients who have childcare concerns to attend. A program shorter than 3 days was ruled out for reasons of course effectiveness.

Most SVRP courses are conducted in conjunction with a referring agency or private therapist who brings his/her own group of clients to Outward Bound. On all SVRP courses, a pre-course consultation is performed with the referring agency or private therapist. The clinical background on each client is obtained, and the goals for each client are blended into the design of the course. Clients attend an orientation to the Outward Bound course to assist them in preparing for the experience.

The design for each 3-day SVRP course is flexible. A typical course may include the following adventure components, depending on client needs: trust activities, group initiatives, ropes course elements, rock climbing and rappelling, orienteering, snowshoeing, cross-country skiing, or a solo. Agencies and Outward Bound staff work together in developing a design that will appropriately address the issues of the client group. Activities are sequentially designed, and the skills learned in one component are used in the next. During summer months, the groups camp outdoors; in the winter months, rustic dormitory accommodations are available.

Group process sessions occur during the debriefing of each activity and also each evening. These sessions are an integral part of the course and help clients to focus on transferring the learning from the course back to the home environment. Each 3-day course culminates in a closing ceremony that includes a Certificate of Completion and an Outward Bound pin. The ritual of a closing ceremony honors the work that clients have done on their course and is used to symbolize what they have learned to assist them in their future.

Follow-up interventions are performed by the referring agency or private therapist in client sessions following each SVRP course. Accompanying therapists are responsible for providing the link between the Outward Bound experience and clients. A written evaluation is mailed to SVRP clients 6 weeks after their participation in Outward Bound to provide the SVRP with continuous feedback to enhance its therapeutic effectiveness.

Clientele

Participants on SVRP courses are generally women between 20 and 45 years old; however, women from 12 to 68 years old have also participated. Up to 25% of the courses are conducted for survivors under the age of 18. A handful of male survivors and male family members participate on courses each year. Courses are conducted separately for issues of sexual assault, sexual abuse, and domestic violence. Although many of the dynamics on these courses are similar, the differences between client needs necessitate separate courses.

Staffing of Survivors of Violence Courses

All staff who work in the SVRP are competent in Outward Bound procedures. All possess the necessary technical background for working in wilderness settings and each has current American Red Cross Advanced First Aid (or Emergency Medical Technician) and CPR certifications. Although it is not required, many of the staff have advanced degrees in social work, psychology, education, or other human service fields. Since referring agencies send accompanying therapists on the SVRP courses, the program does not expect staff to have degrees in a field of mental health. However, staff in the SVRP are usually senior COBS staff, chosen for their abilities in counseling and facilitation, and have a good understanding of issues related to sexual assault, incest, and domestic violence.

Most courses are staffed with two female instructors. The SVRP occasionally works with male survivors or family units and male staff are available for these courses. If an agency requests a male staff for a women's course, these requests are accommodated.

Funding

Few clients are able to pay for their Outward Bound course. The majority of clients are single mothers, often with low incomes, supporting several children. The SVRP is presently supported through federal Victims of Crime Act funds, local Victim Assistance and Law Enforcement funds, and in-kind support from COBS. Some clients are able to use their Victim's Compensation Funds to pay for the course. Clients may apply for up to 100% tuition assistance for the course.

ISSUES PERTAINING TO SURVIVORS OF VIOLENCE

The effects of sexual assault, sexual abuse, and domestic violence are manifested in individuals in many ways. However, there are some common issues related to survivors of violence. Most survivors experience feelings of helplessness, isolation, powerlessness, hopelessness, and guilt. Many have strong feelings of love and attachment, as well as anger and rage, for the perpetrator (most perpetrators of violence in the United States are known to their victims: CARE Networker, 1990).

Clients often experience feelings of terror when they seek help (Agosta & Loring, 1988). They may experience a variety of symptoms including chronic depression, suicidal thoughts, sexual disorders, difficulties in relationships, parenting difficulties, substance abuse, eating disorders, low self-esteem, somatic disorders, phobias, occluded memory, and co-dependency (Sexual Assault Treatment Services, 1988).

Issues pertinent to working with survivors of violence in wilderness settings include: a) flashbacks; b) dissociation; c) control; d) anger/rage; e) fear; and f) trust.

A. **Flashbacks**—Staff should expect that some clients will experience flashbacks on courses. In adventure programming, the physical situations during activities may evoke feelings similar to those experienced during their sexual assault, sexual abuse, or battering (Agosta & Loring, 1988). Blindfolds, ropes, and wilderness settings may have been a part of the victimization and can be triggers for flashbacks. Adventure experiences are designed to enable the client to appropriately confront feelings and situations differently than in the past. Staff and group members focus on providing support and reassurance to the clients concerning issues of safety during the adventure experience as they may relive the horrors of the past. Staff members must be adept at recognizing flashbacks and feel comfortable with their ability to work with clients during these episodes.

B. **Dissociation**—During an assault, survivors often experience a separation of mind and body (Blakely, 1987). This is a defense mechanism to help the survivor cope with the abuse. However, dissociation may also occur when survivors are confronted by the fear and anxiety that may accompany adventure activities. If this occurs, dissociation becomes a dysfunctional coping strategy. Participants need to be physically present for safety reasons. If dissociation does occur during physical activities, clients can try deep breathing, affirmation statements, and soliciting support. Useful strategies for staff include: 1) verbal interventions to remind the clients of where they are, who is present, and that they are safe; 2) having clients stomp their feet on the earth as a grounding exercise; and 3) encouraging clients to keep their eyes open and focus on group members, asking for their support if necessary.

C.   **Control Issues**—Many course participants feel uneasy about the idea of Outward Bound. They are anxious about their loss of control during the program. Regardless of their orientation to the experience by the referring agency, they are unsure about what is going to happen because not all of the details of the experience can be explained prior to participation.

It is important on these courses to honor clients for ways in which they feel they must take control (saying "no" to an activity, removing a blindfold, etc.) and to remember that clients did not have control during their abuse. Clients should never be forced to take part in any activity. For some clients, it may be therapeutically appropriate for them to take a firm stand in saying "no" to an activity. Staff must be comfortable in working with high levels of anxiety and must be adept at avoiding power struggles. When control is an issue, it is probable that clients are feeling vulnerable. Processing about the need for control may uncover therapeutic material and should be used when appropriate.

D.   **Anger/Rage**—Survivors differ greatly in their response to abuse. Some are enraged while others appear superficially to experience little anger. Others deal with their anger by expressing it indirectly, as in sexual acting out, running away, self-mutilation, perpetration, depression, and suicide (Caruso, 1987). Many clients are able to get in touch with anger and rage during their adventure experience. One aim of therapy is to assist clients in learning to experience and express anger safely (Agosta & Loring, 1988; Bass & Davis, 1988). Feelings of helplessness and powerlessness during activities may be mobilized into expressions of anger and rage. By dealing with these feelings, the experience can become one of empowerment.

Examples of anger/rage have occurred when clients experience difficulties on a ropes course. Clients may feel as though they lack the physical strength to continue. They may have negative feelings about their bodies. If clients have made the choice to continue and become angry about feeling helpless, they may mobilize themselves with their anger to complete the event. This can feel like a powerful release to them. One client stated:

> The activities in the course brought up a lot of anger and other feelings I've not dealt with since my assault. I feel when I was climbing the mountain, I left a lot of pent-up anger on that mountain. I don't think I would have done that on my own to the degree I did on the mountain. I believe I have a renewed strength. (R. L., 1989)

Staff must be prepared to be the target of anger because they represent authority figures and sometimes symbolic perpetrators. If staff recognize this and appropriately avoid power struggles, clients may work directly and positively on relationships with authority figures. These courses offer a healthy opportunity for release of intense emotions, provided the staff are skilled in facilitating these experiences.

E. **Fear**—Clients almost always experience some fear during adventure activities, but this fear should be seen as a chance to explore the choices they have when afraid. Many clients feel that fear controls them, but the activities on the course can help them to make the choice to overcome fear. When afraid, clients can take one step, a deep breath, and use the support of the group to help themselves. As opposed to being paralyzing, fear can be viewed as a way to prepare themselves for challenges.

F. **Trust**—Trust is paramount for survivors of violence. They have good reason to be wary of others and may not see the value in taking the risk of being hurt. This applies not only to difficulties in relationships, but also to issues of self-esteem (Caruso, 1987). It is essential to remember the vulnerability of clients and not to make light of the risks they are taking. It is a good idea to adapt activities on the course based on clients' needs, rather than follow a predetermined procedure.

In addition to the above issues, there is much joy and celebration on these courses as clients discover themselves and their personal power. For some, the inner child who was abused and neglected "comes out to play" while engaged in the adventure program. A strong emphasis needs to be placed on these positive aspects as well as on more difficult material. Clients should experience freedom and multiple opportunities to laugh and have fun. The goals of the SVRP courses are to assist in the empowerment of survivors of violence and to enhance their self-esteem.

RESEARCH ON THE EFFECTIVENESS OF THE SURVIVORS OF VIOLENCE RECOVERY PROGRAM AT COBS

Three research studies have been conducted on the SVRP. Oliver (1988), in reviewing evaluations of former students on SVRP courses, found that these courses are most effective in providing clients with insight, understanding, and helping them work through fearful situations. Data were obtained through a questionnaire survey sent to program alumni. The questionaire included eight Likert Scale questions assessing the effect of an Outward Bound course on issues of self-confidence, trust, communication with others, and response to fearful situations.

In her research of rape victims attending the 3-day SVRP, Pfirman (1988) found that the Outward Bound adjunct had tendencies ($p < .10$) toward: 1) decreasing the level of fear experienced by clients, 2) decreasing the perception that chance and powerful others controlled their lives, and 3) increasing their self-concept. Instruments for measurement included the Modified Fear Survey, the Levenson Locus-of-Control Scale, and the Tennessee Self-Concept Scale. Pfirman concluded that the sequential activities and success-oriented outcomes of the Outward Bound experience had a direct effect on the self-confidence of the participants. Prior to their SVRP experience, the women in the study all tested high on levels of fear. Afterward, every individual demonstrated significant decreases in their overall fears, their fear of rape, and their fear of failure. Pfirman attributed the success of the program to: 1) the combination of structured activities that challenged the women and led to successes, and 2) the support and encouragement offered by group members to confront fears. Clients experienced personal achievement as a result of their participation in the SVRP and they developed a sense of personal power as well as an increased ability to trust others and themselves (Pfirman, 1988).

Israel (1989) conducted a study on the effect of the SVRP on battered women. Research revealed that the 3-day adjunct had significant ($p < .05$) positive effect on increasing battered womens' self-concept and problem-solving appraisal, and decreasing their perceptions that powerful others and chance controlled their lives. These changes remained significant ($p < .05$) one month later. Instrumentation for this study included the Problem-Solving Inventory, the Tennessee Self-Concept Scale, and the Levenson Locus-of-Control Scale. This study concluded that therapeutic strategies, like those found in the SVRP, must give women more power to protect themselves. It also pointed out that the strength of the SVRP group activities facilitated women to take emotional risks, share feelings, and ask for support. Its final conclusion suggested that the participants on the SVRP gained a variety of mental images and metaphors to use as new resources for future problem-solving or self-worth references.

SUMMARY

The 3-day SVRP model, when used as an adjunct to existing treatment, is effective in enhancing clients' self-concept and problem-solving appraisal abilities, and decreasing their perception that chance and powerful others control their lives. Clients experientially confront issues in the program that produce feelings of terror, rage, and helplessness. Unlike more traditional forms of therapy, clients are able to react with action and new behaviors, beginning the process of change in safe and supportive environments. Therapists who have used Outward Bound as an adjunct to traditional treatment with survivors of violence state that the 3-day model often reduces the length of treatment required for many clients (Abarbanel, 1988; Wartik, 1986). One therapist said that "it would take 6 months of therapy to do what we do in a weekend" (DePaul, date unknown). Agosta and Loring (1988) of *Ending Violence Effectively* stated that:

> *Wilderness therapy is a powerful vehicle for experiencing emotions and eventually being able to express them. It is a path to learning pragmatic ways of changing one's behavior, of testing newly learned skills, of stretching, reaching, and growing beyond one's imagination. It seems almost limitless in its possibilities for aiding in the healing process, and it can provide new hope and excitement and expand a person's limits. (p.133)*

Betsy J. Webb, M.S., M.S.W., was the Director of Health and Education Services for the Colorado Outward Bound School in Denver, Colorado. She currently is the Human Resources Director for the Colorado Outward Bound School.

8

THE 4TH FIRE: ADVENTURE-BASED COUNSELING WITH JUVENILE SEX OFFENDERS[1]

ROBERT KJOL
JOHN WEBER

Tommy grew up in a home where sexual abuse was a way of life. He recalls being first abused sexually at age 4 by his 13-year-old brother and 14-year-old sister. When Tommy was 8, this same brother coached him through the sexual assault of a 6-year-old male cousin. This behavior continued for several years and expanded to include the forcible abuse of two younger siblings. Tommy wound up in treatment when his cousin told his teacher about the sexual contact, 5 years after it began. Beyond the incest, Tommy had never been in trouble in his community or school. He is currently 13 years old and is an average student in his mainstream classes.

Bill lured a 10-year-old boy in his neighborhood to his tree house in the woods by telling the boy that he could join his club. Once there, several pornographic magazines were brought out. After several minutes of looking at the pictures, Bill told the boy that part of the club initiation was to try some of the sexual acts shown in the magazines. When the 10-year-old initially said no, Bill threatened him by saying that unless he performed the acts, the boy's parents would find out about his looking at the pornographic material. The sexual abuse took place, the 10-year-old told his family a few days later, and Bill was arrested and court-ordered into treatment. Bill is 15 years old and is in the gifted and talented program at his high school.

Jim showed mild signs of Fetal Alcohol Syndrome. For years he was the victim of sexual abuse by two out of the last three of his mother's live-in boyfriends. For the past 2 years, he has been sexually abusing the 7- and 9-year-old daughters of his mother's friend. He babysits for these children twice each week. A month ago the mother of these children caught Jim in the act of abusing one of her daughters. Although caught in the act and referred to treatment by the juvenile court, Jim consistently states that he was "set up," that these girls asked for and wanted his affection. Jim is 14 years old and has been involved in special education during his entire school history.

These three young men, and seven other adolescent sex offenders, have just arrived at Treetop Adventure to participate in a 5-day workshop that will offer a rich combination of adventure, experience, counseling, and fun. The events over the next 5 days will at times be stressful and frustrating, but also exhilarating and self-assuring.

Adventure-based counseling has been recognized for years as a valuable component in the treatment of the emotionally disturbed adolescent. At Treetop Adventure, we have found this to be particularly true in our work with the adolescent sexual offender. This article will describe the sequential, adventure-based counseling process we use to draw from the participants any additional disclosures of sexual offense that may be in their past. Counseling obviously continues throughout the program, yet topic-specific sessions of high impact are reserved for the evening campfire. On our 5-day programs, the final campfire, called The 4th Fire, is designed to draw as much information from the group as they are willing to admit. Over the past 3 years, this final campfire has resulted in many disclosures of both personal victimization and perpetration from guilt-ridden adolescents who have kept these secrets hidden for as long as 7 years. Because of the intensity of the topic of sexual offense, these youths have to be substantially convinced that revealing these secrets will result in a significant and positive change in their lives.

WHAT IS A SUCCESS?

Involving juvenile sex offenders in adventure education programming is not a "quick cure." The 10 youths now at "camp" may have attended some form of therapy for several months (even years), yet they continue to struggle with their issues. It must also be remembered that all have entered camp with a great deal of fear, apprehension, and shame. They are afraid that others will find out what they have done, and they trust neither themselves nor others when it comes to forming new relationships. Due to this self-doubt, the sex offender has practiced and is usually quite good at keeping any interchange at a superficial level, and is immediately suspicious of any display of warmth or care.

In spite of these obstacles, a great deal of success can occur. Adventure-based counseling can help Tommy to understand his strong need to feel in control of others. It can help Bill to gain the courage to disclose how many other "club members" he has assaulted, and it can help Jim to understand his fear of being physically or emotionally hurt.

To bring any of this out, facilitators must have a clear understanding of their own sexuality and a willingness to delve into the subject matter of sexual offense as comfortably as they talk about the equipment to be used or the need to keep the firewood dry. Facilitators must also understand that they are but one part of a continuum of care. The fruits of their efforts may not be seen during the time that they spend with these youths but may result in the disclosure of other abuse weeks, even months, later. With this in mind, success should be defined as a willingness to supply a comfortable, trusting atmosphere where open discussions about sexual offense can occur. For many offenders, this atmosphere may aid them to simply say their victim's name aloud. By doing this, their victim leaps from the safe classification of an object to the more vulnerable classification of a person. Empathy can now begin to be developed and the internal wall of denial can begin to crumble. The tears shed can wash away some of the fear, guilt, and shame.

Because their secrets have been hidden so deeply, for such a long time, we feel that a truly successful experience is one that entails a 5-day, or longer, high-impact schedule. The group arrives on Monday at base camp and will leave on Friday evening. The participants will canoe, camp, climb, and cook together for the next 120 hours. Providing a workable schedule and a high expectation of success is mandatory from the staff. Success cannot always be measured on a graph, though it can be felt in the heart.

THE VALUE AND USE OF PROCESSING

There is little difference between the adrenalin rush experienced when riding "The Edge" at Great America or when leaping to a trapeze from the top of a "Pamper Pole." Both involve a perceived risk and a great feeling of pleasure when your feet finally touch the ground. Both "rides" can be undertaken just for the fun of it. What makes adventure-based counseling stand out as a solid treatment tool is the processing that occurs after the ride. Without it, the ropes course is just another amusement park, something that Tommy, Bill, and Jim will experience and then leave. They may leave with a desire to return, to see if they can make it through the elements again, but little more. All three boys have experienced similar feelings in the past following new and unique experiences, including sexual offense.

At Treetop Adventure, an introductory session is held where all participants share with one another a little information about themselves. By stating the fact that all participants share a common problem, the leader can encourage the group to begin sharing information about their sexual offenses. Ask for a brief statement from each regarding his/her most recent offense that includes the very basics of what was done and to whom. This does not need to be long and drawn out. The purpose of this early session is to establish the fact that sexual offense is a topic that will be talked about many times during the next few days. This group also serves as a tension release valve for most of its members. One of the things most feared as they enter camp is quickly eliminated, and that is: "Are these guys going to find out what I did?"

Once this initial disclosure is out, it is important to establish the concept that with some work and by taking some risks in disclosing past behavior, they can gain control of this behavior. This can be a hard statement to sell, particularly to offenders who have already failed while in some form of treatment. Before they said it to anyone else, they have already told themselves, and possibly even their victim(s), that they would never offend again. As a result of their repeated failures to keep this promise, many sex offenders begin to believe that there is no escape from this behavior pattern. Getting "healthy" is something that they will never be able to accomplish. For this reason, a major task for facilitators over the next few days is to help Tommy, Bill, and Jim to start to believe that they can accomplish almost any task that they are willing to commit themselves to and *try*.

Much of the processing during the week should be centered around the reactions that these youths display during stressful situations. Just arriving at the campsite will be highly stressful to some of the participants as they stand in the woods and watch their parents drive away. From the start, they will be engaging in games that result in a great deal of body contact and touch. Working together on the Trolleys is but one example of this. Jim may feel anxious because of his past history of abuse and his distorted perception that any physical contact is sexual in nature. Bill may become uncomfortable because he swore to himself that he would stop abusing others and now feels himself gravitating toward Jim. Tommy may have feelings of shame because he finds himself enjoying and getting "turned on" by all the contact.

Tommy, Bill, and Jim will be hearing about something called a Trust Fall where they will be asked to fall backwards into the outstretched and waiting arms of people they barely know. They will learn about being a "spotter" and experience other people "spotting" them as they work through some of the low elements. They will be hoisted, pulled, and grabbed as they attempt to get over the "Wall." From the point of view of touch alone, there will be no shortage of stress during this 5-day program. Add to this the typical feelings of fear and vulnerability experienced while on the high elements, rock climbing, and/or rappelling, and one will see the sex offender react. What will be common and should be looked for is an active attempt to regain a feeling of control. The adolescent sex offender is a master at orchestrating some form of control. Even if they are only in their mid-teens, many of these boys have been actively practicing how to sexually gain control of someone else for years. They, like anyone else, revert back to what they do best when the need to feel in control arises.

Sexual offenders are also good planners. Bill was not in camp 5 minutes before he concluded that Jim would be his easiest target to control sexually. It is important to talk (and talk early) about all of these factors. Talk about touch and get Tommy comfortable with sharing how he feels when being touched by others. Have Jim describe how he reacts when he feels afraid or alone. Identify sexual offense as a behavior centered around the need to feel in control of someone else. Have Bill share how much he felt in charge when he was able to get his victim to head into the woods with him toward his tree house. Relate the feelings associated with the experiences of the day to sexual offense, then move on to a specific offense of one or more members of the group.

Processing occurs throughout the day. Topic-specific processing should be planned for in advance and attempted at a time when discussion can be complete and no one feels that he/she must rush in order to remain on schedule. We have always reserved the most intensive processing sessions for the evening campfire. The combination of the relaxation generated by a campfire, an atmosphere where youths feel it is safe to share their feelings, and the skillful direction of a trained facilitator can bring about phenomenal results. Under these conditions, we have witnessed some guarded individuals take a chance and begin the process of getting better.

In no way should this be interpreted as an easy task. The secrets that these youths carry are entrenched in guilt and shame. In cases like Tommy, he will be asked to examine and reject a lifestyle that dates back to his earliest memory. The fear of rejection will be high, not only from the facilitator, but also from others far more significant such as parents, siblings, and victims. Acknowledge all of this in your work with this group, but then press on.

Topic-specific processing should be attempted in the areas of victimization, anger management, vulnerability and control, trust (and the betrayal of trust), and the cycle of sexual offense. This may sound like a lot of information to cover in 3 nights of campfires and it is. However, this subject matter is so intertwined that it is nearly impossible to discuss one topic without including another. The cycle of sexual offense is fueled by anger and the desire to feel in control. Any form of victimization involves the betrayal of trust and a great deal of anger. Once the talking starts, it will not be hard to touch on all of these topics, and more.

The campfire following a day of rappelling is a good time to zero in on the issue of trust. What each youth felt as he/she stepped to the edge of the rock and, trusting the facilitator's knowledge, was coached into the proper position to begin the descent is still fresh. No one would argue that there is a great deal of trust involved here. It's time for a few "What ifs?". What if the facilitator had given a little push to get you started? He promised to ease you into the proper position. What if he pushed you? How would you feel? What if he apologized; convinced you that it would not happen again; got you out on the rock again and pushed you a second time? How might you feel then? How does this relate to your sexual offense? This situation takes about 5 minutes to set up and usually results in a discussion that continues well into the evening. The issues of trust, anger, victimization, guilt, premeditation, control, vulnerability, and more, all come out and can be processed. The intensity of such a session can be extremely high.

THE 4TH FIRE

The most intense session usually occurs at the last campfire of this 5-day workshop. During the previous three campfires, a tremendous amount of sharing and risk taking has occurred. More discussion surrounding the issues of sexual offense has occurred during this concentrated time period than may happen in many weeks of conventional outpatient treatment. At the same time, many of these youths have physically and emotionally accomplished more than they ever dreamed possible. The time is right to offer the possibility of freedom from the burden of carrying any more secrets and to begin the process of truly getting better. At The 4th Fire we always ask for the disclosure of any unreported sexual offenses. Most of the processing that has been accomplished over the past few days has been related to sexual offense. The huge risks taken at those times now seem small when compared to the feelings experienced during the first few hours of the workshop. By pointing this out and drawing a parallel to the risks taken during the week while on the ropes course or rock climbing, facilitators can help many offenders sitting around this last campfire to conclude that the benefits far outweigh the risks.

An intense workshop like this almost always results in at least one participant disclosing further abuse. It is important that you have a plan to deal with this additional information regarding sexual offenses. Facilitators may be approached by a youth stating that he/she will disclose a sexual offense if he/she is promised that it will stay just between them. Those treatment providers not having a clear plan of action at the start of the workshop may wind up debating with themselves over whether to grant such a request. The law in Wisconsin (a law by no means unique to Wisconsin) states that even suspicions of sexual offense are to be reported to the proper authorities. The sexual offenders participating in your group should be made aware of this fact at the outset of the workshop. Do not apologize for exercising this responsibility. The purpose of this planned program is to stop further victimization.

THE VALUE OF PLAY

Finally, as serious and intense as a workshop such as this can and should be, do not overlook the importance of having fun. An experienced leader should look for and find the appropriate opportunities for a positive, humorous undertone in planning the week's program. Play, in itself, is a type of rehabilitation. It can ease the tension surrounding the stressful topic of sexual abuse. There is usually an underlying reason why someone cannot laugh easily; or reasons that sexually-oriented jokes and games are the only things that cause them to laugh. Intentionally humorous games are a way to portray play as a healthy, purposeful element in therapy and everyday life. Members may be more familiar with negative, sarcastic humor used to put down peers in a group. Laughing with others and at oneself is an extremely positive therapeutic tool that many kids at-risk have seldom experienced.

Some of the activities that we have found to be most helpful in allowing the group get to know one another, foster group cooperation, reduce initial tension, and just plain have fun, include the Blind Polygon, the A-Frame, Touch My Can, and the Name Game. A good reference book is Silver Bullets, by Karl Rohnke.

SUMMARY

Keep in mind that you will be dealing with individuals who are scared. The new environment in which they find themselves is frightening. Facilitators must provide an atmosphere of safety at the outset of the program and maintain this throughout the week. Participants must feel safe from rejection, safe from further abuse from others, and safe in knowing that their own behavior will be closely monitored. Sexual offenders not only have a great mistrust of new people whom they meet (particularly other sex offenders), they also do not trust themselves.

It is important to have a good understanding of each participant's sexual abuse/offense history. There must also be the willingness and ability to ask and answer a variety of questions surrounding sexual offense. If you do not know the answer to a specific question, you are far better off acknowledging this and working together on a plan to obtain the accurate information. As stated earlier, it is also important to have a clear plan to handle the disclosure of sexual abuse. Make the group aware of this plan from the outset.

A clear majority of the sex offenders that enter camp have a strong yearning to get help and begin (or continue on) the long road of recovery. Even though many may have been in some form of treatment in the past, a sequentially programmed, adventure-based counseling format similar to the one outlined in this article may well be the first, high-impact opportunity for these youths to find a listening ear, a safe environment to share their feelings, and a chance to finally break the cycle of failure. Be patient.

Robert Kjol established treatment-specific programming for sex offenders at the Homme Home for Boys in Wittenberg, Wisconsin, in 1985, and he co-facilitates these programs at Treetop Adventure.

John Weber is Director of Treetop Adventure and has 12 years' experience facilitating adventure-based counseling programs.

Footnote

[1] The article was originally published in the 1990 Journal of Experiential Education, 13 (3), 18-22.

9

BUILDING FAMILY TEAMS: AN ADVENTURE-BASED APPROACH TO ENRICHMENT AND INTERVENTION

CYNTHIA L. CLAPP, L.S.C.W.
SUZANNE M. RUDOLPH, ED. D.

Introduction

Within the last 2 decades there has been a dramatic shift in the structure of the traditional American family. This shift has included an increase in divorce, single-parent households, and dual-career families (Glick, 1984). Demographics on family patterns indicate that between 40% and 50% of all marriages end in divorce (Guidubaldi & Cleminshaw, 1985) and 80% of all divorced persons remarry within 4-5 years (Hayes & Hayes, 1986). It is anticipated that by the year 2000, single-parent and remarriage families will outnumber the nuclear family in the United States (Pill, 1990).

An important factor to consider is the ability of families to effectively cope and adapt to the stress associated with these transitions. Divorced, remarried, single-parent, adoptive, and dual-career families experience stresses and strains that can tax a family's ability to cope. Although some families may demonstrate flexibility in adapting to life changes in healthful ways, others are likely to experience difficulty. There is ample evidence that suggests that the percentage of children, adolescents, and adults affected by changing family patterns is increasing (Herr, 1989). There is a strong need to establish preventive programs designed to enhance family functioning and expand skills and strategies for coping with stressful family and life circumstances.

An early response to this need for preventive programs has come from the professional area of marriage and family enrichment (Denton, 1986; Mace, 1979; Smith, Schoffner, & Scott, 1979). These enrichment programs are designed to assist families in developing their resources for dealing with difficulties before they became critical. Historically, enrichment programs have predominantly offered services such as adolescent groups, parent education classes, or couples groups to segments of families (Evanson, 1980). The first family enrichment programs were established in 1970 through the founding of the Family Clusters model by Margaret Sawin and, in 1971, a similar model was developed by Herbert Otto.

A common goal of family enrichment programs is to help participants to discover the resources they already possess as opposed to teaching them new abilities. Enrichment can be defined as "the process of strengthening marriages and families, of deepening attributes that persons and family systems already possess, to provide further growth of the individual, marital, or family system" (Sawin, 1979, p. ii). Mace and Mace (1986) state:

> Enrichment is not the process of pumping in, from the outside, something that is not already there. It is rather a matter of drawing out inner resources that the family members already possess, but they have been unable to use in order to achieve what they really want in their shared life. (p. 8)

Enrichment programs are preventive in nature, designed to assist families in discovering and enhancing their strengths and resources (Denton, 1986). Traditionally, these programs have been limited to couples and families who are "healthy" or define themselves as "well functioning"; however, there is recent evidence that indicates that distressed couples or families can benefit from enrichment as well (Giblin, 1986).

Since 1975, there has been an increase in family enrichment program models (Sawin, 1986). However, the majority of these models have been in religious settings that frequently only reach those who are affiliated members. Sawin (1986) suggests that there is a need for community agencies to adopt enrichment programs in order to increase the number of families who could benefit from these services. In addition, the majority of providers have limited enrichment services for "normal or healthy families" (Giblin, Sprenkle, & Sheehan, 1985; Hillman & Evenson, 1981; Mace, 1979; Mace & Mace, 1986; Otto, 1975; Sawin, 1986).

ADVENTURE-BASED PROGRAMMING

One innovative approach to enrichment and intervention can be found in adventure-based programming. Although the therapeutic benefits of this approach are still being explored, there is a growing body of research supporting the use of this program model. In recent years, adventure-based programs have gained recognition as a valuable therapeutic intervention. These programs have served as interventions for populations such as youths at-risk (Gibson, 1981; Weeks, 1985; Wright, 1982), recovering alcoholics (Kirkpatrick, 1983), cancer victims (Harris, 1982), hearing-impaired people (Luckner, 1989), victims of rape (Pfirman, 1988), and adults in transition (Votraw, 1984).

The use of action-oriented, adventure-based activities offers an alternative to "traditional" therapeutic approaches that rely on verbal and cognitive processes. Adventure-based programs are based on the belief that therapeutic change can be facilitated through behavior, action, and reflection (Winn, 1982). An underlying assumption of this philosophy is that insight into the nature of problems does not produce positive change by itself. Change can best occur from processes of translating insight into action through the active experiencing of new situations. The experiential learning philosophies have become a fundamental building block of many family enrichment programs (Evenson, Evenson, & Fish, 1986).

The concept of using adventure-based programming with families has, until recently, been overlooked by professionals in the field. Despite the increase in attempts to develop and deliver programs for families, written information on the subject remains limited. The positive outcomes of previous studies on adventure-based programming with other populations support the need to document and investigate the potential benefits of an adventure-based approach to family enrichment and intervention. The following is a description of the intervention efforts developed by one adventure-based family enrichment and intervention program, The Family Challenge.

PROGRAM DESCRIPTION

The Family Challenge program initially began as a pilot program for families who had adopted older or special-needs children and has since expanded to serve all types of families. It is a short-term, therapeutic enrichment program for families that uses team-building activities and games to enhance communication, cooperation, and problem solving. It teaches families ways in which they can improve their interactions to be a more effective family "team." In the program, families learn to set goals for themselves, observe themselves in action, and try new behaviors or ways of interacting with each other to enhance their effectiveness in managing family relationships and situations. The experiences in the program are used as metaphors for the challenges each family faces in its ongoing life together.

The Family Challenge employs a multifamily group model, working with three or four families at a time. Families are grouped together according to commonalities in family constellation (i.e., single parents, stepfamily, adoptive, traditional), the children's ages, and family issues (mental illness, substance abuse, etc.). This group formation helps to place families in situations where they can enhance the opportunities for mutual aid and support between one another. The program is staffed by professionals experienced in family counseling and recreational therapy; the ratio of staff to families is 1:1, ensuring that each family is given thorough, individual attention.

The program is open to all types of families. A "family" is defined as anyone who lives in the household and/or has close emotional ties to each other. Guidelines for family eligibility to the program include: a minimum age of 7 years for each participant, a commitment from every family member to attend all meetings, no active suicidal or violent behaviors, and an openness to learn about and improve family interactions. In addition, the parents must have some ability to manage their children's behavior. Families that are unmotivated, chaotic, or are experiencing severe difficulties needing specialized treatment are referred for therapy. The cost of the program is determined by a sliding-scale fee based on family income.

Referrals to the program come from a variety of sources, including therapists, social workers, and the families themselves. An informational meeting is held with all family members who will participate in the program. Families referred to the program are requested to participate in an intake interview prior to the first Family Challenge program session. The purposes of this initial interview are to build rapport and to gather initial information pertaining to the family's identified issues, concerns, needs, and goals. During the intake interview, the program director and the family discuss the program with respect to the family's needs and determine whether there is a match between what the family wants and what the program can provide.

The program serves a number of functions. The program can be used as an enrichment experience for families who define themselves as "well functioning." In these cases, the program has the potential to enhance family relationships, accentuate family strengths, and normalize family concerns about negotiating life transitions.

The program can also be used as a component of therapy to enhance therapeutic results and/or serve as a tool for assessing and gathering additional information about family member patterns of interaction. Adventure activities provide a flexible context to explore how a family operates as a working system. Issues and dynamics that could take several therapy sessions to observe or uncover are viewed clearly in the way a family approaches and performs these activities. The setting and atmosphere of the program is relaxed, casual, action-oriented, and different from typical therapy settings. Therefore, the families are more likely to show their usual behaviors and interaction patterns with less defensive filtering. Families referred to the program by their therapists are asked to sign a release of information. The program director initiates contact with the client's primary therapist two to four times throughout the program to discuss the family's goals for The Family Challenge program in relationship to the family's goals for therapy. Staff use this information to tailor experiences to be supportive of the family's therapeutic goals.

The program can also be used as a short-term therapeutic intervention for families experiencing mild to moderate levels of distress. The information learned about themselves can help a family to define and clarify problem areas and treatment goals, and can motivate them to use therapy in a more effective and self-directed manner. The objectives of The Family Challenge program include:

1) increasing family skills in problem solving, communication, and cooperation,
2) increasing team work, trust, and flexibility within the family,
3) empowering families to identify salient issues and goals, and identifing what the members can do to attain them, and
4) enabling families to have fun together.

PROGRAM STRUCTURE

The Family Challenge uses a five-session model. These five sessions take place in a 3-week period and include three consecutive Wednesday evening sessions, each 2½ hours long, and two consecutive Saturday sessions, each 5 hours long. These five sessions are referred to as a "sequence." All sessions take place at Hale Reservation, an outdoor education center outside of Boston, Massachusetts. The evening sessions are held indoors in a building at the center. These evening sessions are used to build familiarity between the families, determine and evaluate individual family goals, reflect and process the learning and experiences of the previous Saturdays, and discuss how families can apply what they have learned to future challenges their family will face. During the Saturday sessions, families perform various adventure challenge and team-building activities with the multifamily group.

SESSION CONTENT AND OBJECTIVE

Session One

Session One is held indoors. The purpose of this meeting is to: (a) give the families an opportunity to begin to get to know each other and identify commonalities within the larger group, (b) introduce fun and non-threatening activities designed to build trust and safety, and (c) provide a vehicle for individual families to establish initial goals for the program.

This session begins with a discussion of ground rules about supporting and respecting each other's differences and strengths. A commitment is made by all participants to refrain from unsupportive criticism, to compliment people whenever possible, and to be respectful of the rest of the group. Expectations of the participants are clarified, reinforcing the guidelines that no one has to do the activities but everyone will be encouraged to **try** everything to the best of their abilities. A series of icebreakers and warm-up activities are introduced after the instructions to the multifamily group. Examples of these activities include Moon Ball, Name Game, Group Juggle, Commonalities, and People to People. These activities are briefly discussed, primarily to give participants an introduction to questions which focus on their self-observation skills. Examples of questions include: "What did you notice about yourself?" "In what ways did you participate?" "Did you help anyone or did anyone help you?" "Did you express your ideas?" "What was fun for you?"

The majority of this first session is spent working with individual families, helping them to develop family goals for the program. A discussion about basic goal-setting principles is held followed by a period where the families break up into individual family groups and decide upon specific family goals. One staff person stays with each family to monitor and assist them in this process. These family goals provide a focus for the activities and discussion on the first outdoor day. The families then come together in a large group and share their goals with each other. This sharing makes it possible for everyone to support each other on their goals and enhances the cohesiveness of the multifamily group.

Session Two

Session Two is held outdoors. The purpose of this meeting is to continue to build trust, safety, and support within the multifamily group and individual families, and to provide families with an opportunity to begin to work together on some problem-solving activities. The session begins with several multifamily activities and games and a few trust-building activities. These activities have a family focus and symbolism, such as pairing with family members for Hog Call, one family being the blob in Blob Tag, or family teams for Giants, Wizards, and Elves. The trust activities consist of paired trust falls and the group circle pass. In paired trust falls, each person in the family takes turns being the "faller" and the "supporter" so that everyone has a chance to be in each role. This activity provides a frame for observing and discussing with the families issues of safety, trust, support, and responsibility for others. In the circle pass, the group supports one individual who is gently passed around the circle. This activity builds trust and support on the multifamily group level.

After these activities, information is presented to the group on steps of effective problem solving. The families then separate so that each family works individually on one initiative activity for the next block of time while the other families work together on an activity. All the families rotate through the day so that each has an opportunity to do an activity by themselves and with another family. This gives each family and the staff an opportunity to observe every family alone. Several aspects of the family system are closely observed (e.g., problem-solving style, communication, adaptability, roles, structure, frustration tolerance, and cooperation). Each activity is carefully supervised and debriefed by one or two staff members.

Following the completion of each task, family members are encouraged to reflect, analyze, and describe what they have just experienced. Solutions to the problem and the strengths of the family and individual members are examined. Questions asked may include: "What did you notice about your family and yourself?" "What strengths did you see in your family and yourself?" "What does this tell you about your family and yourself?" "How do you as a family account for your ability to successfully complete this activity?" "How is this similar to or different from the way you approach solving problems at home?" Participants are also encouraged to look at the changes they would like to make to enhance their effectiveness in solving future problems. Participants are provided with time for reflection and articulation to enhance the potential for changes to occur in their perceptions and behavior.

The day ends with a discussion as a multifamily group about the day's experiences and learnings. The focus is on areas of insight or change in relation to the families' goals.

Session Three

Session Three takes place indoors. The purpose of this meeting is to reconnect as a multifamily group, reflect on the learning and observations of the previous Saturday, and to refine individual family goals with a focus on strategic and structural changes.

The meeting opens with several games to get the group reacquainted. Video footage taken of each family the previous Saturday is then viewed by the whole group. This video provides a vehicle to help families recall their experiences and to observe themselves from the "outside." It is anticipated that the process of viewing themselves in action may provide family members with additional perspective that can expand family member perceptions and clarify family patterns of interaction. The staff use this as an opportunity to encourage participants to exchange their perceptions of the experience and provide feedback.

The families then break up into individual families and, with a staff person present, they review their previous goals and make any changes or adjustments based on their experiences on the first outdoor day. Being as specific as possible, the families decide what changes they would like to make and consider new behavioral options which would help them toward their goal. For example, if the family's goal is for the father to take more leadership, behavioral options might be that the mother is given limits on how much she can talk and the children are blindfolded so they are more dependent on their father's guidance. Any new goals and strategies developed by a family are used by the staff to decide on specialized activities for each family to do on the following Saturday.

At the end of this meeting, all families are given still photographs of themselves involved in the activities the previous Saturday. They are assigned the task of making a family collage, using these photographs, which represents their Family Challenge experience. The collages will be shared with the whole group at the final meeting.

Session Four

Session Four is held outdoors. The purpose of this session is to work more intensively with individual families and to introduce strategic and structural changes in family patterns by providing opportunities for families to "try on" new behaviors through activities specially designed to address the family's goals.

As always, the meeting opens up with several multifamily activities and games. The majority of the day is spent in individual families, working closely with a staff person. This is a more intensive day as the families are asked, through the activities, to try different ways of interacting, communicating, and problem solving together. Throughout the day the activities are strategically designed to assist the families in attaining their goals. The term "strategic" implies deliberate, planned intervention where the facilitator/therapist initiates what happens during the session and designs an approach to using exercises that bring about change in the family's system of interaction, thereby achieving their desired goals (Haley, 1973). Activities are selected based on the possible lessons to be learned from the exercise, the expressed goals of the family, and the creative ability of the facilitator to strategically design the activity either by introducing the activity as a metaphor or by structuring the exercise itself in such a way that it resembles a family problem. One example could be when the facilitator assigns specific roles to family members and directs the flow of communication. The strategic use of the exercise creates a context for change by expanding family patterns of "viewing" and "doing" by empowering families to access their resources, strengths, and creativity, and to discover their own problem-solving abilities (O'Hanlon, 1988). Change occurs when rigid patterns of interaction are interrupted through a change in behavior or in the family's perception of the problem. The intensity of this action-oriented approach, coupled with an element of perceived risk, tends to create a heightened level of emotional arousal and constructive anxiety for the participants. This added element of stress may impel the family out of their comfort zone and motivate them to try new behaviors to lessen these feelings of discomfort (Nadler & Luckner, 1989). Each exercise is carefully structured and debriefed to focus the family's attention on the effects of their new behaviors and the ways in which these new behaviors could be incorporated into their family's life together at home.

The day ends with a multifamily group activity, either a game or a group initiative task, such as The Wall. The day is discussed, and families share the highlights of what they have learned.

Session Five

Session Five is the final session and is held indoors. The purpose of this meeting is to: (a) review what families have learned through The Family Challenge experience, (b) help families to think about how they might apply this learning to other areas of their life, (c) celebrate their successes, and (d) leave the program.

The meeting opens with large group activities, usually playing some of the group's "favorite" games again. The families then discuss their experiences on the previous Saturday in terms of their goals, what they learned, and how this can be applied to their ongoing life as a family. A list of "things learned" in The Family Challenge and "things that helped" in the activities is generated and displayed for all to view. Through a final discussion, families are assisted in clarifying what they have learned and how they can apply what they have learned to future "challenges" they will face as a family, from the struggles of daily living to major family challenges.

The meeting then focuses on celebration and closure. The family collages are each presented by a family member who explains the process by which it was made and the meaning behind it. Each family is given a Certificate of Completion and every participant receives a Family Challenge T-shirt. Participants are given an opportunity to give positive feedback to individuals and families as a whole.

After completion of The Family Challenge, a program summary is written for each family, which highlights their family goals, the activities they did, and what they learned. A brief assessment of the family as a whole and each family member is included. If a therapist or family has requested particular issues to be addressed in The Family Challenge, they will be discussed in this summary. The summary is sent to the families and other people to whom the family has given permission to send it (e.g., referring therapists, school counselors). A program evaluation is sent to each family about one month after completion of the program. Each family member is asked to fill it out and return it by mail to the program director.

SUMMARY

The Family Challenge addresses the need for developing innovative approaches to family enrichment and intervention. The focus of this program is on identifying and improving family strengths and skills to effectively cope and adapt to the stress associated with family life. The Family Challenge has the potential to expand the skills and resources of family members to manage challenging situations and stressful events. Adventure-based activities are used as a medium for families to observe themselves in action and to experiment and practice new behaviors. The Family Challenge offers an extension to adventure-based programming practices and an alternative approach to building family strengths.

A pilot study designed to assess the effects of participation in The Family Challenge was conducted using six families that participated in two program sequences. Pre- and post-test data were collected using the McMaster Family Assessment Device (Epstein, Baldwin, & Bishop, 1983) and the F-Copes Scale (Olson & McCubbin, 1985). Significant positive increases were found in the post-test scores in the areas of family problem solving and general functioning skills. A significant increase was also found in the families' ability to use reframing (the ability to redefine stressful events) as a coping strategy (Clapp & Rudolph, 1990). Preliminary program research indicates that The Family Challenge may offer an effective enrichment and intervention method for families. Further research and application of this approach are encouraged.

Cynthia L. Clapp, M.S.W., created and directed The Family Challenge program for the Protestant Social Service Bureau in Wollaston, Massachusetts, from 1986-1990. She has also worked for the Hale Reservation, Department of Mental Health at Westboro State Hospital, and the Hurricane Island Outward School.

Suzanne M. Rudolph, Ed. D. received her doctorate in counseling with specialization in marriage and family therapy from Northern Illinois University. She has worked as the Program Administrator for the Northern Illinois Corporate Adventure Training Teambuilding Program, Coordinator of Project TAPE, and as an instructor for the Voyager Outward Bound School.

10

THE THEORETICAL FOUNDATIONS FOR ADVENTURE FAMILY THERAPY

MICHAEL A. GASS, Ph.D.

Introduction

The study of human behavior, particularly in the therapeutic world, can be viewed from a variety of perspectives. One perspective possessing particular relevance is the systems approach. With theoretical origins in medicine and biology, this approach does not deny the existence of an individual's influence on her/his own behavior. It does believe, however, that the relationships and interactions within the entities of a particular "system" play a large role in the causes of behavior. For example, instead of focusing on a juvenile's actions in a particular act of delinquency, the system theorist would wish to examine the interaction of the youth with other significant members in his/her life and societal influences to determine causes of dysfunctional behavior and potential avenues for habilitative or rehabilitative measures.

The systems perspective holds particular importance for the social institution of the family. Long recognized as a critical part of the field of human development, the field of family therapy has evolved from the perspective of marriage counselors, psychiatrists, and researchers focusing on schizophrenia (Brown & Christensen, 1986). As a systems theory, the field of family therapy recognizes that an individual's actions cannot be understood separately from his/her interactions with other members of the family. Family therapists recognize that the <u>context</u> of social interactions between family members plays a major role in determining each individual's behavior. They also recognize that if change occurs in one person, it will affect every other family member.

Other advances in therapeutic perspectives have also led to the development of new methods of delivering therapeutic services. One

123

recent advance has been the adaptation of adventure experiences to reach therapeutic goals (e.g., Gillis & Bonney, 1986; Mason, 1987). These experiences are generally not used as a replacement for therapeutic goals or frameworks, but as a means to enrich and facilitate therapeutic strategies. Adventure experiences have generated some influence in psychotherapeutic approaches, and their application to family therapy possesses a great deal of promise.

The purpose of this chapter is to describe the theoretical basis of such a marriage—the integration and enrichment of family therapy with adventure experiences. This objective will be reached by briefly outlining common approaches to marriage and family therapy and illustrating how adventure experiences can be used as a means to reach the therapeutic objectives of these two approaches. The two approaches used for this illustration are structural (Minuchin, 1974, 1981) and strategic (Haley, 1988; Madanes, 1988) family therapies. A case example will be used to outline how adventure experiences can be used to enhance these specific approaches. Potential contraindications of adventure experiences with family therapy and elements needed for a healthy interaction between the two fields will also be discussed.

ADVENTURE EXPERIENCES WITH STRUCTURAL FAMILY THERAPY

Structural family therapy is a theory focusing on the assumption that "families are evolving, hierarchical organizations with rules, or transactional patterns, for interacting within subsystems" (Fish & Piercy, 1987, p. 122). Dysfunctional patterns are often attributed to inappropriate hierarchies, rules, and boundaries between **and** within a family's subsystems. The major goal of the structural family therapist is to reorganize the family's structure by actively directing changes in these issues and interactions. Fish and Piercy (1987) describe these processes of change in terms of structural therapy:

> *Joining and accommodating to the family, structural therapists use direct techniques to create workable realities, reframe present behavior, and intensify stress. Reorganization of the family's structure, synonymous with change, occurs when therapists interrupt dysfunctional sequences and provide alternative transactional patterns for the family. The structural therapist helps support the continual experimentation of alternative transactional possibilities the family can accept, until new patterns emerge which become self-reinforcing. (pp. 122–123)*

There has been some effort to link the concepts of adventure therapy to certain concepts of structural family therapy. One example of this integration is Kirkpatrick (1984), where the author found a strong relationship between the concepts of adventure therapy and the structural family therapy concepts of intensity, unbalancing, joining, boundary making, focus, complementary patterning, and restructuring.

Two important techniques of structural family therapy include: 1) analyzing a family's interaction through a process of **assessment**, and 2) changing the family structure to induce direct change in family interactions, often by increasing their intensity, through processes like **restructuring**. To illustrate how adventure experiences can enhance these structural family therapy techniques, the following case study is offered:

> Jane Merdock (38) had contacted the program, stating difficulties with her marital relationship and family issues. This was the second marriage for both her and her husband, Kevin (42). Kevin and Jane had been married 3 years and both had brought children into their new marriage. Steve (16) was Kevin's biological son and Bill (10) and Craig (9) were Jane's biological children.
>
> Jane complained that Bill was experiencing difficulty in school and starting to use drugs. Steve was also distancing himself from any family interaction and "finding a hard time coming out of his shell." Jane also stated that a number of problems seemed to stem from the children not feeling connected to their respective stepparent. This was often evidenced by Bill's failure to respond to Kevin's disciplinary requests and Steve complaining that he didn't have enough time with his father, blaming Jane for this. Jane also was finding that problems in the family were creating crises in her relationship with her husband Kevin.

ADVENTURE EXPERIENCES FOR ASSESSMENT

In assessing cases, the focus of the structural therapist is to gather certain information about a particular family. Minuchin (1974, p. 130) identifies these areas to be:

(a) **Structure**—The family structure, its preferred transactional patterns, and the alternatives available.
(b) **Flexibility**—The system's flexibility and its capacity for change through processes of elaboration and/or restructuring. This is accomplished by analyzing what alliances, coalitions, and subsystems exist and how they affect family behavior.

(c) **Resonance**—The system's resonance, looking at its sensitivity to individual family member actions.

(d) **Context**—The context of the family's lifestyle, looking particularly at sources of support and stress.

(e) **Life cycle issues**—The family's developmental stage and its performance of tasks appropriate to that stage.

(f) **Symptoms**—The ways in which individuals experiencing problems are used for maintenance of the family's preferred transactional patterns.

In order to acquire this information, the structural therapist often employs several verbal techniques to observe how family members discuss particular issues and how these discussions are accomplished. However, several problems can result in this process. Issues concerning how the family will accept the therapist into the family structure, failures to recognize certain family subsystems, and the possibility that verbal techniques will not uncover critical issues of the family all present major problems for the structural therapist (Minuchin, 1974).

Therapeutic adventure experiences can overcome these difficulties by having the family actually perform an unfamiliar task that requires communication and problem-solving skills to accomplish. This experiential process causes family members to actually display their structure, behavior patterns, rules of interaction, and methods of communication. Such a process eliminates many of the difficulties stated above and the structural therapist will be presented with clear representations of family interactions.

One adventure activity that could be well suited for the assessment of the Merdock family would be the "All Aboard" initiative task (Rohnke, 1989) (see Figure 1).

Figure 1 – The All Aboard initiative task

The objective of this initiative is to balance the entire family on a 1' × 1' square board without any family member touching the ground for an identified period of time (e.g., 10 seconds, the length of time it takes the family to sing one verse of "Happy Birthday"). If one member of the family touches the ground, the entire family must begin the initiative over.

The focus of having the family perform this element is not for recreational purposes. This process, when appropriately challenging, serves the family therapist by providing a rich combination of the current state of family hierarchies and transactional patterns. This is possible because how the family decides to get on and stay on the All Board initiative is analogous to how the family structures itself when confronted by a difficult problem. Interaction by any member of the Merdock family affects the entire family in their home as it does on the square board. As the family is presented with the problem and begins the process of achieving the goal of the task, they project their hierarchical structure and transactional patterns on to the process of completing the initiative. Rich nonverbal actions, as well as verbal ones, are displayed for the therapist. Transactional patterns and boundaries, leadership roles, and the consistency of nonverbal and verbal actions, are all available for the therapist to begin construction of the family map for future therapeutic use.

ADVENTURE EXPERIENCES FOR RESTRUCTURING THE FAMILY

As structural therapists assess family interaction and issues, they also develop processes for transforming apparent dysfunction patterns based on the construction of a particular family's map. A second area where adventure experiences can be used to enhance structural family therapy practices is in the process of therapeutic intervention. This process is called **restructuring** and is specifically meant to present challenges to families in order to produce desired changes. Minuchin (1974) identifies seven categories of restructuring that are used by structural family therapists to produce change. These are: (a) actualizing family transactional patterns, (b) marking boundaries, (c) escalating stress, (d) assigning tasks, (e) utilizing symptoms, (f) manipulating mood, and (g) supporting, educating, or guiding.

In the Merdock example, there are several issues in need of structural change. Two predominant themes are the confused and unclear boundaries between the parental and sibling subsystems and the lack of blending between the two old families into the structure of one new family. A structural diagram of a family facing these issues can be seen in the diagram outlined in Figure 2 on the following page.

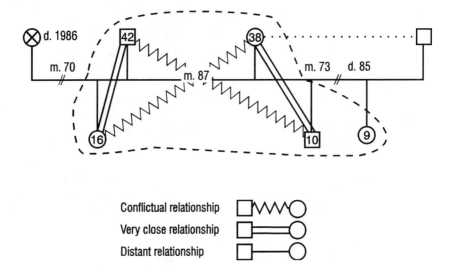

Conflictual relationship

Very close relationship

Distant relationship

Figure 2 – Genogram for the Merdock Family

In this figure, one can see the diffuse boundaries that exist between the parental and sibling subsystems. The children, particularly with their biological parent, are allowed unlimited access into the parental subsystem. This often sabotages the parental roles and creates dysfunctional cross-generational coalitions, undermining parental control as well as the development of autonomy by the emerging adolescents. Restructuring operations need to be implemented to focus on strengthening the parental dyad and decrease cross-generational coalitions by involving the disengaged parent in parental roles with the distant child.

An adventure activity that would provide an excellent vehicle for restructuring the family with these presenting symptoms might be the "Wild Woosey" ropes course element (Rohnke, 1989). The purpose of this activity is for "two individuals [to] creatively and physically support one another as they attempt to traverse the lengths of the two diverging cables that are tautly strung between supports about 12" above the ground" (Rohnke, 1989, p. 110) (see Figure 3).

Figure 3 – The Wild Woosey ropes course element

In this diagram, also note the importance of two sets of "spotters"—one set underneath the two participants as well as one set on the outside of the wires. Both of these sets of spotters work to protect participants from physically hurting themselves in case of a fall. Without the support of the spotters, the participants would be injured if they fell off of the wires.

The key to the successful implementation of this ropes course element is in the appropriate framing around the principles of restructuring outlined by Minuchin (1974), particularly with the issues of strengthening the parental dyad and increasing interaction between each parent and their stepchild. When introducing the element to the Merdock family, the structural family therapist would recommend that the parents attempt the element first, with the children spotting underneath and the therapists spotting on the outside. In performing the element, the children are serving to support the parents, but they are instructed not to speak during their parents' attempts to accomplish the initiative. Structuring the element in this manner lays the groundwork for strengthening the parental subsystem.

Kevin and Jane are attempting to complete a problem that they cannot accomplish alone. Their ability to successfully complete the initiative is directly related to their ability to successfully work together as a couple. Their children are an important part of their system in accomplishing their task (i.e., support), but are not allowed to interfere in the interactions between their parents as they attempt the task.

When the parents complete the task, Bill and Steve are invited to attempt the task blindfolded. Here the parents are asked to spot their stepchildren on the outside of the wire and offer suggestions only to the individual they are spotting. As Bill struggles with completing his initiative, Kevin is available in offering assistance since he has experienced what is successful in accomplishing the task. The more Bill asks for assistance, the more his stepfather can help and the greater his degree of success. This reciprocal arrangement is also set up for Jane and Steve. Errors made in interacting to get to the end of the wire are meant to parallel errors in failing to communicate in the family. Success is only achieved through the interaction of the whole family; stepparents giving guidance, other family members spotting underneath, and efforts for reaching out for assistance made by growing adolescents. This interactive success is designed to begin a process of functional interaction between children and their stepparents.

This element is a structured metaphor of change for the Merdock family, and is enhanced through the focused transfer of such newly learned skills into the home environment (Gass, 1985). Videotaping the initiative is also suggested for families so that they can review the tape with the therapist (either on the ropes course or in the therapist's office) to explore and reinforce the positive changes that occurred. Assigning tasks that focus on building on these types of behaviors outside of the therapeutic sessions (e.g., homework assignments) is also critical to ensure permanent change (Minuchin, 1974).

ADVENTURE EXPERIENCES WITH STRATEGIC FAMILY THERAPY

While structural family therapy sees that dysfunctional patterns are caused by inappropriate family structure, strategic family therapists see that dysfunctional symptoms displayed by families are caused by ineffective solutions to problems they encounter. Strategic family therapists view the sequence of these dysfunctional symptoms and problems as mutually reinforcing, often supporting and compounding one another. The focus of a strategic family therapist is to interrupt these maladaptive sequences to change the way people interact (e.g, Haley 1988; Fish & Piercy, 1987).

The interruption of these sequences is usually accomplished through **straightforward** or **paradoxical** directives given by the strategic therapist. Straightforward directives are based on the family complying with therapist's interventions to bring about change (Papp, 1980). These interventions are usually accepted or followed by the family, and are given to "involve previously disengaged family members, promote agreement and good feeling, increase positive interchanges, provide information, and help a family organize in more functional ways" (Madanes, 1989, p. 24).

Paradoxical directives are designed for those situations where families are focused on defying or rebelling against the creation of change by the therapist. Providing a straightforward directive in this case would only polarize the situation more, causing a greater level of homeostasis and resistance to change. Seeing this situation, the strategic therapist gives a directive as a strategy "designed to provoke a family to change by rebelling against the therapist" (Madanes, 1989, p. 7). The paradoxical directive places the family in a therapeutic double bind where the family is given one message that contains two conflicting elements. As stated by Madanes (1989):

> The messages "Be spontaneous," "Don't be so obedient," "I want you to dominate me" are common paradoxes in human relationships (Haley, 1963). They are paradoxical because if the receiver of the message complies with the request, he [sic] is not complying with the request. The paradox occurs because one directive is qualified by another, at a different level of abstraction, in a conflictual way. (p. 7)

Both of these types of directives are important techniques for strategic family therapists and they can be enhanced through adventure experiences. Certain concepts of adventure therapy have been linked to some degree with certain concepts of strategic family therapy. Bacon (1983, 1989) and Gillis and Bonney (1986) have aligned elements of adventure therapy with strategic family therapy, centering on the concepts of reframing, the use of paradox, and the directive role of the leader. Reasons why elements of adventure therapy seem to mirror the use of strategic directives include the facts that: 1) directives are acted out in a committed fashion rather than just verbally responded to, 2) the consequences of family behaviors are observable and immediate, 3) there is a wide-ranging capacity to construct highly analogous or isomorphic learning tasks in the variety of adventure experiences available for the therapist, and 4) there is often a high degree of motivation intrinsic to adventure experiences.

ADVENTURE EXPERIENCES AS STRAIGHTFORWARD DIRECTIVES

One example of how an adventure experience can be used as a metaphor to enhance a straightforward directive can be seen when the task of belaying is used to address the symptom of the Merdock family's incongruous hierarchy. A relatively simple task to learn, belaying is a prerequisite skill for any individual participating on high ropes course elements, top-rope rock climbing, or other adventure experiences where safety systems must be used in case of a fall by the participant. The system is manually operated by a person who feeds rope out to the climber through a series of commands and signals. In the process of belaying, it is important to recognize that before a person may start a climb or ropes course element, he/she must be given the "okay" by the belayer or be unable to proceed with the task. The belayer is responsible for the participant's life and keeps control of any potentially dangerous situation through clear communication. When done correctly, belaying creates a strong connective bond between participants taking the risk and the belayer supporting their risk by acting as their safety system in case of a fall. Belaying can also serve as a strong metaphor for strong yet flexible boundaries between people.

With the Merdocks, one presenting problem is the question of "Who is in charge of the family?" Various symptoms of this problem are apparent, one being Bill's delinquent behavior. Supporting this mutually reinforcing sequence are: 1) the lack of understanding between the parents on what behavior they expect of their children, 2) the mixed messages they send their children, and 3) efforts by the children to keep the parental alliance separated and confused in order to maintain their own power. In order to change the sequence of symptoms and problems, a task requiring belaying (e.g., the Multi-vine Walk; Rohnke, 1988) is framed around the straightforward directive of clearer communication (see Figure 4 on the following page).

In this particular exercise, the adolescents of the family are invited to participate in the Multi-vine exercise that has been re-labeled "The Adolescent Wire" for this family. On this element, each rope hanging down for use by the adolescent has been given a name for a particular issue that member of the family is addressing. As taught in a previous learning exercise, before proceeding up the initial tree to accomplish their goal through the confrontation of their "issues," the adolescents must go through several specific communication sequences with their belayers, who for this activity are their parents. The communication sequence begins with the participant (i.e., the adolescent) asking the belayers (i.e., the parents) for permission to proceed. After the parents, in their roles as belayers,

132   *ADVENTURE THERAPY*

Figure 4 – The Multi-vine Walk ropes course element

have checked and agreed with one another that it is safe for the adolescent to proceed, they give their okay.

　　With this healthy and functional communication sequence in place, the adolescents begin their walk on the "Adolescent Wire." As they approach problems (e.g., having to let go of one wire to reach another), they look to the parents for support. This sequence of (a) an adolescent asking, and (b) parents providing permission, guidance, and support only after established criteria are met for the safety of the adolescent, is enhanced by the heightened eustress of the activity. By successfully encountering and overcoming this stress, the communication sequence is further reinforced.

In this situation, the belaying has been framed around the healthy sequence of adolescents reaching for independence while parents hold a superior hierarchical position. Because of the danger of falling, the consequences of not obeying belayers/parents are unthinkable for the climber/adolescent. This component of the activity reinforces the need of the adolescent to obey the parental alliance and for the parents to provide clear and consistent communication as a team.

ADVENTURE EXPERIENCES AS PARADOXICAL DIRECTIVES

As stated earlier, while straightforward directives will be helpful for families in certain cases, there are a number of times when families are resistant to such efforts. In these cases, the strategic therapist may need to implement paradoxical directives. Suppose that it becomes evident to the strategic therapist, through assessment procedures and stages of gathering information, that the Merdock family is extremely resistant to changing their incongruent hierarchy. It also becomes evident that they

Figure 5 – The Trust Fall initiative

sabotage efforts of any member attempting to implement change in the dysfunctional family system. This becomes particularly apparent with issues of trust and support. A common element many adventure therapists might use to address this issue would be the Trust Fall (see Figure 5).

In this element, the group offers its support to help an individual to overcome issues of trust and fall backward into the group's arms. This adventure experience is often preceeded by several other easier and less threatening tasks designed to teach necessary spotting skills. These tasks allow individuals to progressively build trust in themselves and each other (e.g., Willow Wand and Trust Circle exercises).

However, in a highly resistant family such as the Merdock's, it becomes painfully obvious in these progressive activities that the adolescents may often sabotage efforts focused on parental success. Trying to develop trust through the Trust Fall initiative, as it is traditionally designed and led, only leads to greater sabotage by the adolescents, higher parental frustration, and maintenance of the symptom and problem sequence. This occurs because the family is in a negative double-bind situation. Agreeing to the parental wishes of success challenges the adolescent power in the family. By failing to heed their parents' wishes, adolescents frustrate the parental alliance and maintain the incongruous hierarchy. The greater the parental division, the greater the power of the adolescents.

In order to break this negative double-bind situation, the adventure therapist must act to destabilize the family, which is often stabilized around the identified patient and the problem behavior. With this adventure activity for the Merdock family, the adventure therapist must frame the activity as a paradoxical intervention, prescribing the symptom of the family and directing the identified adolescent not to do the behavior. To accomplish this, the adventure therapist will lead the family to the log where individual family members will take turns falling off the standing log into their family's arms. Parents and other family members will be allowed to participate, but it should be explained that Bill (i.e., the adolescent causing trouble by being uncooperative or noncompliant) should probably not participate in this event because the family needs the people with the most influence in the family to stay on the ground to organize the spotting. Having Bill fall from the log would really be too risky because the family couldn't be organized without him directing the spotters or challenging the family to be on their best behavior to compensate for his sabotage. The adventure family therapist should also recommend that Bill stay on the ground to continue to distract the family, without physically touching anyone, since this behavior will help the family pull together and always be on guard in case something happens. In fact,

Bill should be encouraged to try harder to sabotage family efforts, because the Trust Fall is even more difficult and dangerous than initiatives that they have done in the past. If he isn't trying hard enough to sabotage the spotting, his parents should recommend ideas to him.

Very rarely would any person leading adventure experiences think of leading the Trust Fall activity in this manner. However, in this case, it presents the Merdock family with a paradox that destabilizes their current negative state. Who in the family wants to fall off the log with Bill trying to sabotage the spotters? They have three courses of action, all of which will have benefits for destabilizing the family's current negative state. These are:

1) If the family follows the course of action directed by the adventure therapist, the parents will be placed in a position of directing Bill's behavior and Bill in the position of following his parental directions.
2) If the family rebels against the statement of the therapist, they will choose not to do the initiative because Bill's behavior is too disruptive, a healthy boundary for the family to establish.
3) Bill and his family may rebel against the therapist's directive, enabling Bill to experience the opportunity to trust his family and the family may experience supporting Bill's independent decision.

If either of these last two options occur, the strategic family therapist should not reinforce the change, possibly stating that the family was fortunate this time, but given another chance they will revert to their old behaviors. Restraining the family from changing blocks potential relapse of behaviors and continues to strengthen the paradox. This eventually leads to the family evolving into a functional system.

It is important to note several critical factors in using paradoxical directives with adventure experiences. First is safety. It is counterproductive, and also dangerous, to prescribe a symptom that can physically or emotionally hurt a family or individual. Adventure experiences, when operated under certain guidelines, are extremely safe (Hale, 1988). Changing the safety procedures to make them less safe through a directive is inappropriate. Second is the need to be non-confrontational in offering the directive. Offering the paradox in a "matter-of-fact" manner allows the therapist to avoid an adversarial position, credit any change that occurs to the family, and permit the family to prove the therapist wrong (Haley, 1988). Third is to ensure that a trusting relationship has been established between the family and the therapist before using paradoxal directives. Delivering such directives without a trusting relationship between the family and therapist will only dissuade the family from returning to treatment (Haley, 1988). Fourth is to recognize that a therapist needs to be sincere in choosing to use paradoxical directives. While a paradox is offered in a "matter-of-fact" manner, it should be well planned and only used when appropriate.

CONCLUSION AND RECOMMENDATIONS

The use of adventure experiences in family therapy creates a strong, synergistic method of reaching therapeutic objectives. Family therapy provides a framework that looks systemically at dysfunctional issues. Adventure experiences are inherently rich with processes that can foster realism and a sense of empowerment rarely achieved in other therapeutic processes. When combined, powerful and lasting changes can result. Together they provide an exciting focus of change needed by many dysfunctional families.

The use of adventure elements with two family therapy frameworks was outlined in this paper. The reader should be aware that these frameworks are commonly combined for greater utility. If this is done, predetermined guide-lines like those by Stanton (1981) and Lebow (1987) need to be followed. Contradictory elements of the structural and strategic family therapies also need to be addressed to ensure that therapeutic intervention is not diminished (Fish & Piercy, 1987; Frazer, 1982).

Caution is also warranted for those adventure therapists not adept at family therapy techniques as well as family therapists not trained in the use of therapeutic adventure experiences. If family adventure therapy has the potential to bring about the type of changes outlined in this paper, it also has the potential to damage families to the same degree. It is important to note that these activities should not be conducted out of the "context" in which they were created. Adventure experiences, as well as family therapy interventions, need to be properly sequenced to achieve desired results. Not following this principle is physically and emotionally dangerous as well as therapeutically inappropriate.

Concern over the ethics of involving families in therapeutic adventure experiences must also become a priority in the therapy field. Families entering therapy are often systems suffering a great deal of conflict and abuse. Entering therapy is often frightening enough without placing the family in even more unfamiliar settings like adventure experiences. Family therapists leading adventure experiences possess a great capacity to bring about change. It must be recognized that inappropriate practices with such programs hold an even greater risk of emotional turmoil for the family (Creal & Florio, 1986). Factors such as the therapeutic needs of the client, safeguarding the rights of families and their members, the powerful change created by adventure experiences, and the rapidity with which critical issues are brought out in adventure experiences need to be considered as part of the treatment planning process. The training and background of the family therapist also needs to be adequate in conducting family therapy, adventure experiences, **and** the interacting processes between these two fields. It is hoped that this paper is a starting point for the critical process of addressing this important interaction.

SECTION 3

PROGRAMMING OF ADVENTURE THERAPY EXPERIENCES

Colorado Outward Bound School Photo

11

PROGRAMMING PRINCIPLES FOR SUCCESSFULLY IMPLEMENTING ADVENTURE THERAPY

MICHAEL A. GASS, Ph.D.

Introduction

As stated previously in this book, the goal of adventure therapy is to create healthy, constructive change with clients and ensure that such beneficial change will continue once it occurs. Previous sections of this book have provided some of the theoretical reasons for why adventure therapy "works," as well as a sample of various programs. Associated with the "why" of adventure therapy are certain programming principles, or "how" it works. Successfully implementing such principles plays an important role in creating and maintaining positive changes in and from adventure therapy experiences. The purpose of this section of the book is to outline some of these principles. In order to highlight the importance of such factors, a short discussion of the concept of change in adventure therapy will be illustrated.

THEORY OF CHANGE AND ITS RELATIONSHIP TO ADVENTURE THERAPY

As outlined by Nadler in the first section of this text, the concept of change is a major focus for most adventure experiences. Change is a process where all individuals, as well as the social organizations of which they are a part, are constantly in some state of evolution. While a clear definition of change in any context almost seems paradoxical (i.e., how can one define something that is always evolving into something different?), there are certain components that interact with one another to allow adventure therapists to use specific information to help clients[1] in issues, areas, and directions where they would like assistance. One perspective of viewing the process of change with a client in therapy is to see him/her as a person who is in a "relationship" with one or more unhealthy behaviors and is either unable (i.e., "motivated client") or unwilling (i.e., "unmotivated client") to break this relationship and establish patterns of interaction with healthier behaviors. The relationship of clients with their behaviors is homeostatic in nature (i.e., resistant to change and self-reinforcing in a linear and/or cyclical sense), yet evolving due to life ongoing events (e.g., personal and environmental stressors). "Problems" or "symptoms" arise when the behavior resulting from this interaction is more unhealthy than healthy in the clients' living environment and is often labeled by someone (usually the clients, other individuals, or an agency) as being detrimental. Change, regardless of whether it is therapeutic, does not occur unless the reason or motivation for change is compelling enough to where subscribing to a new "reality" makes more sense for the client. When this occurs, the client responds by forming a new "relationship" with the new reality (and hopefully more healthy behavior) that is designed with the assistance of the therapist.

An example of this can be metaphorically visualized with the illustration of a three-stranded rope. In this illustration, shown below, the white colored strand represents the client, the gray strand represents unhealthy behavior, and the black strand represents a more healthy behavior.

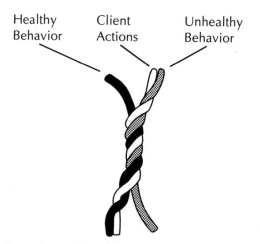

Healthy Behavior   Client Actions   Unhealthy Behavior

When clients begin therapy, they are generally in a homeostatic relationship with their unhealthy behavior (i.e., the beginning of the process represented by the interwoven connection of the gray and white rope). The connection to this behavior may be unhealthy for each client, but it usually makes "sense" at one level or another (e.g., the system of which they are a member), usually at a level possessing the most influence or "power." The premise of therapy and the associated interventions becomes a method of entering into the client's reality (e.g., joining), gathering appropriate information (e.g., assessment) to establish direction of change (e.g., hypothesizing, creation of treatment goals), and creating a stronger "relationship" between the client and a healthier behavior that leads him/her away from the unhealthy behavior (e.g., intervention). The stronger the "weave" that the client and therapist are able to make between the client and the healthier behavior, the more likely the client is to leave unhealthy behavior and not regress or relapse. It is imperative that the client and therapist use interventions and other techniques that are system-changing and self-reinforcing in the client's reality. Without this type of intervention, permanent client change does not occur and the client will return to his/her old relationship with the unhealthy behavior.

What many professionals using adventure therapy have discovered is that one of the most valuable methods that therapists can use to create conditions that will produce this type of change is through the intentional use of eustress (i.e., "positive stress"). This can be accomplished in a number of ways (e.g., unbalancing, punctuation, reframing, prescriptive adventure experiences), but the more appropriate the use of this stress, the more effective and efficient it will be in achieving success. Further illustration of the actual application of this concept can be found in the section of this book on processing, particularly in the article on "Enhancing Metaphor Development in Adventure Therapy Programs" (Chapter 23).

The material contained in this section of the book attends to some of the principles that lead to creating appropriate conditions for change in adventure therapy. It is obvious that these principles should be considered before the adventure therapy experience is conducted. In the first article in this section, entitled "Apples and Onions," Cline points to the need to differentiate between the types of clients with whom adventure therapists work and how a particular diagnosis will drastically affect the type of programming that is possible. Kimball points to the need to consider adventure therapy as a tool for assessment rather than as merely a method of intervention. This consideration obviously changes the manner in which adventure therapists implement experiences with clients. At the conclusion of his article, he outlines an example of a possible diagnostic survey that can be used for assessing clients during adventure experiences; interested professionals should consider adapting this survey to use in their programs or to combine with other therapeutic assessment tools when applicable (e.g., DSM IIIR). Stich and Gaylor point to the need for adventure therapists to understand the interactive effect between clients and adventure programming, providing examples of how climate, medication, and psychological contraindications can occur. While not a complete list of these contraindications, it does demonstrate the need for adventure therapists to be aware of such contraindications, emphasizes the necessity for all adventure therapy programs to have a well-established risk-management plan, and provides a general outline of some features that an adventure therapy program should consider when difficulties arise.

Along with these planning principles, there are several perspectives in programming that influence how each individual is affected by the adventure therapy experience. Many of these features represent the broader "system" of which each client is a part, having a present as well as future effect on their behavior. The article by McPhee and Gass shows how the evolution of a group during an adventure therapy experience influences the behavior of each individual group member. It also provides a five-step model for therapists to gauge the individual's and group's progress in adventure therapy experiences. It alerts professionals to several elements (e.g., individual development, rate and direction of growth, adding and removing members from groups, characteristics of group members) that influence group development. The article by Farragher, Harman, and Bullard outlines how dysfunctional multigenerational family themes possess a particularly strong influence on the behaviors of clients and describes the implications of these themes for treatment. Bowne identifies how the adaptation of one particular element of adventure programs (i.e., the equipment) can serve to enhance the therapeutic aspects of the adventure experience. This premise alone should encourage adventure therapists to re-think the idea of "progress" in the pursuit of treatment goals and therapeutic interventions.

Two articles that outline the actual aspects of program implementation complete this section of the book. Roland et al. illustrate how one adventure therapy program was implemented and has evolved at a private, psychiatric, community-oriented hospital. Areas that are particularly noteworthy in this chapter include a description of components that were incorporated into the adventure therapy program, how the program has evolved, the administrative challenges of the program, staff-training issues, and implications for other practitioners. Gilliam, in her article, outlines the current issues faced by mental health and psychiatric programs that offer adventure therapy as part of their services. Some of the areas addressed in her chapter include the perception of ropes courses by administration, the current directions of treatment, referral issues, the need for prescriptive processing, the resolution of staff conflict, program evaluation, and the standards and guidelines for ropes courses at adventure therapy settings.

In conclusion to this introduction on principles for successful programming in adventure therapy, there are certain concepts, adapted from Curtis and Stricker (1991), concerning change that professionals should remember. Some of these concepts include:

1) **There are no rules of change that will work all of the time**— There are no "ground rules" other than to attend to the specifics of each situation. Any attempt to impose inflexible and predetermined structures in therapeutic practices runs the chance of failing.

2) **Assessment is critical**—Adventure therapists must understand the conditions of particular situations. Details within each client's environment will always vary, and attending to these will often be the key to understanding client behavior and working with the client to produce healthy change.

3) **People are in a "systemic relationship" with their "behaviors"**—Change only happens through clients working on changing specific behaviors (e.g., first-order change) or the spontaneous shift to a newer system of behaviors (e.g., second-order change).

4) **Change always disrupts an equilibrium**—There are pressures, arising from within the clients and in their living environment, that will work to undo change and restore older and unhealthy behaviors. Clients must change to a new behavior where they are in a more favorable "position," one that makes more sense, and where newer and healthier behaviors can be maintained. Until this stage is reached, the person or other factors producing change cannot rest and they (or it) must continue to be implemented in order to assure that change to the newer, more healthy behavior is maintained.

5) **Change is rarely purely voluntary**—"Just say no" or "just do it" is rarely effective for unhealthy systems. People generally behave in ways that make sense to them and for reasons that appear to be the "best alternatives" of the choices available to them. Adventure therapists need to recognize that if they are asking people to give something up, something else will initially be expected in its place which should be more rewarding. Obviously, this can be difficult if it is something that they're in love with, crave, or are rewarded to do.

6) **Implementing change is an ethical decision**—This is especially true with people who are unwilling or unknowing of the change that is occurring (e.g., gentle conspiracies). This point raises some

interesting ethical dilemmas for the field, particularly given the strength of the intervention.

7) **Change must be internalized to have a lasting influence**—As stated by Curtis and Stricker: "If one is to design a lasting influence process, the value of external interventions lies in their impact on internal structures" (p. 213).

8) **Self-education is ultimately the best vehicle for a client to achieve lasting healthy change.**

9) **If you have any questions on these rules, see rule #1!**

Footnote

[1] The term client is used to represent a broad-based spectrum of one individual or many individuals, which could include one person, several people, couple(s), or families, and the interaction of these subsystem(s).

12

APPLES AND ONIONS[1]

FOSTER CLINE, M. D.

I want to tell you the bad news before I tell you the good news. First of all, I'm an outsider. Second of all, I'm a child shrink. Third of all, I've never been on an Outward Bound course. Fourth of all, I'm a Freudian. Fifth of all, I might be an "air head." I don't know, but I could be. In our program at Evergreen, Colorado, we work with extremely difficult youths. The kids in our program have usually been through four or five different foster homes, in prison, or something along those lines before we get them. This is the first outdoor education program to which I've been exposed. From my initial exposure to programs like yours, it seems that there are some things that could be accomplished in outdoor adventure and outdoor experiences that excite me very much.

This brings us to the issue of terminology. Terminology has been thrown around as being "bad news." Outward Bound programs are supposedly working with delinquents. Well now, calling someone a "delinquent" or a "law breaker" is, of course, the same as telling a doctor that somebody has a "limp." Delinquency is a symptom, not a diagnosis. I'm from the old school that says we've got to have a diagnosis because we don't know whether the guy's limping because he dropped a hammer on his toe last night or because he has a hip arthroplasty. *It makes a critical difference in how he should be treated.*

So many times in the mental health field (and I hope this doesn't happen in your programs), it doesn't matter what the problem is. If a person goes to a T. A. place, they get T. A. therapy, they talk about Parent, Adult, Child. If they go to a Freudian place, they lay down on a couch. If they go to a Gestalt Institute, they start hating their mother in a chair. If they go to Outward Bound, they're going down the river. Well, the point is to arrive at some kind of differential diagnosis. Within your program, you should have particular techniques that are going to help particular people in different yet appropriate ways. If you say, "We're here to work with delinquents," that's like saying that you work with limps and you don't know whether you need slings, or crutches, or better shoes, or simply more time. Therefore, I want to stress the importance of terminology: it should provide us with a handle on diagnosis. An intelligent diagnosis gives us a handle on treatment. With proper treatment, we can be effective.

The world is filled with two kinds of people. When people are called delinquents, it's because they have done something to break the law. It's defined legally. They are, however, one of two types of "delinquents": the person is either an Apple or an Onion. There are ways of looking at apples and onions, but what makes an apple an Apple and an onion an Onion? One's a fruit and one's a vegetable; one has a core and the other one just has a lot of layers. Everybody in this room is an Apple. If we weren't Apples, we wouldn't be holding down a job or having friends. We have some kind of good core inside us and an important defense mechanism called projection. If we go through the world as an Apple and we know we have a good core, then we unconsciously think that everybody else has a super good core. We think everybody else is an Apple. That means that when Betty hits John really hard, or when John smashes Mary with a swing, or when one kid shoots another, we say, "Why did he do that awful thing?" Because we're Apples and good souls, we tend to think, "Oh, that's a core crying for help." Much of that is ridiculous because if they're an Onion, it is not a core problem! Now there are many Apples who work with Onions. Unfortunately, when they peel the Onions apart looking for that good core, they end up in tears in search of a core that doesn't exist.

We need some way of separating the Apples from the Onions. Most programs do not know how to work with Onions. When you develop a particular way of working with these difficult kids on Outward Bound programs, you must create interventions that are effective with Onions. As a matter of fact, there aren't many places that can work with Onions. It is important to know whether kids are neurotic or conflicted (i.e., Apples), or character-disturbed or sociopathic (e.g., Onions), because it makes a difference where you put them in the canoe as well as how you direct their therapy. When Apple kids act out or have problems or do something self-destructive, it's the result of a neurosis—there's always a conflict within them. Deep inside their hearts, they feel like jerks. The conflict is often between the Parent and the Child parts. That conflict causes pain, and when a person has a pain they don't like it; somewhere inside, they want help. That's an easily workable situation. The things that will help in this situation are high confrontation combined with high support. I'm sure the best adventure therapy professionals are the ones who put their arms around kids while kicking them in the seat of their pants. You don't want to be milk givers because that will only help a few people some of the time. You don't want people running around kicking people in the seat of the pants since that also will only help a few people some of the time. You really want to be good therapists. You want to be someone who can put your arms around a person while giving hard confrontation about how unacceptable their behavior is. "I'm saying this because I like you." "Oh, you are?" That's what I mean.

With Onions, you may honestly begin to feel that there may not be a lot of good in that person. One of the things about character-disorders that will help you out in your differential diagnosis as you're floating down the river or taking them up the hill is that the better you know them, the less you like them. At first, the person may seem super. There's a statement that says a really good psychopath looks good until you get to know them. The better you get to know the person, the less you like them. Another little important point about being around a psychopath is that pretty soon you feel crazy. You tend to say, "What am I, crazy? Why am I doing this?" I'll explain what's going on here with this type of person in a T. A. sense. They have a fairly good Adult, but not an okay child. There's a big strong Child there, a not-too-well-formed Adult, and no Parent. So the person is not shooting you in the back, dumping the raft, or letting go of a rope because they're in some conflict. They're not up there holding the rope saying, "I love him so much and I hate him so much, I can't stand it—I'll let him go." If you have a character-disorder holding the rope, he says, "That son of a bitch down there is going to make us wait two hours to eat. I want to eat now. Bye!"

The way you handle these groups of people must be different when you have them on your trip because you're not going to be able to relate with the conflicts that they have. In essence, you have to almost re-parent them. Inside all the little Apples is a core of "trust." There is no core of trust in character-disorders or Onions. If I won't trust you, if I'm a character-disordered kid and I don't trust you, then in no way would I willingly let you have control. I'll say, "I don't want you to have control of the situation because I don't trust you. If I'm put into a situation where I have to be controlled by you, I experience rage because I think I'm going to die, because I've never trusted anyone in all my life, and now I'm in a situation where I must trust somebody." It makes me angry and I say, "I'm not climbing down that rope with you holding it." I know one thing that won't work is having a couple of fine leader Apples, who don't know about Onions, in charge of a whole bunch of character-disorders on a trip. I hope you're going to have a mixed group because if you have a whole group of character-disorders, you're in for an awful time on that outing. I know because we work with these kinds of kids. In our group homes and foster homes, we have Onions all over.

It's important for you to check out who's who before you take on delinquents; it's a super dangerous situation. If I don't trust you, I will not let you have control; but in Outward Bound, this is the beauty of these experiences. You have a situation where they must let someone be in control in certain situations. They have got to put their lives in somebody else's hands. You're going to have to force a character-disorder to do that. They do not do it willingly. They fight it. They hate it. They're going to be screaming as they're rappelling, "Son of a gun, I can hardly wait till I get down. This is the stupidest thing I ever did!" They're going to be in a rage. Then when they get down and their feet touch the ground, as a good professional you'll put your arm around him and say, "George, you did super," and he'll say, "I did?" Then they're ready to internalize that particular person as some type of good figure in their life and form some kind of relationship. They must go through that terrible experience, where they had to allow someone else to gain control, but then the controlling person gives them a lot of support and they're able to internalize it. If you try to form a relationship with people like this before they go through that type of experience, forget it.

The two groups have to be treated differently. Is it easy to differentiate between the groups? Yes! You don't have to be some kind of diagnostic wizard to separate the Apples from the Onions; you just need to know how to do it. You need to know how to take a really good history and look carefully at the first years of their life. You also need to find out whether they have had any long-term relationships. These are factors— there's a whole list of factors—that go into the making of a fine Onion or a good Apple. You need to check out whether those factors are present in that particular delinquent. Then you'll know what you're dealing with.

If you think you'll be able to tell what they're like by sitting down and having a chat with them, you will be wrong. A good psychopath would just look you in the eye and say, "I'm so thankful for this Outward Bound experience. You know I've been through a lot of different programs in my life, but I really think this one will help me a lot. I'm so thankful you guys are offering it; it's going to be super." Then who's going to fall through on the contract, shoot you in the back, let go of the rope, or tip the canoe? At that point, you will say, "But I thought he would be perfect for it." So, there is the other clue about a psychopathic kid: what you see in front of you is so good, yet the record is so bad! We tend to believe our senses with these kids and say, "Boy, this is really a neat kid. I don't know what was wrong with the County Mental Health Center."

In summary, I would like to say that I hope from now on you will regard the word "delinquent" with some suspicion. It does not tell you a darn thing. Maybe the kid did his legally antisocial behavior because he was conflicted; because he was crazy; because his parents just got a divorce; or, more hopefully, with good reason, because he simply hated the other kid. Now, are you going to put these kids in the raft based on their legal diagnosis of delinquency or do you want to arrange them according to their personality structure? This is an important question for you to think about, and I hope you will give it a lot of thought.

Dr. Foster Cline is a consultant for Evergreen Consultants on Human Behavior, located in Evergreen, Colorado.

Footnote

[1] This is a transcript from an address given by Dr. Foster Cline at a one- time work session of the Adventure Alternatives in Corrections, Mental Health, and Special Education of the Assocation for Experiential Education in March 1979. The workshop, entitled "Beyond Kelly and Baer," was jointly sponsored by the Association for Experiential Education and the Colorado Outward Bound School. A set of papers from the Conference is available from the Colorado Outward Bound School, 945 Pennslyvania Street, Denver, CO 80203.

13

THE WILDERNESS AS THERAPY: THE VALUE OF USING ADVENTURE PROGRAMS IN THERAPEUTIC ASSESSMENT

RICHARD O. KIMBALL, Ph.D.

There is great pressure in our society to find a quick fix for social ills—delinquency being one of them. Unfortunately, wilderness therapy as a "pill-popping cure" doesn't work. For the most part, long-term behavioral change is a long-term process.

Of course, we can all point to exceptions to this statement. Many youths commit one-time situational delinquent acts. Not suffering from any significant pathological disorder, these individuals are best served by the least restrictive intervention. In these cases, according to the National Council on Crime and Delinquency, wilderness experience alternatives avoid the contaminating effects of institutional care that often result in the development of antisocial attitudes which undermine an individual's sense of self.

However, delinquent acts must be viewed in the context of each individual's needs and the totality of environmental stressors. These stressors can include poverty, poor housing, low educational levels, unemployment, cultural conflict, dysfunctional family situations, and child abuse. Most behaviorally disordered youths are depraved because they are deprived, and the power of a 150-foot rappel often fades in light of this.

While recognizing that long-term therapeutic change avoids quick fixes, it has become increasingly important to appreciate the value of wilderness adventure experiences as being an invaluable tool in psychological evaluation. The first step in therapeutic change is diagnosis or an evaluation of an individual's strengths and weaknesses. In traditional clinical settings, this generally includes the client's history, objective testing results, a family history, and a DSM IIIR classification.

While this information is valuable and should not be dismissed, it can possess serious limitations. First, it is garnered in a clinical setting where past behavior is merely reported but never observed. Second, objective psychological measures are limited to assessing certain a priori defined traits or functions. Third, the client often has a fairly clear idea of what the examiner is "testing." This is particularly true on so-called "self-concept" tests.

For all these reasons, adventure therapy programs can be used as a valuable diagnostic test. One example of this can be seen through the use of adventure experiences in assessing youths by the New Mexico Bureau of Mental Health and Department of Corrections. The counselor's client report is used to supplement forensic court evaluations. New Mexico judges often rely upon written evaluations from these experiences as a deciding factor in sentencing. Likewise, the New Mexico Parole Board may require a wilderness evaluation report prior to parole.

Successful completion of the course serves as an excellent litmus test of an individual's ability to function as a positive member of society. Conversely, in over 5 years of testing, the Santa Fe Mountain Center in New Mexico has found that failure on a wilderness course correlated almost 100% of the time with subsequent recommitment.

RATIONALE FOR USING ADVENTURE THERAPY AS AN ASSESSMENT TOOL

In the process of assessment, wilderness adventure experiences can be viewed as similar to projective psychological tests. The basic assumption underlying the use of projective techniques is that clients reveal a composite picture of their global personality in the ways in which they respond to tasks, demands, and stimuli.

Unlike a clinical setting, however, the testing demands of the wilderness are capricious and require adaptability. Although expectations are made clear during the wilderness expedition, a whole range of responses is possible. Personal characteristics and behaviors emerge in sharp focus.

Like the well-known Rorschach ink blots, wilderness challenges are high in ambiguity. Clients must interpret or structure the task demands as well as their own responses to it. The challenges of the wilderness expedition offer great latitude in response. The greater the latitude and the higher the stress, the more likely the client will "project" unique and individual personality aspects into the "test" situation.

By careful observation of the client's responses to a multitude of "diagnostic" situations (e.g., rock climbing, route-finding, water rationing), the skilled mental health counselor can identify lifelong behavioral patterns, dysfunctional ways of coping with stress, intellectual processes, conflicts, needs, and emotional responsiveness. When properly observed, recorded, and articulated, this data can be the basis for long-term therapeutic goals. A sample guideline for recording the assessment of particular traits is included at the end of this article.

While behavioral change and therapeutic growth usually do occur, at a minimum adventure therapy programs can guarantee that critical diagnostic information will be collected when the programs are properly implemented. An evaluation outline serves to aid counselors in reporting both *psychological processes* as well as *behavioral content*.

Unlike an institutional environment or a clinician's office, there is no way to fake one's way through a wilderness adventure experience. More than once, clients have been model citizens before a judge or in a correctional facility, but reveal total sociopathic behavior during the stresses of the wilderness. On the other hand, obstreperous and contumacious individuals, who may react against the stifling authoritarianism of institutional rules and confinement, have revealed flexibility, compassion, and control under the more open rigors and demands of wilderness courses. The lesson is that institutional conformity is a poor predictor of autonomy and adaptability—necessary traits for success in the real world.

THE ROLE OF STAFF IN THE ADVENTURE THERAPY PROCESS

In terms of successfully achieving a comprehensive, mental health-care program, it is essential for an adventure therapist to view him/herself as a counselor/therapist first and an outdoor instructor second. This does not mean that a lower level of technical wilderness skills is expected, but it reminds professionals that the therapeutic means (e.g., the wilderness) are secondary to the therapeutic ends (i.e., therapy/evaluation). For example, analytical ability, writing skills, and familiarity with basic psychotherapy are just as important as rock-climbing or mountaineering skills.

To successfully bridge the gap between the community mental health system or the corrections system and the outdoor world, adventure therapists must be bilingual. This is to say, they must be able to discuss the American Psychological Association's DSM IIIR classifications just as coherently as they could perform the necessary anchors on a tyrolean traverse. Too many therapeutic adventure programs view themselves as an "alternative to the system," whether it be corrections or mental health. We choose to see the Santa Fe Mountain Center as within the system. Some of our most worthwhile and innovative projects have evolved in conjunction with outside agencies, hospitals, or groups.

By viewing each program and population individually, adventure therapists are able to develop experiences for sex offenders, rape victims, schizophrenics, and families-in-crisis. In each case, the wilderness is simply a component part of a larger therapeutic plan. In many cases, psychologists or therapists accompany clients on wilderness experiences. In other cases, the evaluation report from the adventure therapist provides continuity to the therapist in the traditional mental health setting.

Models such as these have allowed for exciting innovations and keep therapeutic change in the context of a long-term process. Such coordination of services ensures that client groups are received at a point of psychological readiness and commitment to change.

There is no magical formula to replace this motivation which is often the key to change. This concept is summed up in the joke, "How many psychologists does it take to change a light bulb?" Answer: "Only one, but the light bulb has to really want to change." For a client who has insight and motivation, wilderness experiences can be an extremely powerful metaphor for personal growth.

CONCLUSION

One of the premises of adventure therapy is the assumption that experience can be more therapeutic than analysis. While many clinical approaches use counseling to change attitudes in order to modify behavior, I believe that attitudinal change can best follow experiential exploration of new behaviors. It is the role of adventure therapists to help clients to draw insight into areas of dysfunction.

The most distinctive contribution that adventure therapy can make to the field of mental health is to dramatically demonstrate areas of power and competency, as opposed to merely concentrating on dysfunction and failure. Furthermore, because of the strong bonding that usually takes place between counselor and client, many ancillary areas of mental health can be explored (e.g., the mind-body connection, the role of fitness, nutritional awareness, and diet).

Adventure therapy programs have much to contribute to the field of mental health. However, a few caveats come to mind:

1) Do not overstate the impact of what adventure therapy can offer. Post-course outcomes are idiosyncratic and hence, programs should not simply claim to address one psychological variable like self concept or social competency.

2) Don't totally reject the traditional. Understand and be familiar with the medical model. Develop projects in conjunction with ongoing groups that can provide long-term therapy—both as preparation and as follow-up.

3) Recognize that by working with special populations, adventure therapists must operate with the tools and understanding of both the wilderness instructor and the mental health professional.

Richard Kimball earned his doctoral degree from the University of Colorado School of Education in 1978. For the next 10 years, he worked in the clinical mental health system of New Mexico as the Executive Director of the Santa Fe Mountain Center. He is currently a Partner in the Inventure Group, a national consulting firm specializing in career renewal, self-leadership, and executive assessment and coaching. He is also a member of the adjunct faculty at the Center for Creative Leadership where he works as a psychologist providing individual assessment and feedback.

SAMPLE CLIENT EVALUATION
SANTA FE MOUNTAIN CENTER

Purpose: While many wilderness adventure counselors are excellent at providing outdoor leadership and conducting safe, therapeutic courses, too many fail to appreciate the importance of the client evaluation. The client evaluation is the link between the Santa Fe Mountain Center, the referral source, and all subsequent agencies who may deal with the client. The gifted counselor will garner critical evaluative data which, if properly recorded and articulated, can be the basis for long-term therapeutic goals.

FORMAT (Per Example)

I. **Introduction**—The introduction is similar from one course to another and includes:
   (A) A description of the Santa Fe Mountain Center's Wilderness Experience
   (B) Breakdown of clients and referral status
   (C) Location and format of the course
   (D) Dates of the course
   (E) Egregious incidents experienced by the entire group

II. **Course Participation**—This section is usually short and is, relative to other sections, the least important. The section summarizes each individual's ability to accomplish the various phases of the experience. It also details highlights and valleys of the physical/mental challenges.

III. **Socialization**—This section makes comments on interpersonal characteristics.
   (A) With authority
      1. Does the client seek approval?
      2. Is the client hostile, contumacious, obstreperous, resistant?
      3. How does the client react to counseling?
      4. How does the client react to criticism?
   (B) With Peers
      1. Can the client share material items? (cooperation/ sharing)
      2. Does the client contribute to group problem solving? (assistance/resistance)
      3. What role does the client assume in the group? (group role—leader, follower, active, passive)

4. Was the client accepted or rejected socially? (in-group/out-group)
5. Does the client seek intimacy or distance from others? (interpersonal space)
6. How does the client react to interpersonal conflicts? (appropriate/inappropriate)
7. Can the client show compassion and empathy for others? (sociopathy)
8. Does the client accept individuals in group across ethnic backgrounds? (prejudice)
9. Can the client take emotional or physical risks? (trust)

IV. **Observations**—This is an open area and the section's content is determined by the major behavioral patterns which emerge as an individual's themes.
   A. Exaggerated coping devices displayed on the course such as:
      1. dependency on staff or others
      2. hyperemotionalism—tearfulness, instability
      3. hypoemotionalism—lack of appropriate effect
      4. restlessness, insomnia
      5. excessive worrying, paranoia, bad dreams
      6. preoccupation
      7. passive aggression
      8. somatic complaint, hypochondriacal
      9. explosive temper
   B. Personal Traits
      1. ability to channel or direct energy
      2. positive/negative attitude
      3. open and flexible or closed and rigid
      4. impulsive or deliberate personality
      5. over-incorporates or under-incorporates information
      6. immature or mature
      7. sense of values, spirituality
      8. internal or external locus of control
      9. superficial or honest in self assessment
   C. Task Performance
      1. ability to follow directions
      2. attention span
      3. initiative
      4. ability to deal with structured tasks
      5. ability to deal with unstructured tasks

D. Physical Manifestations (related to diagnosis)
1. physical appearance
2. eye contact
3. quality of speech—intensity and level, relevant, coherent
4. thought pattern—logical or loose associations
5. reality orientation—awareness of time, place, and person
6. coordination and balance

V. **Recommendations**—The purpose of this section is to indicate those measures which the evaluator feels need to be taken as the next step in the client's therapeutic struggle. Because there are different categories of clients, there are many different needs, ranging from family therapy to drug counseling or vocational training. The recommendation section is particularly important for a client who is in transition—about to be paroled, about to leave a group home or residential treatment center, etc. It is also critical if the client is in limbo, such as a probation violator, a pre-sentence referral, or a client who is serving an evaluation/diagnostic period, etc. In these cases, the evaluator must be candid and honest or it jeopardizes the credibility of future evaluation.

14

RISK MANAGEMENT IN ADVENTURE PROGRAMS WITH SPECIAL POPULATIONS: TWO HIDDEN DANGERS[1]

THOMAS F. STICH, M. S.
MICHAEL S. GAYLOR, M. D.

The purpose of this chapter is to address two significant risk management considerations in conducting an adventure program in a therapeutic setting. The first section will focus on the potential hazards of psychiatric medications and their limitations on program activities. The second section will address psychological emergencies and how to manage them from a practical standpoint.

MEDICATION OVERVIEW

For staff working in outdoor settings with people who are either physically debilitated (those with chronic diseases such as alcoholism, diabetes, or heart disease) or those who are taking prescribed medications for medical or psychiatric reasons, climatic conditions and potential medication side effects play a significant role in choosing the intensity and duration of program activities. The Outward Bound Mental Health Project, a collaborative effort between the Hurricane Island Outward Bound School and the Department of Psychiatry, Dartmouth Medical School, has been conducting Outward Bound sessions for mental health patients on a regular basis since 1975. Of those patients referred to the Project, a majority are using some form of psychoactive drug. A psychoactive drug is one that acts on the central nervous system. Psychoactive drugs do not cure mental illness, per se. They are used to relieve agitation and anxiety, as anti-depressants, and to control psychotic symptoms such as hallucinations and delusions. During the past 9 years, we have spent over 4,000 student program days in the outdoors with patients, some of whom are over 70 years of age and many of whom have accompanying medical problems. By attending to the appropriate use of medication, thermo-regulation, and fluid intake, we have experienced no medication or medical problems in the field to date.

CLIMATIC CONSIDERATIONS

The hypothalamus is the body's major center for thermoregulation. Body temperature is maintained within a narrow range despite extremes in physical activity and climatic conditions. Important factors in this regulation are fluid and caloric intake, vasoconstriction and vasodilation, thyroid functioning, excessive sedation, and degree of physical activity. Certain psychoactive drugs may disrupt thermoregulation at hypothalamic as well as peripheral levels, leaving medicated individuals vulnerable to high or low environmental temperatures (Shader et al., 1970; Exton-Smith, 1972).

Heat

The hypothalamus prevents overheating of the body both by increasing perspiration and by radiating heat from the body surface through peripheral vasodilation. Even with normal activity levels, heat stroke kills more than 4,000 people per year in the United States, with most deaths occurring coincidentally with increases in humidity (Clowes & O'Donnell, 1974). Individuals at risk for heat morbidity are those who are predisposed by chronic diseases or fluid depletion, or those exposed to excessive thermal environments, either passively or through an increase in physical activity. Phenothiazines, tricyclics, or antiparkinsonian drugs may decrease the body's ability to regulate temperature by inhibiting sweating. Therefore, patients under treatment with these medications require extra caution.

Drug-induced heat stroke usually results in a sudden loss of consciousness, preceded by a brief period of confusion and irrational behavior. The classic sign of heat stroke (i.e., the cessation of sweating) may not be present (Zelman & Guillan, 1970). A case report from the American College of Physicians, for instance, reviewed the death of a 21-year-old psychiatric outpatient who was hospitalized in a coma with a temperature of 108° F following mild activity on a day when the average temperature was 87° F and the average relative humidity was 19%. The patient's comatose condition developed quickly and was preceded only briefly by profuse perspiring and incoherent speech. The patient was on several medications which placed him at risk.

162

During excessively hot weather, medications can be decreased slightly in anticipation of the experience with increased safety and no adverse clinical effects.

Cold

The hypothalamus conserves our body heat in adversely cold situations by stimulating adrenergic systems to produce a vasoconstriction in an effort to conserve heat, and by initiating the shiver response that produces heat.

Propranlol, a drug used to treat high blood pressure, cardiac problems, and certain types of anxiety, can be particularly problematic in cold environments since it suppresses the body's adrenergic (mediated by adrenalin) response to the cold. Other sedative drugs can interfere with central hypothalamic cold regulation if used in sedating doses. Phenothiazines, tricyclics, and antiparkinsonian medications can also decrease the body's response to cold.

Altitude

Any pre-existing condition and all of the conditions mentioned in this paper are exacerbated by changes in altitude. As cases of pulmonary edema have been reported at as low as 8000 feet above sea level, consideration of this factor is essential.

SIDE EFFECTS OF MEDICATIONS

Orthostatic Hypotension: Orthostatic hypotension is a naturally occurring rapid change in blood pressure associated with changes in posture. A transition from lying down to standing up too quickly may cause an individual to experience a transient dizziness or faintness. This is caused by a drop in blood pressure that will temporarily decrease circulation to the brain. This phenomenon is exacerbated by many psychoactive drugs, as well as by changes in fluid and caloric intake. This set of circumstances must be understood well because one often sees a patient on medication (with or without a decrease of fluid or food intake) belaying on a ledge and then standing up too quickly and becoming dizzy, or standing up too quickly after a rest stop on a trail that is adjacent to a steep drop-off. Tricyclics, antiparkinsonian, and some anti-psychotic agents are particularly problematic, though usually only in the elderly and at the inception of therapy with the medication.

Extrapyramidal symptoms: Many anti-psychotic agents are able to induce a variety of involuntary disorders of movement (Shader, 1975).

1. *Dystonia:* Patients on anti-psychotic medications occasionally develop dystonic reactions which usually occur within 4 or 5 days (sometimes sooner, particularly in younger patients) of initiating drug therapy. Difficulties are characterized by disordered muscle movement, bizarre posturing, or rigidity.

2. *Akathisia:* Can be experienced by 15% to as many as 45% of patients on anti-psychotic medications. Symptoms occur as an involuntary motor restlessness and are experienced as an inability to sit still, often accompanied by tremor. Akathisias are most commonly seen after several weeks of treatment and can occur in any age-group.

3. *Pseudo-Parkinsonism:* A triad of akinesia (immobility), rigidity, and tremors (especially at rest), can cause some patients to appear as if they had Parkinson's disease.

4. *Tardive Dyskinesia:* This is a slowly developing neurological syndrome associated with long-term anti-psychotic drug use. Clinical manifestations appear as repetitive involuntary movements of various muscle groups, particularly of the mouth, tongue, and torso.

   Extrapyramidal syndromes will often occur at the time that the patient is beginning medication, with a significant increase in medication, or as a slowly developing problem. Dystonia, akathisia, and pseudo-Parkinsonism can disappear spontaneously or be treated by antiparkinsonian agents. These agents, however, increase the hazards of hypotension and heat stroke. Symptoms may significantly affect balance and agility. Rock climbing, rope courses, or any physical activity might be extremely difficult to perform if extrapyramidal problems are not adequately treated. Therefore, activities should be chosen judiciously for clients for whom treatment has been recently instituted. These patients may need to be closely monitored during activities that require balance and agility. Staff should always be in a position to assist the patients, including being able to lower them to the ground   immediately.

5. *Sun and Light Sensitivity:* For the few patients (5%) on phenothiazine medications that may produce sun sensitivity, sunscreening agentsshould be provided. For those agents that might produce light sensitivity via pupilary dilation (phenothiazines, tricyclics, and antiparkinson agents), sunglasses should be provided.

164

6. *Dry Mouth:* Some medications dry the mucous membranes and will decrease normal secretion. However, fluid and electrolyte balance remain unchanged, though "dry mouth" is being experienced. Rather than unnecessarily increasing fluid intake, sucking on hard candies is the best way to alleviate the situation.

Recognition of the potential hazards from medications and weather is a key element in providing a safe, therapeutic experience. From a practical standpoint, it is necessary to be familiar with all referred clients' medical histories, particularly for potentially limiting factors, secondary medical problems, and medication issues.

PSYCHOLOGICAL EMERGENCIES

In psychological emergencies, as in medical emergencies, prompt treatment frequently decreases a potential problem's severity. Proper management of an individual significantly reduces emotional distress. There are two types of psychological emergencies: primary and secondary. In primary emergencies, emotional illness produces the symptoms. In secondary emergencies, the behavior is a manifestation of a medical problem (Soreff & Olsen, 1975). Recognizing the indicators of emotional or medical illness and properly labeling a problem as either medical or psychological is an important first step in dealing with the situation. Following these basic guidelines should be helpful to the instructor who may be called upon to deal with such problems in the field.

Distinquishing between medical and psychological problems can be done by performing a simple, mental-status examination. Disturbances of cognitive functioning (thinking processes) indicate a potential medical rather than psychological problem. Despite the stresses of a highly charged emotional environment, individuals should not lose their ability to perform simple calculations or remember simple facts. Very often disorientation, confusion, and profound inability to remember simple facts is misattributed to psychological causes. For example, an acute cognitive impairment due to hypothermia or a toxic drug is frequently incorrectly viewed as a psychological problem.

ASSESSMENT PROCEDURES

I. The Mental Status Examination: This is performed to quickly assess cognitive functioning:
   A. Orientation: An individual should be oriented as to person, place, and time. Persons will **rarely** forget their names, and it would be unlikely not to know generally where they are. It would be unusual for psychological conditions to cause this, as a lack of orientation is a general indication of a medical problem.
   B. Imprinting
      1. An individual's short-term or recent memory should be intact. For example, one should be able to remember and repeat five objects after several minutes, spell a simple word backwards, or repeat an entire series of five numbers after they have been presented slowly with a pause between each number.
      2. Calculations: An individual should be able to perform simple calculations.

II. Emotional Distress: An important indicator of the onset of emotional stress is a gradual change in an individual's functioning:
   A. Sleep pattern
      1. The individual will not or cannot sleep, even when tired.
      2. The individual needs an excessive amount of sleep.
      3. The individual appears to be functioning in a sleep-deprived state, unlike other members of the group.
   B. Diet
      1. Loss of normal food and fluid intake or appetite.
      2. Loss of normal energy reserves.
   C. Social Interactions
      1. Overly intense.
      2. Unusually withdrawn.

III. Symptom Assessment:
   A. An individual may be subtly cognitively impaired, requiring a more formal assessment, if:
      1. He/she is unable to make a point.
      2. Others are unable to follow his/her line of thought.
      3. He/she has a short attention span (e.g., difficulty comprehending instructions).

4. He/she is talking very rapidly or is hyperactive in an atypical manner.
5. He/she has a perseverating preoccupation with an emotion, an incident, or the environment.

If a cognitive impairment seems to be present, it strongly suggests a medical problem; the appropriate action is evacuation and medical evaluation. Let the experts determine the exact nature of the disorder and the ultimate disposition of an individual.

INTERVENTION

I. Keep the individual under observation and monitor behavior.

II. Evacuate:
A. If the episodes of abnormal behavior are of increasing intensity, frequency, or duration.
B. After 12 hours of consistently abnormal behavior.

III. Interview the individual:
A. Use open-ended questions initially (e.g., "How are things going?").
B. Point out your observations (e.g., are your observations consistent with the individual's perceptions?).
C. There may be someone else in the group who has more rapport with the individual and is in a position to be more supportive.
D. Eliminate the audience unless otherwise indicated. Some attempt should be made to neutralize their anxiety.

IV. Result
A. If the individual responds favorably, continue your approach because what you are doing is apparently helpful.
B. If the individual responds unfavorably and becomes worse, discontinue your approach and try something new.
C. If the individual is unresponsive, attempt to determine what the cognitive (internal: thoughts and feelings) or environmental (external: interpersonal) contingencies are that are causing the distress.
D. If the individual attempts to respond but cannot, or is non-compliant, an assessment must be made of cognitive functioning (e.g., Is the individual cognitively intact but angry? or is he/she impaired through some toxic or medical process?).

V. If the problem is situational, the individual will most likely respond to the above. The instructor can also try to:
   A. Use the group as emotional support for the individual.
   B. Pair the individual with a supportive figure.
   C. Redesign or reconceptualize the experience to increase the likelihood of the individual re-labeling the experience as positive rather than negative.

EVALUATION OF INTERVENTION

I. Evacuate the individual if:
   A. The abnormal behavior continues or worsens despite all of the above attempts.
   B. His/her behavior absolutely dilutes the meaning of the experience for the rest of the group. The staff must not collude in making the entire content of the course the distorted thinking processes of a distressed participant because it will be at the expense of the other members' experience.

II. Leaving the course is a learning experience for everybody; it requires processing.
   A. Use the group to debrief. This is a superb opportunity for personal growth on everybody's part.
   B. The situation can be used by the staff as a therapeutic object lesson. That is, one can consolidate the learning and generalize from it.

SUMMARY

In conclusion, this paper has addressed two critical risk-management issues in conducting an adventure program in a therapeutic environment. Recent advances in psychiatry (in particular greater understanding of the biological basis of some psychiatric symptomatology) suggest that more individuals will be taking some form of psychotropic medication as an adjunctive treatment.

As medical science advances, it is clear that now, and in the future, wilderness therapy programs must take into account medications (psychiatric and medical) and their side effects when designing specific curricula intended to be therapeutic and safe. Psychological and medical emergencies which are bound to emerge in the field can be managed by the instructor by using common sense and following a coherent evaluation and intervention strategy. With the basic guidelines outlined in this paper, an instructor should be able to manage difficult situations in a professional and sensitive manner.

At the time this article was written, Tom Stich was the Coordinator of Human Development for the Norton Company, and was formerly the Director of the Hurricane Island Outward Bound/Dartmouth Medical School Health Project. Michael Gaylor was Medical Director of the Dartmouth Institute for Better Health and Associate Professor of Clinical Psychiatry for the Dartmouth Medical School. He also served as Director of Counseling for Dartmouth College Health Service and is a consultant to Outward Bound.

Footnote

[1] This article first appeared in the 1984 Journal of Experiential Education, 7(3), 15-19.

15

A GROUP DEVELOPMENT MODEL FOR ADVENTURE THERAPY PROGRAMS[1]

PAMELA J. MCPHEE, M.S.W.
MICHAEL A. GASS, Ph.D.

The use of small-group development has often been recognized as one of the cornerstones of adventure therapy programs (e.g., Walsh & Golins, 1976; Jensen, 1979; Kalisch, 1979; Buell, 1983; Landry, 1986). Central to this development are the various stages each group encounters in its evolution. The purpose of this article is to apply a conceptual model of group development theory to the processes used in adventure therapy programs. The focus of such a model builds upon the past successes and techniques of leaders in the field and provides adventure therapists with a framework to enhance the structured and intuitive strategies currently used in their programs.

USE OF MODELS IN GROUP DEVELOPMENT

It is commonly accepted that as individuals work in groups, they progress through a series of developmental stages. As the group evolves in each stage, unique characteristics arise that indicate the group's progress. Awareness of these stages provides leaders with a framework to judge when actions are needed to help a group to confront or overcome an obstacle.

In viewing fields that use small-group development, one theory that offers assistance for the formation of a model in adventure therapy is the one proposed by Garland, Jones, and Kolodny (1973). This framework identifies five central themes that focus on the stages through which groups progress as they develop. These stages are: 1) pre-affiliation, 2) power and control, 3) intimacy, 4) differentiation, and 5) separation.

Each of these stages can be defined in the following manner:

1) **Pre-affiliation**—During this initial period of association, group members strive to become familiar with one another and their environment. Close and efficient associations have not developed and relationships among individuals tend to be superficial and stereotypic. Members are generally ambivalent toward involvement and often experience some kind of anxiety about participating in the group. Individuals' past experiences with other groups (e.g., classrooms, churches, clubs, sports teams) influence how they view this new, small-group environment. Members also attempt to use these past experiences to help them in the processes of group exploration and affiliation.

2) **Power and Control**—Once it has been established that the group is potentially safe and worth emotional investment, members begin testing group power and control issues. Issues can include, but are not limited to, problems of status, communication, and defining group values. It is at this stage in the group's development that familiar frames of reference may not be satisfactory for governing current behaviors, and new behaviors are often implemented in their place. In developing these new behaviors, issues concerning the balance of individual versus group needs occur. The amount of control that members have on deciding and planning group activities is also a central issue of this stage.

3) **Intimacy**—In this stage, members have decided to "affiliate" with one another and must contend with "sibling-like" rivalries and deeper emotions that are characteristic of close relationships. Members are more invested in the group and there tends to be a greater proficiency in planning and conducting projects as a group. There is also a greater desire to immerse oneself in group life and to share emotions arising out of common experiences.

4) **Differentiation**—At this point in the group's development, roles and status of group members tend to be less rigid. Individual differences and personal needs are accepted more freely and the group becomes more functionally autonomous from the leader(s). The group has created its own identity and members often compare themselves to other groups and previous social situations. The group is seen as being cohesive, yet is able to identify both individual and group needs.

5) **Separation**—The final stage represents the conclusion of the group experience and members are placed in a situation where they must find new resources for meeting their needs. The task of separation can be accomplished in a positive manner (e.g.,

172

reviewing experiences to analyze benefits of the group, incorporating growth of group experiences into future interactions) or in a negative one (e.g., denying that the experience is over, regressing to previous negative behaviors as the experience draws to a conclusion).

The main strengths of this theory lie in its applicability to therapeutic group development and its ability to provide useful information concerning the progress of the group for the facilitator. Because of these strengths and the structure of the five stages, this model has been chosen to provide a framework that illustrates small-group development in adventure therapy experiences.

It is important to note that, depending on the goals of the adventure experience, the: 1) structure of the stages, 2) style of instructor intervention, and 3) types of participant development will be different for each group. Participants in adventure therapy programs all progress through some degree of these five stages, yet the practices used with these groups vary according to the goals set for the particular population.

Based on the need to be flexible yet prescriptive, the authors have constructed a model where the five stages represented by Garland are applied to the central focuses of adventure therapy. While other focuses exist, these areas represent the intent of most adventure therapy programs currently being conducted. For use in group development, adventure therapy programs can be defined as *those programs that focus on changing specific behaviors in order to address an identified dysfunction.* Common examples in the field of adventure therapy include programs for adolescents identified as "juvenile offenders" or programs for individuals suffering from drug dependency.

GROUP DEVELOPMENT MODELS FOR ADVENTURE THERAPY

Given these five developmental stages, this section of the paper will (A) provide a further description of these areas for adventure therapy, (B) show the application of group development for each area in adventure therapy, and (C) outline a model that summarizes group interaction and instructor roles for each developmental stage.

A. Description

The main focus in the therapeutic group is the purposeful changing or directing of behaviors to create a healthier social structure for an individual. Specific behavior changes and treatment plans are implemented to remedy inappropriate behaviors. The group often forms an entity where individuals are held accountable for their behavior and its effect on others. The instructor often uses the strength of the group to help create behavior changes in individuals. The direction of this change is often determined with the help of a medical or therapeutic model.

B. Stages of Therapeutic Group Development with Adventure Therapy Programs

1. **Pre-affiliation**—The leader and the group begin this stage by examining goals and expectations of group members. During this process, individual similarities and differences are explored in conjunction with directions the group can take. Through this process of clarification, the leader helps the group to understand the needs of the individuals and the expectations of the organization of which they are a part. For example, the judicial system conducting a wilderness program for juvenile offenders expects certain standards to be followed during the course to help in the therapeutic process of each individual.

2. **Power and Control**—The leader attempts to clarify the issue of "power and control" and relate it to the purpose of the group. Rules and requirements are again agreed upon by members. Shulman (1984) stresses that any group rules should emerge from the function of the group, rather than from the authority of the leader. For example, a rule of no physical contact might be imposed because if people get hurt in the backcountry, the group must carry them out. This rationale is apt to be more effective than a rule based upon no fighting because it will be considered an assault and you will be punished.

3. **Intimacy**—In this stage, the leader attempts to diagnose problem areas and present them so that new perspectives may be seen. By using clarification and confrontation, the leader and group explore possible ways in which individuals can meet their needs without compromising the rights of others. For example, if Joe hits Sam, a series of questions might be asked: "Joe, what did you want when you hit him?" "What is another way of getting Sam's attention?" "Which method would get you Sam's attention and still maintain your friendship?" "Why is it hard for you to ask to be noticed?" "What can the group do to help you feel as though you belong?"

4. **Differentiation**—The leader clarifies what progress has been made in the group and helps individuals to transfer this knowledge to other situations outside of the group. The leader remains supportive yet begins to represent the point of view of others outside of the group. An example might be, "We've agreed that it's all right to swear while we are in this group, but if I were a potential employer and heard you using that kind of language, what do you think I would think of you?"

5. **Separation**—The leader helps to clarify the gains that have been made and encourages members to transfer these methods to other situations. The leader also provides members with alternative methods to the group to meet the needs that have been fulfilled by the group; for instance, a student leaving a therapeutic wilderness course for alcoholics being integrated into a local group of Alcoholics Anonymous.

C. Outline of an Adventure Therapy Group Development Model

	Group Indicators	Instructor's Role
1) Pre-affiliation	1) anxiety	1) clearly define program goals and expectations
	2) fear of expectations	2) solicit individual's fears and hopes
2) Power & Control	1) individuals seek boundaries and an affirmation for their behavior	1) relate issues of power and control to the purpose of the group
	2) ambivalence to joining the group; "What will I get out of it?"	2) help to clarify what is appropriate and acceptable behavior
		3) enforce limits when needed
3) Intimacy	1) individuals have formed a group and have established norms and values	1) support positive achievements
	2) begin to question the role of the leader	2) suggest areas where growth is needed
		3) help to clarify the function of the group

	Group Indicators	Instructor's Role
4) Differentiation	1) individuals understand the different roles that each plays	1) leader begins to relate the new behaviors to situations outside of the group
	2) individuals understand how the group is different from other groups	2) encourages individuals to be flexible in their group's roles
		3) is supportive yet begins to represent more societal views
5) Separation	1) individuals may feel lost without the group	1) leader helps to clarify gains that have been made
	2) individuals may regress or flee in attempts to deny the emotional impact of the group	2) helps to prepare individuals on how to meet their needs without the group
	3) members often review their experiences in a comparative manner	3) encourages individuals to continue the gains they've already made

CONSIDERATION AND CONCLUSIONS

Adventure therapy has grown to include a variety of applications and mediums. Central to the value of these programs is the use of a small-group environment to aid in the acquisition of therapeutic goals. As members participate in these programs, they progress through series of stages of group development. Given knowledge of group development stages, instructors of adventure therapy programs are provided with

176

valuable information to assist the participant in reaching his/her desired goals. In using the information provided by the group development models, it is important for leaders to be aware of several other factors:

1) **Individual Development**—While the model focuses on the group's development, the instructor must also be aware of the unique needs of each participant. The model presented here focuses on the development of an individual as a group member. Participants may have goals separate from the group that need to be considered.

2) **Rate and Direction of Growth**—It is important to remember that groups will progress through the stages of development at different rates and that individual members within the same group grow at different speeds. This variation in development often makes it important to allow for different individual outcomes to an activity. For example, some participants may progress to a point in a group where they feel comfortable, whereas others may still be questioning whether they are willing to make a commitment to the group. It is also important to recognize that group members can regress as well as advance through these stages. For example, regression to earlier stages is often evident in therapeutic programs as participants approach the end of the experience.

3) **Adding and Removing Group Members**—Inserting or removing members from a group will affect its development. Every participant plays a role within the group and when someone is added or removed, a restructuring of the group will occur. This often results in the group regressing to an earlier stage of development.

4) **Characteristics of the Members**—Other characteristics such as the age of group members or the cognitive and integration abilities of group members will also affect group development. It is imperative to take into consideration all of these factors when implementing this model for group development. In the past, leaders have often relied on "what our program has done in the past" and the "magic" of groups to reach their intended goals. By understanding the five-stage model of group development, it is hoped that instructors will choose activities that are appropriate for the needs of the group at each particular stage. When this is done, the program "flows" or has a sense of natural timing, allowing the participants to get the most from the experience. Groups develop regardless of instructor involvement; knowledge of how the instructor can affect this growth is often the difference between providing a valuable therapeutic experience and just "surviving" an outdoor program.

Footnote

[1] A form of this article first appeared in the 1987 <u>Journal of Experiential Education</u>, <u>10</u>(3), 39-46.

Pamela McPhee is the Co-Coordinator of Outdoor Education at the University of New Hampshire in the Department of Physical Education. She is also Director of the Fireside Program and Ropes Course at UNH. She received her M.S.W. from the University of Connecticut and is a Certified Trainer for Project Adventure, Inc.

A biography of Michael Gass is listed on the back cover of this book.

16

LIKE FATHER LIKE SON: THE ASSESSMENT AND INTERRUPTION OF MALADAPTIVE, MULTIGENERATIONAL FAMILY PATTERNS WITHIN A THERAPEUTIC WILDERNESS ADVENTURE

BRIAN FARRAGHER, M.S.W.
SCOTT HARMAN, M.S.W.
MARTIN BULLARD, M.S.W.

Introduction

This chapter outlines the assessment of significant generational patterns during a 6-day, wilderness backpacking course. The participants consisted of a group of adolescent boys in residential treatment at the Julia Dyckman Andrus Memorial. The trip also revealed how the wilderness leadership experience impacted three of the residents.

During this experience, clients were placed into various leadership roles to identify multigenerational family themes that were dysfunctional and often the reason for their ineffective/inappropriate behavior. The opportunity to lead a peer group in unfamiliar surroundings was a unique experience for these boys. Faced with this challenge, they employed leadership styles that were most familiar to them. In doing so, these clients assumed many of the characteristics of the parent with whom they had had the greatest conflict. Based on this presented behavior during the trip, the staff were able to make initial assessments and interventions in attempts to interrupt these dysfunctional patterns.

This paper provides a description of the organizational structure and process of this type of wilderness experience and how this design facilitated the exposure of maladaptive family themes. After an initial introduction, the first section outlines the "family legacy" concept and its relationship to bio-psycho-social characteristics which repeat through several generations, giving particular emphasis to specific dysfunctional patterns of relating within family systems. Potential treatment interventions and further implications for ongoing treatment are then reviewed for appropriate implementation by other therapeutic adventure programs.

BACKGROUND

The Julia Dyckman Andrus Memorial is a private, residential treatment center within an expansive and wooded suburban setting. The agency serves 65 emotionally disturbed boys and girls, ranging from 4 to 18 years in age. It is a comprehensive treatment program designed to meet the educational, clinical, and recreational needs of the residents.

The agency accepts children with a variety of presenting problems. The majority tend to exhibit passive and dependent qualities reflecting ego deficits such as low self-esteem, weak impulse control, poor judgment, and low motivation. These difficulties, often coupled with overwhelmed family systems, necessitate residential placement. Once accepted, the resident's length of stay is approximately 18 months. Long-term goals include resolution of the presenting problem and reintegration of the child into the family and community.

One component of the adolescent boys' treatment program is a wilderness backpacking trip. The children receive instruction in outdoor skills prior to their departure. Part of their training for this 6-day experience is an overnight backpacking trip.

In 1989, 9 residents participated in the wilderness experience. The 6-day backpacking expedition covered approximately 25 miles in New York's Adirondack Region. During the 3 travel- and 2 rest-days, the group climbed mountain peaks and endured inclement weather. The children used tarps for shelter and stoves for cooking while practicing guidelines that reflected minimal environmental impact.

THE CREW SYSTEM

Before leaving for the wilderness trip, the staff organized the boys into three independently functioning groups. The reason for breaking the larger group into smaller, more manageable units was to enhance communication and interaction between clients. This appeared both practical and desirable for: 1) gathering and distributing of information with nine group members, and 2) allowing the three crew leaders to be placed in leadership positions (Cataldo, 1982).

The crew format provided other individual and group benefits. The residents enjoyed a greater sense of independence throughout the trip as staff members shared their information and power with the resident crew leaders. Furthermore, the crew system gave a greater number of residents the opportunity to function in a leadership role. Finally, each crew relied on the cooperation of its members, enhancing the opportunity for self- and group responsibility, peer bonding, and participation.

In these types of experiences, it is important to allow residents to assume formal leadership roles as often as possible. Given this priority, a crew size of three has been found to be the most optimal. When a crew has only two members, individual contributions are easily blended into a crew consensus. The addition of a third member disrupts this equilibrium and forces greater reciprocity among the crew members (Walsh & Golins, 1976), and groups of a larger size do not modify the nature of these interactions proportionally (Simmel, 1973). Therefore, the use of three-member crews provides the greatest opportunity for leadership without significantly compromising the crew interaction.

In selecting the crew leaders, the staff identified several criteria. These included: 1) the resident's personal and family history in an attempt to decrease harmful conflicts, 2) cottage residents who had prior camping and/or backpacking experience, and 3) the existing influence that cottage residents already possessed within their social system at the Hospital. While tension within a crew should not be completely eliminated, efforts to limit destructive interactions should be made. For instance, a child frequently made a scapegoat should not be placed with a boy who often victimizes others. With decreased direct staff supervision of daily activities, special attention must be paid to crew structure in order to reduce potentially serious repercussions.

THE CREW LEADERS

As discussed earlier, three residents acted as crew leaders. The following synopsis describes how each boy's personal and family history impacted his leadership role during the wilderness experience.

Neil

Neil, a 16-year-old white boy, had been in treatment at Andrus for 4 years at the time of the trip and had participated as a crew leader on a similar, less structured trip 2 years earlier. During his stay at Andrus, he had one brief, psychiatric hospitalization in response to an acute psychotic episode. Prior to placement, Neil lived with his mother who both neglected and physically abused him. She is also chemically dependent.

Both of Neil's parents were raised in state institutions for developmentally disabled children. Neil's mother abandoned Neil and his brother, leaving them with the boy's natural father. As Neil's father was unable to provide an adequate level of supervision, he filed a court petition to have Neil placed in care.

Treatment issues at the time of the trip included extreme levels of dependent and passive behavior, low frustration tolerance, lack of impulse control, and low motivation.

Bob

Bob, a 14-year-old male, had been in treatment at Andrus for approximately 9 months at the time of the trip and was the only African-American in the group. Bob's natural mother died of a drug overdose while he was very young and at the age of 6, he was adopted by an older, middle-class, African-American couple who reside in an affluent New York City suburb. Bob's adoptive father is a recovering alcoholic and both parents appear to be emotionally withholding and extremely rigid. Bob was referred for residential treatment for a variety of school-related, behavioral problems. Treatment issues at the time of the trip included open defiance of authority, gender and racial identity issues, extreme mood swings, and a general state of depression.

Richard

Richard, a 17-year-old male, had been in treatment at Andrus for 3 years at the time of the trip and had been a crew leader on a previous wilderness experience. His family came to the United States from Southeast Asia when he was 7 years old and had difficulty assimilating to the new culture.

Richard's family had spent several years in refugee camps before coming to the States. After reports of physical abuse by his father, Richard was referred for placement in Andrus. Differences in cultural values seem to have contributed significantly to the stressors placed upon Richard's father and further fueled the physical abuse.

Treatment issues at the time of the trip included substance abuse, explosive anger, continued parent-child conflict, and extreme avoidance of and resistance to exploring these issues.

These family histories indicate significant themes that had a great impact on leadership styles. While Richard's history includes physical abuse and Bob came from a substance-abusing family, Neil's family exhibits both of these destructive tendencies.

FAMILY LEGACY

For decades, researchers have recognized a multigenerational pattern or "family legacy" existing within several fields of study. Medical scientists, for instance, point to a genetic link in the transmission of many biological diseases from parents to children. There is little doubt, for example, that illnesses such as diabetes, heart disease, and Huntington's disease have a strong genetic component and are passed from parents to offspring through a genetic code. Likewise, in psychiatry, observations indicate that conditions such as schizophrenia, bi-polar disorder, and depression continually occur in certain families (Rosenthal, 1970). There is a strong indication that these conditions are also genetically linked and, like other illnesses, can be exacerbated by unfavorable environmental conditions.

In addiction studies, the term "family legacy" has been used to describe the tendency for drug and alcohol use to recur within the family throughout several generations. It has long been understood that chemical dependency runs in families, but only recently has research indicated a possible genetic predisposition for the disease of addiction (Heath, 1986; Woodside, 1986). Once again, this condition will be more likely to manifest itself if environmental conditions permit.

Research indicates that social problems such as physical and sexual abuse also seem to recur in families throughout several generations (Holmes et al., 1976). This family legacy appears to be a result of a learned response on the part of children of abusive parents who repeat this abuse with their own offspring. We learn to parent from our parents and, as a result, dysfunctional parenting styles tend to prevail generation after generation.

While the above evidence does not indicate a genetic code for parenting per se, it does suggest that methods of discipline, means of expressing emotion, and patterns of communication do recur within multigenerational family systems. These patterns, coupled with genetic loading for emotional instability or addiction, place many of these children at risk for repeating destructive and dysfunctional family patterns. Unfortunately, these maladaptive tendencies are rarely uncovered until individuals reach adulthood and begin to raise their own children, thereby reintroducing the continuing cycle of dysfunction.

Within such families, members often become locked into set patterns of interaction where potentially dysfunctional patterns are used as survival skills and employed when facing stressful and painful events. These coping mechanisms help to balance the dysfunctional system and maintain the family homeostasis (Black, 1986). It is only when a family member steps out of his/her system and into another that it becomes clear the significant toll these maladaptive interactions have had on the individual's capacity to interact with others in an adaptive and productive manner.

As crew leaders, residents gained insight into the impact of their family's legacy on their leadership skills. Given the parallel between crew leadership and parenting, this experience served as a foreshadowing of future parenting roles because many of the tasks that are performed by crew leaders in relation to their crews resemble the tasks parents face in relation to their children. As a parent oversees family functioning, crew leaders must ensure the smooth and efficient functioning of their crew, including delegation and completion of tasks. While performing their functions, crew leaders were to keep the best interest of their crews in mind, necessitating clear assessment of each crew member's capabilities. Managing interpersonal problems and their effects became an additional important leadership function because the crew leader had to ensure that the basic needs of crew members were met (i.e., food, shelter, safety, etc.) as well as manage feelings within the crew which might threaten group cohesiveness.

Clearly, many of the issues the crew leaders faced were quite similar, if not identical, to those that must be managed by parents. Having been thrust into this role, leaders were able to identify how much their reactions resembled those of their parents and, indeed, how similar they are to their parents.

This experience allowed residents to witness how their family's maladaptive patterns have had an impact on their personalities as well as on their leadership styles. With the help of the treatment staff, they were able to gain insight into the similarities between crew leadership and parenting, in addition to recognizing their potential strengths and weaknesses within this role. Having confronted how they transferred these maladaptive family patterns into other relationships, these residents now have the opportunity to process these issues, make appropriate changes, and break their family's generational legacy before they are in a position to repeat this destructive behavior.

LEADERSHIP STYLES AND SKILLS

Each of these crew leaders' family histories clearly influenced their behavior. The three crew leaders on the wilderness trip manifested the maladaptive parenting styles common to chemically dependent and physically abusive family systems. Despite similarities, individual leadership styles and crew management skills varied between the leaders.

In leading his crew, Neil was passive and dependent, becoming quickly overwhelmed by the demands placed upon him by both his crew and the staff. As he became neglected, Neil would neglect the needs of the crew and become angry and frustrated with his inability to provide effective leadership. He would express his anger and frustration by distancing himself from his crew which further impaired the crew's ability to perform. This created a cyclical pattern which continued until Neil would lash out at his crew members in an ineffective attempt to restore order and provide direction. Neil's efforts were coupled with threats of physical harm and violence.

Bob's leadership style differed somewhat from Neil's. He was harsh, overly critical, and impatient with his crew members. Not unlike his own parents, Bob was rigid and intolerant of his crew's mistakes, becoming completely self-absorbed and disregarding the welfare of his crew. He would often leave his crew and fail to communicate information passed on to him by the staff. Upon his return, Bob would become physically and verbally abusive to his crew members and use threats and ridicule to persuade them to attend to the necessary tasks. By the trip's end, Bob had all but abandoned his crew.

Richard's leadership style contrasted greatly with that of the other two leaders. He was heavily invested in maintaining the crew's cohesion and did so by fulfilling a caretaker role for his crew. In doing so, Richard put the physical needs of the group before his own. Crew members were fed first, tasks were delegated, and crew-related needs were tended to before individual needs. Much like his father, Richard viewed the value of the crew's cohesion as a priority over the crew's overall welfare. Richard was a harsh, punitive, and critical leader in his efforts and used his authority in a ruthless manner.

The connection between these boys' leadership styles and how they were parented is undeniable. Neil's pattern of neglect and abuse replicated the pattern he learned from his mother. Bob borrowed his hypercritical and rigid manner from his adoptive parents, and when extremely stressed, he abandoned his crew as he had been abandoned by his biological mother. Richard placed a strong value on the crew's cohesion which was consistent with the culturally-based family values of his father. Both father and son were willing to maintain group cohesion to preserve what they valued, even at the risk of physical harm.

A powerful result of this process involved the residents' own identification of these multigenerational family patterns and their replication of dysfunctional coping mechanisms. Although each boy experienced this realization in varying degrees, the expectation of becoming like their parents created sufficient discomfort to promote motivation for change.

IMPLICATIONS FOR TREATMENT

The assessments and observations made during this wilderness experience suggest implications for individual treatment, programming within the agency milieu, and future wilderness trip designs. The primary implication for individual treatment is the use of a wilderness trip as a method for helping the child not only to identify and alter dysfunctional patterns of relating, but also to recognize the source of such maladaptive tendencies. Although the crew leaders made initial attempts to alter their own styles of leadership on this trip, these efforts proved to be ineffective due to the brevity of the outing (6 days). A trip of this duration does not allow adequate time for the crew leaders to benefit from the positive changes in leadership styles and the more effective patterns of relating to crew members. Longer trips of 10 to 14 days would provide more time for dysfunctional patterns to emerge as well as time for crew leaders to recognize the benefits of altering these unproductive methods of leadership. In addition, shorter but more frequent trips (2 to 3 days, once or twice a month) might help to provide the leaders with a recurrent forum in which to confront their maladaptive patterns of relating and to practice more effective interpersonal skills.

The emotionally and physically demanding nature of the shared wilderness experience also helped to open a dialogue between the staff and the crew leaders. Within this context, the leaders were able to recognize their family's ineffective and maladaptive methods of relating. This insight provided the residents with the opportunity to identify with their parents and, as leaders, empathize with the difficulty their parents experienced in managing their own troubled family systems. Clearly, the opportunity to lead a group of peers and the framing of this experience by the staff enhanced this awareness.

Even without further wilderness trips, this 6-day experience provides a rich assessment and focus for more traditional treatment in the hospital. Treatment within the agency milieu is greatly enhanced by the residents' and staff's understanding of the family legacy. This knowledge, applied to more traditional group settings, can promote increased processing of dysfunctional behaviors that are impulsive or irrational. In addition, the communication of such information can enrich ongoing family interventions provided by the clinical treatment team. Finally, consistent positive reinforcement of new and more productive methods of relating as well as continual confrontation of former, ineffective coping mechanisms may increase the likelihood of breaking the family cycle of dysfunction.

ADVENTURE THERAPY

Unfortunately, these destructive patterns of relating often remain hidden within the daily routine and structure of the agency. Wilderness trips provide the residents with the opportunity to display these tendencies in a setting that lacks the limits and restrictions often felt within the boundaries of the institution. The physical and emotional intensity of the outdoor experience, coupled with the means of the wilderness to ensure uncompromising natural consequences to crew dysfunction, produces the level of discomfort necessary to promote change. Such trips force residents and staff to step outside the limits established by the institution and confront new challenges and responsibilities. The stressful demands placed upon participants can not only expose individual or group pathology, but can also introduce a powerful new vehicle for change.

Brian Farragher received his M.S.W. from Fordham University in 1984 and is currently the Director of Residential Treatment Services at the Julia Dyckman Andrus Memorial.

Scott Harman received his M.S.W. from Fordham University in 1992 and was formerly the Program Director of the Adolescent Boy's Cottage at the Julia Dyckman Andrus Memorial.

Martin Bullard received his M.S.W. from Smith College in 1992 and was a child care worker at the Julia Dyckman Andrus Memorial. He has also been an instructor for the Pacific Crest Outward Bound School.

17

HOW TO USE EQUIPMENT THERAPEUTICALLY[1]

DOUGLAS BOWNE

In adventure therapy programs, equipment plays a crucial role in the individual and group treatment experience. The selection of sleeping bags, tents, and cooking utensils is a variable that may be altered to facilitate treatment goals.

Traditionally, equipment has been viewed from a management perspective as requiring significant financial and logistical resources. However, beyond the utilitarian function of the equipment lies a vast therapeutic potential. The use of expensive, high-tech gear does not guarantee quality programming. In fact, an inverse relationship exists between treatment impact and technical sophistication of the equipment used when properly cared for by the instructor/therapist.

The purpose of this article is to share the therapeutic and economic practices surrounding equipment as exercised at the Higher Horizons Program. Simultaneously, fellow educators, therapists, and administrators are encouraged to explore the relationships between equipment selection, program goals, and clients.

THE PROGRAM AND YOUTHS

Higher Horizons is a part of the New York State Division for Youth (DFY). It is a therapeutic adventure program derived from the philosophy of Outward Bound, working primarily with adolescent males and females remanded to the DFY by the Family Court System. Higher Horizons offers a spectrum of courses year-round to address the special needs of the DFY population, ranging from one-day rock-climbing experiences to 38-day alternatives to institutionalization.

As with many adventure therapy programs, the delinquent youths who participate are distinguished by a general distrust of and antagonism toward authority. They are unwilling to assume responsibility for themselves or others in socially acceptable ways. Violence and defiance tend to be their modes of problem solving.

The primary goal of the intervention and treatment is to create a socializing experience or, in broad terms, to habilitate. This is achieved through the adventure process by providing concrete learning experiences that enable clients to make positive changes in themselves, teaching decision-making and problem-solving skills, and cultivating responsibility for self and others.

THE EQUIPMENT

The equipment provided to Higher Horizons participants is the most rudimentary, durable, and least expensive that can be found, allowing marginal comfort without compromising safety.

The packs are World War II vintage, constructed of laminated wood. Shelter is created with a sheet of plastic and a ball of string. Food utensils consist of one cup and spoon per person. No flashlights, knives, or other unnecessary tools are issued to the youths.

These items are purposefully selected to support and enhance the treatment goals when carefully integrated by the adventure therapist. That the equipment is durable and economical is of secondary importance.

TREATMENT THEORY AND PRACTICE

Current adventure therapy models are sophisticated in that the treatment elements—season, environment, program activities, clients, and treatment goals—are orchestrated. Consequently, no two programs or courses will be alike and the therapeutic applications of equipment are unique for each program. However, generic formulas can be outlined.

The equipment previously described is chosen to promote achievement of the habilitative goals. The army packframes necessitate lashing on a laundry bag or stuff sack to carry clothing and gear. They require the use of knots which are learned by following instructions and frequently asking others in the group for assistance. When not attached properly, the load falls off, compelling the group to wait while the negligent individual reties the pack. While this could be considered a real inconvenience, in this context it is a planned learning experience. The difficulty that arises requires clients to attend to their equipment so that they don't become a burden to others.

The plastic "tents" serve as a good example of how equipment and objectives interface. Each group of 6 people is given a sheet of plastic, 12' by 14', and a ball of string. This, they are told, will be their shelter while in the program. They are given instruction in set-up and how a stone or a ball of leaves will secure the corners. Beyond this, the group must work together and creatively fashion their shelter. When they have done so properly, they will remain warm, dry, and relatively comfortable. When they do so improperly, they will find that the tent may flap in the wind, or the ends may open up, permitting rain to seep in and, finally, to collapse the structure. Such an experience demands that the occupants critically assess their behavior, accept responsibility for their actions, and work together.

Participants are outfitted with surplus wool clothing, ponchos, "Mickey Mouse" boots, and any other simple items demanded by the season. The clothing selected is functional and provides ample protection from the elements. It is also bulky, adding another element of stress with which participants must contend. The strategic use of specific types of clothing and equipment fosters the program goals of providing concrete learning experiences that teach decision making and problem solving and cultivate responsibility.

MEETING BASIC NEEDS

A deeper understanding of equipment as a treatment medium can be reached through Abraham Maslow's Hierarchy of Human Needs Model. According to Maslow, all human beings are guided by a hierarchy of needs, beginning with survival needs, then moving on to safety, belongingness, ego-status, and finally self-actualization. One can never successfully move to a higher-level need until the lower-level needs are satisfied.

The vast majority of delinquent youths have been deprived since birth and consequently have not had the opportunity to satisfactorily meet their most basic needs. Survival, safety, and belongingness are clearly unresolved issues.

When clients begin an adventure course, they enter a new environment—the "wilderness." This environment immediately impels them to become concerned with the basic survival needs of water, food, and shelter, as well as safety needs. The small peer-group and experiences like solos encourage the confrontation of belongingness or social needs. This model is also helpful in understanding how ego-status needs are met through activities such as rock climbing, and self-actualization needs are addressed through service.

The relationship of food to survival needs makes it a powerful therapeutic force in the wilderness program. Programs can supply freeze-dried foods that are prepared merely by adding water. On the other hand, providing unprocessed foods creates a total group experience when they are prepared with a common cook pot, group spoon, and knife. Learning to cook with the most simple equipment and to satisfy one's hunger with wholesome foods teaches participants tangible survival skills transferable to their home life.

The basic need for safety is addressed continually in the adventure experience. The wilderness is perceived by most clients as a hostile and dangerous environment. In this setting they face their fundamental fears directly. As clients learn to manage their equipment and clothing effectively, they learn that they can control their own safety in a socially acceptable manner.

INTRINSIC REWARDS AND SANCTIONS

Each Higher Horizons course is divided into phases having specific treatment and programmatic objectives. The first phase focuses on learning the basics of wilderness living and social interaction. At this time, participants are issued equipment that they perceive as second-rate. They are told that if they "respect" these items by not damaging or losing them, they will earn newer equipment. The gear is shown to them so that they are aware of what they are working for.

The second phase of a course emphasizes applying the newly acquired skills while dealing with the increasing physical and emotional challenges of rock climbing, mountain ascents, etc. At this time clients are rewarded with modern frame packs, synthetic sleeping bags, and nylon tarps.

Structuring a course in this manner achieves several significant treatment objectives. Clients are concretely rewarded for learning to care for their equipment, and the traditional value of working for one's equipment is emphasized.

Client/therapist rapport is not sacrificed when care and use of equipment is intertwined in the total therapeutic process. Clients care for their equipment because it meets **their** needs rather than meeting an administrative mandate to keep operating cost down.

Providing the minimum amount of equipment also addresses these objectives. One cup and spoon are given for the duration of a course. If lost, the participant can carve a spoon or eat from a tuna fish can. Accountability for one's possessions becomes extremely clear.

For both the therapist and program administrator, the care and use of equipment is an excellent barometer of the achievements of the clients. Excessive equipment damage frequently indicates that the clients have been unable to contend with the challenges of the experience. When clients end a course with the equipment neatly organized and accounted for, their spirits and sense of accomplishment and responsibility are high.

THE THERAPIST

The therapist has two primary responsibilities with respect to equipment and the client. First, he/she must allow the experiential process to work, providing the opportunity to learn from mistakes but not permitting the client to experience overwhelming failure. The cumbersome equipment initially requires an attentive instructor/therapist to teach its proper use and to manage individual and group frustration to ensure a positive learning experience.

Secondly, through group and individual discussion, the therapist must make clients aware of the growth that occurs. Clients with histories of failure frequently deny success. When it is acknowledged, they need help in transferring the significance of the learning into their future.

WHY NOT HIGH-TECH?

State-of-the-art equipment can actually undermine the clients' therapeutic development. Outdoor equipment advertisements highlight the "convenience," "ease of handling," and "comfort" aspects of their products. The "go it alone," "get away from it all" advantages are stressed. Yet the goal of adventure therapy programs is to promote interdependence rather than independence.

Comfort can minimize stress, and stress, when properly managed, is a forceful motivator for growth and change. For instance, when using heavy, awkward packs, the first major crisis on a course frequently takes place in the first mile or two. Almost immediately the therapeutic process can begin.

Convenience also undermines the learning of basic skills, such as learning to tie knots on a pack or to cook meals. The convenience of a tent undermines the need to be creative and deal with the environmental consequences of inattention.

State-of-the-art equipment is also designed to maximize safety in high-risk environments, under adverse weather conditions. However, operating in highly rigorous conditions before the client has cultivated an appreciation for good equipment and for the objective environmental dangers is potentially injurious. In short, the best equipment money can buy is of no value if the client has lost it, broken it, or is refusing to use it.

EQUIPMENT FOR THE FUTURE:
A STEP BACK IN TIME

Future trends in equipment management at Higher Horizons will be directed toward involving program participants in making their own gear; for example, Adirondack pack baskets, utensils of wood, and dishes of clay. Approaching the habilitative process from this perspective significantly deepens the clients' involvement in the wilderness experience. Participants gain vocational skills through fabricating the equipment used to ensure comfort and sustain their lives. Making their own possessions, which are used in a wilderness experience and then taken home upon graduation, has great treatment potential. The equipment would act as a constant reminder of their new-found competencies.

The degree to which equipment is utilized to further the therapeutic process depends largely on the expertise of the instructor/therapist and the goals of the program. From an economic standpoint, the systems discussed are cost-effective. The ultimate challenge for adventure therapy programs is to continue to manage equipment in a way that protects the safety of participants and meets program objectives, while enhancing the treatment process.

Douglas Bowne has been active in experiential programs with special populations within the New York State Division for Youth since 1971. He is currently in the process of developing a new program near Plattsburg, New York, called Adirondack Wilderness Challenge. This program will be comprised of a 12-week adventure residential program followed up by a 3-week wilderness program.

Footnote

[1] This article first appeared in the 1986 Journal of Experiential Education, 9(3), 16-19.

18

EXPERIENTIAL CHALLENGE PROGRAM DEVELOPMENT IN THE MENTAL HEALTH SETTING: A CASE STUDY[1]

CHRIS ROLAND, Ph.D.

A major movement today is the development and implementation of "adventure" and "challenge" programs in mental health settings. Program titles and descriptions vary from agency to agency, creating a somewhat confusing lexicon. Terms include Therapeutic Adventure Program (TAP) (Kidder, 1987), Adventure Therapy (Stitch & Senior, 1984), Challenge Therapy (Castle & Eastman, 1985), Camping Therapy (Collingwood, 1972; Polez & Rubitz, 1977), Wilderness Therapy (Kimball, 1983; Bernstein, 1972), Outdoor Therapy (Smith, 1980; Smith, 1982), Experiential Therapy (Stitch, 1983), and Experiential Challenge Program (ECP) (Roland, Summer, Friedman, Barton, & McCarthy, 1987). Challenge/ adventure programs have been developed in a wide range of mental health settings, including community mental health agencies, special schools, and private psychiatric hospitals. Within these settings, there appear to be three approaches to program development: 1) creating programs on-site, where agency personnel are trained to lead the different program activities (Roland, et al., 1987; Witman, 1987); 2) offering programs off-site, led by agency personnel (Ferguson, 1983; Hauser, 1987); and 3) offering programs off-site, led by outdoor challenge consultants/specialists (Chase, 1981; DeSantis, 1988; Kimball, 1983; Stitch & Senior, 1984).

With such a range of program titles, there is a corresponding range of program development processes. Differences include whether activities are sequenced, and if so, which sequences are used. Other differences include activity length, activity sites, staff training programs, indoor versus outdoor activities, and use of debriefing and processing techniques.

NASHUA BROOKSIDE HOSPITAL

Nashua Brookside Hospital (NBH) is a private, free-standing, community-oriented hospital owned and operated by Psychiatric Institutes of America. The hospital offers comprehensive care and professional treatment for individuals and families throughout New England. Currently, adolescents and adults are served on both an inpatient and outpatient basis.

In the fall of 1986, the Director of the Activity Therapy Department began to research the options for the development of a challenge program. Although the director had participated in numerous challenge education workshops and seminars, she was uncertain of the specifics of creating a challenge program in the clinical setting in a semi-urban environment (minimal land with no trees). Consequently, she and her staff researched, via the local and national therapeutic recreation network, realistic and affordable program development options.

Staff members agreed that the Brookside program, initially referred to as "Adventure Therapy," would include the following components:

1. A sequential model, as outlined by Roland et al., (1987), would be followed. This model is shown in Figure 1. Activities are divided into five progressive levels: (a) Goal-setting (e.g., contract writing), (b) Awareness (e.g., stretching exercises), (c) Trust (e.g., blind trust walk), (d) Group Problem Solving (e.g., the 12-foot wall), and (e) Individual Problem Solving (e.g., low challenge course events).

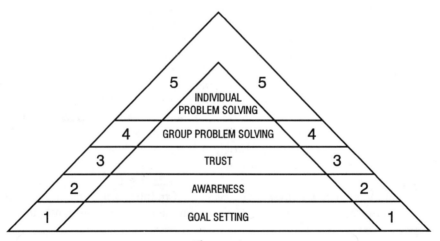

Figure 1

2. Staff would be trained on-site as well as at recognized regional training programs.
3. The program would be interdisciplinary: activity therapists, psychologists, occupational therapists, and mental health workers would all have the opportunity to be trained as program leaders.
4. An advisory board would be created to help with program development, implementation, and evaluation. Board members would represent other psychiatric hospitals, independent consulting firms, and local colleges and universities.
5. A low challenge course utilizing free-standing platforms and telephone poles would be constructed on the hospital grounds.

PROGRAM DEVELOPMENT PROCESS

After the hospital's administration gave full approval for the proposed program, confusion became apparent regarding terminology. "Adventure Therapy," "Therapeutic Adventure," and "Experiential Therapy" were some of the terms that were used simultaneously throughout the hospital. One of the first program development steps was to agree on one term that most succinctly described the program. Since the program was being based on the model in Figure 1, it made sense to use the same term, "Experiential Challenge Program," or "ECP." The new program was initially introduced via an in-house newsletter, The Brookside Report, sent to every department in the hospital. One purpose of the newsletter was to educate staff members, for example, that the ECP would be an actual part of patients' overall therapeutic programs, and not simply a series of diversionary activities.

ADMINISTRATIVE CHALLENGES

When NBH decided to integrate challenge programming, the administration needed to carefully research and then monitor the services. In much the same way that sequencing was emphasized in the process of Experiential Challenge, it was emphasized in the evolution of the ECP at Nashua Brookside Hospital. When NBH initially explored the prospect of a challenge program in a private psychiatric/chemical dependency hospital, two questions required answers: 1) What legal liability issues needed to be addressed?, and 2) What type of "challenge" programming was most appropriate for the population served by the hospital? By working in conjunction with the hospital's parent organization and the company's insurance representative, the necessary documents related to confidentiality and liability were developed. The following is a partial list of these materials:

1. Program description (for patients and parents).
2. Release for Participation (for patients and parents).
3. Consent to be Videotaped While Participating in the ECP.
4. Consent to Participate in Research.

There was considerable discussion about the direction of the challenge program. The Hospital Administrator and Medical Director had had experience with this type of programming and their concern was that the evolution of the NBH program be conservative. Therefore, the decision was made to develop and implement low-level challenge activities, including a low outdoor challenge course and in-house team-building equipment.

The discussion regarding the direction and rate of implementation became crucial to the survival of the concept within a multidisciplinary program. The treatment goals of the patients combined with the need to maximize available resources became the determining factors in deciding upon the direction of the program. Staffing for the ECP would be interdisciplinary; thus, the program became a part of the treatment in those participating Clinical Programs. The Director of Activity Therapy became the responsible person for administering the ECP services. Clinical issues were channeled to the Program Director for each of the Clinical Programs which is consistent with the Matrix Model of Management adopted by the hospital. By integrating staff members from other disciplines, the therapeutic value of the service was maximized. Clinicians who worked with the patients daily were trained to be leaders and co-leaders in ECP groups. This was especially effective in developing a therapeutic continuum in which the objectives of a patient's treatment, as well as patient and milieu issues being addressed in treatment, are brought into and taken away from ECP groups.

As the ECP sequencing evolved, a set of policies and procedures was established for consistency in service delivery and as part of the program monitoring system. Included were patient criteria, goals and objectives of the program, safety procedures, referral procedures, instructions for the use of challenge equipment, and documentation standards.

STAFF TRAINING

Once the policies and procedures were developed, the need for staff training was addressed. Initially, three Activity Therapy staff members participated in a 3-day training program offered by an established, challenge education training firm. The three staff members had not been exposed to challenge programming prior to the training and returned with mixed reactions. Their comments ranged from describing it as a great personal growth experience to voicing concern about being able to apply the experience in a therapeutic group in an inpatient setting. The one common comment was that the experience was extremely powerful yet had an equally dangerous potential.

The critical element was a staff trained in the theory and practice of the ECP combined with advanced clinical skills, especially in the area of group therapy. Two categories of qualified staff were established: leaders and co-leaders The leader was required to have completed an intensive, residential training program in leading the ECP. The co-leaders were hospital staff members who were interested in assisting with the ECP. They were required to attend a one-day training program in the theory and application of the ECP at Nashua Brookside Hospital. The co-leaders could not run ECP groups without a qualified leader. Both leaders and co-leaders also received further on-site supervision and training from an outside consultant periodically throughout the year.

AN ACTIVITY PROCESS MODEL

After the first 6 months of programming, NBH staff members felt the need to expand upon the original ECP model. They felt that this model helped to set the stage for initial program development by categorizing the numerous challenge activities, especially regarding the order of difficulty. However, facilitators realized that every challenge activity in fact had components of all five levels. For example, a Trust Circle required individual and group initiative (e.g., use of spotters), and individual initiative (e.g., the "faller"). Thus an "Activity Process Model" was developed as shown in Figure 2. In addition, facilitators began to use the ECP as a diagnostic/prescriptive tool for use in treatment.

Facilitators first identified issues that were the result of a group's participation in previous low-level challenge activities. Facilitators then prescribed a sequence of activities that promoted the awareness and discussion of these issues. For example, one common treatment issue was a group's inability to function as a unit. This was rapidly seen in initial awareness activities: patients rarely helped one another and often refused to cooperate. Thus, a series of activities that focused on trust, cooperation, and group initiative were chosen and implemented. This process was critical in order to make the ECP a therapeutic experience.

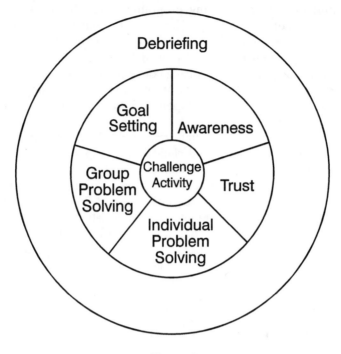

Figure 2

Debriefing becomes the outer ring of the Activity Process Model. Debriefing is a form of group processing where the treatment focus of the ECP is formulated. Facilitators are expected to interpret and apply the performance of the group to the overall treatment program. Observations, interpretations, and interventions need to be precise and reflect the goals of the ECP as well as each patient's program. Facilitators often guided groups by the use of metaphor (e.g., Bacon, 1983), illustrating how patients' behaviors demonstrated/reflected the treatment issues being addressed. Additionally, a cognitive hierarchy in formulating probing questions (Quinsland & Van Ginkel, 1984) was often followed. This is where the clinical skills of the facilitators were put to the test. Patients were quite manipulative in these instances by denying or avoiding issues relating to themselves. The more facilitators knew about their patients and their treatment program, the better equipped they were to recognize this manipulation when it occurred and to make the appropriate interventions.

200

HIGH CHALLENGE ACTIVITIES

Throughout the program development stages, staff members continued to discuss whether a high ropes course should also be constructed on hospital grounds. Some activity therapists had significant experience with this type of high-challenge pursuit. They felt that this component would enhance the overall program, especially with the development of self-esteem of patients. Yet the hospital administration's concerns were the expense of materials, staff training, and whether the patients would indeed gain from the experiences. Since many hospitals may encounter this same issue in the program development process, a closer look is in order.

The perceived need for high-adventure activities has been well documented. The vast majority of adventure and challenge programs include some type of high-adventure activity, whether it be rock climbing, whitewater canoeing, kayaking and rafting, rappelling, or "high ropes coursing." The need for individual risk-taking is often the major goal for such programs. In addition, the need for "risk-exercise," especially for adolescents, is frequently cited. Rosenthal (1980) noted:

> *Risk Exercise (RE) on a well-calculated basis invigorates one physically and mentally and produces a state of well-being and elation, often times bordering on euphoria. All this adds up to a sense of joy and happiness, a renewing of one's courage and vigor, a peace of mind. (p. 37)*

Program descriptions of organizations that offer high-adventure experiences often portray numerous benefits to participating individuals. One of the more recognized organizations, Outward Bound, Inc., gave the following description in one particular brochure:

> *...Outward Bound is a unique educational experience which leads to a new understanding of yourself, and the fact that most of your limits are self-imposed. Through Outward Bound, people give themselves a chance to step out of their old routines and ordinary surroundings—if only for a week or two or three—and some amazing things happen. Fearful people find inner strengths. Loners discover the joy of working with others. People who've always said "I can't" find a way to say "I can!" Outward Bound yields joy after hardship, builds confidence through experience, brings high adventure from hard work, provides challenging opportunities for you to find out who you really are.... (p. 1)*

Conversely, there is increasing agreement in the field that outdoor practitioners are often faced with difficult decisions that may have undesirable outcomes (Havens, 1987; Havens & Fain, 1986). Ewert (1987) explained that some outdoor pursuits in a given situation at a particular time may affect a participant's self-concept in a negative way. As an example, he noted, "Little is known about what happens to an individual if he/she fails to complete a course component such as rock climbing" (p. 21).

Literature cites the need for proper program sequencing (Havens, 1985; Roland & Havens, 1983; Smith, 1985). Programs being operated today include the "immersion" experience where a participant finds him/herself on a mountain peak, rappelling platform, or zipwire in the early stages of the program. For many individuals, this approach is valid—they can, and sometimes do, learn a great deal about themselves and others. For other individuals, this immersion approach can be detrimental. The Roland Report (1985) gave the following case study of a high-school student participating in an adventure program as part of a physical education program:

> ...A sophomore class was instructed to solve a problem: to safely negotiate, as a team, an underground drainage pipe, about three feet in diameter. The group needed to crawl approximately thirty yards from one end of the pipe to the other—all in total darkness.
>
> The group began without any difficulty.... Halfway through the experience one girl became very emotional. She began screaming and was apparently out of control. She also began to hit her head on the concrete pipe. After much chaos...the group made it to the other end.
>
> The next day the teacher talked with the girl. He discovered that when she was four or five years old, her uncle, as a joke, locked her in a suitcase for a few seconds. She said it was a terrifying experience but had forgotten about it—that is, until that pipe. (p. 5)

Thus, depending upon a participant's background, including skill level, emotional stability, etc., there is always the possibility that one may perceive a "low" challenge activity (as seen by an instructor) as a very "high" challenge activity. Leroy (1983) noted:

> [A Challenge Education student] began my interest in the nature of adventure by teaching me a valuable lesson. Back on the

glacier, what I perceived as a simple stroll Priscilla perceived as a high adventure, full of danger, difficulty, and the unknown. Priscilla taught me that when we try to understand "adventure," the physical magnitude of the peak, pole, lake, or trial is no more important than the emotional response the task elicits. (p. 18)

After much analysis by reviewing the above advantages and disadvantages of high-adventure programming, and after lengthy discussion with the advisory board, the Brookside staff decided to take a careful, middle-ground approach. Instead of initially constructing a high-challenge course or vertical, indoor climbing wall, an "Adventure Experience" would be offered. This experience would be held off-site and include top-rope rock climbing and rappelling. The Adventure Experience was developed and led by a consultant who had an extensive background with the practice and teaching of rock climbing.

The introductory rock-climbing program included and integrated all of the elements found in the ECP model. These included such elements as individual and group goal setting (e.g., some patients may plan to only touch the rock), awareness (e.g., becoming comfortable with a different outdoor environment), trust (e.g., of leader, peers, equipment), group problem solving (e.g., deciding which route to select), and individual problem solving (e.g., the actual individual climb).

The teaching of basic rock climbing began indoors at the hospital. First, the use of technical equipment (e.g., ropes, carabiners, seat harnesses) was reviewed. For example, patients learned the technical strengths of each piece of equipment as well as how to fit a harness. Next, usually on the day of the actual experience, patients organized the technical gear, extra clothing, and food. This involved all the members of the group having to work together, dividing the community equipment, and sharing the effort. Backpacks were filled and traded within the group. Once the group was transported to the climbing site, the instructor then constantly demonstrated the correct use and holding abilities of the equipment. Whereas the exact strengths were not generally retained, the overall effect was to increase trust in the equipment.

The correct and accepted methods of belaying were taught, demonstrated, and reinforced, making the participant an active part of the safety system. Only mechanical methods of belaying (e.g., Sticht plates, Munter hitches) were used in order to allow any member of the group, under the instructor's supervision, to belay another. The actual knots to attach the rope to the climber were taught, practiced, and finally inspected each time by the instructor.

The program then moved on to the teaching of the actual techniques of movement on the rock. Climbing, properly executed, does not use just physical force to ascend, but more importantly, cognitive thought, body movement, and balance. A selection of appropriate climbs were necessary—climbs that were challenging yet within the climber's ability. A selection of easy to moderate climbs no more than 75 feet in height was chosen for each experience. With group support, placement of the appropriate safety systems, and the necessary technical training, the patients then ascended. The instructor made sure that each patient understood that the only expectation was to try. Once again, not everyone in the group climbed. Climbing brings out real fears that must be addressed. Many sessions may be needed before one is comfortable enough to even try. Just tying into the seat harness, attaching the rope, and then touching the rock was a real and gratifying success for some patients.

Group support was vital to a successful experience. Being quiet and respectful enabled the instructor to give feedback, directions, and support while the patient was on the rock. Group understanding of a good effort by a fellow patient who did not climb or reach the top was also essential. Prior to the return trip to the hospital, a thorough group debriefing was held. The major focus was on how the rock-climbing experience can be associated with patients' therapeutic goals and objectives. Metaphors were constantly used; for example, helping the patient to make the link between taking the risk to climb the rock and taking the risk to stay drug-free when back in the community.

After approximately 6 months of the rock-climbing program, therapists, administrators, and patients agreed that the program was safe and extremely beneficial. However, climbing would be curtailed during the cold, New England winter months. Thus, the decision was made to design and install an indoor climbing wall in the hospital's multipurpose room.

The rock-climbing consultant and hospital staff members designed the wall with the following criteria: 1) no blocks would be bolted directly into the walls; 2) the wall would attractively blend with the multipurpose environment; and 3) every possible safety feature would be integrated in the design, including lack of access when the wall was not in use.

The final product was a unique, state-of-the-art climbing wall. Installed in one corner of the multipurpose room, plaster handholds were bolted onto painted plywood installed at a slight angle. The design included a storage area with a locking door for the climbing gear. The wall has numerous levels of difficulty to challenge patients (and staff) of all ability levels.

With the addition of these programs, an expanded version of the Activity Process model evolved, as shown in Figure 3.

Figure 3

It was apparent that the Adventure Experiences did not constitute a new segment, but an actual perimeter; their activities were "all-level inclusive" (i.e., every activity had elements of goal setting, awareness, trust, group problem solving, and individual problem solving). The key concept was that the "inner core" had been initially developed (appropriate for both adolescents and adults) while the "outer core"—the adventure experiences—was developed later. This perimeter was thus dependent on the core, but the core was not dependent on the perimeter.

Implications for Practitioners

Developing and implementing a challenge program in the hospital setting is obviously a complex task, requiring the cooperation of numerous professionals. The following are additional guidelines and suggestions to help with the development of future programs or with the enhancement of existing programs.

A. Staff Training
   1. Key staff members need to attend a 3- to 4-day, residential training program. This program needs to focus on professional growth rather than interpersonal growth, and it needs to be directly applicable to the patient populations being served.

2. All staff members who may be involved with the ECP need periodic (e.g., once a month) training with one-on-one feedback sessions (from one to 3 hours).
3. Proficiency standards need to be established and staff periodically evaluated based upon these standards.

B. **Program Development**
1. An in-house marketing strategy should be developed. Included should be a "sales packet" containing program philosophy, the selected program model, published articles about similar programs, and a "quote sheet" with quotes from patients of other programs relating their experiences in the ECP.
2. Challenge equipment needs to introduced in a careful, sequential order. With the latest developments in low-level, group-oriented activities, including portable group initiatives, a challenge program can be implemented in a timely fashion. Staff members who did not participate in the training program and who may be skeptical initially, will first see their patients highly involved with trolleys, spider webs, portholes, etc. When this approach is taken, comments from nurses, psychologists, and social workers have included, "Hey, these folks are having fun and learning about team work," and "This challenge stuff is interesting—it makes therapy fun and relevant."

   A next step would be the installation of outdoor, low individual and group initiatives—possibly followed by the installation of high equipment. When low, teams, and high equipment are installed simultaneously, too often the skeptics will focus their gaze on the high events, with resulting comments including, "I don't see what all of that has to do with therapy," and "You'll never see my patients on those high wires." In some hospitals, the high course has become the proverbial white elephant—it is simply not used due to the negative attitude of the staff.
3. Regarding the installation of high events, the following should be taken into consideration:
   a) Is there full administrative support?
   b) Are there committed staff members willing to sign a 2- to 3-year contract with the hospital? Too often staff are extensively trained and then leave.
   c) With shorter patient stays, limited therapy periods, and greater staff workloads, is there realistically sufficient time to implement a high-ropes program?

206

d) Is the administration willing to investigate therapy session options—from one to 3 hours?
4. An effective marketing technique, especially aimed at the managerial level, is to offer an experiential management training program. Since similar activities and debriefing techniques are used, management personnel may gain a better understanding of the experiential process. Evaluation data of this type of managerial program have indicated specific instances of transfer to the workplace (King & Harmon, 1981; Roland, 1982).

CONCLUSION

Through the combined efforts of Nashua Brookside Hospital staff members and outside resources, two models in challenge programming have evolved. Though numerous mental health programs in the United States and Canada utilize some or all of the components in these models, a standard model has not been established. The whats, whys, and hows of a specific program development process are now better defined. Since many professionals are undoubtedly struggling with some of the issues that were faced at NBH, perhaps this program development synopsis will help. Program title, activity sequence, low- and high-challenge courses, on-site/off-site activities, etc., are all subjects that need to be addressed before any challenge program can materialize.

The goal of any Experiential Challenge Program should not be to change an existing treatment program on a particular hospital unit, but to offer a specific tool to the treatment program to complement what already exists. This is a critical and most delicate key to the potential success of the ECP. Though one needs to exhibit high levels of enthusiasm for the ECP, there is also the need to be careful not to suggest that this particular treatment modality is of greater value than other, perhaps more traditional, modalities. Facilitators need to carefully plan the activity sequence, not only for patients but also for other staff members. Initially engaging patients indoors with basic problem-solving activities tends to be more effective in selling the program than higher-level, outdoor challenges. Once the program becomes an accepted treatment modality, having accumulated an impeccable safety record, then numerous on-site and off-site adventure experiences can be offered. If the initial program development phases are not taken slowly and are high adventure-oriented, there is a good chance that the entire program will be viewed as diversionary and not therapeutic.

Dr. Chris Roland is President of Roland and Associates, Inc., in Keene, New Hampshire.

Footnote

¹ An earlier version of this paper was published in the 1989 <u>The Bradford Papers Annual</u>, <u>Volume III</u>. Martinsville, IN: Bradford Woods Outdoor Center.

19

WHAT HAPPENS WHEN ROPES COURSES MOVE FROM THE WOODS TO PSYCHIATRIC TREATMENT FACILITIES?

NANCY GILLIAM, Ph.D.

Introduction

Ropes courses have been introduced in a variety of mental health and psychiatric settings as a form of patient treatment. These hospitals and treatment centers have recognized the experiential, physical, and therapeutic value of adding such interventions to their treatment options. Despite this growth, there have been few studies on issues related to ropes courses in psychiatric settings (Gass & McPhee, 1990).

The purpose of this case study was to describe the experiences of staff and patients at five psychiatric hospitals and treatment centers where ropes course activities are used for treatment. The goal of this investigation was to discover how these treatment facilities have integrated ropes courses into their programs.

METHODS

The primary methods of data collection were interviews and observations. Interview questions focused on such topics as funding, goals, liability issues, administrative support, therapeutic uses of the course, staff and patient views of the course, and significant staff issues such as training and safety. The facilities interviewed were located in the eastern and southeastern United States. At each site, interviews were conducted with administrators or assistant administrators, activity therapy directors, ropes course directors, two or three staff members who facilitate the course, three or four therapists, and three or four patients. Interviews lasted from 30 minutes with patients to 1 or 1½ hours with staff.

In addition, staff were observed at each site conducting ropes course experiences for 1½ to 2 hours. The processing related to these experiences was usually part of the observation. The total time spent at each site was between 2 and 2½ days. Content and qualitative analyses were used to study patterns of experience for patients, staff, and administrators.

RESULTS

The results suggested that ropes courses at all five facilities were accepted as a valuable treatment strategy. Problems that were identified were staff training, marketing, educating the hospital community, underuse of the course, and scheduling. The results of the interviews also revealed that all five of the facilities implemented the course as a treatment tool, but several also used the ropes course as part of a marketing strategy to assist them in a competitive health care market. Funding had not been a problem with the courses and liability issues tended to center around trespassing concerns. Other comments focused on the following four areas:

1. **Use of Course**—Support for the ropes course was critical to its success. The amount of support the course received from within the facility varied from site to site. The perceived danger involved with the ropes course was cited as the biggest impediment to supporting it, and each site had developed strategies to educate and reduce the perception of fear among hospital employees. The amount of support the course received directly affected the use of the course.

2. **Treatment Direction**—There was little agreement in these five sites on how the course should be used as a treatment tool. Most staff agreed on medical and psychological criteria for participation, but not on the age of participants. The course was used most often for adolescents. There was no agreement about how often patients should be on the course or for how much time. Roles of the facilitators varied from being a part of the unit to being more a part of a separate Activity Department. Processing styles varied from having no therapeutic focus to being strongly recovery-oriented; there appeared to be no standard model for how to use the course therapeutically. However, when staff, therapists, patients, and administrators were asked about their perceptions of the course, most favored the use of the course and potential expansion of these activities for treatment.

3. **Purpose of Ropes Courses**—While activity therapists tended to be the initiators of building a ropes course, the goals held by administrators and therapists differed. Administrators stated that goals were related to marketing or community relations. Therapists possessed more treatment-related goals. For individual patients, these goals included increasing self-

210

confidence, trust level, and self-awareness. For groups, the goals included increasing leadership skills, giving and receiving feedback, a sense of community, an appreciation of differences between individuals, and group problem-solving skills.

4. **Major Concerns**—Despite the overall support, many concerns remained. Chief among these were how to resolve program leadership problems, how to make the course more intense, and how to take advantage of underutilized high events. Another critical issue was the processing of ropes course events. Although staff felt technically trained in actual ropes course skills, they were less sure of their preparation in group-process skills, understanding group dynamics, and psychotherapy. Many staff felt the integration of the ropes course experiences into the patient's treatment in the facility was weak. Issues about safety also existed.

Funding for the course did not seem to be a problem, but patterns of generating revenue from the course did vary. Use of ropes courses as marketing tools seemed to be increasing. All sites stated that insurance coverage was not a problem since their existing policy was sufficient. Liability issues were reviewed, but trespassing was the issue most often brought up by administrators.

RECOMMENDATIONS

As observed from these four conclusions, a number of difficulties arose in these programs. The potential avenues for resolution of these difficulties include: 1) referral issues, 2) prescriptive processing, 3) congruent vision between the ropes course and administrative staff, 4) the resolution of staff conflicts, 5) focuses for staff orientation, 6) gender issues, 7) program evaluations; 8) standards and guidelines; 9) job burnout; 10) use of the high ropes courses; and 11) increasing course use. Suggestions for resolving these issues include:

1) **Referral issues**—Several therapists were concerned about referring clients to the course, wondering how therapeutically useful it was for clients. One answer to this question may depend on the insight and talent of the facilitator. How well the facilitator can help patients to translate the event into applicable, personal, and meaningful insights seemed to be an important quality in determining the value of the therapeutic experience. If significant and sensitive time is not spent integrating the experience, the experiences from the course may not generalize. Stich (1983) emphasized the need for both a therapist and an outdoor leader to be present to maximize therapeutic benefit. One therapist stated that the course was too intense for some clients and felt that this issue needed

to be addressed. To answer these concerns, it was felt that staff training needed to focus on developing additional skills in: (a) group process and group dynamics, (b) the individual patient's diagnosis, and (c) the necessary skills to make an activity relevant to recovery.

2) **Prescriptive processing**—As indicated by what was already occurring at staff trainings, more emphasis should be given to designing activities to fit the particular population (Deal, 1983; Gass & McPhee, 1989; Roland, Keene, Dubois, & Lentini, 1989). For instance, the method used to describe and process an activity for adult children of alcoholics should greatly differ from that used for the same activity with women who have been sexually abused (Roland, Keene, Dubois, & Lentini, 1989). As mentioned earlier, Bacon (1983) and Gershenfeld and Napier (1983) have written practical works which help facilitators to understand group process. These skills of "creating metaphors" and "design" not only aid in understanding the nature and dynamics of groups, but give one the ability to make activities relevant to recovery (Deal, 1983).

3) **Congruent vision between the ropes course and hospital staff**— The processing style used at a particular site should be congruent with the goals of the organization. If the organization sees the ropes course as being for fun rather than therapy, it obviously won't receive much support. Within each treatment setting, there seemed to be the following continuum of perspectives about how the course is viewed:

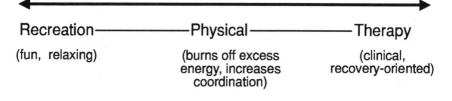

Among the five sites, there was extreme variation in perception of the course. For instance, some staff felt that the ropes course's primary use was for adolescents, to get them out of the hospital and burn off excess energy. As can be predicted, these sites limited the number of populations using the course. At other sites, the perception of the course was much more clinical. At these centers, more populations used the course sites. At some sites, the course was initially seen as recreational, but its clinical use was in the process of evolving.

One conclusion of the study is that if the entire hospital community viewed the ropes course as a valid treatment strategy, then it was more likely to be processed therapeutically. A mixture of processing skills generally reflected the various perspectives of the course. Sites with more emphasis on the clinical use of the course placed a higher emphasis on process training.

4) **The resolution of staff conflicts**—Another important topic found by the study included the resolution of conflict between co-facilitators. Most often, conflicts occurred around one or two primary issues: (a) a safety issue, or (b) an interpersonal issue. Regarding conflict around safety issues, it was interesting to observe the process when two co-facilitators disagreed about how an activity was being conducted. Although guidelines that have been approved by the administrators did exist about how to handle these problems, there were some situations that did not fit existing policies and procedures. One contingency for this was evident at the North Carolina Outward Bound School, where if such a disagreement occurred and where safety was the issue, the conservative opinion ruled. It is vitally important to spend staff training time on such questions and to develop clear and proactive guidelines for dealing with situations of this sort.

With interpersonal conflicts (e.g., a disagreement between partners on how to facilitate a group) Stich and Gaylor (1983) recommend the use of an atmosphere that is supportive where conflict can be dealt with openly. Another method for this could include staff training on how to use disagreement creatively. This would include an agreement ahead of time, as co-facilitators, that disagreeing is okay. In this light, staff disagreement could serve as an opportunity to model open, honest disagreement for patients who frequently have difficulty with self-expression, assertiveness, and anger. When two people in authority are disagreeing and work through it in front of the group, it can be a powerful and healing experience for the patients.

5) **Focuses for staff orientation**—Required training of internships for new staff could also be a useful addition to staff training. Since the ropes course learning is a process that is based on experiential education, staff seem to best learn facilitating by working with other facilitators. As a part of ongoing training, it may also be important for staff to appropriately work on their own issues.

6) **Gender issues**—At these five sites, men led therapeutic processes more often than women, and this may be a concern for certain therapeutic populations. It is also important to note that because some programs (e.g., Outward Bound) were originally designed for men, many programs are still heavily laden with male images and values; staff need to be aware of this inherent sexism. The ropes course can be a powerful tool for addressing gender issues with patients and awareness of these issues is important.

7) **Program evaluations**—An annual evaluation of the ropes course program is helpful in discovering problems, addressing them, and

increasing the productivity of the course. Every aspect of the program needs thorough and continual review. One method to accomplish this is to create an evaluation process that includes external experts in ropes-course building as well as training in order to provide detailed feedback. At least one of these experts must have advanced skills in both ropes courses and psychotherapy. This approach has many advantages: it helps to keep programs current on safety, insurance, group-processing, ethics, and technical issues; and it supports fresh and ever-growing ideas and visions.

Another advantage to having an evaluator analyze the program is to keep up-to-date with current safety recommendations in the field. Because ropes courses are a new form of treatment for mental health patients, there are few published evaluations. For the most part, safety recommendations vary with the experience of the ropes course leaders. As a consequence, it is difficult for decision-makers to be aware of new safety data. Evaluators can detect flaws in equipment or design and offer alternatives that would greatly decrease the possibility of injury to the participants.

8) **Standards and guidelines**—National hospital-accrediting groups may soon be setting standards and guidelines for treatment settings with ropes courses. This is a needed step to ensure both the safety of patients, emotionally and physically, and the success of ropes course programs as a treatment tool. A concern that this accrediting group may have is whether qualified staff are actually at the site doing therapy, particularly if hospitals are billing for third-party payment for ropes course time. Staff may soon be required to have advanced training in ropes courses, degrees in counseling and psychotherapy, and licenses as helping professionals in their state to qualify for insurance reimbursement.

It is also important that one person at each ropes course facility be designated as the Ropes Course Supervisor for all units using the course and be responsible for all aspects of the course. This person should maintain high standards of facilitation and safety and be familiar with technical and training issues. In this way, patients, staff, and the program are at less risk.

9) **Job burnout**—Job burnout can and does happen with the ropes course as it does with any job. Staff must continue to feel challenged and excited by their work. The previously mentioned suggestions of expanded staff training and regular evaluations would help to accomplish this, as would providing educational opportunities for staff. By doing this, administrators would not only demonstrate their caring for the staff, but would also retain staff longer, a great advantage when weighed against the lengthy and costly process of training new staff.

Another suggestion to avoid staff burnout is the diversification of their job responsibilities. Several sites had recreation therapists who also served as counselors in the unit and at group therapy. The staff felt more current with patients' needs and more a part of the hospital community when they handled a variety of responsibilities, and the patients benefited from the continuity and connectedness they felt with the staff.

10) **Use of high ropes course**—For those facilities looking into ropes courses, a good approach is to put in a low course before deciding to put in a high course. For a facility with high events, the factors contributing to it being underused are a fearful staff, insufficient time, and uncertainty about how to make the high events applicable to recovery. Networking with sites that do use their high events is beneficial; discover how they have resolved the issues. Get additional support and training for staff. Support those staff who are fearful and provide ways for them to work through their issues. Their personal growth will provide them with richer strategies to use in processing with patients who have the same fears.

11) **Increasing course use**—A frequently asked question by staff and patients alike was, "Why is the course not being used more?" Gaining support for the course so that more units will use it has been a key factor in its degree of integration into the facility, although this varied from site to site. When administrators see the course as useful in only one way, the course will not likely expand to other populations. However, when key people at two sites challenged the existing thinking about ropes courses, the use of the course did expand. For instance, ropes courses can be used not only with youths, but also, as is suggested in previous literature, with families (Cole, 1989; Kirkpatrick, 1983; Roland, Dunham, Hoyt, & Havens, 1989). As Mason (1981) reported, this can be a rich opportunity to increase the understanding of family dynamics and facilitate bonding. Using the course on weekends would increase the likelihood that families could participate.

Another concern voiced by staff was the frustration of increasingly shorter length of stays for patients. Yet one Program Director saw the ropes course as a credible answer to this prevalent problem with inpatient programs. Hospitals and other mental health facilities are being forced to look for alternative treatment strategies that can achieve effective treatment change in shorter periods of time. Due to their intensity, ropes courses have the ability to achieve what other mental health models take longer to accomplish. Ropes courses build trust, community, and bring issues to the surface more quickly. Because of these qualities, ropes courses may actually become more prevalent in these types of mental health settings to answer this issue.

CONCLUSION

Research has been done on wilderness programs and Outward Bound, but there is a paucity of research focused exclusively on ropes courses as a treatment strategy. Further research and evaluation is needed on this topic. Researchers need to develop a consistent set of measurement tools so that effectiveness and ineffectiveness can be investigated. Topics could focus on such issues as the long-term effect, if any, of the ropes course on mental health patients. Does the course create change? Specifically, how is the course affecting patients? For what length of time does the impact remain with patients? How is it best used in conjunction with other therapies? What are the types of changes that are most frequently seen? What are the precise therapeutic gains from the course? What factors influence whether the course is therapeutic? Future studies need to look at more settings for a longer time. In addition, future studies need to do a feminist critique of gender issues in staffing, story lines, and processing.

Future investigations could do comparisons of ropes courses. For example, researchers could create a study utilizing two treatment groups: the experimental group would use the course and the control group would not. Comparative studies could look at ropes courses being facilitated by recreation therapists and those being facilitated by clinical therapists. Comparative studies could also explore ropes courses used for recreation and those integrated into the treatment model.

The interviews and observations in this study have only begun to expose some of these factors. It was beyond the scope of this project, which was designed to provide a preliminary overview in an area where there has been little previous research, to address these questions. It is hoped that the issues illuminated in this project will stimulate further research.

Nancy Gilliam, M. Ed., Ph. D., is a practicing psychologist as well as a consultant to psychiatric treatment facilities that are developing adventure therapy. She trains therapists to use and maximize adventure therapy.

REFERENCES

Bacon, S. (1983). *The conscious use of metaphor in Outward Bound*. Denver: Colorado Outward Bound School.

Banaka, W. and Young, D. (1985). Community coping skills enhanced by an adventure camp for adult chronic psychiatric patients. *Hospital*

SECTION 4

PROCESSING OF ADVENTURE THERAPY EXPERIENCES

Craig Dobkin

20

THE EVOLUTION OF PROCESSING ADVENTURE THERAPY EXPERIENCES

MICHAEL A. GASS, Ph.D.

The processing of adventure experiences is generally recognized as one of the most valuable skills of an adventure therapist. A therapist's ability to augment the therapeutic quality of the experience or direct clients to areas of functional change through processing techniques often determines whether the adventure experience will be successful in empowering clients to reach their therapeutic objectives.

While some professionals (e.g., Quinsland & Van Ginkel, 1984) have defined processing as "an activity that is used to encourage individuals to reflect, describe, analyze, and communicate what they have recently experienced" (p. 9), its use in adventure programming (particularly in therapeutic groups) is generally much more extensive. Processing can occur prior to, during, or after adventure experiences to appropriately enhance therapeutic processes. Processing techniques can be used to: 1) help clients focus or increase their awareness on issues prior to the experience (e.g., framing, briefing, metaphoric introductions); 2) facilitate or direct change while an experience is actually occurring (e.g., punctuation, stop action, reframing, suggestions); 3) reflect, describe, analyze, or discuss the experience after it is completed (e.g., debriefing, journal writing, reframing, solo experiences); and/or 4) reinforce change and provide integration in clients' lives after the experience is completed (e.g., transfer of learning, subsequential therapy sessions). Viewed in this manner, a broader definition of processing adventure therapy experiences is required.

Given the need for a broader and more inclusive perspective, processing can be defined as *those techniques that are used to augment the therapeutic qualities of the adventure experience based on an accurate assessment of the client's needs*. The goals of processing are to: 1) enhance the present therapeutic value of the adventure experience, and 2) increase the positive integration of functional therapeutic change for future use by the client. Processing techniques are generally verbal in format, but can also take the form of non-verbal strategies such as drawing, journal writing, or solo experiences (several examples of these are presented in the chapter by Tom Smith in this section of the book). While therapeutic adventure experiences can naturally occur without processing (e.g., see Bacon and Kimball's description of "spontaneous metaphoric transfer" in the First Section of this book), these occurrences are too infrequent, and it is generally felt that processing provides a series of invaluable steps in reaching the two goals mentioned above.

One way to view the role of processing in adventure experiences is to compare the creation of a therapeutic adventure experience to the process of taking a picture. Depending upon what "picture" a client needs, the therapist helps to structure the medium the client requires in a manner that will work best for the client. When it comes time to take the picture, a number of adjustments may need to be made in order for the client to obtain the picture he/she desires. In many ways, this portion of processing is like the interworkings of a camera, providing the means by which the adventure therapist helps to clarify the appropriate focus for the client, enough light to illuminate those features that need highlighting, shading to give the picture appropriate perspective, and sometimes even some "touching up" in the development of the experience to provide the picture with a more complete view of the situation. While not as important as the experience itself, the processing "camera" provides the necessary adjustments for clients to receive pictures of their present as well as intended landscapes.

BACON'S EVOLUTION OF PROCESSING TECHNIQUES IN ADVENTURE PROGRAMS

While the complexity of processing techniques in adventure therapy experiences can be quite extensive, their applications for adventure therapy programs have evolved a great deal since their introduction in the 1960s. Probably the most detailed and complete effort in chronicling this development has been accomplished by Bacon (1987). This author has highlighted the evolution of the "curriculum" of adventure programs, and his model is nowhere more evident than in the development of processing in adventure therapy programs. His evolution includes three stages: 1) the "Mountains Speak for Themselves" (MST) curriculum model, 2) the "Outward Bound Plus" (OBP) curriculum model, and 3) the "Metaphoric" curriculum model. Each of these models is discussed, highlighting the reasons for their use and outlining their potential weaknesses.

THE MOUNTAINS SPEAK FOR THEMSELVES (MST) MODEL

This model represents the first type of processing used in all adventure programs when they were initially introduced to North America. It follows the approach to processing that was (and, to a major degree, still is) being used in adventure programs outside of North America (e.g., outdoor pursuits programs in England). First outlined in written form in a paper by James (1980), this type of processing relies upon the experience itself to be so powerful or influential that it produces the global change and integration necessary to achieve the specific therapeutic objective. The model also deemphasizes discussion and processing techniques by the instructor and generally relies on clients to extract the insight and learnings from the adventure experience and apply them to their particular issues. As stated by Bacon (1987): "The Outward Bound [adventure experience] is so positive, profound, and powerful, that it will automatically generalize to the student's daily life; instructors need not be excessively concerned about [facilitating] transfer" (p. 6).

The strengths of this model mirror the strengths of the professionals who use this model. Many individuals who used this model in the early adventure therapy programs, as well as those who continue to use this method, are well trained in providing safe and progressively challenging adventure experiences. Adventure experiences have a strong, intrinsically motivating structure and often result in "a sense of mastery and peak experiences" (Bacon, 1987, p. 5).

Usually practitioners of this model avoid the processing techniques found in other models (e.g., framing, debriefing, structured discussions) for one of three reasons: 1) the instructor or program does not believe that such efforts are necessary, appropriate, or valuable; 2) the instructors are not trained in the use of adjunctive therapeutic skills and stay clear of entering areas where they lack sufficient training or competence; and 3) the instructors simply are not aware that other types of processing techniques exist.

While its methodology is still used (often for one of the three reasons listed above), there are certain limitations of the MST processing model. Bacon identified these limitations as: 1) the adventure experience is not structured to meet the specific therapeutic needs of the client, 2) the general goals achieved on the adventure experience (e.g., increased self-concept, self-efficacy) do not translate into specific therapeutic changes, and 3) the adventure experience could be more effective for treatment if there was a focus on integrating or transferring the experience into the future of the participant.

THE OUTWARD BOUND PLUS (OBP) MODEL

As detailed by Bacon, the second development in processing evolved from attempts to resolve the criticisms of the first model as well as from the type of professionals who were attracted to the increasing use of adventure experiences. This natural evolution occurred as professionals with different backgrounds and training (e.g., psychotherapists and educators rather than mountaineers and wilderness instructors) began to enter instructor positions for adventure programs. Because of their background and insight into what occurred on adventure experiences, these "new types" of instructors placed a value on the importance of using cognitive, reflective techniques to assist in highlighting critical areas of development during the experience. The focus of these instructors was not to ignore the proper delivery of experiences that were appropriately being accomplished by their colleagues, but to add techniques to increase a client's understanding and integration of the learning found in adventure experiences. This focus on "adding to" the experience in this manner led Bacon to label this type of processing as the "Outward Bound Plus" (OBP) model.

Samples of the type of "imported" or additional techniques that became attached to adventure experiences conducted with therapeutic populations included Reality Therapy, Alcoholic Anonymous techniques, Rogerian reflective techniques, learning stages based on Bloom's taxonomy of cognitive objectives, etc. Instructors in adventure therapy programs that used these techniques increased their responsibilities. As Bacon pointed out, not only did instructors need to direct a good course, but they were also expected to be "knowledgeable about the background and daily functioning of the population they were serving" (p. 9).

There were several advantages to using this method of processing. As identified by Bacon, professionals started to find that this method increased the effectiveness of the "imported techniques" for many of the reasons identified in the first section of the book (e.g., it "broke down" inappropriate client defenses, it highlighted the concrete representations of issues, it enhanced an already supportive atmosphere, it made better use of the "renewal feelings" provided by wilderness settings).

While these advantages have seemed to increase the richness of adventure therapy experiences, several disadvantages have also come to light. In his article, Bacon pointed out three of these disadvantages. They include:

1) The OBP model becomes too "techniquey," meaning that a dependency on these imported techniques may result in the loss of the unique nature and intricacies of adventure experiences to produce change.

222   *ADVENTURE THERAPY*

2) This type of processing can be difficult and confusing for the instructor, especially entry-level instructors. Processing in this manner asks instructors to be quite knowledgeable about the clients with whom they are working. This may be too difficult for certain instructors, particularly given their sometimes limited training, background, and lack of organizational support.

3) In extracting a large degree of learning from post-experience discussions, this type of processing draws the focus of treatment away from being experiential.

In summarizing these thoughts by Bacon, it becomes quite evident that this type of processing can run the risk of steering away from the strength (i.e., the experiential nature) of adventure experiences. By overfocusing on the spoken words about the experience, the possibility arises that the power of the experience can become diluted. In its worst case, this could turn into a sort of "analysis paralysis," where the therapeutic processing actually detracts from or contraindicates the treatment gains of the adventure experience, which for many people serves as a major source of strength in their efforts toward therapeutic change.

It also becomes evident that this type of processing is more of a reactive than proactive technique. While clients might make statements in OBP processing methods about how they are "going to change" based on what they did in the adventure experience, actual change is never observed nor do they ever "try out" this change unless it is done in a subsequent adventure experience. While some leading adventure therapists who use OBP processing have come up with techniques to implement change in further adventure learning experiences [e.g., the "adventure wave" concept from Schoel, Prouty, & Radcliffe (1987)], there is the potential loss of clients never actually "walking their talk" or working on using new and more functional behaviors in the adventure experiences.

This type of processing also requires participants to place their emotions into cognitive representations (e.g., words). For some clients, the requirement of placing emotions into cognitive expression can assist them in their change processes, but for other clients this process can be difficult and overwhelming. There is also the question of whether addressing adventure experiences in cognitive terms truly addresses the emotional or affective elements that could produce change. It is obvious that some clients may thrive in the OBP process where these discussions become even more important for therapeutic change. However, it needs to be recognized that such a focus on these discussions can hinder, impair, or negate change for other clients.

Despite these disadvantages, the OBP model represents a highly functional and sophisticated manner in which to process adventure experiences. It can also provide guidance for the debriefing portion of the third model, although as pointed out in the next section of this introduction, the debriefing used in the metaphoric model is often quite different than the debriefing experienced in the OBP model. It is also quite probable that the majority of adventure programs, including therapeutic ones, currently rely on this particular method of processing. Professionals interested in this type of processing are encouraged to carefully read the chapter by Heidi Hammel in this section of the book. It presents one of the best detailed frameworks, based on the work done by Quinsland and Van Ginkel (1984), on how the OBP is accomplished. The following chapter containing Clifford Knapp's lists of possible questions for use in debriefing also provides one of the best single sources of questions to use following adventure experiences.

FRAMING OR THE METAPHORIC MODEL

The third model of processing centers on having the clients focus on the relevant therapeutic issues in such a manner that they can work on changing their unhealthy patterns of behavior during the activity. In order to accomplish this, the adventure therapist "frames" the outlook of the clients before the activity, directing their attention to issues that are most relevant for them. Bacon has referred to this model as the "metaphoric model," and while all frames are not metaphorical in content, they often possess analogous structures between the adventure experience and the clients' issues.

As with the changes from the first to second model of processing, the evolution from the second to third model has focused on integrating the strengths of previous works. The focus of this third model is to advance the processing skills detailed by the OBP model yet maintain the "experiential nature" of the MST model. Bacon states that "the third generation model must attempt to conserve the OBP gains in specificity and transferability while simultaneously reasserting the primacy of the experience" (p. 11).

Bacon highlights the differences between these three models by using an example of the "Wall" activity with corporate groups (p. 13), but these differences are equally evident in therapeutic settings. For instance, an adventure therapist is working with a group of alcoholics. Based on an accurate assessment of their needs, it is determined that one focus of treatment should address the changes required to move from a dysfunctional, abusive lifestyle to one that centers around a life of sobriety. The MST model of processing would try to incorporate adventure experiences that focus on empowering clients, one of which might be the Trust Fall. In this activity, the client group would gather around an object approximately 4 feet 4 (e.g., a stump, table) and take turns voluntarily standing on top of this object and falling backwards into the arms of the group (e.g., in a "zipper" fashion—see Webster, 1989, p. 16–17). The hope of this adventure therapist would be that the power of such an experience, as well as other adventure experiences conducted during the treatment, would produce positive changes in the clients and enable them to change their behavior.

The adventure therapist using the OBP model would conduct this experience in a similar manner, and would then initiate some sort of discussion about which elements of the Trust Fall related to the treatment issue. In this case, the focus of the discussion might be the changes necessary for clients to make to change their alcoholic lifestyle. Part of this discussion might center on how difficult it was to fall backwards off the log and how that could be compared to how difficult it is to leave their alcoholic lifestyle behind and enter one of sobriety.

Adventure therapists using the third model would instruct the group on safety procedures prior to the activity and would answer initial questions on the mechanics of the activity just like the adventure therapists using one of the other two processing models. However, before the activity began (based on an assessment of the needs of the clients), the adventure therapist would make a statement like the following:

> Probably lots of you think that this exercise has something to do with trusting others, or with knowing that people will support you if you let them. And that's a fine meaning to get out of this activity. But our purpose in choosing this exercise is actually pretty different; we picked it because we feel there is an even more important lesson here. And that lesson concerns letting go of an old lifestyle. Let me tell you a bit more about what I mean.
>
> Each of you will be getting up here and holding on to this tree before falling backwards. Before you fall, I'm going to ask you to close your eyes and imagine that the tree is that part of your personality—that piece of you most responsible for your drinking and drugging. I don't want you to think of this as a tree anymore; I want you to think of it as the most powerful factor responsible for your using. And I want you to hug it like you love it—like it's all you've got.
>
> Because after you hold on to it for awhile, for 30 seconds, I'm going to ask you to let go—to give up and let go of whatever it is that keeps you drinking and drugging. You'll just lie

back and fall towards these people. And don't be surprised if you feel a little nervous. Any alcoholic/addict has at least some love for his/her old lifestyle, no matter how much he/she really wants to change it. And there's always some degree of hesitation to committing to a drug-free life. 'Cause you don't know what it is like. So I'd be surprised if you didn't feel some kind of nervousness about falling. (COBS Staff; in Gass & Dobkin, 1991, p. 11–12)

There is the possibility that many of these details could come out in either of the previous styles of processing. This **might** be achieved in the MST style through an individual's spoken or subconscious insight into the connection of the activity with recovery or by informally sharing his/her thoughts with other clients. This **might** also be achieved in this manner in the OBP type of processing, but in that type of processing the instructor would probably lead the group to this area of discussion based on their presenting treatment needs. The adventure therapist would probably spend time discussing issues in the activity specifically related to sobriety and substance abuse, particularly focusing on clients' attachments to dysfunctional areas. In such discussions, clients would urge each other to do those things in their lives necessary to stay sober.

However, with the third style of processing, the presentation of this information would have been provided before the experience began. Instead of the activity serving as a means to provide discussion material, it would serve as a means to **foster actual change during the activity**. Not only would clients be directed toward working on those issues of greatest importance to them, but they would also use the strongest part of the adventure experience (i.e., the experience itself) to work on resolving this issue.

One way to view how these processing models connect yet build on one another is to view each in the following manner:

1) The MST model focuses on the process of "learning by doing" with no imported or adjunct instructor feedback provided outside of conducting the actual adventure experience.
2) The OBP model centers on "learning by doing" and then thinking and talking about how the experience relates to treatment through an instructor-organized discussion.
3) Framing experiences, or using the metaphoric model, focuses on actual "change by doing" and reinforcing this change through self-directed but instructor-supported integration.

Bacon clarifies the differences between the second and third types of processing in the following statement:

> The difference between the approaches is that the second generation (OBP) students do not realize the metaphoric nature of the Outward Bound event until the post-activity debriefing. Conversely, third generation (metaphoric model) students perceive the metaphoric qualities of the experience as they pass through it; their post-activity discussion focuses on how they reacted to the metaphor, not on how they reacted to the literal experience [of the Trust Fall]. (pp. 12-13)

In this quote, Bacon acknowledges the strengths of the metaphor model where the adventure therapist "briefs" the clients about the issues at hand in order to focus their attention on the treatment issues. Resolving the adventure experience becomes parallel to resolving the treatment issues, using the action-oriented portion of the adventure therapy treatment (i.e., the experience) to create change.

As with other models, there are potential weaknesses with the metaphoric model. Some of these potential disadvantages include:

1) **Complexity**—As with the movement to the second form of processing, change to the third form of processing places additional responsibilities on the adventure therapist. Not only does the instructor need to perform all of the responsibilties of the first two forms of processing (e.g., properly assessing the needs of the client, conducting safe adventure experiences, providing an appropriate structure for integration at the end of the experience), he/she must also provide appropriate framing and structuring of the experience for the client. An adventure therapist must add these responsibilities to his/her treatment concerns, as well as examine how introducing these techniques influences the context of other variables in the adventure experience. While this enhances the effectiveness of treatment, it can exponentially add to the complexity of accomplishing such a task.
2) **Greater amount of assessment**—To produce this type of change through framing, adventure therapists must be more prescriptive in their techniques. This often requires a greater level of assessment concerning the needs of the client and what the context of change means to the client. Without this knowledge, this type of processing can become a hit-or-miss intervention.
3) **Ability of clients to see parallel structures**—The use of framing, particularly if it incorporates metaphorical thinking, requires

the client to recognize the connections between the structure and change in the adventure experience and the structure and change in the therapeutic issue. A client's inability to match the frame of the adventure experience with the frame of his/her reality will probably result in some level of client confusion or an experience where the client will dismiss the presented frame because it didn't make sense to him/her. When this occurs the adventure therapist will generally be able to fall back on the OBP style of processing, but might have missed an opportunity to center on certain critical issues for the client.

4) **Delivery of introductions**—Delivering appropriate frames and structures also requires an ability of the adventure therapist to match the client's reality. While knowing the language and background of the client is important, framing requires much more than merely placing labels or images from the client's environment on to adventure activities. Kolb (1991) cautions professionals not to underestimate the importance of truly comprehending the client's context or reality in order for metaphors to be isomorphic.

Introductions must match the present reality of the client through appropriate language, pacing, style, and context as well as offer opportunities to isomorphically change to a healthier solution in his/her own reality. This process is described through the metaphor of a three-stranded goldline rope, discussed in Chapter 23, "Enhancing Metaphor Development in Adventure Therapy Programs."

5) **Accounting for individual differences**—While this is true in the MST and OBP model, it also needs to be accounted for in the metaphoric model. In a group situation, there will very likely be individual differences between clients. Creating frames that enable clients to internalize their own perspectives and outcomes will lead to a greater ability to produce change with each individual.

6) **Greater attention to ethical considerations**—It is obvious that there are several ethical concerns that are brought to light by this type of processing. One concern that is particularly relevant is that the adventure therapist is actually narrowing the focus of the experience by using this processing technique. This focus helps the client to center on the issues that have been identified as the critical areas of change for the client. In doing so, however, it is highly likely that other areas will not receive as much, if any, attention. Other concerns are highlighted later in this book by Creal and Florio.

Two articles are included in this section of the book that detail and describe this type of processing. The first article is Gass's chapter which outlines a seven-step process for creating metaphors and other framing processing techniques for therapeutic change. Other sources that detail examples of creating frames for this type of processing include Gass and Dobkin (1991) and Bacon (1983).

The second article is Bacon's work in the area of paradox and double binds. This area of processing has demonstrated the potential of adventure therapy to incorporate even more advanced therapeutic skills to enhance the empowering qualities of adventure experiences. Bacon's chapter is recommended for those professionals willing to advance into this territory. As highlighted later in the final section of this book, as the techniques involved in adventure therapy advance, there must be a greater level of commitment and training by professionals in the field.

21

HOW TO DESIGN A DEBRIEFING SESSION[1]

HEIDI HAMMEL

Chances are you and I already agree that experiential education is a valuable form of education. I wouldn't have written this chapter and you probably wouldn't be reading it if we didn't both agree that there is tremendous potential for human development and growth in carefully designed, safely executed, and thoughtfully processed experiences. As you are reading this particular article, the chances are also good that you have some ideas and some questions about how you, as a leader or teacher, can maximize that growth through thoughtful processing or debriefing.

The primary purpose of debriefing is to allow participants to integrate their learning, thus gaining a sense of closure or completeness to their experience. In order for participants to take what they have learned in an outdoor experience and use it effectively in their everyday lives, they must think about it and interpret its meaning for themselves. As a leader, you can facilitate this process by:

1. Setting aside enough time to reflect on the experiences.
2. Asking the right questions.
3. Planning appropriate activities that will help participants to reflect on their experiences.
4. Listening to the participants carefully.
5. Supporting each participant's unique learning.

This debriefing guide provides some ideas for doing these things, but a word of caution is necessary: this is only a guide, not a set of rules to be followed exactly. The joy of designing a quality debriefing is that each one will be different because each group you lead will be different.

STAGES OF LEARNING

In designing a debriefing you are guiding people through a potentially complex learning process. In order to do this effectively, it can be helpful to understand how people learn. How do we piece together information gained from experience, instruction, or reflection? How do we get to the point where we can say, "I learned that . . . ."?

One way to describe how people learn is Bloom's Taxonomy of Educational Objectives, which delineates six levels of learning (for more information about applying this concept to experiential education, read Quinsland and Van Ginkel, 1984):

> **KNOWLEDGE** (memory level)—remembering information by recognition or recall.
>
> **COMPREHENSION** (understanding level)—interpreting or explaining knowledge or learnings in a descriptive or literal way.
>
> **APPLICATION** (simple usage level)—correct use of knowledge (e.g., to solve rote problems or answer questions).
>
> **ANALYSIS** (relationship level)—breaking knowledge down into component parts and detecting relationships between them (e.g., identifying causes and motives).
>
> **SYNTHESIS** (creative level)—putting parts together to form a whole (e.g., to formulate a solution).
>
> **EVALUATION** (opinion level)—making judgments about the value of ideas, solutions, events.

What does this mean? It is simpler than it looks. At first we are concrete in our thinking about our experiences. We remember the events and their associated feelings. ("Today we sweated it out on that hike. I remember feeling as though it would never end!") When we have refreshed our concrete memories, then we can look for patterns or relationships between recent and past events and feelings. ("I felt today as I've felt before when there is an enormous unknown in front of me— tired, grouchy, excited all at once. I felt all those things because I didn't know what to expect.") Only then can we move to more abstract thinking and consider what we have learned from an experience, how we might apply that learning in other situations, and whether we like what we have learned. ("Maybe tomorrow I can look at the map in the morning, compare tomorrow's proposed distance with today's, and then gauge my strength. I don't like feeling overwhelmed by not knowing what to expect, so I can inform myself and get a handle on what's coming up.")

APPLYING STAGES OF LEARNING

The following is a chart to show how these stages of learning relate to the stages of debriefing.

Learning Stage	Debrief Stage	Sample Questions & Activities
Concrete Knowledge Comprehension Application	**Review/describe** events feelings thoughts problems	**Questions:** What did you do when...? What happened when . . .? How did you feel when . . .? What did your group do when...? **Activities:** Guided blind review *"I'm proud that I . . ." whip (can substitute happy, scared, excited, disappointed, pleased)
Abstract Analysis Synthesis Evaluation	**Identify patterns** **Make comparisons** **Relate to daily life** **Propose solutions** **Examine values**	**Questions:** What was the highlight for you? The most challenging? Do you see any patterns? Does this remind you of anything? Have you ever faced a similar challenge/ problem/feeling? How? What did you do then? Have you learned anything here that you could use when that happens again? Have you learned anything about yourself through this experience? **Activities:** **Human tableaux Pantomime highlight/challenge ***Place in the circle ***Self shield *Rogerian listening on group issue *"I learned that I . . ." whip Choose & share two objects which represent self of before and now Multi-media sharing—imagine the highlight/challenge; draw it; share drawing; write about the drawing; share the writing.

```
  *   Values Clarification
 **   Playfair
***   NCOBS Field Manual
```

By recognizing the stages of learning as your groups go through them, you can design or modify your session to make it more effective. Different groups spend more or less time in each stage, so you must pay close attention. If you stay in the describing stage too long, you may notice people yawning or appearing bored or restless. It is obviously time to move on to questions or activities that get people to make comparisons or identify patterns. On the other hand, a group that has not had enough time to review their experiences will often not be able to move on to the next stage. They will return to descriptions even though you have asked them to start comparing or looking for patterns. This means you'll need to give them more time and/or ways to finish that stage. A group that is still discovering patterns and making comparisons will not want to move on to thinking about how to apply their knowledge to their everyday lives, nor will they want to describe how they feel about what they have learned. Your job is to sense when they are ready to move forward or when you are moving too quickly and need to slow down.

FOCUSING A DEBRIEFING

Once you understand that your debriefing session needs to follow the stages of learning from concrete to analytic to abstract, you may be tempted to pull together a list of all the questions and activities you know and start designing. Wait! There is more to consider. How do you know which activities will work? How do you know which questions to ask or how many or to whom? It is time to start focusing.

ASSESSMENT OF PARTICIPANTS

The first step is to assess the needs and abilities of your group, as individuals and as a group. Ask yourself: How involved is each person? How involved is the group? What kind of personal impact is this experience having on these people and the group? How self-aware are they? How well are they able to verbalize their feelings and thoughts? How comfortable are they sharing those feelings and thoughts with each other?

For instance, how would you rate your group and the individuals in it on the scale of possible responses seen in Figure 2? Asking yourself these questions will help you to select appropriate questions and activities for your group's debriefing. If your group has just spent an entertaining but uneventful day rock climbing, you would hold a matter-of-fact, brief session, including questions and activities, to review the day

234   *ADVENTURE THERAPY*

FIGURE 2

Level of participant response
bored .... actively resistant or .... there, but just .... totally focused
                    passively noncommital tentative, hesitant

Personal impact of the experience
ho hum .... a few pleasant experiences .... oh WOW!

Level of self-awareness
I'm not feeling ...... I don't know .... I'm not sure, but .... I'm feeling proud,
anything   what I'm feeling   I think I'm ...   sad, pleased, mad,
                                                              frustrated, etc.

Ability to verbalize feeling and thoughts
silence .... vague, mumbled words of   specific, clear,
                    unclear sentences,   descriptions or explanations
                    hard to understand

Level of comfort with sharing
resistant .... uncomfortable .... chosen silence ...... tentative ... spontaneous
refusal to   silence   I'm not ready to   sharing   outpouring
share   share that much

and a few questions or activities to allow them to reflect on the meaning of the day for themselves. Since their level of involvement and the impact of the experiences was low, they will not need or want a lengthy, soul-searching session.

On the other hand, after a fear-filled day on the rocks, be prepared to allow time and support for people as they look back on that harrowing experience, relive some of the events and feelings from the safety of solid ground, sort out their feelings, and try to learn from them. How do you know whether to use planned activities or ask questions? The amount and type of structure you use will depend on your participants' needs as you have assessed them. The more unaware, inarticulate, and uncomfortable your group is, the more structure you will need to provide. To ask people who are just beginning to recognize their feelings to describe the difference in these feelings from the first to the last day may be asking the impossible. If the group is just becoming aware of those feelings, they may not yet have words to describe them. They may well have forgotten their feelings from the first day since they don't have words to pin them down.

You know that the group has felt many emotions from observing their faces or listening to the tone of their voices, but how can you help them to recover those feelings? A structured activity or question may help them to remember or label their feelings. After reviewing the events of the day, you could start a whip going quickly around the circle using a specific feeling ("I was scared when . . . .") or ask "When did you feel proud of yourself on this trip?" or "You looked disappointed up there. Were you?" (Always check your interpretation of an emotion that you think you have observed.) In this way you have given the participants a hint, a piece to work with, so they can find a way into themselves. If you use too broad a question ("How did you feel today?"), they may muddle around and perhaps feel embarrassed or angry because they cannot answer your question. By asking that, you have blocked instead of aided their transfer of knowledge from the field to daily life.

With a group that is uncomfortable with sharing their thoughts and feelings, try working in pairs to defuse the risk of sharing in a large group. Give a writing assignment, clearly stating that it can be shared or not. As a rule, the participants should always know that they may pass their turn. Do a short round robin or a positive, non-threatening "whip" in which each person completes a short statement like "I'm glad that I . . . ." A quick, clear whip can often loosen people up and focus their attention. Because everyone is on the spot very briefly, they may be willing to risk sharing a small piece of themselves.

If a group is shy or tense, pushing them to disclose their feelings will probably have the opposite effect. You can model self-disclosure for them by talking about your own feelings. "The first time I did that, I felt . . . ." Ask for concrete feelings about specific events, not global feelings: "How did you feel when you got to that hard part?" instead of "How do you feel about rock climbing?" Provide gentle and small opportunities to disclose, and then reward the group by thanking them for talking or by restating what they said in a supportive way. Each small disclosure, if it falls on supportive ears, can build trust within the group.

You may find, on the other hand, that you have a group that talks easily and articulately. For them to have a high-quality debriefing, you may only have to plant a few questions and then facilitate the spontaneously unfolding discussion. It may be enough to ask key questions at the right time. "How was that for you today?" "Do you see any patterns in those feelings?" "Have you noticed any parallels between your feelings here and those in your daily life?" "Do you think you can use what you have learned today when you are at home?" In fact, the participants in such a group will probably pose those questions to each

236

other or answer them before they are asked. Responding with a supportive nod may be all you have to do to keep the ball rolling. The most important contribution you can make is to be sensitive to your group's needs and abilities, both in planning the debriefing and in the midst of it.

BALANCING VARIETY, FLEXIBILITY, TIMING, AND LOCATION

The final four things to consider in planning your session are variety, flexibility, timing, and location. Used with sensitivity, these can contribute to a smoothly flowing and enlightening debriefing.

There are an infinite number of questions and activities to include. Vary them, play with them according to your group's needs and abilities. Do activities alone, in pairs, in trios, or with the entire group. Talk, touch, smell, act out, write, draw, pantomime, sing. Address matter-of-factly both the positive and the negative aspects of the experience, the comfortable and the uncomfortable, the pleasing and the repulsive. Be loud and quiet, big and small, active and still, slow and fast, silly and serious. A wisely chosen variety of activities and questions keeps the participants' attention engaged, which leads to more productive processing of the experience.

In planning and leading a session, be flexible. Try to assess your group accurately, but be prepared to change if you discover that you have been mistaken. Remember, the participants are right. If your debriefing flounders, you have simply chosen an inappropriate set of activities or questions for that group of participants. If your group is not comfortable with the level of self-disclosure or self-examination that YOU want, adapt your goals to fit their abilities. Meet them where they are.

Timing and location, too, are crucial. Schedule a time and pick a place that will maximize your participants' ability to focus. Discomfort, fatigue, hunger, cold, or bugs practically preclude awareness of feelings or abstract thinking. If you talk before lunch, will the group be able to pay attention? How hungry are they? If you wait until after lunch, will they be asleep? Is it too dark, too buggy, too cold, too late? When WILL be a good time? When could you MAKE a good time?

Remember that experience itself does not guarantee growth. Growth occurs when people recognize, articulate, and reflect on the feelings that are a result of experience. A good debriefing can pull together all the wildly flowing feelings so that they make sense. It can crystallize those feelings into kernels of knowledge.

Heidi Hammel has worked in the field of education since 1977. She has taught in the classroom, worked as Dean of Students, instructed for a variety of outdoor programs, and acted as the program director for an outdoor leadership training program. She is currently the Director of A.B.L.E. (Adventure Based Learning Experience) at the Delaware Valley Friends School.

Footnote

[1] This article first appeared in the 1986 Journal of Experiential Education, 9(3), 20-25.

22

DESIGNING PROCESSING QUESTIONS TO MEET SPECIFIC OBJECTIVES

CLIFFORD E. KNAPP, Ph.D.

The ultimate goal for experiential educators is to assist participants in learning from their experiences. Participants should be taught how to apply the skills, concepts, and attitudes that they have learned to future life situations. Experiential educators can improve their ability to process or debrief experiences by being clear about their objectives and by planning strategies to meet them. Processing helps people to reflect on experiences and to facilitate specific personal changes in their lives. The skill of processing primarily involves observing individuals, making assessments about what is happening, and then asking appropriate questions. There are many personal and group growth objectives that can be achieved through adventure and other types of experiential programming. Among the more important objectives are: communicating effectively, expressing appropriate feelings, listening, appreciating self and others, decision making, cooperating, and trusting the group. If the leader has one or more of these objectives in mind, the observations, assessments, and processing questions may be better directed toward achieving these ends. The underlying assumption of this article is that if the leader and participants know where to go and how to get there, the participant is more likely to arrive. The following questions, organized by specific program objectives, are designed to assist leaders in more effectively processing experiential activities for personal and group growth.

COMMUNICATING EFFECTIVELY

1. Can anyone give an example of when you thought you communicated effectively with someone else in the group? (Consider verbal and non-verbal communication.)

239

2. How did you know that what you communicated was understood? (Consider different types of feedback.)
3. Who didn't understand someone's attempt to communicate?
4. What went wrong in the communication attempt?
5. What could the communicator do differently next time to give a clearer message?
6. What could the message receiver do differently next time to understand the message?
7. How many different ways were used to communicate messages?
8. Which ways were most effective? Why?
9. Did you learn something about communication that will be helpful later? If so, what?

EXPRESSING APPROPRIATE FEELINGS

1. Can you name a feeling you had at any point in completing the activity (for instance: mad, glad, sad, or scared)? Where in your body did you feel it most?
2. What personal beliefs were responsible for generating that feeling? (What was the main thought behind the feeling?)
3. Is that feeling a common one in your life?
4. Did you express that feeling to others? If not, what did you do with the feeling?
5. Do you usually express feelings or suppress them?
6. Would you like to feel differently in a similar situation? If so, how?
7. What beliefs would you need to have in order to feel differently in a similar situation? Could you believe them?
8. How do you feel about the conflict that may result from expressing certain feelings?
9. How do you imagine others felt toward you at various times during the activity? Were these feelings expressed?
10. What types of feelings are easiest to express? ...most difficult?
11. Do you find it difficult to be aware of some feelings at times? If so, which ones?
12. Are some feelings not appropriate to express to the group at times? If so, which ones?
13. What feelings were expressed nonverbally in the group?
14. Does expressing appropriate feelings help or hinder completing the initiative?

DEFERRING JUDGMENT OF OTHERS

1. Is it difficult for you to avoid judging others? Explain.
2. Can you think of examples of when you judged others in the group today? ... when you didn't judge others?
3. What were some advantages to you by not judging others?
4. What were some advantages to others by you not judging them?
5. How does judging and not judging others affect the completion of the activity?
6. Were some behaviors of others easy not to judge and other behaviors difficult?
7. Would deferring judgment be of some value in other situations? Explain.
8. Can you think of any disadvantages of not judging others in this situation?

LISTENING

1. Who made suggestions for completing the activity?
2. Were all of these suggestions heard? Explain.
3. Which suggestions were acted upon?
4. Why were the other suggestions ignored?
5. How did it feel to be heard when you made a suggestion?
6. What interfered with your ability to listen to others?
7. How can this interference be overcome?
8. Did you prevent yourself from listening well? How?
9. Did you listen in the same way today as you generally do? If not, what was different about today?

LEADING OTHERS

1. Who assumed leadership roles during the activity?
2. What were the behaviors which you described as showing leadership?
3. Can everyone agree that these behaviors are traits of leaders?
4. How did the group respond to these leadership behaviors?
5. Who followed the leader even if you weren't sure that the idea would work? Why?
6. Did the leadership role shift to other people during the activity? Who thought they were taking the leadership role? How did you do it?

7. Was it difficult to assume a leadership role in this group?
8. Why didn't some of you take a leadership role with this group?
9. Is it easier to take a leadership role in other situations or with different group members? Explain.
10. Did anyone try to lead the group, but felt they were unsuccessful? What were some possible reasons for this? How did it feel to be disregarded?

FOLLOWING OTHERS

1. Who assumed a follower role at times throughout the activity? How did it feel?
2. How did it feel to follow different leaders?
3. Do you consider yourself a good follower? Was this an important role in the group today? Explain.
4. How does refusal to follow affect the leadership role?
5. What are the traits of a good follower?
6. How can you improve your ability to follow in the future?

MAKING GROUP DECISIONS

1. How were group decisions made in completing the activity?
2. Were you satisfied with the ways in which decisions were made? Explain.
3. Did the group arrive at any decisions through group consensus? (Some didn't get their first choice, but they could "live" with the decision.)
4. Were some decisions made by one or several individuals?
5. Did everyone in the group express an opinion when a choice was available? If not, why not?
6. What is the best way for this group to make decisions? Explain.
7. Do you respond in similar ways in other groups?
8. What did you like about how the group made decisions? What didn't you like?

COOPERATING

1. Can you think of specific examples of when the group cooperated in completing the activity? Explain.
2. How did it feel to cooperate?
3. Do you cooperate in most things you do?

4. How did you learn to cooperate?
5. What are the rewards of cooperating?
6. Are there any problems associated with cooperation?
7. How did cooperative behavior lead to successfully completing the activity?
8. How can you cooperate in other areas of your life?
9. Did you think anyone was blocking the group from cooperating? Explain.

RESPECTING HUMAN DIFFERENCES

1. How are you different from some of the others in the group?
2. How do these differences strengthen the group as a whole?
3. When do differences in people in a group prevent them from reaching certain objectives?
4. What would this group be like if there were very few differences in people? How would you feel if this were so?
5. In what instances did being different help and hinder the group members from reaching their objectives?

RESPECTING HUMAN COMMONALITIES

1. How are you like some of the others in the group?
2. Were these commonalities a help to the group in completing their task? Explain.
3. Were these commonalities a hindrance to the group in completing their task? Explain.
4. Do you think you have other things, not yet found, in common with some of the group members?
5. How did this setting help you to discover how you are similar to others?

TRUSTING THE GROUP

1. Can you give examples of when you trusted someone in the group? Explain.
2. Is it easier to trust some people and not others? Explain.
3. Can you think of examples when trusting someone would not have been good idea?
4. How do you increase your level of trust for someone?

5. On a scale of 1–10, rate how much trust you have in the group as a whole. Can you explain your rating?
6. What did you do today that deserves the trust of others?
7. How does the amount of fear you feel affect your trust of others?

CLOSURE QUESTIONS

1. What did you learn about yourself?
2. What did you learn about others?
3. How do you feel about yourself and others?
4. What new questions do you have about yourself and others?
5. What did you do today of which you are particularly proud?
6. What skill are you trying to improve?
7. Was your behavior today typical of the way you usually act in groups? Explain.
8. How can you use what you learned in other life situations?
9. What beliefs about yourself and others were reinforced today?
10. Would you do anything differently if you were starting the activity again with this group?
11. What would you like to say to the group members?

Clifford E. Knapp is currently a professor of outdoor teacher education in the Curriculum and Instruction Department at Northern Illinois University. During his educational career, he has taught in public and private schools in grades K–12 for 9½ years. Dr. Knapp earned his master's and doctoral degrees from William Paterson College in New Jersey. He has conducted teacher workshops in outdoor/environmental education across the nation and abroad for more than 25 years and has written numerous articles, book chapters, and books on teaching environmental ethics, human relations, community building, and nature awareness.

23

ENHANCING METAPHOR DEVELOPMENT IN ADVENTURE THERAPY PROGRAMS

MICHAEL A. GASS, Ph.D.

One rapidly growing area of experiential learning has been the use of therapeutic adventure programs. These programs have the ability to create empowering experiences, often achieving therapeutic levels of change that would be difficult to reach without such interventions.[1] However, it is becoming increasingly evident that adventure therapists must tailor experiences to the specific needs of participant groups to foster growth and ensure the successful integration of therapeutic changes into participants' lives (e.g., Durgin & McEwen, 1991; Ewert, 1990). One critical element in achieving this integration is the process of transferring clients' learning and insights gained during the adventure program into functional therapeutic changes in their actual life situations. This process is called the transfer of learning and occurs on one of three levels: 1) *specific transfer*, 2) *non-specific transfer*, 3) and *metaphoric transfer* (Gass, 1985).

Specific transfer occurs when the *actual products* of learning (e.g., skills such as canoeing, belaying, reading) are generalized to habits and associations so that use of these skills is applicable to other learning situations. *Non-specific transfer* occurs when the specific processes of learning are generalized into attitudes and principles for future use by the learner (e.g., cooperation, environmental awareness). *Metaphoric transfer* occurs when *parallel processes* in one learning situation become analogous to learning in another different, yet similar situation. While the transfer of learning can be positive, negative, or non-existent between learning environments (Hunter, 1986), one of the central purposes of adventure programs is to develop a positive transfer of learning to the future lives of clients. Without positive transfer, programs have little or no long-term value for participants.

While all three types of positive transfer can occur from adventure experiences, therapeutic programs generally place a great deal of emphasis on positive metaphoric transfer. Metaphoric transfer is facilitated by appropriately "framing" or structuring each experience to directly assist clients with integrating functional changes into their lives. Appropriate framing can enhance the therapeutic value of the adventure experience, enabling it to be more prescriptive and specific in its application and use. The proper structuring of metaphoric adventure activities for therapeutic purposes is often the key to creating valid therapeutic experiences and lasting change for clients. In the attempt to incorporate the concept of metaphoric transfer with therapeutic adventure experiences, it is possible that many professionals overlook several critical concepts in their efforts to use this therapeutic approach. Framing is often used to go over the standard logistics and rules of the activity, inform clients of the new terms they will be using (e.g., belaying, spotting, debriefing), remind clients of their therapeutic goals, or motivate them to complete the physical tasks that are ahead. These framing techniques are generally presented in a similar manner for all groups. One current example of framing adventure experiences can be found in Schoel, Prouty, and Radcliffe (1988) with the "visualization" technique:

> You have climbed up to the Hickory Jump. You see the trapeze. You see the arms of the group held out to catch you. You feel the butterflies in your stomach. You are focused on the trapeze. You are coiling your legs to jump. You are jumping out with all your effort. You feel your hands get a hold of the bar. You are feeling the group congratulate you, hold you, and let you down. (pp. 91–92)

This introduction, and others similar to it, are examples of how many programs prepare clients to address therapeutic issues. While these techniques may be quite valuable in motivating clients to participate and successfully complete initiatives like the "Hickory Leap," they ignore some critical concepts that are necessary for therapeutic change to occur. The lack of attention to a specific framework designed for a particular client group and to the interaction that exists between therapeutic issues diminishes the therapeutic value of the activity.

The purpose of this article is to address these problems by: 1) providing a brief overview of the use of therapeutic metaphor with adventure experiences, 2) presenting an actual example that appropriately demonstrates the process of framing a therapeutic adventure experience, 3) analyzing the specific factors that lead to the successful implementation of therapeutic metaphors, and 4) outlining a seven-step approach that provides a practical framework for creating isomorphic adventure experiences for therapeutic populations.

OVERVIEW OF THE USE OF
THERAPEUTIC METAPHOR

The use of metaphoric structures has been outlined by a number of therapists outside of the field of adventure therapy. Probably the individual credited most often with the development of therapeutic metaphor is Milton Erickson. In his work, Erickson (1980; Haley, 1973) found that using metaphors instead of direct therapeutic suggestions reduced clients' defenses to functional change and enhanced therapeutic interventions. De Shazer (1982) and Minuchin (1981) also stated that when metaphors contained linking "isomorphs" (i.e., possessed "equivalent structures") to therapeutic issues, they offered powerful vehicles for therapeutic change. Isomorphism, a concept initially developed by scientists and mathematicians (Hofstadter, 1979), occurs when two complex structures of different situations can be mapped on to one another so that similar features can be linked together. Once the connection of these features is made, the similarity of roles they play in their respective structures creates a medium for change. This medium provides possible connections for the transfer of valuable information learned in one environment for future use in another.

Bacon (1983, 1987) has provided a bridge for the use of metaphors in the development of therapeutic adventure experiences. In creating such experiences, he states that four key components must occur in order for the metaphor to be effective. The metaphor must: 1) be compelling enough to hold the individual's attention (i.e., it must be related with appropriate intensity), 2) have a different successful ending/resolution from the corresponding real-life experience, 3) be isomorphic, and 4) be related in enough detail that it can facilitate a student's "transderivational search" (i.e., a process by which the client can attach personal meaning to the experience). Bacon states that when these four conditions are met, adventure experiences provide more successful resolutions to formerly unproductive and dysfunctional behaviors, creating opportunities for positive therapeutic change within clients.

While other forms of therapy (e.g., psychotherapy, family therapy) follow similar steps in the creation and use of metaphors (e.g., de Shazer, 1982; Haley, 1988; Minuchin, 1981), properly constructed therapeutic adventure experiences possess inherent qualities that build on these steps and create strong potential for the development of highly successful metaphors. Two of these qualities are: 1) the ability of appropriate adventure experiences to produce *client-motivated responses* to therapeutic issues rather than relying on external motivation for change, and 2) the fact that most adventure experiences are oriented toward successful endings.

The concept of how adventure therapy and the use of therapeutic isomorphs create change can be illustrated through the structure of a goldline rope (see Figure 1). In this diagram, the white strand represents the therapeutic needs of the client, the gray strand represents their present dysfunctional behavior, and the black strand represents an appropriate metaphoric adventure experience. While all three strands have somewhat different structures, their initial patterns are isomorphic because of their similarities.

Therapeutic   Client   Dysfunctional
Adventure   Behavior   Behavior
Isomorphs   Isomorphs   Isomorphs

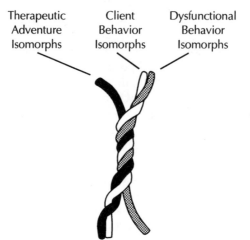

Figure 1—The interconnectedness of therapeutic isomorphs

Note that as the adventure experience produces successful change with clients, the strand of client behavior follows the success-oriented strand of the adventure experience and not the dysfunctional behavior that is creating difficulty for the client. While it is nearly impossible to create exactly identical isomorphic structures between the adventure experience and client needs (see Figure 1), the closer the adventure experience mirrors the pattern of client treatment, the more isomorphic and therapeutically relevant the adventure experience becomes in reaching treatment objectives.

Critical to this view is the belief that with the use of appropriate isomorphs, behavior is primarily changed *within the context of the adventure activity* rather than through analogies created by reflective techniques conducted after the experience (e.g., debriefing). Both activity and reflection are important for therapeutic change to occur, but it is the strands of isomorphic connections within the adventure experience that make metaphoric transfer possible and "pull" client behavior toward more functional change. Debriefing, while serving an important function, becomes more

                                                      ADVENTURE THERAPY

of a reinforcement of behavior changes that occurred during the activity than the primary medium for producing new functional behaviors.

Framing metaphors *before* the experience represents quite a different approach from the processing procedures followed by many therapists currently conducting adventure experiences. For example, Kjol and Weber (1990, pp. 19-20) argue for the common approach of "debriefing after" (or "Outward Bound Plus" model; Bacon, 1987), emphasizing that "what makes adventure-based counseling stand out as a solid treatment tool is the processing that occurs after the ride" (i.e., the experience). The use of metaphors with adventure experiences differs from this approach in that it recognizes the experience as the actual medium that creates therapeutic change. The framing done *before* the activity provides the critical conditions for change to occur during the experience.

While some adventure therapy programs have begun to use framing techniques to produce therapeutic change, the difficulties presented earlier in the Hickory Leap activity point to problems in creating truly appropriate metaphoric transfer. The most difficult tasks in creating metaphoric transfer in adventure programs generally lie in: 1) constructing therapeutic metaphors that are isomorphic to client needs, 2) framing experiences in a manner that can be interpreted and integrated into clients' perspectives, and 3) using appropriate debriefing techniques after the experience to reinforce change. The following illustration is designed to depict how therapeutic adventure programs can overcome these obstacles.

AN ILLUSTRATION OF USING THERAPEUTIC METAPHORS

The following description is an example of how an adventure experience has been structured to create therapeutic change for substance abusers through metaphoric transfer.[2] Traditionally, this "Maze" activity is conducted by creating a maze of rope connected in and around a group of trees at the waist level of participants (Rohnke, 1989, pp. 103-104; Webster, 1989, p. 34). Individuals are blindfolded, introduced to the initiative through a description of their task (i.e., finding their way to an exit while blindfolded), and led by instructors to various points in the Maze.

In this example, the title, introduction, logistics, framework, and associated debriefing of the initiative have been changed to create stronger therapeutic isomorphs for clients with substance abuse problems. The therapeutic goals of this initiative, presented in this manner for this population, emphasize: 1) the ability to ask for help, 2) the ability to set appropriate boundaries around issues of recovery in order to maintain abstinence, and 3) the elimination of dysfunctional behaviors that undermine the ability to maintain abstinence (e.g., placing the needs of others ahead of the need to stay sober).[3]

A sample introduction by a therapist focusing on the particular isomorphs of this activity for this client group could proceed in the following manner (Note: All participants put on their blindfolds prior to this description):

> The next activity is called the "Path to Recovery." It's called that because a number of the obstacles you'll encounter are very similar to obstacles many of you are currently encountering in your addictions. Our addictions often blind us in our path to a substance-free lifestyle, and we often fail because we don't remember to live by principles that will allow us to free ourselves from abusive substances.
>
> After my description of this activity, we will place you on the road to recovery by putting your hand on a rope. This rope leads you along a path of indeterminable length. Along your journey to recovery, you will meet a variety of other people going in different directions. Some of these people will be in a great hurry, showing a lot of confidence. Others will be tentative, moving cautiously. Some will seem to know the right direction, whereas others will seem lost. Don't let go of the rope, because if you do, you will lose the path and we will have to ask you to sit down until the initiative is over.
>
> The goal of your journey is to reach one of the exits to abstinence. There are several exits in this maze, and as you reach one of these exits, I'll be there to ask you to make an important choice. The choice will be: 1) whether you wish to choose to step out of the maze. If you make this decision, I'll ask you to remove your blindfold and sit quietly in the abstinence area until this initiative is over; or 2) you may choose to go back into the maze to help others. If you choose to go back into the maze, you run the risk that this particular exit may be shut when you return and you will have to find another exit.
>
> If at any time during this activity you would like to receive help, all you need to do is ask for it and guidance will be provided. Otherwise we would like everyone not to speak throughout this initiative until it is completed.
>
> Remember the rules of the initiative: follow the safety rules we've provided; no speaking unless you want help; I will be waiting for you at the exit of the maze and ask you to make your decision. After approximately 30 minutes, I will ask those of you still in the maze to remove your blindfolds for a small break.

After delivering this introduction, instructors distribute clients throughout the maze and tell them not to move until the "go ahead" is given. When all of the clients have been placed in the maze, they are told to search for an exit. In this initiative, however, the exits remain closed until each person asks for "help." The exit only opens up for the person asking for help.

After clients ask for help, they are informed that they have created a pathway from their addictive process and they are ready to make an important decision for themselves. If clients choose to step out, they are asked to remove their blindfolds and step aside to observe others in the maze from a designated "abstinence area." It is important for these clients to remain in the abstinence area and silently observe the rest of the process. If clients choose to go back into the maze, their blindfold remains on and their exit closes and remains closed until they ask for help again. If clients become grouped near an exit, each person is informed that they must make their own decision independently from others.

The initiative is usually stopped after 30 minutes even though some clients may still be in the maze (usually because they keep going back in to rescue others). At this point, the clients still in the maze are asked to quietly remove their blindfolds and join the rest of the group in a circle.

ANALYSIS AND INTEGRATION OF THE ACTIVITY

Different issues arise within each group during the debriefing of the exercise, but it is usually advisable for the therapist to begin the process by asking people to relate their experience in the initiative to their experience in trying to reach or maintain sobriety. Given the treatment orientation and objectives described earlier, discussions generally focus around: 1) how asking for help assisted people in this initiative, 2) people's choices at the exits, and 3) what "failing to hold on" to the rope represented.

In the beginning of the debriefing, clients are informed that the exits will not be opened until someone asks for help. The clients who called for help are asked to describe how this assisted them in finding their exit. They are also asked to elaborate on why they asked for help and what it felt like to receive assistance. The objective of including this dynamic in the initiative is to enhance the isomorph of people with substance abuse issues asking for help, particularly when feeling lost or "blinded" by their addictions.

The "choice" decision is meant to be isomorphic with a critical boundary issue for these clients, since their recovery process must be considered first in any decision. Stepping out of the maze is isomorphic to a healthy personal decision. Choosing to go back in is isomorphic to a dangerous decision, one where they may never have the opportunity to achieve an exit to abstinence again.

Sometimes people (e.g., adolescents) state that they stayed in the maze because "stepping out" would be "boring." This is a key issue to emphasize in the debriefing since abstinence may seem less exciting than "being in the game." This "exciting" game, however, possesses tragic consequences for many substance abusers. Some other important metaphors to discuss may include:

- To "let go" of the rope is to lose a chance to achieve abstinence
- The feelings of abstainers observing others "lost" in the maze of abusive substances
- Metaphorical techniques participants used to "find an exit" to abstinence (e.g., the struggle of searching)
- Interaction with others searching for abstinence in the maze
- The inability to communicate while searching for abstinence
- The role of hospitals/treatment centers in "placing" clients on the road to abstinence and the role of the client in following the path and making choices.

ANALYSIS OF ISOMORPHS

It is important to note that the goals for this particular activity are meant to be isomorphic for clients focusing on the first and second steps of the AA process (e.g., Alcoholics Anonymous, 1976). If the needs of clients differed (e.g., focusing on 9th or 12th step issues), the initiative would obviously be structured differently. Therapists with other orientations or theoretical structures for treating substance abuse issues would obviously frame their isomorphs differently based on the treatment objectives. It is critical for therapists using this technique to be clear on the objectives of therapy; otherwise, the use of therapeutic adventure experiences becomes a "hit or miss" strategy for intervention.

The creation of therapeutic isomorphs can also vary based on the characteristics of the therapeutic population. This example has been used successfully with a variety of client groups, including adolescents and adults, men and women, and clients from African-American, Anglo, or Latino cultures. Individuals possessing various interpretive frameworks require different therapeutic introductions and adventure experiences to produce equally beneficial results. Just as this article points to the need for adventure therapists to tailor experiences to specific therapeutic goals, it is equally important to consider each client's background in the assessment and prescription of therapeutic interventions.

The Path to Recovery initiative is conducted quite differently from the way the Maze activity is traditionally presented. Some of these differences, outlined in Figure 2, point to how the specific needs of clients and the resulting treatment objectives should change the way each initiative is presented and structured.

Concepts	Traditional Maze Activity	Revised Path to Recovery Activity
Verbally asking for help...	...is generally downplayed if not given a negative consequence.	...is the most important objective for participants to accomplish. Participants not allowed to continue in initiative if this is not accomplished.
Choosing to go back into the Maze...	...is often rewarded as positive, healthy, altruistic, and self-sacrificing behavior that commonly serves as a pivotal point for group success.	...is a dysfuntional and detrimental attribute when considered in relation to maintaining sobriety.

Figure 2

The ability, as well as willingness, to adapt the presentation and structure of adventure experiences allows therapists to create appropriate isomorphs that make critical differences for specific client needs. The Hickory Leap example presented earlier illustrates that without the proper framing of the appropriate isomorphs, there often fails to be a strong metaphoric connection between the adventure experience and the therapeutic needs of the client. This failure inhibits the likelihood of positive changes occurring through metaphoric transfer as depicted in the goldline rope analogy.

One reason why metaphoric transfer often fails is that therapists using adventure experiences do not consider the positive or negative "content" of treatment objectives (the objective may be to encourage or discourage particular behaviors). Interventions need to mirror these qualities in order to be isomorphic. For example, implementing the Maze activity in its traditional manner for this particular population fails to pay attention to this concept by giving the request for help a negative consequence, the result being an actual contraindication of the desired treatment objectives (see Figure 2).

It is also important to recognize that often more than one therapeutic objective exists in treatment, especially when the multiple diagnoses and resulting complexity of some therapeutic issues are considered. Adventure therapists must consider the relationship that exists between multiple treatment objectives and the resulting series of isomorphic connections as well. These relationships are just as important to consider in framing therapeutic adventure experiences as is the proper identification of each individual treatment objective.

The need to address the content and relationship of multiple treatment objectives can be observed in the Path to Recovery initiative (see Figure 3). In this initiative, the three treatment objectives focused on issues of: 1) asking for help, 2) making healthy choices for a functional recovery process, and 3) avoiding behaviors that could undermine the recovery process and the ability to maintain abstinence (e.g., placing the needs of others ahead of maintaining one's own abstinence). The first two objectives possess positive focuses for recovery while the last one involves avoiding a negative and dysfunctional issue. For this particular stage of treatment, it is important to recognize the order of these three objectives and their relationship with one another.

Figure 3 displays the hierarchy, content, and relationship of the three treatment objectives. In this illustration, the three therapeutic objectives (white bars) are isomorphically matched with three components of the

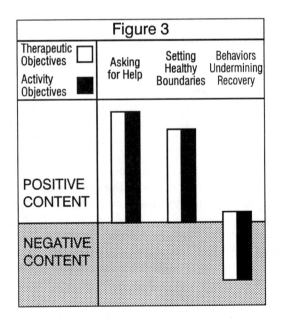

therapeutic adventure experience (black bars). Two of these goals represent "positive" content in the therapeutic intervention (i.e., those isomorphs representing healthy behaviors for the client) while the third represents a predominately negative behavior (i.e., those isomorphs representing dysfunctional behaviors for the client). Along with viewing the content of each goal, attention is focused on the relationship between the three objectives. As seen in the illustration, the therapeutic objective of "asking for help" is more important in relation to the other two isomorphs, and the adventure experience is conducted to represent this interaction (i.e., clients cannot address the issues of the second and third treatment objectives until they address the therapeutic issues of the first objective). It is the relative content and interactive relationship between the isomorphs in metaphoric transfer that create a tighter "weave" of the connection between the treatment objectives and the therapeutic adventure experience.

SEVEN STEPS TO CREATING ISOMORPHIC EXPERIENCES

Given the need to adapt adventure experiences to target specific therapeutic issues and populations as illustrated in the Path to Recovery initiative, a seven-step model has been developed for creating appropriate metaphoric experiences. The seven steps in this model include:

1. **State and rank goals**—State and rank the specific and focused goals of the therapeutic intervention based on the needs of the client.
2. **Select metaphoric adventure experience**—Select an adventure experience that possesses a strong metaphoric relationship to the goals of therapy.
3. **Identify successful resolution to the therapeutic issue**—Show how the experience will have a different successful resolution from the corresponding real life experience.
4. **Strengthen isomorphic framework**—Adapt the framework (e.g., title, introduction, rules, process, etc.) of the adventure experience so that it becomes even more metaphoric and the participant can develop associations to the concepts and complexity of the experience. Make sure that the isomorphs creating the metaphoric process possess the appropriate content (e.g., positive or negative focuses) and relationships with one another.

Figure 4

Application of the seven step process for creating metaphoric transfer to the Path to Recovery activity

1. State and rank goals	(a) Ability to ask for help (b) Set healthy boundaries around recovery issues (c) Eliminate specific dysfunctional behaviors (e.g., rescuing, enabling)	(e) Create abstinence area where clients can still be present near individuals "using" (f) Create other relevant analogies
2. Select isomorphic experience	The Maze activity (Rohnke, 1989)	(a) Use an appropriate progression of activities that lead up to this activity (b) Review level of group development (c) Ensure that clients feel relatively comfortable when blindfolded (d) Review verbal framework to ensure its esmorphic connection between adventure experience and treatment objectives
3. Identify successful resolution to the therapeutic issues	(a) Asking for assistance (b) Choosing behaviors that place abstinence first (c) Avoiding rescuing and enabling behaviors	
4. Strengthen isomorphic framework	(a) Create description that is analogous to the current state and needs of client (b) Make exit from Maze dependent upon each person's ability to ask for help (c) Revise choice decision to mirror client's choice to abstinence or continual "blinding" addiction process (d) Make choice decision mirror negative consequences of rescuing or enabling behaviors	
5. Review client motivation		
6. Conduct experience revisions		(a) Make necessary safety with adjustments (b) Provide appropriate reframing
7. Debrief		(a) Center discussion around treatment objectives (b) Use debriefing to punctuate isomorphic connections

256

5. **Review client motivation**—Double check to make sure that the structured metaphor is compelling enough to hold the individual's attention without being too overwhelming.
6. **Conduct experience with revisions**—Conduct the adventure experience, making adjustments to highlight isomorphic connections (e.g., appropriate reframing).
7. **Debrief**—Use debriefing techniques following the experience to reinforce positive behavior changes, reframe potentially negative interpretations of the experience, and focus on the integration of functional change into the client's lifestyle.

To show the actual use of this model, Figure 4 illustrates how the planning of the Path to Recovery initiative used each of these steps to reach its treatment objectives. Adventure therapists are encouraged to use this type of checklist as a guideline for creating appropriate interventions.

CONCLUSION

One important benefit of using isomorphic frameworks in therapeutic adventure experiences is that change primarily occurs during the activity and not after it through connections made during a facilitated debriefing session. This approach is quite different from the "debriefing after" approach to processing currently used by many therapeutic adventure programs. Debriefing following the metaphoric experience becomes more of a reaffirmation and reinforcement of behavior changes that occurred during the activity, rather than the primary medium for producing new functional behaviors. The experience of behavior change during the activity may also enhance learning and transfer even further for those clients who have difficulty expressing their growth verbally in a debriefing.

The approach presented in this chapter also differs slightly from the metaphorical approach outlined by Erickson (1980) and Bacon (1983, 1987) in that it connects the debriefing process to the actual adventure experience and does not see debriefing as a separate experiential change process. Debriefing is used as a means to punctuate isomorphic connections and reframe negative interpretations, not as a separate course experience. It also differs from these approaches in that it recognizes the need to identify the content of the isomorphs and the relationship that exists between therapeutic objectives, particularly when working with complex therapeutic issues.

Isomorphic frameworks can also be applied to other types of adventure programs with different objectives (e.g., education, organizational development, and service learning programs). Further investigation of this concept with these populations is needed.

As the number of applications of adventure programs has grown, so has the need to develop greater sophistication in prescribing specific practices for particular populations. Positive change can be achieved more often by using methods that address the specific needs of the population rather than by the blanket application of any adventure experience to any therapeutic issue. Creating the change through metaphoric transfer of learning by addressing isomorphic connections is one critical method which merits attention.

Footnotes

[1] For further references and readings in the area of adventure therapy, the reader is encouraged to explore the following resources: Bacon and Kimball, 1989; Gass, 1991; Gillis and Bonney, 1986; Schoel, Prouty, and Radcliffe, 1986; and Tobler, 1986.

[2] It is important to recognize that as initiatives and ropes course elements are adapted for specific educational or therapeutic uses, the field must not forget the debt it owes to the originators of these activities (e.g., Rohnke, 1989) who made such powerful media possible. These activities are not adapted to minimize the creative work these pioneers have accomplished, but to build even greater bridges for educational and therapeutic change.

[3] This activity is used most appropriately after a series of progressive activities that allow participants to look at such powerful issues in a safe manner. For example, it should be used with groups who have: 1) worked together for an appropriate period of time, 2) already established a sense of group identity, 3) members who can feel relatively comfortable and safe when blindfolded, and 4) experienced previous adventure activities involving issues of trust, support, risk, and challenge. To introduce an initiative with this much confrontation to unprepared clients would contraindicate treatment and would also be unethical.

24

PARADOX AND DOUBLE BINDS IN ADVENTURE-BASED EDUCATION

STEPHEN BACON, Ph.D.

Abstract

This chapter describes a way of integrating paradoxical and double-bind techniques into adventure-based education. The emphasis is on a skill-building approach focusing on offering examples, responding to practitioner concerns, and addressing common mistakes. In addition, the theoretical foundation of paradox is examined, particularly in terms of its historical roots and the rationale underlying its claims of effectiveness. The specific techniques covered include: 1) predictions of failure, 2) restraining comments, and 3) the utilization approach. The paper concludes by discussing the likelihood of a significant integration of paradoxical techniques into adventure-based education.

INTRODUCTION

The ability to enhance student motivation is one of the most important skills of an Outward Bound instructor. Personal growth at Outward Bound is dependent on concrete achievements, through the mastery of difficult or apparently impossible challenges. Without sufficient motivation, students will not exert the effort and take the risks required for this mastery.

In general, instructors enhance student motivation via four techniques: 1) inspiration, 2) support, 3) reasoning, and 4) confrontation. In inspiration, the instructor helps students to move past their limits by empowering them with uplifting ideals, such as the benefits of risk taking or the rewards of adventure. Many of the readings commonly employed on Outward Bound courses are good examples of the use of inspiration. When instructors are practicing support, it is likely that they will encourage students by techniques such as physical closeness, speaking in a calm or soothing tone of voice, and offering verbal reassurances. Reasoning includes techniques such as the presentation of reasons explaining the benefits of taking part in the course activity. Finally, the use of confrontation involves actions such as pointing out that certain choices will not lead to desirable goals, stating that a student's behavior is inappropriate or maladaptive, or setting clear limits.

The judicious employment of these four techniques often enhances student motivation; experienced instructors have numerous anecdotes that describe how support, inspiration, reasoning, or confrontation helped their students to attain Outward Bound objectives, However, while these techniques are clearly both effective and useful, they do have one significant drawback: they tend to be quite predictable; that is, students are often familiar with these approaches and expect them to be present at Outward Bound. Of course, fulfilling such expectations is not necessarily bad; acting in a predictable manner in the midst of a high-stress situation is often comforting to students. However, one can run into difficulties with this predictability when working with "problem" students—students who have long histories of avoiding success. Moreover, any student can act like a "problem" student given enough stress.

These four common motivational techniques (i.e., inspiration, support, reasoning, and confrontation) do not only characterize Outward Bound, they are also present in the "real world." Virtually everyone has received a mixture of advice, heart-to-heart talks, firm limits, second chances, people who "believed in them," and so forth. What is so noteworthy about individuals with chronic problems is that they continue to manifest their inappropriate behaviors despite repeated exposure to contrary messages from others. They have often spent years being unresponsive to the usual ways that people try to change others; they frequently have sophisticated, well-established defenses against motivational statements of inspiration, support, reasoning, and confrontation.

Of course, a heavy enough dose of these direct techniques or statements will often break through defenses; in fact, the efforts of many therapy and substance-abuse treatment programs are firmly based on that assumption. Unfortunately, breaking through defenses by this sort of frontal assault can take a long time and involve many setbacks. Moreover, some people are so skilled at resisting direct approaches that they successfully resist changes regardless of the amount of pressure applied to them. Their level of resistance is such that if it were being manifested for positive reasons, it might even be considered heroic or praiseworthy!

260

Given this profound ability to stay the same, there is little wonder that treating such people is often so frustrating for therapists.

Recognizing the seriousness of this kind of resistance and the difficulties inherent in changing it by direct techniques, one school of psychotherapy has attempted to develop novel approaches that can surmount these defenses efficiently and effectively. Some leading figures in this strategic or paradoxical school include Milton Erickson, Jay Haley, Paul Watzlawick, Cloe Madanes, Richard Fisch, and John Weakland. Their approaches are often called therapeutic paradoxes or therapeutic double binds because they tend to place the client in a special position—one of apparent contradictions.

Before explaining their approach in detail, it is useful to first examine some of the problems one can encounter when trying to use direct techniques with resistant clients. One of the hallmarks of such clients or students is their rather remarkable ability to transform helpful suggestions into "lose-lose" double-bind situations. An Outward Bound example of this ability—the capacity to transform a simple directive into a negative double bind—can be offered using the case of an imaginary delinquent adolescent.

When an instructor asks this adolescent to put on his pack and hike, this request potentially places the adolescent in a dilemma. If he complies with the instructor's suggestion, he is obeying an adult order. Not only has the delinquent had many experiences that have taught him that following an adult's advice often leads to problems, he also has typical teenage developmental needs to defy adults in order to sustain his newly formed sense of individuation. In addition, he belongs to a peer culture where he gains status by resisting adult directives. If the delinquent complies with the request, he will feel as if he is betraying his individuality, losing status, and trusting problematic advice. However, if he defies the request, he will reap the instructor's displeasure and is likely to become the recipient of a variety of negative consequences. In addition, he may lose the benefits of the Outward Bound course.

The adolescent is in a lose-lose situation. Given the way he sees the world, he has no choices that lead to clear success and satisfaction. He has succeeded at transforming a helpful, direct suggestion (i.e., put on your pack and participate in this program) into a non-therapeutic double bind. It is no wonder that such adolescents are marked by hostility, distrust, depression, labile affect, and other negative emotions and behaviors. Their worldview and the typical responses of others to that perspective frequently double binds them into lose-lose situations.

Strategic therapists address this sort of negative double bind with another type of double bind—a positive or therapeutic double bind. In the negative double bind, the situation is structured so that no matter what choice is made, the individual experiences significant loss or damage. Conversely, a positive double bind exists when individuals are placed in a position where all of their options lead to beneficial results.

A therapeutic double bind can be illustrated by using a group of adolescents on a troubled-youth course. Imagine that the course has been going well and that the group is almost through the initial acting-out stage and is beginning to settle into the Outward Bound routine. However, as usual, a number of the students continue to be prone to antisocial behaviors.

In this sort of situation, the instructors might choose to tell the group something like the following:

> It's nice to see that you're all settling into the course at Outward Bound and you seem to be doing very well, but I have one concern. At Outward Bound, especially after things start going well and people are getting more motivated, the pace of the course sometimes gets faster; the group hikes farther and more quickly, climbs more, and so on. This increase in pace tends to make some folks nervous because some students start to wonder if they are going to be able to keep up; they start to worry that they might be the ones who will mess up and slow the group down.
>
> In some groups, it often happens that students solve this concern by having one or two students be the regular "screw-ups." These are the people who always get up late, or complain, or hike slowly, or forget something. On the surface, it may seem as though these people are messing up badly, but actually they do a lot for the rest of the group. First of all, it reassures the other students to know that they aren't the worst group member—the screw-up has being in last place all locked up. In addition, the screw-up usually distracts everyone from their own problems; there's nothing like finding a scapegoat to blame for everything when you're feeling blue.
>
> (At this point, the instructor stops and asks a few questions about scapegoating to ensure that the students understand these points. Following this brief discussion, the instructor continues by pointing out that although the screw-ups help everybody else, they also tend to lose out pretty seriously.) Most of the time, people are mad at them. So, while this group may choose to have a scapegoat to gain the benefits, maybe the only fair thing to do is to be willing to share the screw-up role around equally—kind of like latrine duty is shared. Everyone could take a turn. One of the things that I am wondering is, who is going to volunteer to be the first screw-up?

262

By providing a rationale requiring group members to act out, the instructor has created a different kind of double bind—a therapeutic double bind. At this point, the group can follow directions—an atypical act—and cooperate by having a member function as the scapegoat, or it can defy the instructor and refuse to allow any group member to assume that role.

It is most probable that the students will unite against the instructor and this "crazy" request and refuse to allow anyone to volunteer to be the scapegoat. Even if someone does volunteer, his/her misbehaviors will be pseudo-misbehaviors, not the real thing. The group is in a win-win situation; any choice it makes leads to success.

If a student does begin to act out genuinely, the instructors can comment that someone has decided to volunteer to help the group by being the scapegoat after all. This reference brings some humor into a typically tense, confrontational situation and provides an easy way for the acting-out student to apologize without losing much face. The students can agree that, yes, they were just doing a bit of spontaneous volunteering. Finally, if the situation continues to escalate, the group can be asked to view the misbehavior from a different context. They can be questioned about whether they really need this student to help them in this way. The students will probably respond in the negative and proceed to confront the misbehaving student about his unsolicited assistance and inappropriate behaviors.

One of the significant benefits of using therapeutic double binds is that they are unusual and unexpected; it is unlikely that a person who has chronically maladaptive personality strategies has ever encountered this type of intervention. As mentioned earlier, such people do have sophisticated ways of resisting typical change strategies, but they are usually defenseless against the paradoxical qualities of the double bind because they have simply never encountered it before. After all, how often is an adolescent asked to volunteer to act out?

While this quality of unexpectedness is valuable, it does not fully explain the efficacy of the double-bind approach. More importantly, it does not outline its "paradoxical" quality—its ability to reorder the student's worldview. In following a set of paradoxical directives, the student is impelled into a perspective that contradicts his/her normal way of structuring reality, a worldview that does not support the continuation of the student's problematic behaviors. This implicit reordering of reality is illustrated by the following example of an anxious student on an Outward Bound course who is worried about an upcoming climb.

Imagine that students receive a standard Outward Bound intervention for anxiety; that is, suppose that they are supported.

Typically, this support takes the form of comforting messages such as assuring them that the climb will be easy, telling them that they will be helped by the instructor or the patrol, or suggesting that they have the qualities needed to handle the challenge. While this type of support will be effective with many students, individuals who use anxiety to maintain a maladaptive personality will not respond in a positive manner. Often they will resist the support with statements such as "It's easy for them but impossible for me," "They can't understand how I feel," "I've never done anything like this before," "I know I can't do it," and so on.

The more support such people receive, the more they argue how hard it will really be for them. Their strategy is quite effective, at least initially, in terms of achieving love, attention, and repeated assurances from others that they are accepted. Unfortunately, it also makes them feel weak and helpless, especially since their role in the dialogue requires them to argue the position that they are inadequate. The sign of the depth of their commitment to these maladaptive strategies is that they are capable of becoming more helpless regardless of the amount, quality, and type of help offered. Everything leads them to assert their inadequacy: inspiration makes them feel weak, support causes them to claim they are not worth all the fuss that is being made over them, and confrontation generates tears plus an implicit or explicit counterattack accusing the confronter of a deficit in empathy.

To understand how a practitioner could use paradox to break this cycle, it is important to understand how anxiety is commonly conceptualized. Anxiety is perceived as one of those negative emotions that is beyond one's conscious control: it is "thrust" upon a person; there is no say about whether it comes or goes; the victims are not responsible for their own anxiety experience. A number of other problems are similarly defined: people with a hot temper claim that their anger "makes" them blow up; people with depression argue that their melancholy "overcomes" them no matter how much they resist; and shy people state that their nervousness "renders" them incapable of social intercourse.

A paradoxical approach will often focus its intervention on this involuntary quality of anxiety. As will be illustrated below, there is no direct confrontation with or attempt to minimize the person's anxiety; rather, the paradoxical approach actually encourages the student to experience anxiety. However, the encouragement is offered in such a manner that it becomes difficult to continue to experience real anxiety.

Suppose that the instructor suggests that the student's anxiety is rooted in reality. The climb will be challenging, and the instructor is happy to see that the student is really thinking about it and seriously considering all of the problems that could arise. However, perhaps the student needs to think even more about the difficulties; perhaps he/she needs to try to become more anxious. After all, anxiety is the root of caution and caution is a critically important quality on an Outward Bound course. Therefore, during the next 3 days, the instructor would like the student to schedule three 45-minute periods each day to do nothing but worry about the upcoming climb. These scheduled "anxiety meditations" will guarantee the student's ability to successfully avoid all dangerous actions.

If the student attempts to follow these instructions sincerely, it will be impossible for him/her to have a genuine anxiety attack. Since, by definition, anxiety is something that arises without solicitation—something that is neither invited nor welcomed—the consciously created anxiety generated through this assignment is not "real" anxiety. One cannot experience genuine anxiety if one invites it, one can only have a sort of pseudoanxiety. Worries come by themselves; trying to worry makes it impossible to truly worry. In sum, the paradoxical instructions have made it impossible for this student to manifest normal anxiety. Either the student can have a pseudoanxiety experience or he/she can decide that the whole assignment is silly and not waste his/her time with anxiety. In this second choice, the student has shifted his/her efforts from resisting anxiety to resisting the assignment.

Sometimes beginners who use paradoxical approaches believe that they are effective simply because people are polarity responders; that is, people tend to do the opposite of whatever they are told. However, the preceding example illustrates a deeper, more sophisticated, and more fundamental aspect of paradox: its ability to utilize the student's worldview in such a way that either the worldview must be abandoned (the student gives up perceiving himself as an anxious person) or the literal experience is abandoned (he/she has a pseudoanxiety attack instead of a genuine anxiety attack).

Paradox is defined in the dictionary as "an argument that derives self-contradictory conclusions by valid deduction from acceptable premises." The therapeutic paradox above was built on an acceptable premise (i.e., caution is important in Outward Bound) and it had valid deductions (i.e., your anxiety is positive because it leads to caution; please practice it frequently) and it reached a self-contradictory conclusion (i.e., invited anxiety is not real anxiety). The self-contradictory nature of the experience is so uncomfortable or so freeing that the student either abandons the problem entirely or redefines it drastically (usually the drastic redefinition eliminates the problematic aspect of the situation).

Paradox is not a new way of changing human perceptions and behaviors. The Zen koan of "the sound of one hand clapping" is an example of a spiritual paradox designed to alter an individual's perception of reality. The martial arts practice of using an opponent's own momentum against him- or herself is another example. Therefore, while the use of paradox may not be new from a historical perspective, it is new to modern psychotherapy. The introduction of indirect techniques has offered a significant challenge to an almost-century-long dependence on direct techniques of facilitating human growth and learning.

PREDICTION-OF-FAILURE DOUBLE BINDS

Obviously, paradox and double binds are advanced techniques. It does not take much imagination to realize that there are a number of ways a beginner can get into trouble with such approaches. Realizing this, most therapists who use paradox have been trained for years in its employment and know when, how, and with whom it will be successful. Outward Bound instructors would probably do well to refrain from using these techniques unless they have had special training and supervision in paradoxical psychotherapy.

However, while the advanced paradoxical techniques may be beyond the reach of the average instructor, there are simple and safe forms of double binding which can be used by any Outward Bound staff member, even one who has had little or no training in this area. Perhaps the simplest paradoxical technique is the prediction of failure.

A prediction of failure is usually presented as part of an introduction to an Outward Bound activity. It has three components: 1) a rationale for the prediction of failure that is so convincing that it cannot be discounted or ignored; 2) a compelling description of ways in which the students are likely to fail in the upcoming activity; and 3) a suggestion that it will be difficult and/or unlikely for the students to avoid these particular ways of failing.

The paradoxical technique of predicting failure is only successful if the instructor is able to make such a profound connection with the students that his/her message cannot be ignored. A simple prediction alone is unlikely to be effective; one must "hook" the students. If the instructor can deliver the prediction in such a manner that the group can now refute, ignore, or forget the instructor's insights and rationales, then they pass through the Outward Bound activity in the context of the prediction. Instead of their behavior being simply a reaction to whatever course event they encounter, the behavior will be a reaction to the course event as framed by the prediction.

Effective pacing is the primary technique responsible for forming this kind of profound connection between the course event and the prediction. Good pacing requires delivering the rationale for the prediction so that it is comprehensible, matches the students' current worldview, and is irrefutable. The most common error is to toss in a quick prediction during an introduction without making a serious effort to "sell" the concepts to the listeners. For example, a simple statement that the group will probably fall apart and fight during a peak climb will have little impact. Contrast that quick prediction with the following concluding remarks to a peak climb introduction.

> *I'd like to say one final thing before we begin the climb. All of you look rested and very enthusiastic right now, and I have heard a number of you saying things about supporting each other and making it to the top together and really being up for this. And I appreciate those ideas. But I wouldn't be giving you the whole story if I didn't tell you about something that you're probably going to face during the climb.*
>
> *As each of you moves up the mountain, you're going to experience your own individual encounter with the stress of climbing. For some of you, that stress will be mostly physical. As you move up, you'll become more and more tired until it seems like a huge effort to simply place one foot in front of the other. When that happens, you might start blaming yourself for slowing everyone down and wish that you had never come, or even wish that they would leave you behind. On the other hand, you might get angry with the rest of the patrol for going too fast or with the instructors for placing you on a peak that was obviously too much for you. Rationalizations for why you should quit will be running through your mind: "I'm not into mountain climbing" or "I've always had a physical problem with my knee, or my ankle, or whatever." Or you may have all these things going on at the same time: you might be depressed and blaming yourself or angry and resentful, and you could have lots of rationalizations about why you should quit.*
>
> *Others of you will have a different experience. While you might get a bit tired, you won't be even close to exhaustion. You may look at the slow people and wish they weren't holding everything up so much; you want to get to the top and get it over with, and they just won't move. You might sprint ahead and get separated from the group. Or maybe you'll stay near the slow ones but the comments you'll make about their pace will let them know you're angry with them.*
>
> *I guess what I'm trying to tell you is that you have more than a mountain to climb out there. This experience is going to tell you something about yourself, and how the whole group interacts is going to say something about this patrol. I wish I*

could be optimistic and predict that everything will come out all right; there are ways to have a successful peak climb as an Outward Bound patrol. But some small signs that I've observed thus far on the course make me believe that people will be thinking more of themselves than of others, and more of their own physical comfort than of the real purpose of the climb.

Note how much effort was made in this prediction to align it with the experience of the students. It began by assessing their present level of enthusiasm accurately. Beginning an introduction with an accurate reflection of the students' current feelings makes it likely that they will accept the instructor's estimates of their future feelings and reactions. Including explicit, concrete details like "huge effort to place one foot in front of the other" increases the probability that the students will begin to experience those feelings in their imagination. As they listen, some may think, "That's me" or "I could do that." This kind of reaction helps to make the prediction salient during the actual climb. The students will encounter this particular peak in the context of the predictions offered in the introduction.

One useful variation on the prediction-of-failure paradox is to add a comparison between this particular patrol and the average patrol, or to describe the odds of success explicitly. This variation could have been included in the peak climbing introduction by concluding with something like the following:

I would like to hope that you will be able to master this peak climb without squabbling and falling apart as a group. However, I've done this climb with students several times before and I have to tell you that only a few groups are able to complete it without a major fight, getting strung out on the trail, or two or three of the slow people feeling completely abandoned by the faster members. So I want to wish you luck, but I also want to let you know the real odds you're facing.

Obviously, in using this approach, one hopes that the students will be motivated by the challenge of beating the odds and proving that they are among the few patrols that can climb the peak and simultaneously maintain a sense of group harmony. Just as obviously, this kind of "competitive" prediction must be used carefully or it can backfire and result in a counterattack from students who dislike being compared with other groups.

268

RESTRAINING COMMENTS

Another useful paradoxical technique is the restraining comment. In the restraining comment, the instructor acknowledges that the patrol has been doing quite well; however, the instructor goes on to say that he/she is concerned that they are making progress too quickly, that they are doing too well. The instructor concludes the restraining comment by advising them to grow or learn or succeed at a slower pace.

At times the instructor may even suggest that it will be necessary for the patrol to prepare themselves for a relapse into their former, less positive behaviors. In extreme cases, he/she can ask the patrol to stage a literal relapse. This rather surprising suggestion is often justified by the rationale that the patrol needs to understand their past behaviors in detail before giving them up forever. Restraining comments are particularly useful when a patrol has had a success experience after the instructor predicted failure. If, for example, the patrol described above has completed its peak climb successfully, the following restraining comment might be included in the introduction to, say, a day of hiking through difficult terrain.

> I know that yesterday I told you that you all were going to have lots of difficulty with controlling your emotions and with cooperating as a group as you climbed that peak. And as we all know, you proved me wrong. And of course, I'm glad that I was wrong.
>
> Well, today we are going to be hiking and orienting our way through some difficult terrain. While it will probably be physically easier than yesterday's climb, it may be harder because there will be some mystery, some ambiguity, about it. You may not always be sure you are doing the right thing. And that's a potentially stressful situation, a time when if you don't pull together tightly, you can really fall apart in a big way.
>
> Well, I guess I just want to say I'm happy about how well you did yesterday, but I'm concerned that your success on the mountain may set you up, because you might expect that you'll do as well today as you did yesterday. I feel that I need to prepare you for some other behaviors because there's a good chance that they may occur.
>
> You see, it's kind of unnatural for a group of students to move through an entire course without some kind of fairly major interpersonal conflict; in fact, we count on that as part

of what helps you to grow. So please don't be surprised if you have some difficulties keeping yourself centered or have a hard time cooperating. Yesterday was really excellent, but in a way it was almost too excellent. We're a bit worried that you are getting along too well. Most of all, we're worried that you will expect this kind of success as part of your typical functioning and be disappointed when you have some troubles.

Effective restraining comments create a typical positive double bind; a win-win situation. If the students continue to succeed, the instructor can know that part of their success was due to his/her ability to enhance their motivation. If they relapse, they are prepared to handle the failure more effectively. Failure is most devastating when it comes about unexpectedly; restraining comments prevent that sense of surprise.

Another benefit of restraining comments is that they often create powerful debriefs. In the example above, any negativity during the hiking day is already framed as a relapse into non-team-oriented behaviors. Beginning the debriefing within that context helps the group to focus immediately on key issues and is conducive to positive group-process outcomes.

THE EMPLOYMENT OF PARADOXICAL TECHNIQUES

Chronic resistance on the part of students can often be attributed to the overuse of direct methods with people who have learned that responding to this type of approach is unhelpful or even dangerous. This kind of overuse is equivalent to using the "right" thing with the "wrong" people. There is an axiom from psychotherapy that speaks to this strategy: "If what you are doing is not working, try something else." While this saying is simple and logical, it is surprising how frequently it is ignored. Often, instructors continue to use a direct approach ad nauseam, even after it has failed repeatedly. With this in mind, paradoxical techniques can be the "something else" that will succeed when standard approaches have repeatedly run into a brick wall.

When should this "something else" be employed? Obviously, an instructor does not want to overuse the paradoxical approach. If failure was predicted for every activity, the power of the predictions would be lost by the repetition of the technique.

An often cited rule of thumb is that double binds should only be invoked when the instructor believes that inspiration, support, reasoning,

270

and confrontation will not work. *Use the direct approaches whenever possible; reserve the indirect or paradoxical techniques when nothing else is effective.*

While this suggestion is both simple and appealing, some paradoxical experts have argued that it is useful to apply these techniques even when a direct approach would be effective (Fisch, Weakland, & Segal, 1983). According to this point of view, paradox works well with dysfunctional individuals but works even more effectively with high-functioning people. In other words, paradox can contribute to the efficiency of the Outward Bound course by allowing students to learn certain lessons more quickly.

Probably the most pragmatic answer to "when" is that it depends on an instructor's experience and style. When instructors first begin to use paradoxical approaches, they tend to employ them primarily after the failure of traditional techniques. As they gain experience and skill, they try them in a variety of situations, including ones where direct approaches would work. Finally, their experience and natural inclinations dictate how often and with whom they practice the model.

Instructors who are not familiar with paradoxical approaches may be concerned that the effects of these techniques will fade over time. It can be argued that a double-bind success is not a real success; that somehow, the reliance on paradox will make the achievement forced, artificial, and hollow. According to this belief, only a student who does it all on his/her own (i.e., who is unsupported by the extra motivation generated by paradox, and who is completely free to fail) has earned a real success.

This argument fails to recognize the essential legitimacy of the Outward Bound experience. The course challenges are so real that any attempt to "fake" one's way through them will fail; the activities are so demanding that only a deep and sincere alignment with one's own strengths leads to success. A success in this context stands on its own. It has a basic integrity—an integrity that cannot be touched by varying instructional styles or techniques.

Furthermore, regardless of what pedagogical model is employed, all Outward Bound instructors attempt to enhance student motivation. Motivating students does not cause their successes to be "artificial" or "hollow"; these feelings generally occur when the instructor does not allow the students to operate with sufficient freedom. Neither the paradoxical nor the traditional approaches advocate this type of overinvolvement.

Another criticism of the paradoxical approach is that it may enhance the probability of success so effectively that students will not learn how to handle failure. While that would be a lovely problem to have, paradox is simply not effective enough to eliminate all failure! An Outward Bound course is so complex and demanding that there will always be plenty of opportunity to learn from mistakes.

If paradoxical techniques are employed unskillfully, they can seem sarcastic or uncaring. The key to avoiding this dilemma is to choose one's words carefully and attempt to understand how they will sound from the student's perspective. One should also stay sensitive to more subtle factors such as tone and style; even if the words are correct, poor delivery can still irritate some listeners. One of the best guidelines for avoiding problems with tone and style is to avoid using these techniques with students that one dislikes. The dislike will tend to come through regardless of attempts to mask or hide it. At best, the resulting paradoxical communication will be ineffective; at worst, it may damage the instructor/student relationship.

There is some debate among adherents and opponents of the paradoxical approach about whether it is honest. Critics have argued that the indirect approach is manipulative and deceitful; some clinicians have even claimed that paradoxical therapists lie to and mislead clients. Obviously, these issues of integrity and trust are fundamental for any therapeutic or educational relationship.

One of the most effective ways to avoid ethical problems is to ensure that all predictions of failure and restraining comments are strictly honest and accurate. Do not predict failures or suggest that a patrol's progress is too rapid unless those failures are likely and the progress actually has been impressive.

The more one works with reframing, the more difficult it becomes to believe that there is only one way to understand a situation or that only one way to present the facts is correct and complete. Effectively pacing a student's worldview often moves instructors far away from their own way of seeing a situation. Building the rationale that underlies successful employment of paradoxical techniques frequently requires an instructor to adopt a radical perspective on the behaviors of a student. In the context of this sort of reframing, simple definitions of truth begin to fail.

Instructors need to work with these techniques and then make ethical decisions from their own experience. Perhaps, though, one rule could be emphasized. If instructors feel manipulative or believe that they are lying to the students, that quality of manipulation or deception will be transmitted. In this situation, paradoxical techniques will not lead to positive outcomes.

THE UTILIZATION APPROACH

Most of the preceding section on double binds concentrates on how to employ the paradoxical approach **prior to** a course activity; this section on utilization concentrates on how an instructor can operate paradoxically **in the midst of** an activity. Utilization, paradox, and double binds are highly similar concepts; in fact, some professionals use the terms interchangeably. However, for the organizational convenience of this paper, utilization will be reserved for interventions performed in the middle of course events.

From a historical perspective, the utilization approach is the primary forerunner of modern paradoxical methods. Developed by Milton Erickson, its emphasis is on using whatever behaviors are presented by the client as fulcrums for change and growth. Since these behaviors are "used" by the therapist—as opposed to the more traditional tactics of ignoring, replacing, or fighting them—the approach is called the utilization method.

Milton Erickson was a hypnotherapist in the early and middle parts of this century when not much was known about trance work. In those days, the only way to induce a hypnotic trance was via direct suggestion. For example, therapists would tell their clients that their eyes were getting heavy, they were unable to move any part of their bodies, and they were sinking into a deep sleep. While this approach worked well with some of their patients, a significant percentage of people were unable to attain trance via such direct suggestions. Erickson first shocked and then stimulated the field of hypnosis by developing a set of techniques which could take almost any behavior and use that behavior to induce a trance. Using an Ericksonian approach, it was no longer necessary for the clients to follow rigid suggestions and to enter trance via a predefined sequence of events; instead, almost any set of behaviors could be used as the basis for hypnosis.

One well-known Ericksonian anecdote illustrating the utilization method concerns a man who came to Erickson convinced that he could not enter a trance because his mind wandered rapidly from point to point. Erickson utilized this presenting behavior and helped the man to go into hypnosis by focusing his attention sequentially on a number of items in his office such as the shape of the file cabinet, the sound of the cars in the street outside, the smell of the roses on the desk, the weight of his body sinking into the chair, the warmth suffusing his limbs as he noticed their stillness, and so on. As Erickson proceeded, he chose focal points conducive to entering a trance, altered the rhythm of his client's mental wandering, and interspersed indirect suggestions about relaxation. Soon the man entered a trance.

One vital factor in this induction was Erickson's ability to build rapport with this man by reframing his tendencies toward mental wandering as useful and admirable. Erickson told him that the mental wandering indicated that the man was innately curious, and that curiosity is positive in that it provides knowledge and information.

Furthermore, he told the man that he should not fight this tendency; rather, he should practice it more wholeheartedly. This reframe increased the man's trust in Erickson and minimized his anxiety about entering trance. Of course, while the continuation of the behavior was encouraged, there was a slight but significant difference: the man's mind was compelled to wander under Erickson's direction. The induction was so successful because the patient was predisposed to cooperate with his natural behavior patterns.

This anecdote reveals all of the essential principles of the utilization approach. First, a decision is made to avoid using a direct approach to change a client's problematic behavior. As mentioned above, direct approaches refer to common-sense, logical, and straightforward techniques like inspiration, support, confrontation, and reasoning. Such approaches are problematic in that they may lead to denial, defensiveness, and resistance. It is time consuming, energy intensive, and difficult to surmount this resistance. If it is anticipated that these types of problems will occur, it is best to bypass them by choosing to use indirect techniques.

Second, since it is likely that the problem behavior will occur regardless of anyone's attempt to stop it, the practitioner of a utilization approach does not fight the inevitable. In fact, he generally encourages the client to continue to emit the particular behavior. However, the meaning, the context, the amount, the duration, or the exact form of the behavior is altered so that manifesting the behavior no longer has the same results.

Third, both the encouragement of the behavior and its alteration are justified by reframing. Often this reframing is based on a rationale describing the positive aspects of practicing the behavior. Not only does such a rationale motivate the client to follow the paradoxical therapist's directives, it also builds rapport.

Fourth, the eventual result of the utilization approach is either a minimization or cessation of the behavior. This occurs because the therapist's encouragement of the action and/or the subtle modifications of its practice have made it unappealing. Or, and this is an even more elegant result, the meaning of the behavior becomes significantly altered— altered to the point to where emitting it is now therapeutic.

In this Erickson anecdote, it is possible to see the sequencing of the four steps of the utilization approach. First, Erickson accepted the fact that it would be difficult to change the client's proclivity to mental wandering by a direct approach; therefore, he decided to use indirect techniques. Second, he encouraged the client to continue the problematic behavior: the mental wandering. However, the wandering was subtly changed; the man's attention wandered under Erickson's direction. Third, Erickson achieved a quick rapport with the client by implicitly reframing the problem behavior as positive. Not only did the man relax a bit, he was also motivated to follow Erickson's subsequent directions. Fourth, the problematic behavior of a restless mind was eliminated as the man relaxed into trance.

When the utilization approach is dissected, it appears simple and straightforward. However, this apparent simplicity tends to mask a vital point: utilization techniques are almost always based on a creative leap where the very behavior that has been cast as the problem now forms the basis of the solution. What makes Erickson's intervention so brilliant was not his specific actions; instead, it was his ability to design an intervention that was unbounded by formal traditions. Clients and students tend to be fixated on one way of understanding their behaviors; unfortunately, therapists and instructors can become equally fixated. The most challenging aspect of the utilization approach is its requirement that one be capable of radical shifts in perspective.

I once had an experience with an alcoholic student on an Outward Bound course which provides a good illustration of the utilization approach. The man was a scientist who prided himself on his rationality and self-control. He had been very detached from the course and had not been significantly moved by any of the individual or group challenges.

This man had a strong and genuine fear of heights. We were about to do the ropes course and it was clear that he would have an extremely difficult time with certain events. His fear seemed so powerful that there appeared to be little hope of minimizing it through supportive techniques such as offering encouraging comments. My co-instructor and I decided to practice a utilization approach that we hoped would enhance his ropes-course experience. We also hoped that the intervention would deepen his involvement with Outward Bound and his recovery process.

As we had expected, he was extremely anxious as he began the ropes course; however, he managed to inch himself through the first few, relatively easy events. But when he came to the high beam, he was stymied. He had great difficulty letting go of the tree that anchored one end of the beam. When he did move six inches away from the tree, he immediately clutched the overhead safety wire and refused to proceed. He was visibly trembling and sweating, the epitome of anxiety.

Instead of trying a predictable intervention such as attempting to talk to him through it, the following suggestions were offered:

> *Mike, I want you to continue holding on to the safety wire and listen to me for a moment. I have something to say that may surprise you a bit. In a kind of strange way, I'm pleased that you are as nervous as you are. Keep holding on while I tell you why I'm pleased that you're so nervous.*
>
> *In attempting to become sober, you're trying to do one of the most difficult things you've ever done. You know it won't be easy, and you know you're going to have to work hard and overcome lots of obstacles to make it. No matter how much you want to do it, there will come a time when it will feel impossible—when you know you can't stay sober. You have a chance today to learn how you react when faced with those feelings.*
>
> *I'd like you to stop a second and think a bit and then tell me a few changes you really want to make in your life around sobriety. (He told me that: 1) he wanted a reconciliation with his son; 2) he wanted to maintain his sobriety; and 3) he wanted to be more genuine in his interactions with others at work.)*
>
> *Okay, Mike, those sound like great goals. Now in a moment I'm going to ask you to say a sentence about one of those ideas. For example, say: "I'm going to quit drinking because I want to be a better father to my son," or "I'm going to be real with the people at work." And after you say that sentence, I want you to take your hand off the safety wire and move one step closer to the other end of the beam. And then say another sentence relating to one of your goals. And again, I want you to master your belief that you can't do something, and take another step. Do you understand what I'm saying? (Mike indicated he did.)*

Mike followed the instructions and made a statement with every step. While he did grab for the safety line several times, he made it across. And he did it under his own power, without any other support. The experience moved him deeply as well as the other alcoholics. Watching a trembling, almost paralyzed man make a statement about sobriety and then temporarily master his fear and take a step forward had a profound impact on them.

276

In this example, the four utilization steps were employed as follows. First, his fear was strong and relatively resistant to direct change methods; therefore, we decided to utilize it for therapeutic purposes. Second, the behavior was encouraged; we told him we were pleased that he was afraid. We also changed the expression of the fear slightly; he was to combine it with a statement about sobriety. Third, the encouragement to perform the behavior was based on a positive reframe. His fear was no longer seen as a nervousness about heights—something that was embarrassing or uncomfortable; rather, it was a profound and meaningful opportunity to test his ability to move forward in the face of feelings of hopelessness. The reframe was partly accomplished by our verbal messages and partly by requiring him to precede each act of courage with a statement about sobriety. Fourth, the meaning of his experience had now been sufficiently altered so that his formerly problematic action—the fear—was now a therapeutic opportunity.

Most utilization approaches seem simple and obvious in hindsight. However, at the moment they are needed, in the heat of an ongoing Outward Bound activity, it is often difficult to resist responding in a traditional way to a problem. It was tempting to suggest that Mike use deep breathing; we also thought about climbing into the trees with him and talking him across the beam. While these methods might have worked, at least to some degree, they would not have resulted in the deep level of involvement and commitment elicited by the utilization approach. Of course, it is possible that the same approach would backfire with another student. For example, Mike could have discounted the instructions completely by saying that his sobriety and his relationship with his son had nothing to do with walking the high beam. If he had responded in that way, the instructors would have looked like simplistic moralists.

In this example, the key to success was our judgment that the intervention would be well received—that Mike was open to this frame of his problem. We guessed that he felt guilty about his alcoholism and his relationships at work and with his family. Successfully passing through the painful experience on the high beam would not only give him an empowerment experience, it would also function as a kind of "penance" for his guilt. In sum, there were several subtle reasons why we believed that Mike would be receptive to these instructions.

Another example of the utilization approach occurred during a Trust Fall activity. A woman had become nervous about falling backwards and repeatedly hesitated each time she attempted to drop into her teammates' arms. All of the males were trying to help her by making a variety of suggestions and supportive statements. Significantly, the female members of the group were less active. The more help that was offered, the more stuck the woman appeared to be. After a number of failed attempts to get her to fall, the group was close to becoming frustrated. Some felt like continuing to support the woman; others appeared to be on the verge of confronting her; and almost everyone was uncomfortable. At that point, I stepped forward and made the following suggestion:

> Kathy, I can see that you are stuck up there and I know it's a lousy feeling this early on in the course to have already run into a problem. Now, I don't really know what it is that you are trying to let go of up there, but I want to suggest that what you need to let go of is something really important for you.
>
> Just hold the tree and listen to me for a second. I've been watching what's going on here and what I see is a lot of guys giving you a lot of support and encouragement. And in general, I think that kind of support is great. But I'm afraid that even when you do fall, it won't be as though you did it by yourself; it'll be more like you did it with all these people's support and encouragement. And I feel somehow that it would be especially good for you to do something for yourself, by yourself.
>
> But in another way, I'm a bit hesitant to ask you to do that because you might be giving up a lot. It's really hard in our society to be a strong woman who's capable of taking care of herself; in fact, lots of men don't like that kind of woman. And if you learned to be strong and independent up here, I'm not sure how many problems you'd run into back home with your new, assertive behavior. A pretty, helpless, and dependent woman can have a smooth ride in this world, but an assertive and strong one is pretty often called a bitch.
>
> So even though I know you don't really want to, I could understand if a part of you wished to stay helpless and dependent. And I mean that seriously; I know that the other choice—to be independent and strong—could make your life much harder. I'd like you to think about it for a moment.
>
> After a bit—a minute or so—someone down here will count to three and you will either choose to fall or not. If you don't fall at three, I'm going to ask that you simply come down and rejoin the group without making any more attempts. Also, I'm going to ask the patrol to be quiet and stop helping you.

The woman fell easily on her next try. She was angry with me and explained that she had long ago made up her mind to be strong and independent. All that had stopped her from succeeding on the Trust Fall was that the support from all the men had distracted her.

The patrol was not sure if my interpretation had been accurate, but they did stay sensitized to her in terms of dependence/independence issues. Later on in the course, they confronted her about these issues during a debriefing. She had not pulled her share of the sled during a ski trip, and the group felt that she was using her femininity to manipulate them and get out of work. She resisted the confrontation briefly, but then admitted that they were right. Following this admission, she resolved to demonstrate a new commitment to self-reliance and independence on the upcoming ropes course.

The next day she impressed everyone with her courage, resolve, and independence as she made a voluntary choice to attempt some of the most difficult ropes course events. She moved through the challenging activities virtually without support even though they were quite difficult.

Once again the four steps of the model were employed. First, direct approaches were being practiced ad nauseam by the men in the group and no progress was being achieved; therefore, an indirect approach was chosen. Second, her behavior was reframed positively. Her hesitancy was not seen as being indicative of a fear of heights or falling; rather, it was seen as a commitment to a life strategy that enabled her to relate to men successfully. Third, the behavior was encouraged—it was "understandable" that she wanted to get along with men. However, a not-so-subtle alteration in the meaning of "getting along with men" was offered, equating her male relationship strategies with dependency and helplessness. Fourth, the alteration in meaning was so unappealing that she chose to abandon the behavior. Her motivation to fall was partially fueled by her anger at me; my reframe clearly made me an enemy, someone to be proved wrong. This anger made her polarity response— her tendency to do the opposite of what I had suggested—particularly powerful.

The key to the successful employment of the utilization approach is the creative ability to view apparently negative behaviors in a different, usually positive, frame. There is a beneficial aspect to even the worst actions; if one is capable of seeing the behaviors from another perspective, from within the student's worldview, some kind of redeeming value will emerge.

Prior to this kind of positive reframe, almost everyone else who has reacted to the behavior has concentrated on pointing out its negative aspects. This feedback causes the student to hold on desperately to the positive aspects, knowing that he is the only one who perceives them.

When the instructor supports the positive aspects, the student can relax his grip on them for a moment and be free to experience the negative side. This may be the first time he has seen the whole picture. Since, in general, the negative aspects of the behaviors are much stronger than the positive, the experience of a holistic viewpoint can lead to quick change.

Of course, this reevaluation process does not necessarily happen consciously; it will often occur outside of the student's awareness. The fact that these processes do operate at the unconscious level so frequently is one of the reasons that paradox and utilization have earned a reputation of operating like "magic."

CONCLUSION

Erickson gained the reputation of being a therapeutic "wizard" for his creative and effective employment of the utilization approach. He was consistently doing something unexpected, looking at a situation from a perspective that was unconventional or even weird, achieving results that were difficult to explain through traditional models. This aura of "magic" made the utilization approach daunting to other professionals; as a result, especially in Erickson's early years, few therapists attempted to replicate his techniques.

Even the modified Ericksonian techniques described in this article might seem somewhat overwhelming to an Outward Bound instructor. It may be tempting to dismiss them, believing that they lie in the purview of the trained psychotherapist, beyond the scope of the average instructor.

That rejection, however, would be a mistake. While paradox appears to be difficult initially, a limited amount of practice will reveal that it is simply another form of common sense. The rules may differ slightly from the ones governing direct techniques, but in their own context, they are just as logical and straightforward.

It is simpler to learn to use a paradox if one begins with introductions and then moves on to the utilization approach. Introductions tend to be easier because one can prepare them ahead of time. Using prediction-of-failure introductions provides experience in terms of perceiving the positive aspects of seemingly negative behaviors. After practicing this perspective in introductions, it will be easier to be sensitive to similar patterns in the midst of a course activity. Then one can implement a utilization intervention in a spontaneous and natural manner.

Both paradox and the utilization approach are intended to complement and supplement the interpersonal methods currently practiced at Outward Bound. In general, the courses will be most effective

280   *ADVENTURE THERAPY*

if these direct techniques continue to dominate the way in which instructors interact with students. More specifically, it is not recommended that these methods be replaced by paradox and utilization; in fact, it is suggested that direct techniques continue to be used 80%-90% of the time. However, when one has a feeling that these tried-and-true approaches will not work, or if one believes that an indirect technique will work more quickly or effectively, then these alternatives can be employed.

It is a mistake to conceptualize paradox and utilization as techniques, as one more addition to the instructor's "bag of tricks." Certainly there are paradoxical techniques like "prediction of failure" or "restraining comments," yet one should not simply lump these together with other techniques like group debriefing skills or initiative games. The paradoxical model is different because it is based on different assumptions about how people learn and grow.

Even as Freud and his psychodynamic model challenged the prevailing psychological concepts of his time, paradox confronts current definitions of human learning and development. Freud's major contribution was the concept of the critical importance of childhood experience; his method rested on helping patients to work through developmental traumas. This approach to treatment and personal growth was a radical challenge to the then-dominant paradigms of reason, will, and simplistic empiricism.

The paradoxical approach offers an equally radical challenge to the psychological paradigms that dominate current thought. Paradox is not simply a way of helping a person to change more quickly or more effectively; instead, it is a system that is founded on a different set of beliefs about the capacity of people to learn and grow. To describe these underlying assumptions in detail is beyond the range of this article; interested readers are referred to Zeig (1980), Haley (1973), Madanes (1984), Fisch, Weakland, and Segal (1983), Lankton and Lankton (1983), and Weeks and L'Abate (1982). In an entirely oversimplified form, however, it can be argued that the paradoxical adherents believe that people are capable of making healthy choices, of turning their lives around quickly and relatively easily, if the repetitive strategies that lock their lives into unproductive patterns can be interrupted.

This assumption, and especially its belief that people can change easily, strongly confronts the paradigms that currently rule psychology and human development. It contradicts the medical model and its adherence to the deterministic nature of genes and biochemistry, as well as the psychodynamic model and its belief in the overriding power of early childhood experience.

Outward Bound does not need to subscribe to any one model in order to conduct successful, adventure-based courses. Indeed, it has its own assumptions about how people learn and grow (e.g., Voeky, 1987). However, Outward Bound instructors do operate in the context of prevailing theories about how people change. Those who choose to use the paradoxical approach may find themselves doing more than adding a few techniques to their "bag of tricks"—they may be implicitly embracing a new set of assumptions about human learning.

Stephen Bacon is currently a clinical psychologist in private practice in Santa Barbara, California. He has a long history of working with Outward Bound, beginning his work in 1980 as a residential counselor with troubled youths. From 1984 to 1987, he served as the Vice President of Research and Program Development at the Outward Bound National Office in Greenwich, Connecticut. He has written a number of critical pieces in the field, one of which includes the book The Conscious Use of Metaphor in Outward Bound.

Footnotes

[1] Certain identifying details about the individuals used in examples have been altered to preserve confidentiality.

[2] In this version of the Trust Fall, students are asked to concentrate on what they want to "let go of." The emphasis is on the renunciation of psychological obstacles, as opposed to the traditional emphasis on trusting others.

25

ALTERNATIVE METHODOLOGIES FOR PROCESSING THE ADVENTURE EXPERIENCE

THOMAS E. SMITH, Ph.D.

Most outdoor leaders would agree that one of the important purposes of adventure/challenge experiences is to be a stimulant to personal growth. Goals for "enhancing self-concept," "improving peer relationships," or "developing social consciousness" are often stated as program objectives or individualized educational program goals/objectives. It is further agreed that to maximize the potentiality of the adventure sequence contributing to these goals of personal growth, there must be a meaningful "debriefing" or "processing" of the experiences.

The more traditional procedure for processing is that of the sharing circle. Whether it be a sit-down circle beside the trail, a special meeting at the base of the "Wall," a structured "magic circle" or "medicine wheel," or an evening of sharing by campfire light, there is value in the verbal exchange of feelings, reactions, and awarenesses stimulated by the experiences completed. The processing circle can also provide opportunity for dealing with peer conflicts, group decisions, and the developing attitudes and behaviors of the participants. The role of the leader is to facilitate a meaningful exchange of thoughts, perceptions, feelings, reactions, energies, and support within the group.

The adventure leader's role as facilitator of group processing is a delicate and complex one. The skills required are parallel to those of professional therapists and counselors who have training as group leaders. Few adventure leaders have skill training for dealing with the intensities of personality, emotion, and group dynamics that can unfold in the processing circle. This creates some real conflicts for adventure leaders. On the one hand, they are told of the great value and necessity of the processing component, and on the other hand, they are warned to exercise caution in dealing with the psychological and social dynamics that may become quite intense. On the one hand, the adventure leaders are encouraged to guide participants to become aware of their feelings about trust, risk, commitment, self-confidence, and personal resources; yet on the other hand, leaders are told to beware when dealing with emotional conflicts, interactional difficulties, depressive and self-evaluative moods, and recurrent traumatic memories. On the one hand, the leader is to ensure that all participants have an opportunity to be a part of the processing group, but on the other hand, they have neither the skills nor the guidelines to appropriately direct the over-aggressive, over-reactive, group-dominating individual, or to involve the withdrawn, frightened, untrusting participant.

This leads to a great deal of frustration for outdoor leaders as they search for answers to the important questions of when to process, how to process, how much to process, and how to deal with complex psychological and social dynamics. The experts concerned with leadership training for adventure facilitators usually argue for some training in psychological group leadership. However, because new leaders are being trained in such a wide variety of settings and disciplines, it will be a long time before the majority of them have any significant amount of skill training in psychological counseling and/or group dynamics. (Note: It will be an even longer time before any significant number of the professionals with psychological and groupwork background reach out to tap the tremendous therapeutic growth potential of the adventure sequence.)

Three guidelines for outdoor leaders now in the field may offer some clarification of the frustrations and confusion that surround the whole issue of debriefing or processing:

1. Traditional processing (sharing groups) is of great value at times, and this methodology can be used by the lay leader who is willing to follow some of the basic guidelines for any growth group sequence. Leaders must carefully avoid the errors of "overprocessing" and "underprocessing," and must be aware of a group's readiness and potential for processing.
2. Alternative methodologies for processing the adventure experience are available; they are perhaps more desirable than traditional processing for some groups and at some times. Most of these alternative methodologies do not require the leaders to be as complexly skilled as the traditional sharing circle does.
3. Emergency procedures and strategies for dealing with the individual or group "crisis" in psychological or group dynamics are important. Just as we want leaders to have valid emergency

procedures for dealing with technical problems and physical crises, so they should also be prepared to deal with the "emotional distress" or "psychosocial emergency" of individuals and groups.

The purpose of this chapter is to elaborate on the second guideline above, providing adventure leaders with some ideas for alternative processing. The alternatives are certainly not offered in antithesis to the procedures of traditional sharing circles, and all adventure leaders should keep developing groupwork skills for the traditional style of processing, in addition to developing some alternative methodologies. Therefore, before presenting ideas on some of the suggested alternatives, the following is a brief elaboration on the first and third guidelines above.

TRADITIONAL PROCESSING

The circle-sharing group is the most basic of all groupwork arrangements. The members of the group take "time out" from the essential adventure experiences and share their concerns, feelings, reactions, insights, conflicts, awarenesses, and appraisals of the task. The leader's job is to facilitate an atmosphere of trust and honest communication, wherein all group members find acceptance and understanding sufficient to reveal true feelings, fears, and conflicts. The sharing of these emotions and revelations, with the acceptance/support of the group at hand, leads to personal growth and learning.

There are two problems that good leadership must recognize and avoid. First, there is the problem that can be called "overprocessing." This involves the group, or particular individuals within the group, taking too much time to process. Individuals, or groups, can procrastinate, reiterate, or chatter irrelevantly ad infinitum. They can deal with tangential issues, life histories, and defensive babbling or safe conversation. Granted, groups will deal with these sorts of problems in their own way and in their own time, if that time is available; but in the time-limited typical adventure sequence the leader must assume responsibility for skillfully guiding the group away from the extraneous and toward the timely termination of the processing.

The second problem that good leadership must recognize and avoid is that of "underprocessing." This involves the group, or selected individuals, not taking sufficient time to allow everyone to share and process their feelings and reactions. Some adventure leaders do not fully recognize the value of the debriefing exchange and cut the procedures short. Others may be overwhelmed by the unfolding intensities and will turn the group away from important issues by interventive strategies. There is no easy answer to the question of how much processing is sufficient, for that depends on the group and the situation at hand. However, leaders must come to recognize that there is a time to stay quietly in the process circle and a time to move on to the next adventure activity.

Perhaps even more important than recognizing and dealing with the problems of "overprocessing" and "underprocessing," the leader has the responsibility for setting the climate of the whole processing exchange. Gendlin (1972) has suggested that the leader is really responsible for only two things: to "protect every member's belongingness if it is endangered," and to "protect every member's right to be heard if it is lost."

Carl Rogers (1970) has stated this in terms of his own goals in the group. He writes:

> I wish very much to make the climate psychologically safe for the individuals. I want them to feel from the first that if they risk saying something highly personal, or absurd, or hostile, or cynical, there will be at least one person in the circle who respects them enough to hear them clearly and to listen to that statement as an authentic expression of themselves.
>
> I listen as carefully, accurately, and sensitively as I am able, to each individual who expresses himself. Whether the utterance is superficial or significant, I listen. To me the individual who speaks is worthwhile, worth understanding. Colleagues say that in this sense I validate the person. (n. p.)

The leader's role in creating the atmosphere for sharing and caring, trusting and risking, growing and learning, is delicate and difficult. It requires an awareness of, and an appreciation for, some of the basic ground rules for groups. Leaders should not dictate these basics to the group so much as to be them, to reflect them, to reinforce them, and to be aware of their importance.

1. Everyone belongs to the group just because they are here. No one has to accomplish or meet anyone else's expectations. If everyone in the group gets angry or frustrated with one person, that person still belongs to the group. If someone gives up on him- or herself, the group does not give up on that person. If one member of the group is selfish, unfair, hostile, or withdrawn, the group may say so, but it does not reject him/her from the group.

2. Connectedness is important, and our first goal is to make significant contact with each other. Gendlin notes that "contact is something felt. It is like looking someone in the eyes and knowing he [sic] sees you" (Gendlin, 1972). Once a group begins to connect and everyone feels the acceptance, the safety, and the attempted understanding, then all other purposes and intentions of the group will be possible.

3. Everyone listens to everyone. In fact, some of the early activities for processing groups may be to cultivate good listening skills for all group members. Our listening is a sincere attempt to understand and to really know what is being shared. We listen in a manner that lets others know that we accept their words, their feelings, and their totality as people. Roland has put a primary request on the group leader to "be sure to accept student feelings" (Roland, 1982).

4. Non-verbal language is important, and we attempt to tune in to the cues of body movement, facial reactions, and touches. Early groupwork exercises may seek to cultivate non-verbal communication and break down barriers to the realm of touch. There is often a meaningful communication between group members during periods of inaction and total silence (i.e., interactional touch).

5. Honesty and congruency are our goals in sharing interaction. Each group member tries, as best as he/she can, to get in touch with the reality of his/her own attitudes, feelings, values, and perceptions, and attempts to express them as they are. There is a guideline of "say what you mean and mean what you say," and efforts are made to resolve conflicts between two sets of values or feelings, or between feelings and overt behaviors. It is quite acceptable to be a bit "incongruent" at times, with behaviors, feelings, values, and verbalizations in apparent conflict; but we seek to resolve these conflicts and to express ourselves with greater "congruency."

6. The group has healing capacity. Rogers (1970) has noted that "one of the most fascinating aspects of an intensive group experience is to observe the manner in which a number of the group members show a natural and spontaneous capacity for dealing in a helpful, facilitating, and therapeutic fashion with the pain and suffering of others." This implies, of course, that the leader is certainly not solely responsible for facilitating the growth process.

7. Everyone needs to take part in decisions in some way. Whether we set a format of "decision of consensus" wherein everyone must agree, or a format of democratic majority rule, each member of the group must have input. If we neglect the feelings of any one group member, then that decision may be futile. Even in the situation of autocratic and authoritarian decision making, as when the leader judges that time constrictions require promptness, it is important to discuss the necessity of the decision with the group and allow them to express their feelings about the decision.

Any list of guidelines or ground rules for process groups could be much longer, but the above seven points are basic and important. If leaders understand them, then the group will develop a pattern of meaningful processing in the tradition of the sharing circle.

EMERGENCY PROCEDURES FOR DEALING WITH EMOTIONAL/SOCIAL CRISIS

Adventure/challenge experiences can stir up intense emotions and engender group dynamics crises. Participants may feel panic, emotional collapse, and interpersonal conflict when activities are in progress; some individuals may find themselves in deep emotional arousal and serious anxiety/depression/panic states, or in some intense interpersonal conflict regarding trust or safety. While the processing group can offer an opportunity to defuse some of these distress situations and offer the individuals an opportunity to work through some of the confusion and pain, that same process-group interaction can create an emotional/social crisis. The very intensity of the group experience can foster emotional distress or trigger interpersonal problems.

The adventure leader is not expected to set broken bones, but he/she must be able to make splints for travel and provide effective First Aid until proper attention can be obtained. The teams course leader is not expected to suture the cut or splint the sprained finger, but there must be proper First Aid and follow-up nursing/medical care as necessary. It would seem that outdoor adventure leaders should also have some understanding of what could be called "psychological First Aid," necessary in situations of emotional/social crisis.

In addition to emergency procedures at the time of the adventure experience, the adventure leaders must also have knowledge of available

288

professional consultation as required. Hopefully, as more mental health professionals become familiar with the therapeutic potential of the outdoor experience, they will begin to exchange ideas with outdoor leaders. Of course, as with the leadership training for dealing with medical/physical/ technical/geographic/weather emergencies, there cannot be cookbook plans that cover all situations, and the judgmental competencies of the leader will be called into play. However, we do need to think about some standards and suggested guidelines for dealing with some of the more typical and probable psychological and social emergencies that might occur during the adventure trip as a result of the intensity of group processing.

While one would want to alert adventure leaders to the need for psychological First Aid, that does not imply that leaders cannot facilitate meaningful (and safe) processing groups. That would be a misinterpretation akin to saying that those who advocate standard medical First Aid for the adventure leader taking groups camping are implying that the leaders should not venture where accidents and medical emergencies might occur. Lay leaders can facilitate meaningful process groups, but they should be prepared to deal with potential psychological and social crises.

ALTERNATIVE METHODOLOGIES FOR PROCESSING

One of the most effective ways for the adventure leader to deal with the issue of processing is to make use of some alternative methodologies. Some leaders are simply too uncomfortable with the more intense psychodynamics of the group-sharing circle, and some groups are simply not ready or willing to work in that traditional format. Some situations and time lines do not lend themselves well to group discussion. Rather than bypass or minimize the important step of debriefing or processing, it would be desirable to have alternative methods. Before presenting some suggestions for different patterns of processing, there are clear advantages to these alternatives.

1. Many of the alternative methodologies for group processing are activities in and of themselves and can be especially valuable as warm-up and group-building adventure experiences. If one attends to the important issue of "sequencing" in the development of individual and group readiness for the higher-order risks and adventures, these exercises can be significant. As these adventures build the

group, they can prepare the participants for techniques of processing the adventure later on. (Most of these alternatives are true adventures themselves.)

2. Many of the suggested alternatives for processing are viewed by individuals and groups as quite safe and nonthreatening, yet they do provide for much sharing and basic group interaction. The more traditional sharing circle can be quite anxiety-producing for many, and this anxiety results in withdrawal, defensiveness, or frustration. Groups can be guided to interaction and trust exchanges via activities that are quite acceptable to all. At their best, warm-up and process-readying exercises that the group perceives as light and safe are in reality more complex than group building.

3. Some of the suggested alternatives for processing are more appropriate for individuals than groups because they can be more available and meaningful for those people who are reluctant to interact and share in the group. I have even heard the argument that leaders need not worry about processing at all because what is really important for each individual will surface later on and will eventually be processed by that individual. This is not to say that all individuals will or should be left alone to process their own adventure experiences, but it does point to the need for professionals to acknowledge this role of each client in processing.

4. Most of the suggested alternatives for processing are more structured than the traditional sharing circle, and thereby tend to force involvement from everyone in the group. For those persons who find the unstructured open group quite threatening, the structured interaction of an introspection task does get them involved in the process of focusing on feelings and perceptions. Because of the structure of some of the alternatives, they can be scheduled into the full adventure sequence, thus avoiding imbalances between tasks and processing.

5. Finally, a major advantage of the alternative methodologies is that they require less sophistication of psychological and group dynamics skills. Some years ago, when I began to explore alternatives to standard processing, I was concerned with helping lay leaders to develop strategies that they could apply effectively. Many leaders feel incompetent to facilitate the intensities of the traditional sharing circle and they tend to minimize or avoid a venture sequence. The alternatives as

suggested do not require complex psychological and group dynamics skills; they can be instituted by lay leaders or used by more sophisticated leaders in a more complex application.

Here, then, are a few suggestions for alternative methods of processing. The best way to learn about them is to experience them directly. One might suspect, in fact, that many adventure leaders have already had exposure to many of these exercises, although they may not have considered the possibility of the exercises as processing.

1) **Relaxation/Centering/Introspection**—The intent of historical processing is to provide individuals with insights that can be internally processed and can consequently effect attitudinal, emotional, and behavioral change. There is a component of "introspection" to every processing circle, and each individual will determine, at that time or later, critical issues for themselves.

Therefore, one could consider any situation of individual reflection as a basic alternative to the traditional sharing circle. This procedure has been considered as "relaxation," "meditation," "introspection," or "centering." Most outdoor leaders are somewhat familiar with these methodologies for self-search states. Many leaders use the procedures as warm-up, quiet-time, or journaling assignments. There is a first step, instructionally, of simple progressive relaxation after Jacobsen (1929), with emphasis on breathing to bring the individual to a state of deep inner thought (or even transcendence of thought to a "higher order" consciousness). Two important references are White and Fadiman's (1975) book of activities for awareness via centering. Smith (1981) gives sequential instruction for the phenomena of "gravitational centering," which can be accomplished standing in the forest and seems to have significance as preparation for climbing and other tasks that require balance. Many of the suggested "sunrise exercises," adapted from Native Americans, are also a variation of relaxation, stretching, and energy for personal growth.

In recent years there has been a host of background sound tapes that are designed to guide the listener into greater relaxation. There are tapes of the natural environment, including ocean shores, birds in the forest, loons in the wild, rainstorms, and frog ponds. There are full-tape sequences for relaxation, with verbal instruction to the listener; and there are special "new age" electronic music backgrounds that are designed for body/mind awareness. In case one has trouble finding these special tapes, try the music from Neil Diamond's "Jonathan Livingston Seagull," or Pachelbel's Canon in D.

Breathing is a basic and important dimension of relaxation and centering. Man can survive some 30-40 days without food, perhaps 3 to 4 days without water, but only about 5 minutes without breathing. In the ancient Sanskrit, the word for air translates as "vital energy." To teach individuals to breathe in rhythm with their relaxation is to assist them to better introspective states. A classic reference on the connection of breathing to tension and relaxation is Dr. Bruno Hans Geba (1973).

Like some of the other suggestions to follow, the exercise of relaxation/centering is an activity in and of itself (e.g., warming up before or "energy down" after). As individuals become increasingly adept at finding a centerpoint of balance, relaxation, peace, and quiet, the activity can be used throughout any adventure sequence. The thesis is that important "processing" is going on each time a person spends a few moments in quiet introspection.

2. **Special Adaptations/Extensions of Introspection**—There are a number of special activities that qualify as processing and that are adaptations or extensions of basic relaxation/centering. All of these activities can be sequentially repeated once the adventure program unfolds.

   a) Special places is an activity where each member of the group finds a particular place in the woods or by the shoreline that appeals to them. The early instructions can be to inspect, to feel, to listen, and to become one with that special place. Individuals will find real joy in later returns to that special place for reflection on activities of the preceding time span. A variation of this is to have each person find "my tree" and then use that station for later processing of self-awareness.

   b) Solos have a long history of being used during 3- to 4-week, outdoor adventure trips; they have also been used for a few hours in the one- to 2-day sequences.

One of my own adaptations of the solo has been to require youths to eat their lunch "alone" and in silence when on a one-day trip to the outdoor experience. The solo is a time to learn of self-sufficiency and individual resources, but it is also a special time for quiet meditation and self-searching.

c) Guided fantasy is a powerful addition to the basic relaxation state. The leader gives verbal input or direction that tends to steer the person's thought processes in a certain relationship to eidetic imagery (e.g., Ahsen, 1973). Many of the basic methods of guided fantasy are based on complex Gestalt psychological theory, but there have been many extensions to practical situations.

For example, leaders can use guidepost suggestions as preparation for activities to follow, in a pattern of mental rehearsal for success. For example, track coaches have had success having runners visualize, prior to the race, themselves leading the others down the stretch to the finish wire. Also, this same sort of visualization process by suggestion can help the individual to recapture the intensities of previous moments (e.g., "You are up on that two-line bridge.").

d) Journaling is obviously an activity for self-processing. Just as leaders can assign time for a return to a special place or personal tree, so there can be sequence time for journaling. This can be an "unstructured" journal with creative, free-flowing thought recorded. It has been my experience, however, that most individuals do much better with a "structured" journal, one that has sentence stems, diagrams, and other thought stimulants.

I often prepare a special journal for an adventure trip, with attention paid to the sequence in which the activities will unfold; thus, the pages of the journal are written with an eye to processing the unfolding events. Some growth and adventure sequences have a special theoretical base, and there can be a specific correlation between the journal and the expected activities.

3. **Dyads/triads**—It is possible for individuals to process significantly in small groups of the total adventure tribe. The dyad, or triad, can be practical when there is limited time, for it can allow each person to share feelings and insights with others in a short time span. In this case, the leader is encouraging individuals to share with each other, which brings all group members into the role of the helpful listener. It is possible to group the many available activities for small groups or paired interaction into four patterns.

   a) *Warm-up dyads/triads.* These are for the purpose of developing community connectedness. There may not be as much focus on real process sharing at this level, but it does set the stage for later interactions. An example of an exercise of this pattern would be a simple, "Find a partner, sit down back-to-back, and talk to each other about your favorite place in the world." Then, after the difficulties of the back-to-back conversation are apparent, "Now, turn around, make eye contact with your partner, and talk about the joys of seeing the person you're talking to."

   b) *Developing listening skills.* This is important in early group or subgroup interaction. Individuals seek to share and be heard, to feel that the other person is really listening and making a conscious effort to understand. Being heard clearly is such an important first step, and people do need to practice listening. I like the exercise called "reflective listening," which is for triads. One person is designated as the listener, one as the speaker, and the final person as the commentator. The message sender is instructed to talk freely on a designated topic (e.g., "Spare the rod and spoil the child."). The listener must then reflect back what was heard, and the commentator gives feedback on the exchange. (Did the communicator communicate clearly? Did the listener hear and reflect back what was said without the distortion of his/her own feelings?) This exercise can improve each individual's listening abilities, enriching alternative processing methodologies that will occur later.

   c) *Structured dyads/triads.* There are many activities in which dyads and triads can participate to illustrate sharing. After the Trust Falls, the leader could break the group into pairs and simply instruct everyone to "talk about trusting others." When time is limited, this pattern of processing can provide every participant with a maximum of available time to talk about the completed experiences and personal insights. There are a host of structured interactional exercises, and many are quite appropriate to adapt to the outdoor classroom (Raths, Harmin, & Simon, 1966; Otto, 1972).

d) *Non-verbal dyads.* Although this suggestion requires one to take a "mystical" leap to the notion that energy exchanges can take place without verbal interaction, it can hold promise as an alternative processing method for some individuals. Again, some non-verbal interactions can be used as warm-ups and group connectors (there can be significant, quiet exchange in eye-to-eye contact or in the special sensitive exchange that unfolds in "touching faces"). The exercise of two eye contacters "mirroring" each other's movements without touch is a significant exchange, and people who seem to connect one-to-the-other can share in silence at later points in the adventure sequence.

4. **Group Exercises**—These are structured group interactions which involve everyone in the group process. These exercises can be grouped into three patterns.

a) *Group-building exercises.* Group-building exercises, while not really interactional processing at the time, can set a mood for the group interaction as the sequence unfolds and can also help everyone to develop good group-listening skills. A group can start with a simple task such as writing a personally descriptive adjective on a 3" × 5" card (e.g., the word that best describes you, or the word that describes some feelings that you have that you don't like). The card is then held to the forehead so that others can identify that word with the face below, and people are instructed to simply move about the room contacting each other. There can be a simple task, such as passing a positive word around the circle, which forces even the quiet people to say at least that one word. These patterns of interaction tend to ready the group for affective exchanges later.

b) *Structured feeling exchanges.* These are tasks which can be structured by the leader to focus the group's attention on appropriate material (personal feelings). I have gotten more mileage out of a little deck of about 50 three-by-five-inch cards, each with a feeling adjective (sad, angry, afraid, growing, moody, worried, joyful, bitter, hurt, used, etc.) printed on it, than with almost any other task in my "good medicine bag." I spread the cards about on the floor before the group, and instruct everyone to pick out the word that best describes how they have been feeling over the past few months, or the word that they dislike most, or the word that they most want someone they care for to possess. Then, one by one, all must talk about their choice, and a significant sharing occurs. This exchange creates a new self-awareness in each participant, and it also readies the group for significant usage of the traditional circle of sharing.

c) *Non-verbal group exercises.* These are short but significant steps toward the potentiality of good energy exchange without words. It has been written: "Some of my knowledge comes from not speaking, some of my speaking comes from not knowing, some of my knowledge cannot be spoken...." While non-verbal group exchanges such as "sun-lofting" and "hands-around" massage, as described in my book of articles (Smith, 1981), are trust building, they also provide for an intense interactional exchange. There is something important going on in the awareness and feelings of the receiving individual, and that is a variation of "processing." Perhaps even more exemplifying is the exercise "Center-of-the-Universe," which involves an individual stretching out in relaxation in the center of the group. All others reach out to simply place a hand on the individual and "think good thoughts, give good energy." After a period of silence, the individual may free-associate thoughts, feelings, and awarenesses of that moment, or let recollections from earlier unfold. The leader can even facilitate the group focus to related issues, (e.g., having the person who had some trouble with Trust Falls earlier in the sequence talk about how he/she feels about the group right now).

The list of suggestions for group interaction, dyads/triads exercises, and the many varieties of relaxation/centering, could go on and on. In general, most of the activities suggested by the human potential movement and the humanistic education movement can be adapted as alternatives for processing. References of general importance would include Stevens (1971), and Canfield and Wells (1976). The ideas are out there, and no outdoor leader need avoid the important step of processing because of feeling overwhelmed by the intensity of the traditional processing circle. Use an alternative, modify, or create, but do provide clients with the opportunity to process those important feelings.

Dr. Tom Smith is a retired psychologist/wilderness guide who has been a facilitator for personal growth groups and leadership training workshops. He has been a frequent presenter at national and international conferences on experiential learning and challenge therapy, and is the author of three books. He lives in western Wisconsin and spends time in his tree house reflecting on his many learnings along the way.

Footnote

[1] An earlier version of this paper was published in The Bradford Papers Annual, Volume I. (1987). Martinsville, IN: Bradford Woods Outdoor Center.

SECTION 5

RESEARCH OF ADVENTURE
THERAPY PROGRAMS

Craig Dobkin

26

THE EVALUATION AND RESEARCH OF ADVENTURE THERAPY PROGRAMS

MICHAEL A. GASS, Ph.D.

Introduction

While there are a number of issues in the field of adventure therapy that could be considered somewhat controversial (e.g., a particular therapeutic technique, certain ethical standards), most professionals agree that there is a lack of a strong research base. As the field has evolved, this criticism has changed from there being a lack of research in general (e.g., Shore, 1977) to there being a lack of research that is well designed, meaningful, and applicable (e.g., research studies employing appropriate controls or statistical power) (e.g., Banderhoff, 1990; Burton, 1981; Ewert, 1987; Gillis, 1992; Levitt, 1982; Priest, 1992). While certain critical pieces of research have emerged that contribute to the definition and substantiation of adventure therapy, there still remain a number of gaps in the body of knowledge representing the field. Research concerning the effectiveness of adventure experiences as a therapeutic approach has been somewhat successfully resolved, yet a much broader array of questions still remains unanswered. The failure to answer these questions contributes a great deal to the misunderstanding and lack of clarity surrounding the field.

The purpose of the introduction to this section is to elaborate on the importance of research in the field of adventure therapy, outline some of the current weaknesses, and highlight new directions and resulting questions that will lead to future growth. Following this introduction is a series of articles that does an excellent job of leading the way for the development of research areas and a brief annotated bibliography of some of the research in adventure therapy that is readily available to interested professionals.

RESEARCH AND ITS ROLE IN ADVENTURE THERAPY

Priest (1992) stated that the roots of the term "research" come from the Latin forms of "rescisco" (to find out the facts or to understand and know through inquiry) and "servo" (to watch or observe). The process of research in adventure therapy can serve a variety of purposes, some of which include:

1) evaluating program effectiveness with a particular therapeutic technique or specific population;
2) comparing particular program techniques, using this information to select or enhance those techniques that prove to be most effective, and adapting or eliminating those techniques that fail to produce intended results;
3) communicating to others the effectiveness of a particular program;
4) planning, analyzing, prioritizing, and predicting probable outcomes of a particular approach or program;
5) determining how to create and design new programs or particular program elements;
6) providing information necessary to secure funding or support for program development or continuance;
7) describing the components of certain techniques in adventure therapy and how they are similar to or different from other therapeutic approaches;
8) and identifying certain variables, the relationship between which can accomplish therapeutic objectives.

No matter what the reason for using research, there are prescriptive processes associated with acquiring intended knowledge. The particular research process selected usually depends upon the series of answers sought by the researcher. Many of the differences in the approaches to research can be observed in articles in this section of the book. For example, a survey on substance-abuse treatment programs that use adventure therapy techniques was used by Gass and McPhee (1990) to ascertain the current status of programs that use this approach in a variety of program areas (e.g., staff, participants, treatment approaches). These authors used this approach to describe the current status of this segment of the professional field. Using a series of evaluative measures focused on determining program effectiveness, Wichman (1991) evaluated the ability of a wilderness therapy program to change asocial behavior with

302

youths at-risk. This author sought to determine a series of focused outcomes of one particular program. While both of these studies used varying approaches to answer different questions for different populations, the information provided by each investigation contributes to the field of adventure therapy and serves as a valuable addition to the construction of a comprehensive perspective of the field.

It is the combination and interrelated nature of such pieces of research that formulate and define any professional field. Priest (1992) has outlined how information obtained from research achieves this interrelated quality and construction of a particular body of knowledge. The questions associated with this development include the following segments, where the word "it" is used to represent each category of the phenomenon being researched:

1) **Description**—What does it appear to be?
2) **Differentiation**—What is it similar to?
3) **Relationship**—What is it associated with?
4) **Causality**—What is it influenced or affected by?
5) **Discrimination and Regression**—Can it be predicted?
6) **Experimentation**—Can it be controlled?

To show the interrelated nature of these concepts, Priest (1992) has used the configuration of a pyramid. These concepts can be illustrated in the following manner:

A QUESTION OF RESEARCH

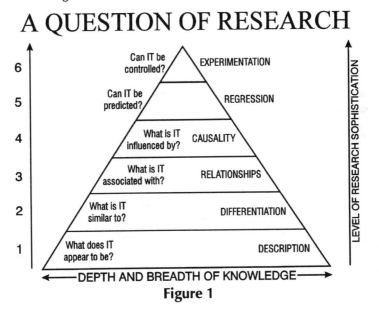

Figure 1

Using the two examples outlined earlier illustrates how the various portions of this research triangle interconnect. The article written by Gass and McPhee provides an understanding of what is occurring with adventure therapy programs used by substance abusers. While the article describes information about the clients using these services, the characteristics of the programs conducting these services, and the staff facilitating these experiences, etc., it does not compare this form of treatment to or differentiate it from other therapeutic approaches. The study does not determine which factors in adventure therapy create effective change, or even that this kind of therapy does create effective change. Instead, this research study represents a foundation of one portion of the field of adventure therapy, describing what this area appears to be.

The article by Wichman represents the other end of the pyramid, presenting one situation where variables are being manipulated to determine specific changes in asocial behavior. As pointed out in the article, the research study shows that a reduction of asocial behavior was achieved, but it cannot answer other associated questions (e.g., What are the specific elements that create the possibility for such change to occur? How are these variables related to other treatment-related issues? Why did change occur and how can it happen again?).

When all of the elements of this "research pyramid" are combined, a valid perspective of the professional discipline is presented. In developing a body of research, areas focusing on the broader research concepts and questions (e.g., description, differentiation) form the basis for producing and answering more focused, specific, and limited research concepts (e.g., experimentation and causality) (see Figure 1). However, without connecting interrelated pieces found through the inquiry process, gaps will still exist in trying to achieve a comprehensive perspective of the field. Without a foundation to describe adventure therapy programming, effective programs lose their ability to interpret and present what is actually being effective in treatment. Without causality, one fails to determine how and if change occurs, and why. As pointed out by Priest, the entire field of adventure learning suffers from not following a progressive investigation of a particular topic area, as well as from not focusing on the "middle stages" of the research pyramid. What is needed to resolve this dilemma is a series of multiple and interrelated approaches (e.g., qualitative and quantitative approaches) to research at all levels of inquiry. When this is accomplished, a clearer and more substantiated base of knowledge concerning what adventure therapy can and cannot truly accomplish will result.

Other difficulties exist in constructing a thorough "pyramid" of research, one of which includes the sometimes vast distance between the researchers of adventure therapy and practitioners who do not have the time, money, interest, or expertise to conduct research into adventure therapy but do need the benefits of research outlined earlier (e.g., substantiation for funding or program continuance). Ewert (1987) has pointed out that much of this difficulty can be attributed to the different needs faced by each group. It is quite common for practitioners to contact researchers wanting "proven statistics" that demonstrate the efficacy of adventure therapy without regard for associated processes or cautioning limitations. Conversely, researchers often approach practitioners to try to gather data, demanding difficult if not impossible stipulations that are necessary for performing "valid" research but are often impossible to accomplish in field settings. Part of the answer to this dilemma requires a proactive and cooperative interaction between researchers and practitioners to determine how the targeted needs of each group can be met.

THE FUTURE OF RESEARCH IN ADVENTURE THERAPY

To resolve these dilemmas, part of the answer lies in mapping out the future direction of the field, determining the critical questions to be asked if such a direction is taken, and identifying where research at all levels of inquiry is needed. In an effort to chart such a future, 27 interested professionals met at a Research Symposium, sponsored by the Coalition for Education in the Outdoors in January 1992, to discuss the current and future state of researching the therapeutic aspects of adventure programs. The discussion covered a variety of issues, but it centered particularly on the research questions that need to be developed and expanded to adequately build the knowledge base of adventure therapy in the next 5 to 10 years. The areas covered in this discussion were organized into six categories of interest and concern. These areas were: 1) treatment effectiveness, 2) issues of training and competence of professionals in adventure therapy, 3) integration of adventure therapy with other therapeutic approaches, 4) treatment issues, 5) clearer definitions of programs, and 6) funding issues.

Each of these issues, their concerns, and areas of research are outlined below. It is hoped that these questions, as well as the resulting inquiries they produce, will assist in providing the direction and impetus for areas of research in the next 5 to 10 years of adventure therapy.

EXAMINING TREATMENT EFFECTIVENESS

In determining the treatment effectiveness of adventure therapy approaches, there is a large degree of concern in demonstrating "what **treatment**, by **whom** is the most **effective** for this **client** with that specific **problem** under which set of **circumstances**" (Kazdin, 1991). Each of these variables, along with the interaction of these variables, needs further examination for the validation as well as the development of therapeutic adventure programs. Some of the questions associated with these analyses could include:

- Are there differences in the effectiveness of inpatient, short-term programs and extended wilderness trips? If there are changes, do they vary depending upon certain population characteristics (e.g., adolescent and adult, acute versus chronic needs)?
- Are there differences in the effectiveness of certain treatment approaches in adventure therapy? For example, do the ways in which adventure therapists process an experience differ (e.g., framing an experience versus debriefing the experience)?
- Knowing that many of the concepts of adventure therapy are based on the idea that activities are "unfamiliar" to clients, what is the appropriate level of "activity sequencing" to use with certain populations?
- What types of research designs would be most appropriate for studying specific types of issues? Alternative designs to traditional approaches to research also need to be explored— these types of designs could include single-subject designs, multiple baseline analyses, case study methods, and qualitative designs. Critical incidents with therapist and clients also need to be further explored.
- What comparisons between other "action"-oriented approaches to therapy can be drawn (e.g., art therapy, expressive therapy, occupational therapy, recreational therapy)?
- Should there be some sort of "Institutional Review Board" for ongoing research in adventure therapy? It could help to direct researchers to critical areas of need in the field, protect clients, and ensure that other ethical practices are being implemented.
- As data bases grow in size, the question of how meta analyses of certain variables and client populations needs to be explored.

ISSUES OF TRAINING AND COMPETENCE OF PROFESSIONALS IN ADVENTURE THERAPY

In this rapidly evolving field, questions have arisen about who is qualified to conduct therapeutic adventure experiences and how this should be regulated (if it should be). This has become a particularly pressing issue given two recent deaths in separate wilderness therapy programs, as well as a move by the Council on Accreditation to regulate the use of adventure programs in group homes. Some of the questions associated with the training of professionals conducting adventure therapy experiences include:

- Who is the most appropriate professional to lead the processing/ facilitating portion of the experience when working with a social service agency (e.g., adventure therapist, social worker, clinical psychologist)? If these groups of professionals work together, what is the best "mix" of talents to achieve the therapeutic objective? Which is "better": to have one person who is cross-trained in providing adventure experiences as well as certain therapeutic approaches, or to have two professionals working in a team relationship to provide appropriate services?
- There are many service providers currently conducting training in adventure therapy practices. Is it appropriate/ethical to conduct "therapy" in these types of experiences as part of the training? If so, what are appropriate guidelines?
- How do we test different training models to prove program effectiveness?
- How do we accommodate different therapist styles in adventure programming?
- Do therapists need a strong background of personal adventure/ challenge experiences? If so, what degree of experience determines an "appropriate" background?
- How long does it take to train an adventure/challenge therapist? Should higher education programs become involved in certifying adventure therapists?
- How do we assess/teach competence in developing profession-als? Is there an appropriate way to conduct self-assessment for therapists? How does the field ensure that professional compe-tence is kept up-to-date?
- Who are the "successful" therapists in our field? Should they be used as mentors for training others? Where are our current leaders coming from? What kind of training did they receive and how do they maintain their professional level of competence?

INTEGRATION OF ADVENTURE THERAPY
WITH OTHER THERAPEUTIC APPROACHES

Many of the current models of therapists using adventure experiences for therapy have been "hybrids" (e.g., outdoor therapeutic recreation, combining social work and adventure therapy, adventure family therapy). As these models are used, a number of questions have arisen:

- What are the potential benefits, as well as concerns, of these models? How can the field best influence more "traditional approaches" to more readily accept them?
- How do we create a positive impact on traditional therapists who work with adventure therapists? What are the best strategies for accomplishing this?
- How can therapeutic adventure programs best interact with insurance companies to acquire/maintain third-party payments?
- How do therapeutic adventure experiences meet/interact with specific diagnostic/symptom criteria (e.g., DSM IIIR)?

TREATMENT ISSUES

Certain issues concerning treatment have arisen in conducting therapeutic adventure experiences. Some of the areas that need further research include:

- What influence do medications have on the adventure process for clients?
- Further investigation is also needed into the influence that adventure programming has on clients receiving medication. For example, effects of heat or cold conditions are known to create potentially negative side effects (e.g., Stich & Gaylord, 1984), but more information is needed to make a final judgment.
- How does the adventure process vary for clients with particular diagnoses?
- What are certain contraindications for therapeutic adventure experiences (e.g., forcing survivors of sexual abuse to perform a Trust Fall)? Should there be identifiable and written "red flags" cautioning the use of certain adventure experiences with certain populations?
- Should there be a "data base" of information identifying certain activities as being most effective with a particular population?

308

- What influence does the composition of a group have on the effectiveness of treatment during adventure experiences? For example, Gass and McPhee (1990) have raised the issue that treatment might be compromised when groups contain members with different treatment diagnoses and when new members are introduced to pre-existing treatment groups. These variables need further investigation to examine the validity of these claims and the potential for concern.

CLEARER DEFINITIONS OF PROGRAMS

There was a concern among the participants at this workshop that the profession needs to be able to differentiate between the types of programs delivering adventure therapy services. If there were to be classifications of adventure therapy programs, some of the areas would include:

- **Length of time of treatment**—Concerns were raised about what can reasonably and ethically be accomplished in a given time frame. This was a major concern of those professionals working in inpatient settings where there has been a decrease in the number of treatment days that insurance companies will reimburse.
- **Goals**—Can similarities be found among programs with the same treatment objectives, whether they be behavioral, psychosocial, or cognitive in nature?
- **Level of the intensity of treatment**—One example currently being advanced is a model proposed by Gillis et al. (1991) of recreational, enrichment, adjunctive therapy, and primary therapy programs. This model needs further investigation.
- **Level of training of professionals**—Does the training background of a professional make a significant difference to the outcome of treatment? If so, where, how, and to what degree do these differences occur?

FUNDING

One of the concluding concerns addressed during the symposium was about funding such research projects: where such monies could be obtained, how quality assurance could be ensured, potential impact on various academic departments as well as on federal agencies, how support could be acquired from corporations and other funding agencies—all of these topics were mentioned.

All of the questions above accentuate the obvious need to further develop research in adventure therapy. Professionals must continue to interact and support each other's efforts. It is my hope that the information contained in this introduction will provide part of the basis for furthering the accomplishments of our field in the next phase of its development.

ARTICLES IN THIS SECTION OF THE BOOK

The articles found in this section of the book are meant to provide the reader not with a comprehensive representation of research in the field, but with an initial familiarity with the current state of research into adventure therapy. The article by Gass and McPhee (1990) is included to describe the current state of the field in one particular area of treatment (i.e., the use of adventure therapy with substance abusers). The articles by Gillis and Simpson (1991) and Wichman (1992) represent the current state of outcome studies on the effectiveness of adventure therapy. The study by Durgin and McEwen (1991) provides an important perspective on the influence of time and external, systemic factors on the lasting effect of the changes that occur in adventure therapy. The article by Braverman (1990) outlines a triangulated method of investigating the changes that occur in adventure programs. Finally, the bibliography by Gillis serves as a rich resource for further investigation into adventure therapy research.

27

EMERGING FOR RECOVERY: A DESCRIPTIVE ANALYSIS OF ADVENTURE THERAPY FOR SUBSTANCE ABUSERS[1]

MICHAEL A. GASS, Ph.D.
PAMELA J. MCPHEE, M.S.W.

Introduction

Substance abuse is a pervasive problem affecting every socio-economic class and ethnic group in American society. In addressing the influences of alcohol abuse alone, a 1987 Gallup Poll (Desmond, 1987) found that:

- One in every four families was affected by alcohol
- 10.6 million adults were alcoholics.
- Alcohol was a factor in half of America's murders, suicides, and accidental deaths.
- The yearly economic costs of alcoholism and alcohol abuse to society were estimated at $117 billion dollars in reduced work effort and $13 billion dollars in medical treatments.

Americans spend over one billion dollars annually to provide treatment for individuals suffering from substance abuse (Desmond, 1987). Despite this investment, actual rates of lasting recovery from substance abuse remain relatively low. Some researchers have concluded that there is no treatment modality for adults that has experienced a participant success rate greater than 35% (Babor et al., 1987; Lord, 1987). Other studies (e.g., Emerick & Hansen, 1983) have found this figure to be even lower, suggesting that 7% represents a more realistic figure for the percentage of adults who achieve lasting abstinence from chemical dependence. The recovery rate for adolescents is believed to be even lower (McLellan et al., 1980; Emerick & Hansen, 1983; Desmond, 1987).

An important issue associated with these figures is the definition of "true recovery." While total abstinence from alcohol or other drugs is generally considered to be the best indicator of a successful response to treatment, Babor et al. (1987) believe that it is also important to examine changes in the psychosocial and behavioral factors related to the illness. They argue that initial abstinence may not affect the factors that contributed to the onset of substance abuse (i.e., family difficulties, interpersonal relationships). Changes in these areas are important for maintaining abstinence and are true measures of determining a healthy recovery process.

In order to increase the recovery rates and take into account these contributing factors, a number of innovative approaches are being explored. One promising approach is the use of adventure experiences as adjunctive or primary treatment with chemically dependent individuals. The first such documented program was established in 1978 by the Colorado Outward Bound School in collaboration with St. Luke's Hospital in Denver (Stich, 1984). Since that time, the number of hospitals, agencies, and treatment centers using adventure experiences as therapy for substance abuse has greatly increased.

Adventure programs generally involve placing participants in therapeutic groups and presenting them with a series of sequential and challenging experiences related to treatment. These activities are processed and debriefed thoroughly, focusing on the transfer of what has been learned in these activities into the clients' lifestyles of recovery (Gass, 1985). Special attention is centered on clients observing and understanding dysfunctional behavior patterns (e.g., ineffective coummunication, inability to accept responsibility) and working through the emotional trauma associated with the disease process (Colorado Outward Bound School pamphlet, 1983). Therapeutic adventure experiences also focus on helping the person to overcome negative personal attitudes and attributes such as low self-esteem, immaturity, and dependency (Colorado Outward Bound School pamphlet, 1983).

Adventure programs with substance-abuse populations have grown in number and size in recent years, and though individual programs have published descriptions of their own treatment methods (e.g., Stich, 1984), there has been no attempt to identify how the field addresses substance-abuse treatment through adventure experiences.

The purpose of this study is to describe how adventure programs approach substance-abuse treatment and, most importantly, to determine critical issues and trends. All of the existing programs that could be identified were surveyed to determine the type of clients in adventure therapy programs, the intended goals of such programs, the models utilized for treatment, the methods of reimbursement, staff information, and program evaluation results. The findings of this survey, as presented in the subsequent results section, provide a general but straightforward description of the current state of work in the adventure therapy field with substance-abuse populations. Each piece of information stands on its own, but it is the subsequent integration of the results that illuminates the strengths and weaknesses of the field and raises some critical issues that must be addressed if adventure therapy is to increase its effectiveness and gain greater acceptance.

METHOD

Subjects. Sixty-one programs in the United States were identified as utilizing adventure experiences with substance-abuse populations based on material supplied by the Association for Experiential Education, agencies involved with adventure and/or substance-abuse programming (e.g., Outward Bound, Healthcare International, Experiential Therapists, Inc.), and literature searches conducted in ERIC, Psychology, and Sociology indexes. Each of these programs was mailed a letter describing the purposes of the study, a seven-page questionnaire asking specific questions about their treatment program, and a self-addressed stamped envelope. Fifty of these programs (an 81% response rate) completed the survey. Of the 11 programs that chose not to complete the survey, only one identified a particular reason (i.e., it was felt that the survey violated client confidentiality).

Questionnaire Development. The questionnaire requested information on five areas of adventure programming for substance abusers: 1) clients (e.g., referral methods, age of clients, screening procedures); 2) program characteristics (e.g., length, types of activities, specific goals); 3) expenses and funding arrangements; 4) staffing characteristics (e.g., number of staff, staff:client ratio, training); and 5) specific program research findings.

The questionnaire also listed the programs involved in the survey and asked each respondent to list any other programs that were conducting adventure therapy activities for substance abusers. Prior to distribution, the questionnaire was sent to five directors of substance-abuse programs for review. The reviewers' comments and criticisms were carefully considered by the authors and appropriate changes were made to improve the survey.

RESULTS

Client Information[2]

Client Problems. Of the programs surveyed, 4% worked exclusively with alcoholics, 8% worked exclusively with clients addicted to other drugs, and 88% worked with both populations. Most programs (88%) also worked with populations other than substance abusers. In fact, the survey identified 26 other groups who were sometimes involved in particular programs. There was an incredible diversity among these groups. For example, 66% of the surveyed programs also worked with emotionally disturbed persons, 58% worked with youths at-risk, 48% worked with survivors of family violence, 44% with persons with eating disorders, and 40% with corporate groups. While the number and variety of these other populations was extensive, substance abusers represented 50% of the total client population of the agencies in the survey.

Client Referral and Screening. Most substance-abuse clients in adventure programs (86%) were referred by medical or therapeutic staff (e.g., doctors, counselors) while only 14% of the clients were self-referred. Of those referred by professionals, 35% were referred by a private doctor or counselor, 25% by public agencies, 20% by private agencies, and 20% by staff within the judicial system.

Many programs required routine medical screenings by a medical doctor before allowing substance abusers to participate in adventure experiences. Clients were rarely excluded from participation due to required treatment medications.

Client Age. The age of substance abusers involved in therapeutic adventure programs ranged from 5 to over 80 years old. Forty percent were between the ages of 15 and 20 years.

Program Characteristics

Size, Experience, Affiliation. The average number of persons participating in a program in a year was 50. On average, the programs for these clients had been in existence for 2½ years. Seventy percent of the programs were affiliated with hospitals or treatment centers.

Program Function. Eighty-two percent of the adventure programs identified their program as performing a therapeutic function, and 18% saw their function as primarily diagnostic. Eighty-six percent of participants were in initial treatment programs and 14% were in relapse treatment. Most of the programs surveyed (86%) did not differentiate between initial and relapse treatment groups when conducting experiences, whereas 14% of the therapeutic adventure programs did separate these groups during experiences.

During therapeutic adventure experiences, 78% of the programs combined people with alcohol and those with other drug problems and 15% offered separate experiences. Twenty percent of the programs in the survey utilized a systems approach to therapy (e.g., included family therapy as part of substance-abuse treatment).

Length. Most programs (64%) conducted experiences lasting less than one day in length. Of course the same group of participants could receive a number of short experiences. Only 10% of the programs used experiences longer than 15 days.

Program Activities. A wide variety of adventure activities was used to achieve the therapeutic goals, ranging from initiative games (92%) to snowshoeing (4%) (see Table 1).

Table 1	
Initiative Games	92%
Low Ropes Course Activities	92%
High Ropes Course Activities	69%
Day Hiking	54%
Meal Planning	50%
Overnight Backpacking	50%
Rock Climbing	44%
Solo Experiences	44%
Orienteering	36%
Journal Writing	34%
Service Projects	30%
Cross-country Skiing	28%
Flatwater Canoeing	26%
Whitewater Rafting	19%
First Aid Training	19%
Whitewater Canoeing	17%
Mountaineering (e.g., ice axe use)	10%
Caving	6%
Downhill Skiing	4%
Snowshoeing	4%

Goals. The study also identified the goals used most often in therapeutic adventure programs. Behavior-oriented and psychosocial goals were more frequent than cognitive development goals (see Table 2).

Table 2

Behavior-oriented Goals

Improve communication skills	96%
Increase individuals' abilities to change their lives in a positive manner	90%
Provide motivation to change existing lifestyles	88%
Teach clients social integration skills	80%
Discover new, positive recreational experiences	80%
Provide greater impact/efficiency to the recovery process (e.g., shorten the length of hospitalization for the client)	68%
Teach clients to find and incorporate appropriate alternative lifestyles	60%
Reduce incidence of problem drinking and/or drug abuse	54%
Teach clients the steps of how to work through social integration skills	46%
Find new lifestyle directions	42%

Psychosocial Goals

Increase self-esteem/concept	98%
Increase levels of trust in others	94%
Increase the ability to accept self-responsibility	94%
Confront fears and feelings	88%
Reassess one's own potential	86%
Increase socialization skills	86%
Increase sense of self-competency	82%
Re-evaluate personal values	72%
Increase autonomy (i.e., independence)	60%
Increase levels of maturity	50%
Let go of past, or accept past	50%

Table 2 (cont'd)	
Cognitive Development	
Teach goal-setting strategies and plan for their results	68%
Teach techniques in stress reduction	68%
Teach about the dysfunctional behavior patterns of substance abuse	38%
Teach the A. A. structure and process	26%
Teach the chemical effects of abusive substances on the body	22%
Teach about the disease process	18%

Admission Timing. Programs also varied in the practice of permitting substance-abuse clients to enter ongoing adventure therapy programs. Most programs (72%) allowed new participants to enter already initiated adventure programs, whereas 28% never added additional participants once a program had started.

FINANCIAL ARRANGEMENTS

Sixty-five percent of the programs stated that fees for services provided in the therapeutic adventure program were simply integrated into the total treatment cost instead of appearing as a separate item. Seventy-six percent of the programs received third-party payments for their services. Third-party funding sources included medical insurance (23 programs), county services (8 programs), and state governments (7 programs).

STAFFING CHARACTERISTICS

Most programs in the survey assigned two staff members to work specifically with their therapeutic adventure activities. One staff member usually possessed a master's degree or higher while the other had a baccalaureate degree. The average length of time that staff members had been directly involved as instructors/therapists in adventure programming for substance abusers was 2 years.

PROGRAM RESEARCH

Only two programs stated they had completed formal research on the effects of therapeutic adventure experiences for substance abusers.

One found "a 10% higher sobriety rate with adventure participants than with a control group," and the other found "enhanced levels of cooperation and trust with a higher orientation to team/group versus individualistic behavior." Three other programs stated that they were currently completing research.

INTERPRETATION

The use of adventure experiences with substance-abuse populations has grown at a tremendous rate since the first documented program in 1978 (Stich, 1984). However, as of 1990, most adventure programs designed for substance abusers had been in operation for less than 3 years. While these efforts have received initial positive recognition, there are several issues evident in the results that need to be considered for the field to develop validity and long-term acceptance.

Inadequate Research Base. The deficiency of specific program evaluation and research work is most evident. Only two programs reported having any research conducted on their program's treatment capabilities. While research may not be a priority for many programs in the survey, without it, it is difficult to determine the effectiveness of adventure programs for substance abusers. It is also important to determine the long-term effects of adventure experiences on treatment outcomes. Could adventure experiences create positive short-term change, yet might the developments fade as the client is unable to reinvest in therapeutic adventure experiences? The answer to this question seems vital to the long-term validity and ethical use of adventure therapy programs.

Interestingly, the lack of research did not seem to have a negative effect on most programs' abilities to receive third-party payments. This may occur because most programs (65%) are able to place payment for adventure services under other more traditional forms of treatment (e.g., occupational therapy, therapeutic recreation).

Need for Program Specificity. While substance-abuse participants represented half of the total client population in the survey, it was found that most programs (88%) also worked with other clients receiving adventure therapy. The development of prescriptive treatment modalities for specific client populations must receive greater attention. Therapeutic adventure experiences, like any form of treatment, need to be tailored to the specific needs of the client. Using "blanket approaches" threatens the potential strength of the therapeutic treatment and could possibly interact in a negative way with other forms of treatment for particular groups or individuals. Further research must be performed on the effects

318

of specific experiences on targeted client needs to enhance the therapeutic capabilities of adventure experiences.

It was also observed that very few substance-abuse clients were excluded from adventure therapy based on age, psychiatric medications, or treatment prescriptions. While it is positive that programs are recognizing the adaptability of adventure activities for all ages and populations, the field must also develop a sensitivity to the potential negative effects of certain components of adventure practices. Stich and Gaylord (1984) have begun this process by identifying certain climatic conditions and potential medication side effects that play a significant role in selecting the intensity and duration of adventure activities. Further work needs to be conducted to identify contraindicating conditions, particularly with the use of certain medications and other forms of primary and adjunctive therapies.

Results from several other factors in the survey also raise questions about who should be involved and when. Most programs did not separate clients based on abusive substance (e.g., alcohol versus cocaine) and did not differentiate between initial treatment and relapse clients. These characteristics would seem to influence the planning of therapeutic adventure experiences, yet most programs failed to differentiate client treatment based on these critical factors. Greater investigation into these programming decisions is needed.

There was also a wide variety of survey responses concerning the introduction of clients into existing groups in adventure experiences. The influence of new members has generally been recognized by group development theorists (e.g., Glasser, Sarri, & Vinter, 1974; Kerr & Gass, 1987; Napier & Gershenfeld, 1983) to have a regressive effect on group members, yet a majority of programs (72%) allow this to occur. While there are obvious practical considerations for such practices, it is possible that the treatment effects provided by therapeutic adventure experiences could be hindered. The benefit or detriment of these policies needs to be examined.

Appropriate Goals and Activities. Another confounding factor is the goals of these programs. It seems that many programs attempt to function as a panacea for all of the issues confronting the substance abuser, although there is a greater tendency to focus on behavioral and psychosocial treatment goals than on more cognitively oriented ones (see Table 2). Kimball (1983) cautions against overstating the impact of therapeutic adventure experiences. A greater level of understanding is needed to determine the process- and product-oriented outcomes that truly occur from such experiences.

The survey also found that only 18% of the programs use adventure experiences for diagnostic functions. The use of such experiences in client evaluation can be extremely beneficial. Kimball (1983) and Stich (1984) have done excellent work in detailing the use of adventure experiences as diagnostic tools and further work in this area is needed.

In viewing the types of adventure activities utilized by programs, it seems that those requiring less wilderness exposure (e.g., initiatives, high and low ropes courses, meal planning) are used more often than other types of experiences where wilderness elements are required (e.g., water activities, backpacking). It was not possible from this survey to specifically ascertain the reasons for these differences, although several factors seem to play a major role in choosing the specific activities:

a) the need for treatment centers to maintain year-round programming,
b) the influences of climate and environmental conditions on programming,
c) the strong influence of adventure associations supporting the use of certain adventure activities (e.g., ropes courses) for therapy,
d) the liability constraints of taking clients off the grounds of the medical facility,
e) and the view by some funding agencies (e.g., insurance companies) that if clients are well enough to travel and participate in certain wilderness activities, then hospitalization is not required.

Research is needed to determine how the selection of certain adventure activities affects the treatment of substance abusers. Creal and Florio (1986) caution therapists in adapting adventure approaches, stating that it can compromise treatment efficacy and that deviations need to be carefully scrutinized.

Descriptive research, like the study presented within this paper, provides the basic knowledge necessary for the pursuit of other forms of research. These forms include the ability to predict, control, and explain phenomena within a field of study (Borg & Gall, 1983). The use of therapeutic adventure experiences is an exciting and important development in the treatment of substance-abuse clients. It is hoped that the information and questions provided by this study will act as a springboard for the further development of this form of therapy. However, the issues above need to be addressed to provide greater hope from this approach for individuals suffering from this debilitating disease and a greater acceptance of adventure therapy as a valid form of substance-abuse treatment.

RECOMMENDATIONS

This study identifies areas that require attention by both researchers and practitioners:

1) The need to document the ability of adventure programs to help clients to achieve and maintain sobriety, including an understanding of the actual changes produced in the factors that contributed to the onset of substance abuse.

2) The need to develop specific treatment approaches in adventure programming for this particular population. It is likely that how an experience is implemented (e.g., metaphoric presentation, specific progressions) is as important as what particular activity is selected for treatment.

3) The need to identify which specific behavioral, psychosocial, and cognitive goals are best enhanced by therapeutic adventure programs for this specific population. As a field, professionals must learn where to focus program energies for the greatest amount of client benefit.

4) The need to determine the potential of certain adventure experiences to be an inappropriate or negative treatment for certain people under particular conditions. If therapeutic adventure experiences have the ability to create positive changes, professionals must also recognize that when used incorrectly, they can produce disastrous consequences.

5) The need to understand when substance-abuse clients should participate or be excluded from therapeutic adventure activities. This issue has legal as well as moral implications for programs.

A biography of Michael Gass is listed on the back cover of this book.

Pamela McPhee is the Co-Coordinator of Outdoor Education at the University of New Hampshire in the Department of Physical Education. She is also Director of the Fireside Program and Ropes Course at UNH. She received her M.S.W. from the University of Connecticut and is a Certified Trainer for Project Adventure, Inc.

Footnotes

[1] This article was originally published in 1990 Journal of Experiential Education, 13(2), 29-35.

[2] If the reader is interested in the specific statistical analyses of the demographic variables in the study, they may contact the authors at NH Hall, Dept. of PE, UNH, Durham, NH 03824.

28

TROUBLED YOUNG PEOPLE AFTER THE ADVENTURE PROGRAM: A CASE STUDY[1]

CAROLYN HUTTON DURGIN, M. S.
DOUGLAS MCEWEN, Ph.D.

Structure is a critical component of any rehabilitation program for troubled young people. Case histories of those who have participated in wilderness adventure courses strongly suggest that without effective structure in the follow-up, the initial gains in positive behavior are short-lived (Hutton, 1988). As Nold and Wilpers (1975) stated over 15 years ago, adventure programs are only one part of the rehabilitation process.

Wilderness adventure programs for troubled young people, particularly those in the correctional system, became popular in the 1970s as correctional officials searched for alternative methods to increase the effectiveness of programming and to reduce the overcrowding in training schools (Kimball, 1980). "The unfamiliar, less secure environment of wilderness encourages developing new perspectives on old patterns and assumptions" (p. 8). Despite the early enthusiasm, many correctional officials remained skeptical of adventure programs because of indications that positive effects lasted no longer than 6 months to a year (Kelly, 1974). While further studies have indicated some positive effects, such as improved attitudes (Golins, 1980), a body of literature has not emerged that conclusively supports the long-term positive changes in behavior for troubled young people as a result of participating in adventure programs (Hutton, 1988).

Part of the responsibility for creating longer-lasting changes in behavior lies in follow-up programs after the course. Peer pressure and stress in the home environment make it difficult for these young people to maintain the positive behavior patterns learned on the course. Immediate follow-up support from community counselors would seem necessary to make the new behavior a part of a daily lifestyle (Golins, 1980).

> Changes in self-image brought about during the Outward Bound course may be dramatic, yet it is unlikely that these changes will be lasting if there is no one to help the juvenile discuss, evaluate, and integrate his [sic] learning into community life. By establishing follow-up programs that help the delinquent make the transition and sustain improved self-image, social workers can make significant contributions to the work with juvenile delinquents (Kaplan, 1979, pp. 45-46).

This article presents four case histories of what has happened to young people after their adventure courses. They raise important questions about the role of follow-up and the long-term effectiveness of adventure programs that need to be addressed by the field.

DOCUMENTING COURSE AND FOLLOW-UP CASE HISTORIES

The subsequent case histories were documented as part of the follow-up program associated with an adventure course for troubled young people offered through the Touch of Nature Environmental Center at Southern Illinois University. The 30-day course consisted of an initial immersion in individual and team initiative courses, backpacking, canoeing, rock climbing, rappelling, caving, orienteering, and basic camp craft. This was followed by a 3-week expedition which included a solo experience. There were 10 to 15 young people in each group. Following the course, a Touch of Nature staff person went to the home community to meet with each young person and his/her family and counselors to review what was learned during the course. Each youth was then assigned an advocate who was a paraprofessional working for the Touch of Nature Center. This advocate would meet with the adolescent on a weekly basis and report on his/her progress toward achieving agreed-upon goals. The advocates worked in conjunction with community social workers from youth-serving agencies to reinforce the skills learned during the adventure course.

As a result of the advocacy program, a quantity of records were accumulated on the progress of each troubled young person after completing the adventure course. Three types of records were extremely important. First, there was the Wickman Andrews Behavior Intervention Scale (WABIS). The WABIS scale contains a rating of 40 behaviors typically exhibited by delinquents and was filled out on a regular basis by the advocate. This rating helped to characterize the young person in relation to his/her progress toward stated goals. The second source of information was the Youth Evaluation Statement (YES), written by the advocate after weekly meetings between the advocate and the young person. It evaluated the progress toward goals set in the areas of family, school, work, peers, and counseling. The third source of information was a fact sheet completed by trip leaders at the end of the adventure course prior to the advocacy program. This listed a number of biographical details on the young person's community and family. The use of three data sources provided a means to cross-check information for consistency.

Records were kept on hundreds of young people who participated in the adventure course and subsequent advocacy program. Unfortunately, most records were not filled out in a complete and orderly fashion. Of all the records accumulated, only four cases could be found with detailed unbroken reports for a period of 6 to 18 months after the adventure course. What follows are these case histories. While one could argue that they are atypical of this population, we do not think so. Most of the other files examined showed troubled young people following similar patterns. Despite the limitations, we believe that these case histories are based on the best records yet reported for a follow-up program for troubled young people.

FOUR TROUBLED YOUTHS

Steve

Steve was a 15-year-old in the eighth grade, who lived with both parents, used marijuana and cocaine, but had no prior court record. From the reports it appeared that the father had a drinking problem and abused his wife. The mother loved Steve, but vented some of her frustration with the family situation on him. Both parents felt that Steve had a poor attitude. Steve's father was concerned about his drug use and his mother agreed to family counseling. However, they were unable to consistently implement suggestions such as father-son talks, recognition of improvements, and required chores.

Steve appeared to change his attitude during the adventure course. He learned to trust the course leaders and spoke to them about his problems. However, he did not improve his communication skills or reduce his tendency to threaten others. The leaders felt that he needed continued counseling support after the course.

Steve's progress was poor after the adventure course. He had a number of absences from school and continued to socialize with friends with known delinquent behaviors. However, one month later, when one of his friends went to jail, he began to think about improving his behavior and selecting better friends. Several weeks later, Steve was assaulted by his father. He left home at this time and continued to make new friends who were in constant trouble. His performance in school deteriorated, so school officials and the advocate recommended that he be sent to a children's home. Here his attitude and behavior improved, but after several months at the children's home, he stole a vehicle and was arrested by the police.

While the records indicate that Steve's undesirable behavior became more frequent soon after the wilderness course, it appears that much of this can be attributed to the poor family environment. Steve is quoted in one of the reports as saying he changed his attitude after the adventure course but the family did not. The family was a definite hindrance to Steve's progress. He did not respect his parents and felt that his mother failed to prevent the father from disrupting the family. Steve tried to change his attitude because of experiences in the adventure course, but these feelings were overwhelmed by anger with the family, and sustained positive behavior never resulted.

Sandra

Sandra was 17½ years old and had completed the 10th grade. Before taking the adventure course, she had no court record, but she did have difficulty with friendships, parents, foster parents, and school. She did not live with her natural parents who were divorced. Her mother abused over-the-counter and prescription drugs, was unemployed, and was not very involved in the advocacy program. There were communication difficulties with her natural father.

During the adventure course it was reported that Sandra became more assured of herself, less afraid of trying, and more cooperative with others. Although Sandra was committed to the goals that she had established on the course, she was sometimes moody and rebelled with no warning. This could be due to the lack of continuity in her life and the fact that many of her foster-home placements were unsuccessful.

After the adventure course, Sandra moved to a new foster home and began school. Three months later she attempted suicide after having an argument with her foster father. She was subsequently placed under psychiatric care for 3 weeks and then moved to a group home. Throughout the follow-up period, she continued to have trouble forming friends.

There was no unusual turning point in Sandra's follow-up program. She continued to have communication problems with her father and felt rejected. This, combined with various disruptions in foster homes and unpredictable emotions, contributed to her overall lack of ability to perform the new behavior learned on the course.

Tom

Tom was a 15-year-old who had completed the eighth grade. He had a history of chronic truancy, disruptive behavior in class, running away, and smoking marijuana. For a period he lived with his aunt and uncle in Florida, but he moved back with his father, stepmother, 17-year-old brother, and stepsister. The stepsister became a drug dealer and moved out, and Tom would join her for extended periods of time. The parents tried to help him by increasing family rules and talks, but these changes were short and inconsistent.

After being charged with battery, the court forced him to enroll in the adventure course as an alternative to jail. Thus Tom entered the course with a negative attitude and felt he had no real problems that needed changing. Throughout the course he exhibited negative behavior that included running away, fighting, not doing his duties, sniffing white gas, and throwing his pack over a cliff. Ultimately, he decided to improve his behavior and complete the course. His instructors felt that Tom had gained some feeling of accomplishment and a new attitude toward home and school. However, they felt he needed constant counseling to complete goals and make appropriate decisions.

After the course, Tom's goals were to attend school, stop fighting, meet weekly with his advocate, and live with his parents. For the first month Tom appeared to make great progress. He and his father gained each other's trust. Tom no longer associated with detrimental friends except for his girlfriend. However, at the end of the first month, he was accused of exposing himself. By the end of the ninth month after the adventure course, Tom had left home and was staying with a transient. Tom knew that he was in error but would not return home to the strict discipline of his parents. He felt that they didn't provide a sincere family environment; they were spending too much time at bars and were not trying to communicate with him.

After Tom ran away from home and refused to attend school, the court initiated a new advocacy program. However, he refused to cooperate, missed appointments, walked out of meetings, refused counseling, refused offers for jobs, and continued to associate with undesirable young people. Much of his behavior at this time could probably be attributed to the use of drugs supplied by his stepsister. Finally, the second advocacy program was terminated and the agency recommended a residential drug treatment program to help Tom overcome his dependency on drugs and work through his many emotional problems.

In summary, Tom had a long history of multiple behavior problems. While the adventure course temporarily improved his attitude and actions, his undesirable family environment and his stepsister's drug culture made it too easy for Tom to regress. He saw no real need to change, and despite constant counseling support, he sunk into a drug culture. The final report described Tom's attitude as "I do not care."

Greg

Greg was a 14-year-old seventh grader living as the only child with his parents in a well-maintained, clean home. The family was poor; both the mother and father worked for minimum wage. However, Greg received an extraordinary part of the family resources. Greg was physically strong and intimidating. He liked sports, but did not accept discipline, fought with his father, had no respect for others, had a severe language-abuse problem, skipped school while his mother was at work, and was hyperactive. He had a long history of social problems.

His parents eventually agreed to family counseling and Greg entered an advocacy program one year before he was referred to the adventure course. During that year, he lived with his parents for the first 4 months. However, after a violent fight with his father, he was placed in a group home where his behavior and attitude improved. Unfortunately, after his return from the group home to his parents' custody, his behavior regressed. Greg, who had been sexually abused by a neighbor, was suspected of being promiscuous with other boys.

Greg participated in a 30-day adventure course. Due to the fact that he was slow, clumsy, and inattentive, he became the group's scapegoat. He also lacked self-confidence and ran away several times. However, by the end of the course he began to assert himself to a greater degree and became less of a scapegoat. The instructors felt that he needed much structure to help confront his problems.

After the course, Greg's goals were to attend school daily, follow his parents' rules, concentrate on his homework, and cooperate with his teachers. Greg's commitment to his goals was weak. He had no self-discipline and no respect for his parents. The parents were unable to consistently practice what they learned in family counseling. In the first month after the adventure course, Greg was placed in a special hospital program for behavior problems. By the second month, Greg's parents could not control his behavior.

His behavior deteriorated in the months following the wilderness course. This was attributed to his being in the custody of his parents. They demanded strict discipline but made inconsistent demands, lacked patience, and refused to believe their actions contributed in any way to his overall behavior.

Despite the constant counseling support and the attempts of his parents, Greg was ultimately expelled from school because of truancy and abusive behavior. He also left the advocacy program. It is assumed that he eventually left home and his fate is unknown.

CONCLUSIONS

It is apparent from these case histories that an adventure course is only a small part of a troubled young person's life and that these outdoor experiences, by themselves, have limited impact upon changing their behavior. The records of other cases reviewed, while not as complete as the four presented, produced similar conclusions. Troubled young people may leave an adventure course with positive behaviors and good intentions to achieve desirable goals, but these changes, no matter how small, are soon lost in the struggle against poor family interactions and negative community environments. The advocacy follow-up program, its counselors, and the youth agencies, simply could not provide the intensive services each young person required. Tragically, Steve, Sandra, Tom, and Greg were unable to sustain a positive behavior pattern in the face of an essentially unchanged home environment and negative peer pressure.

These case studies raise some fundamental questions about the value of adventure programs for troubled young people. It could be argued that it is unethical and inappropriate for any organization to run an adventure program for troubled young people without a strong community follow-up involving significant others. Clearly support from family and peers is a key to sustaining positive changes initiated during the adventure course.

In the face of tremendous obstacles within the young person's home environment, what steps can be taken to improve the effectiveness of an adventure course and follow-up program? While there is a lack of empirical or narrative research to support any strong statements, the authors do wish to offer some suggestions.

First, more care needs to be taken in selecting young people who have the highest prospects for success in adventure courses. One important factor is age. Younger candidates, 10- to 13-year-olds, are probably more able to change than 17-year-olds with criminal records and well-established behavioral patterns. Improved pre-tests of the young people would also be helpful in identifying those most likely to succeed.

Second, longer adventure courses might help to more firmly establish desirable behavioral changes. Reports reviewed in this study suggest that many troubled young people are just beginning to make positive changes when the course terminates. Perhaps more time could be spent at base camp after the field trip to reinforce positive changes.

Third, it is absolutely essential that every adventure course for troubled young people be integrated with a follow-up support program. The advocacy program reported in these case studies is one example and even then, success was often not possible. Follow-up programs need to be strengthened. If the young person's home environment is extremely negative, perhaps direct placement into a sheltered home for an extended period would help to establish positive behavioral patterns and foster some maturity before re-entry. Another possibility is to have short, weekend, follow-up adventure courses to re-establish and/or reinforce positive behavior. These mini-courses could also include family and/or friends to involve all of the young person's significant others in the follow-up.

From beginning to end, each part of the rehabilitation process is essential if lasting changes are to be made in a young person's behavior. Adventure courses can be an important part of that process. However, much more is needed. The trail to success is long and arduous. It appears that we are just beginning to understand how long and difficult following that trail might be.

Carolyn Hutton Durgin completed her M.S. in Recreation from Southern Illinois University.

Dr. Douglas McEwen is a Professor of Outdoor Recreation at Southern Illinois University in Carbondale, Illinois.

Footnote

[1] This article was first published in the 1991 Journal of Experiential Education, 14(1), 31-35.

29

PROJECT CHOICES: ADVENTURE-BASED RESIDENTIAL DRUG TREATMENT FOR COURT-REFERRED YOUTH[1]

H. L. (LEE) GILLIS, Ph.D.
CINDY SIMPSON, ED.S.

Project Choices is a residential treatment program for drug-abusing, adjudicated adolescents that employs the adventure-based counseling model to instill change. Its goals have been to reduce conduct-disordered behavior associated with delinquency and drug use. Thus far, the program has proved effective.

In a recent overview of substance-abuse counseling in community corrections, Haddock (1990) noted options for outpatient programs wanting to initiate effective treatment programs. Many of his suggestions have been incorporated into Project Choices, an adventure-based, residential treatment program for court-involved youths who display alcohol and other drug-abuse issues significant enough to have them come into contact with the state of Georgia's juvenile court system. Project Choices is a program of Project Adventure, Inc., and uses the adventure-based approach to counseling to attack the problem of substance abuse.

PROJECT ADVENTURE

Project Adventure began in 1971 and offers action-oriented experiences on what are commonly referred to as "challenge ropes courses" (Rohnke, 1989). A typical challenge ropes course may bring to mind an obstacle course associated with military training. Most adventure-based counselors, however, have adapted these obstacles to physical challenges that are both individually and group focused. These activities enable clients to achieve specific educational or therapeutic goals (Gass, 1991). When offered as opportunities for personal growth, these activities form a process called adventure-based counseling (Schoel, Prouty, & Radcliffe, 1988).

Adventure-based counseling experiences often begin with warm-ups, structured exercises that allow members of a group to encounter one another, to feel more comfortable interacting as a group, and to begin experiencing the spontaneity of the adventure process (Gillis & Bonney, 1986, 1989). Initial warm-up activities are sequenced to become more physically and psychologically risky, while also communicating a sense of fun and adventure.

The choice to participate when encountering these challenges is seen by most adventure-based counselors to rest with the client. Adventure-based counselors generally follow Rohnke's (1984, 1989) attitude of "challenge by choice." This attitude provides clients with the opportunity to withdraw from an activity at any time. Implicit in the challenge-by-choice philosophy is the guideline that counselors provide the information necessary for clients to make informed choices before an activity begins.

A concept related to challenge by choice is the "full value" contract (Schoel, Prouty, & Radcliffe, 1988). The full-value contract is an adaptation of a therapeutic contract associated with approaches found in Gestalt Therapy, Transactional Analysis, and Reality Therapy (Corey, 1990). With the full-value contract, clients are asked to agree to work together and to work toward their individual as well as group goals. They also agree to adhere to safety guidelines and to a willingness to give as well as receive positive and constructive feedback. Relating these powerful adventure experiences to real-life situations is a primary concern of adventure counselors.

Project Choices attempts to combine effective adventure-based counseling techniques with factors related to effective treatment of drug-abusing adolescents. Prior to developing the program, counselors consulted the research literature to see which elements were necessary to build an effective program for drug-abusing adolescents.

ADOLESCENT ABUSE FACTORS AND SUCCESSFUL TREATMENT

Haddock (1990) noted that the number of individuals in treatment almost equals the number of research articles on substance-abuse treatment. From the sheer number of research articles available, it has been necessary to rely on reviews of literature in the field to make sense of what is state-of-the-art. Several issues raised by reviews of effective programming in substance-abuse treatment are especially relevant to the treatment methods used by Project Choices.

ADDICTION CHARACTERISTICS OF ADOLESCENTS

Newcomb and Bentler (1989), in a review of issues related to adolescent drug use and abuse, noted that the etiology of involvement with addictive substances is related to peer-group drug involvement. Wills and Vaughn (1989) have researched the same issue and found that if the peer group values drug using and abusing and the adolescent has poor relationships with adults (especially family members), he/she is more likely to become involved in abusing substances. A supportive relationship with the family was found to be inversely related to drug use.

Adolescents who use alcohol as a coping mechanism for negative feelings (i.e., anger) and who have positive expectations of alcohol's effects are more likely to follow the path toward alcohol abuse (Cooper, Russell, & George, 1988). Sensation-seeking (Zuckerman, 1979) is also seen as a personality variable related to substance abuse. Here the willingness to risk and the need for excitement have been directed toward uninhibited activities such as excessive drug use. This latter variable is thought to be especially relevant to clients in an adventure-based, drug treatment program because adventure experience is related to positive thrill seeking and risk taking.

The literature suggests the need for treatment programs to 1) teach positive coping skills, 2) foster a peer group that does not value drug abuse but does acknowledge positive sensation-seeking activities, and 3) build a positive relationship with family members that includes positive support and open communication. Haddock (1990) noted that self-help methods like those of Alcoholics Anonymous (1981), and psychotherapeutic methods, such as bibliotherapy, social-skills training, coping-skills training, and individual, group, or family therapy all contribute to effective substance-abuse programs in corrections. The combination of these approaches has also been augmented by alternative programs such as adventure-based treatments similar to what is offered through Project Adventure.

ALTERNATIVE PROGRAMS FOR TREATMENT

Tobler's (1986) meta analysis of drug prevention programs noted that alternative programs that focused on physical adventure (e.g., camping and wilderness activities) were most effective for drug-abusing adolescents. Furthermore, Price, Cowen, Lorion, and Ramos-McKay (1989) described several features of effective prevention programs. Successful programs were found to do the following: 1) focus on a specific target group; 2) aim to promote long-range change by setting clients on a new developmental course; 3) provide an opportunity to learn new coping skills; 4) attempt to strengthen existing support from family, community, or school settings; and 5) collect rigorous research evidence to document their success.

Gass and McPhee (1990) specifically addressed the use of adventure-based therapy for substance abusers. They conducted a survey of existing treatment programs and had recommendations similar to those above. They advocated, among other things, that programs develop specific treatment approaches that use adventure programming for a particular population (adolescents or adults) and that document their ability to help clients to achieve and maintain sobriety (i.e., follow-up). Their research also found that the majority of programs responding to their survey only used adventure-based programming in conjunction with an existing drug and alcohol treatment program and that the most frequent use of such programming was only one day, although multiple one-day use was not accounted for in the survey. The one-day use of adventure programming is perhaps indicative of substance-abuse treatment programs responding to the survey, but not normative for all adventure programming with adolescents as demonstrated by two recent articles.

A SAMPLING OF ADVENTURE PROGRAMS FOR AT-RISK YOUTH

Although not specifically addressing substance-abusing populations, several authors have recently described therapeutic programs for delinquent youths. Clagett (1989) noted the effectiveness of a wilderness experience that lasts from 8 to 18 months. A success rate of 85% regarding recidivism after 6 months is cited as one positive evaluation of this program for adjudicated youths. Successful elements cited in the program include intensive screening for appropriate adolescents, family involvement, and an aftercare component. Similar to other adventure-based (Schoel et al., 1988) and substance-abuse treatment programs (Haddock, 1990), group counseling is used as a primary therapeutic tool.

A program similar to Clagett's is Marx's (1988) outdoor adventure program for adolescents in the state child-welfare system, called Teen Adventure. This 4-month program with an 8-month follow-up consists of wilderness trips and community service projects. Goal-oriented behavioral contracts and home visits are an integral part of the Teen Adventure program. The author reports participant and program success, measured by positive, self-report assessment from participants and their parents. Additionally, the renewed funding by the state for the program contracts was cited as evidence of positive, external evaluation.

Project Choices has attempted to design a program that matches the elements of successful programs for substance abusers and adjudicated adolescents, while extending the length and depth of traditional adventure-based counseling programming to focus on the specific needs of adjudicated adolescent drug abusers.

PROJECT CHOICES

The philosophy of Project Choices uses adventure-based counseling techniques, including challenge by choice and the full-value contract, to encourage young people to develop positive social behaviors and decrease drug-abuse behaviors. This goal is achieved through positive interactions with a firm but understanding staff, along with caring confrontation and consequences given by a group of peers who suffer from similar addictive problems.

Trust in self and others is faster through participation in adventure activities that parallel recovery concepts. Development of this trust is accomplished through designing activities that promote cooperative behaviors between clients. Given a supportive, structured environment where adventure activities are used to therapeutically create positive stress, clients in Project Choices are encouraged to develop increased self-esteem, learn positive coping skills, improve relationships with their families, and value their ability to live drug-free when returning to their home environments.

The incorporation of family dynamics is primary in the Project Choices treatment and transition program. A family atmosphere is created through the use of placement homes and placement-home counselors who serve as "house parents" throughout the treatment and transitional aftercare program. More importantly, clients' family members are included in special weekend programming during the treatment phase of the program and are involved throughout the transitional aftercare program.

ADMISSIONS CRITERIA

The criteria for drug abuse that most Project Choices clients meet come from the Diagnostic Statistical Manual—Revised (DSM IIIR) and include a maladaptive pattern of substance use that includes either 1) continued use despite knowledge of having social, occupational, psychological, or social problems, or 2) recurrent use in situations that are physically hazardous (American Psychiatric Association, 1987).

Most clients are interviewed while in custody at a Regional Youth Development Center (RYDC). During the interview process, background social and psychological information is gathered to 1) determine if the potential client meets admission criteria, and 2) assist in the design of an individualized treatment program. Once accepted into the program, clients live under the supervision of three treatment counselors (two primary and one secondary) assigned to the 8-week treatment phase of the program. The clients reside in Project Adventure placement homes during the 8-week treatment and 8-week transition program. Each placement home and each transitional aftercare home houses up to six clients and is staffed by a placement-home counselor.

PHASE I: TREATMENT

Each treatment day begins with a morning meditation along with individual and group (behavioral) goal setting, and it ends with a Narcotics Anonymous (NA) (1988) meeting and a "debrief." The debrief is a discussion of the processes by which individual and group goals have been met or not met and strategies to improve performances.

Through the use of adventure activities, the group is guided sequentially through simple group and individual tasks to more creative and complex problem solving. The group activities and debriefs are a major therapeutic aspect of the program. Negative behavioral consequences are determined by the group and treatment staff, and they range from a behavioral contract to removal from the program.

The first week of the program is spent camping outdoors. During the first week, pretests are given and clients meet individually with a physician and licensed psychologist for diagnosis. Initial individual treatment plans are written by the treatment staff at the end of the first week, based on background information and diagnostic impressions.

During the second week, the clients participate in numerous drug education lectures. These include the following topics: 1) the disease concept of addiction, 2) denial, 3) family dynamics and chemical dependency, 4) effects of different drugs, 5) drug abuse and AIDS, and

336

6) the 12-step model for recovery (NA, 1988). The lectures are complemented by videotapes and adventure activities. Adventure activities related to substance abuse and recovery topics help clients to visually, actively, and concretely experience their education on addiction issues. For example, an initial adventure activity would ask clients to put on a blindfold to help them understand the concepts of powerlessness and lack of control. Clients are asked to line up in a designated order while blindfolded (Rohnke, 1988). In the group discussion (debrief) that follows, clients are asked to talk of times in their life when they have felt powerless (similar to when they were blindfolded) and times when they have felt powerful (similar to when they found their place in the line-up). The counselors parallel these expressed feelings directly with the drug-education topics of powerlessness and lack of control. The use of adventure activities to parallel addiction concepts is a primary way in which adventure-based treatment differs from traditional treatment of addictions.

The third week is again spent camping. During this period, clients are given increased responsibilities for camp set-up, meal preparation, and clean-up, and they participate in more challenging group activities, which demand increased amounts of cooperative behaviors, increased levels of trust, and more reliance on individual strengths within the group.

The fourth week introduces the first three steps in the 12-step model for recovery and helps clients to look back on their patterns of abuse and determine how their lives have become unmanageable. Individually, clients are responsible for writing their own life story and sharing it with their peers. This ordeal can be a painful look at how their lives have become unmanageable because of their drug abuse.

During the fifth week, the group participates in a week-long backpacking trip. Clients are responsible for planning the menu for the week, organizing the equipment, packing their gear, cooking their own food, setting up their own tents, and generally caring for all elements of the camping experience. The cooperative skills learned during the third week prove to be useful to the group as they deal with backcountry challenges. The attempt here is to teach clients that learning new skills can prove helpful in dealing with later stresses.

In the sixth week, clients are introduced to nonchemical coping skills to prevent relapse. This week is spent developing a specific, individualized plan for dealing with problems when clients are out of treatment and back in their home community. Each client is responsible for identifying his/her triggers that lead to the drug abuse and for developing a checklist of positive actions to replace drug use as a way of coping effectively with their problems.

The end of the sixth week is the family weekend. Clients' family members participate in activities, lectures, and planning sessions designed to promote improved cooperation and communication. The goals for this weekend are to develop strategies for developing a family team. Activities are designed to help families to see their function in their son or daughter's recovery. In individual meetings with counselors, both parents and clients communicate their personal goals following treatment and determine who will be responsible for carrying them out. Educational options for the clients are also discussed, and tentative plans are made for the transitional aftercare phase of the program.

Week 7 is spent developing and implementing two community-service projects intended to demonstrate the need for clients to become responsible members of their community. The first group of clients role-played a drama to elementary school students on the recurrence of addiction in families. After they presented the drama, clients shared some personal life experiences and stressed the need for the young people not to start using drugs or alcohol.

The eighth week involves post-treatment evaluation, testing, and planning for transition to the aftercare program. The transition ceremony includes a brief slide show of activities in which clients were involved throughout the program, awards for the most improved group member, dinner, and progress reports from the staff to the parents and court service-workers in attendance.

PHASE II: TRANSITIONAL AFTERCARE

Clients completing the 8-week residential treatment program move into the transitional aftercare phase for a minimum of 2 months to a maximum of one year. The focus of transitional aftercare is continued recovery through increasing family involvement, practicing relapse prevention skills, exercising independent living skills, and participating in traditional school, GED preparation, or employment.

While residing in transitional care, clients are involved in the following activities: 1) attending group therapy twice a week, 2) attending a relapse-prevention group once a week, and 3) attending a focus group with members of their own sex. The transitional care program integrates the 12-step model of Alcoholics Anonymous and Narcotics Anonymous on a daily basis. The clients are responsible for facilitating a weekly, community NA meeting at the Project Adventure site, which was initially developed by the first Project Choices treatment group.

Family participation is encouraged through visits by the family to the placement home and through clients' weekend passes home. On completion of transitional care, clients return home or are placed in an independent living situation. Completion and placement are decided jointly by the client, a transitional care counselor, a consulting psychologist, the referring personnel, a family member, and an alcohol and drug counselor from the treatment program.

EVALUATION RESULTS

Participant Characteristics

In the first three groups, 29 clients completed the 8-week treatment program, and 27 of the 29 (93%) clients completed a minimum of an 8-week, transitional aftercare program. Of the total number of clients, 17% were women and 83% were men; 38% were black and 62% were white. Project Choice's clients mirror available national figures, which indicate that 93% of juveniles in correctional facilities are boys, 52.5% are white, and 41.4% are black (Bureau of Justice Statistics [BJS], 1990). The average age of the Project Choice client was 15.76 years old, with ages ranging from 14 to 17.

The average number of biological parents in the homes of these clients was 1.18 and the average number of siblings was 1.93. A total of 67% of the clients had only one biological parent in their home, which also mirrors the national average (BJS, 1990). Clients had committed an average of 5.27 offenses, including the admitting offense(s) and violations of probation, with over 50% having committed more than five offenses. This number of previous offenses is slightly higher than the 43% of incarcerated juveniles who have been arrested more than five times (BJS, 1990). The average number of previous hospitalizations for clients was .45, ranging from no admissions for 69% of the clients to two to three admissions for 10% of the clients.

Of the original 29 clients, 79% met criteria for drug abuse, and 21% met multiple drug-abuse criteria. Of the first group, 31% were identified as dealers; the remaining 69% were primarily abusers of drugs. Note that the original admissions criteria included at least one drug offense, and these criteria resulted in the inclusion of drug dealers who did not meet criteria for drug abuse or drug dependence. A total of 61% also met criteria for conduct disorder; other diagnostic disorders included dysthymia, academic problems, and borderline intellectual functioning.

Regarding intelligence levels as measured by the Weschsler Intelligence Scale for Children-Revised (WISC-R, 1979), scores were generally in the average range on the overall verbal, performance, and full-scale intelligence quotient and nearly all subscales. As a group, the clients scored lower on two measures of overall verbal intelligence: *information* (M = 7.00) and *vocabulary* (M = 6.78). Each of these subscale scores is one standard deviation unit (3 points) below the average score of 10 on a subscale, but they are in line with the difficulties the majority of these clients have had with public schools.

The clients who were not enrolled in school at the time of their admittance to Project Choices accounted for 22% of the total number of clients, and 33% of the total number of clients were below grade level. Currently (either in transitional aftercare or placed back in their home environments) 89% of the original 29 clients are attending the local school system, the alternative school at Rainbow Lake (located at Project Adventure's Covington, Georgia, site), or are involved in GED preparation.

As is generally the case among youths who have been adjudicated, these clients scored much higher on performance measures of intelligence than on verbal measures (Sattler, 1982), specifically scoring lower on the comprehension subtest of the WISC-R (*hf* = 6.78). Some authors have speculated that active (less verbal) treatment programs may be more effective than traditional therapies with clients who have higher performance skills due to their inability to have insight into their problems (Hollis & Williams, 1990). This hypothesis deserves further testing. Our current evaluation, supported by Tobler's research (1986), suggests that this hypothesis is correct. One of the ways in which these positive changes is measured is through changes in behavior.

Behavioral Measures

Staff. The Revised Behavior Problem Checklist (RBPC; Quay & Peterson, 1978) was used by counselors as a weekly measure of each client's behavior during the treatment phase of the program. The conduct-disorder scale of the RBPC was used for evaluation of each client's behavior as it was thought to be indicative of the primary problem that leads many of the clients to begin using drugs in the first place. Sample items on this scale included: 1) "Disruptive; annoys and bothers others"; 2) "Selfish; won't share; always takes the biggest piece"; 3) "Blames others; denies own mistakes." Average conduct-disorder scores measured by staff are graphed in Figure 1.

Statistical analysis (ANOVA) for repeated measures revealed an overall significant difference in the scores on the staff's behavioral rating over time, $F(6.96) = 2.38$, $p = .03$. Significant differences were found to exist between Week 2 and Week 8, demonstrating that the counselors noticed specific behavioral changes in the clients over the course of the treatment program. Mean scores for staff ratings as well as peer and self are presented in the figures.

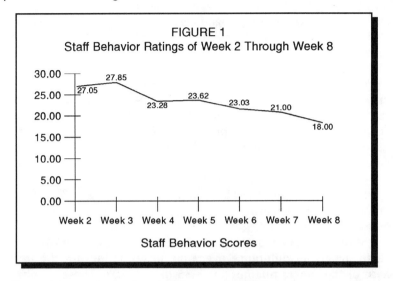

FIGURE 1
Staff Behavior Ratings of Week 2 Through Week 8

Staff Behavior Scores

Peer. A peer behavioral rating was also used as a method of measuring the global behavioral change taking place among clients in the program. Each client was asked to rate every group member on a scale of 1 to 100, with the higher score indicating more negative behavior. Average scores for peer rating are graphed in Figure 2.

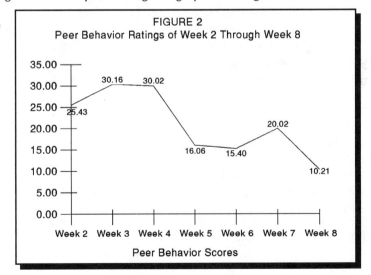

FIGURE 2
Peer Behavior Ratings of Week 2 Through Week 8

Peer Behavior Scores

Statistical analysis (ANOVA) for repeated measures revealed an overall significant difference over time in peer ratings for the treatment phase of the program $F(6.36) = 5.66$, $p = .0003$. These ratings reveal that the clients noted a difference in the behavior of their peers from week to week. There was a significant difference between Week 2 and Week 8, indicating that clients' behavior had improved from the first to the last assessment.

Peer ratings at Week 7 increased from their level at Week 6 and then decreased significantly during the final week. Week 7 followed the family weekend. Perhaps the ratings reflect both the anxiety raised when family members participated in the treatment program and the excitement among the group prior to completion of the treatment phase. It is interesting to note that the staff measures that were more specifically related to behavior and did not reflect a single global score did not reflect the same rise in negative behavior at Week 7.

Self. Self-ratings of behavior reflect the average score clients gave themselves each week, while they were also rating their peers. Self-scores are graphed in Figure 3.

Statistical analysis (ANOVA) for repeated measures revealed an overall significant difference over time in self-ratings for the treatment phase of the program $F(6.36) = 3.35$, $p = .0101$. These ratings reveal that the clients noted a difference in their own behavior from week to week.

The same increase in behavior rating occurred following Week 6 (family weekend) in the self-scores that occurred in peer scores. Again, in consultation with staff (despite their average behavioral rating), these scores were thought to reflect the anxiety many clients felt after having their parents involved in treatment (or in some cases, after not having their parents attend the weekend session). The self-rating score may also reflect clients' anxiety about the transition to the relatively less structured aftercare program that would come at the end of Week 8.

Drug screens and recidivism. Random urine screens for drug use are used during the treatment and transitional phases of the program. At this writing, 99% (112 of 113 total drug screens) of the drug screenings have shown no detection of chemicals. The clients' choice not to abuse drugs and not to enter into conduct-disordered behavior that would lead them back into the jurisdiction of the Division of Youth Services or Department of Correction system is the ultimate behavioral proof of the efficacy of the program.

To date, of the students in the first two Project Choice groups, 87% have successfully completed both phases of the program. A total of 44% have been discharged to their families or guardians and are attending

342

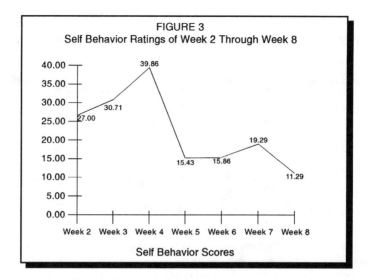

FIGURE 3
Self Behavior Ratings of Week 2 Through Week 8

Self Behavior Scores

school or working. Of the clients still in the transitional aftercare program, 33% are enrolled and attending the Newton County, Georgia, Public School, 5% are in the alternative school at Rainbow Lake, and 5% are in GED preparation.

Contributing to the client's treatment and academic success are other variables that have been assessed prior to and following the initial treatment program. These variables include personality factors and self-esteem.

STANDARDIZED MEASURES

Personality measures. The Minnesota Multiphasic Personality Inventory (MMPI; Hathaway & McKinley, 1982) was used as both a treatment-planning instrument and a pretest/post-test indicator of treatment effectiveness. The significantly different pretest and post-test subscale scores are included in Figure 4.

The decreases in scales of (a) depression (Scale 2: D; pre M = 60.76, post M = 51.83, t = 4.34, p = .0001, (b) obsessive compulsive behavior (Scale 7: Pt; pre M = 60.48, post M = 54.34, t = 3.13, p = .002), (c) disorganized thinking (Scale 8: Sc, pre M = 60.86, post M = 53.55, t = 3.62, p = .0006).

(d) manic excitement (Scale 9: Ma, pre M = 64.31, post M = 60.48, t = 2.49, p = .009), (e) anxiety (A; pre M = 60.48, post M = 53.24, t = 4.33, p = .0001), and (f) control (Cn; pre M = 58.38, post

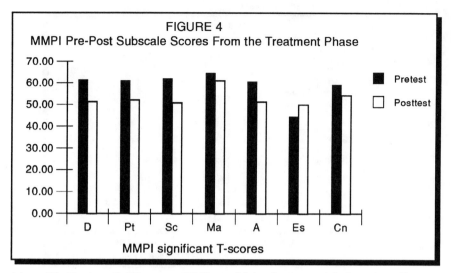

FIGURE 4
MMPI Pre-Post Subscale Scores From the Treatment Phase

MMPI significant T-scores

$M = 52.41$, $t = 3.37$, $p = .001$) could be interpreted that the clients are learning some skills to handle their sad feelings related to alienation from their families and their past failures in school and with DYS.

Note that all of the scores decreased with the exception of ego strength (Es; Pre $M = 42.9$, Post $M = 48.97$, $t = 4.19$, $p = .0001$), which increased from pretest to post-test. This increase in ego strength can be interpreted as the clients gaining skills at benefiting from more insight-oriented, traditional psychotherapy (Archer, 1987). This finding lends credence to the hypothesis that action-oriented, adventure-based therapy may be helpful in allowing adolescents to become more insightful and to benefit from more traditional forms of treatment (Hollis & Williams, 1909).

Self-esteem measures. The Battle (1981) Culture-Free Self-Esteem Inventory was used prior to (pretest) and following (post-test) the treatment phase of the program. As with many adventure programs, self-esteem was shown to increase significantly after participation in activities that encouraged clients to challenge themselves and achieve physically as they had not done in the past. The average scores on the self-esteem inventory are graphed in Figure 5.

Note that the two scores were significantly different ($t = 4.19$, $p = .0001$) and did increase when measured prior to and following the treatment phase of the program. These scores indicate that clients perceived themselves in a more favorable light following participation in the treatment program than they did when they arrived.

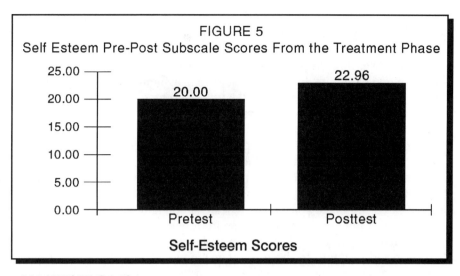

FIGURE 5
Self Esteem Pre-Post Subscale Scores From the Treatment Phase

Self-Esteem Scores

LIMITATIONS

As an evaluation of behavioral and self-reported personality and self-concept changes, this program seems to have had a positive effect on the 29 clients who have participated thus far. Nevertheless, from a research standpoint, these findings lack many of the qualities that could underscore the reliability of the program evaluation. These limitations include the following points: 1) there was no randomization of treatment, because clients were screened for meeting criteria for drug abuse or drug dependence from a population of incarcerated youths in the juvenile system of the state of Georgia; 2) no control group was used with which to compare the behavioral or self-report measures included in this evaluation; 3) using multiple scores from the same test (MMPI) and evaluating them separately with t-tests can produce changes by chance, which might not exist in reality; and (4) because this evaluating was conducted on the first three groups in treatment, small changes in format and content of the programming that took place from the first through the third sessions may have contributed to history effects that influenced the outcome. The programs, though similar in content, did contain slight differences. Despite these limitations, evaluation of the program will continue in an attempt to maximize treatment effectiveness.

SUMMARY AND RECOMMENDATIONS

Project Choices is designed to use the best that adventure education and traditional drug treatment have to offer. Both the observed behavior and self-reported attitudes related to change resulting from participation in this action-oriented, residential treatment program have been evaluated. The data suggests that we are on the right track.

In order for Project Choices to remain effective, the following recommendations are in order. First of all, assuming that the need for residential treatment of adjudicated youths who meet DSM IIIR criteria for drug abuse or dependence remains the same or increases, effective, action-oriented, adventure-based treatment and follow-up must be allowed to progress in order to continue the positive changes in behavior and attitude found thus far. Based on the findings in this study, the continuation of Project Choices may demonstrate the ability of these positive changes to be maintained over time and serve as a more cost-effective means for treating adjudicated substance abusers than incarceration and recidivism. Secondly, with most of the initial clients coming from home environments that have contributed to drug abuse, many of the adolescents treated cannot realistically be expected to return to those same environments and remain drug-free. There is a need to provide long-term transitional homes or independent living situations based on a model similar to what is described here.

Maintenance of these positive changes following discharge from Project Choices and throughout the client's lifetime is the conclusive test of our work. We plan to continue sharing our results in hopes of benefiting from the scrutiny and profiting from the feedback we receive.

H. L. (Lee) Gillis, Ph. D., is an Associate Professor of Psychology at Georgia College and a consulting psychologist with Project Adventure. He works with Project Choices, which has been renamed as Cooperative Treatment Program (CO-OP), as an evaluator, diagnostician, treatment team leader, and group therapist.

Cindy Simpson, Ed. S., is the Director of Project Adventure in Covington, Georgia. She developed Project Challenge, a 6-week adventure program for court-referred youths in 1982, and Project Choices (now CO-OP), which is a 16-week adventure program for drug-involved, court-referred youths in 1990. Both of these programs serve the Department of Children and Youth Services of the State of Georgia.

Footnote

[1] This article was originally presented at the 1991 convention of the American Association for Counseling and Development in Reno, Nevada. Portions of this article were also presented at the Southeastern Regional Conference of the Association for Experiential Education in Charleston, South Carolina, and an earlier version appeared in Project Adventure's newsletter, Ziplines.

30

OF WILDERNESS AND CIRCLES: EVALUATING A THERAPEUTIC MODEL FOR WILDERNESS ADVENTURE PROGRAMS[1]

TED WICHMANN, Ph.D.

INTRODUCTION

Therapeutic wilderness programs involving youths at-risk have always received much popular press because of their dramatic nature; they have been described as one of three models showing promise for the effective treatment of youths at-risk, including violent delinquents (Strasburg, 1978). Psychological data collected in various studies suggest that therapeutic wilderness programs reduce alienation and improve self-concept (Hunter, 1984). Similarly, there appears to be a relatively low rate of recidivism among graduates of therapeutic wilderness programs when compared to control groups or to the 40% national recidivism rate for juvenile delinquents (Kimball, 1980). However, beyond these self-concept and recidivism studies, there is no clear consensus among researchers about why or how to measure short-term, specific behavioral change related to therapeutic wilderness programs. Research tools are lacking, and results are confusing.

There are also few studies of therapeutic wilderness programs that have attempted to measure the effect of process variables on outcome. Bernstein (1973) found that delinquents' performances on 10 wilderness program tasks were positively correlated with the quality of their relationship with their instructors and with the instructors' pre-course expectations for students' performance on the 10 tasks. Andrew (1977) evaluated two therapeutic wilderness programs and found no changes in the self-concept or delinquent behavior of the participants. She also looked at participant-observers' ratings on a "Program Process Checklist" which showed: 1) an inadequate program design, 2) no operational procedures, 3) incompetent staff, 4) no orientation or follow-up, and

5) a lack of understanding of the Outward Bound process. Cave (1979) used a true experimental design to demonstrate that the level of stress on a wilderness course was positively correlated with psychological improvement among young adult males who had been incarcerated in a forensic hospital. Those who went on a low-stress rafting trip did not change, while those in the high-stress mountaineering course improved significantly. These studies suggest that just going camping in the wilderness may not be therapeutic and that it is important to look at the process as well as the outcome.

The research literature presents strong evidence that therapeutic wilderness programs are effective. However, many "compare the impact of the wilderness experience to electricity; we know it works but we are not sure why" (Kimball, 1979). In order to begin to understand why, there must be a theoretical foundation from which specific research questions can be developed that are broadly accepted and highly generalizable. Secondly, research questions and designs must be more than a simplistic look at the effect of the program on self-concept or recidivism (Hunter, 1987).

The purpose of this study was to develop a theoretical model for therapeutic wilderness programs and to explore its validity through multivariate analysis of data collected from the Spectrum Wilderness Program at Southern Illinois University at Carbondale.

Theory

Unfortunately, there is no standard model that describes all therapeutic wilderness programs. Programs vary in length, counseling approaches, client parameters, follow-up activities, and other components. Similarly, there is not a unified theory for such programs. However, the following components, gleaned from the literature, are used by most therapeutic wilderness programs: 1) a wilderness environment (Golins, 1978); 2) a primary peer group (Walsh & Golins, 1976); 3) stress and perceived risk (Cave, 1979); 4) problem solving (Golins, 1978); 5) a humanistic style of instruction (Hendy, 1975); 6) challenge, mastery, and reflection (Walsh & Golins, 1976); and 7) some form of reality therapy (Kimball, 1979). These components have been used, in conjunction with observation of the Spectrum Wilderness Program, to develop a therapeutic wilderness model with two interrelated levels: Level I—the physical environment and increased self-esteem; and Level II—the social environment and reduced asocial behavior. Level I is similar to the model developed by Walsh and Golins (1976) and could be applied to any Outward Bound or adventure program. It is not described in detail here as it is not essential to this study.

Level II of this model, represented in the figure, applies only to therapeutic wilderness programs in which the outcome goal of reduced asocial behavior is highly relevant. The important learning environment in this model is the social one created by the primary peer group. This group must be large enough to generate many complex interpersonal problems, but small enough so that no one can hide.

The role of the instructors is to ensure that this environment promotes growth by creating helping relationships which are genuine and congruent, and by providing unconditional positive regard (see Rogers, 1961).

Interpersonal stress is often the result of a number of factors including physical and psychological challenges, as well as the asocial behaviors students bring to the course.

The wilderness environment often acts as a powerful reinforcer. However, Mother Nature sometimes ignores such asocial acts as stealing food from the group. In fact, the natural consequence for this may be that the perpetrator gets more to eat. Such behavior is dealt with by the group using the Circle. Either students or staff may "call a Circle." All students and staff must stand in the Circle until the interpersonal problem, such as stealing food, is resolved. The process of the Circle is similar to Reality Therapy (see Glasser, 1965). A brief synopsis of such a Circle might go like this:

Instructor:	What are we doing now?
Students:	Joe stole food again, and we are trying to beat him up, but you keep stopping us.
Instructor:	Is this helping to solve the problem?
Students:	No, because it keeps happening.
Instructor:	Can we make a plan to do better?
Students:	What if Joe promises to not steal food?
Instructor:	What are the reasonable consequences if he does steal food again?
Students:	Joe must cook the next meal for the group and give up his rations for that meal.
Instructor:	Can everyone, including Joe, commit to this plan?
Students:	Yes.

If the group, as in this example, confronts the challenge and solves the interpersonal problem, group harmony is increased, stress is reduced, and needs are fulfilled without asocial behavior (see figure on following page). If a group avoids the challenge, the interpersonal problem persists, and fear, discomfort, and stress increase as they stand in a circle in the

Level II of the Therapeutic Wilderness Model:
The Social Environment and Reduced Asocial Behavior

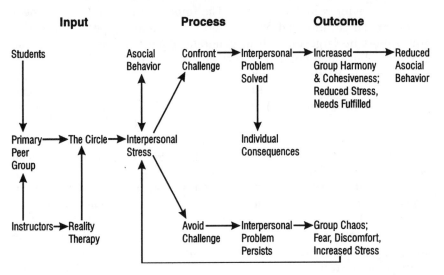

wilderness. It is, in a sense, a metaphor for life. The ultimate goal is to teach students to run a Circle and solve interpersonal problems with little or no input from instructors.

The core of this model involves intense, experiential, interpersonal problem solving. In the lives of many youths at-risk, "doing the right thing" is an order from above. They understand neither what "doing the right thing" is nor how to accomplish it. They lack appropriate role models and tools to develop the ability to articulate interpersonal problems, to conceive of options, to see the necessary means and potential obstacles, and to weigh consequences (Platt & Spivack, 1983).

The experience described by Level II of the Therapeutic Wilderness Model provides the understanding and the tools, as well as the motivation, the support, and the reflection upon experience, necessary to learn these skills. Interpersonal problem solving may be a key to reducing asocial behavior, not only in the wilderness, but also in life. This study was designed to examine some of the key variables in this theory. The purpose of this investigation was twofold. First, it was to determine if the therapeutic wilderness program did reduce the asocial behavior of those youths who graduated. Secondly, it was to see if there were person and process variables from Level II of the Therapeutic Wilderness Model which could predict post-course asocial behavior.

Program

The Spectrum Wilderness Program is a therapeutic wilderness program which offers 30-day courses involving up to 33 clients who are divided into groups of 8 to 11. Three instructors live and work with each group, 24 hours per day. Program staff interview each individual client in the community prior to the course. Instructors also provide a follow-up staffing and individual contract evaluation following the course. Case workers, probation officers, and significant others attend both the orientation and the follow-up sessions. The wilderness course usually includes the seven phases of Immersion, Homebase, Expedition, Solo, Final Expedition, Service Project, and Transition. Typical activities include initiative problems, teams course, ropes course, rock climbing, caving, backpacking, canoeing, and much group processing via the Circle.

Subjects

The subjects for this study consisted of 72 youths at-risk between 13 and 18 years old. Approximately 90% of these young people were referred to the program as a result of a judicial decision, and, therefore, neither random sampling nor assignment was possible. Half of the subjects (N = 36) par-ticipated in the Spectrum Wilderness Program. The control group consisted of those subjects (N = 36) who were placed in the Spectrum Advocacy Program. The Advocacy Program provides a part-time, para-professional adult from the community to spend up to 10 hours per week as a surrogate "Big Brother" or "Big Sister." Since intake into the wilderness program could only occur once each month, the Advocacy Program served as a "holding" program for many youths who would later participate in the wilderness program. The criteria for referral and acceptance into both programs was the same.

The subjects in these two groups were very similar; however, since random assignment to programs by the researcher was not possible, control subjects were treated as a "non-equivalent control group" (Campbell & Stanley, 1963). The subjects in this study had a mean age of 14.9 years. Fifty-eight were male, and 14 were female. Eighty-eight percent (N = 63) were white. Fifty-four percent (N = 39) were referred by the Illinois Department of Children and Family services, while 46% (N = 33) were adjudicated delinquents referred by a probation office. The demographics of the wilderness group and the control group were virtually the same.

RESEARCH MEASURES AND PROCEDURES

The Wichmann-Andrew Behavior Intervention Scale (WABIS) is a 40-item observer checklist designed as a practical, unobtrusive measure of specific asocial behaviors of youths at-risk who participate in therapeutic wilderness programs. Previous research has documented strong reliability and significant validity for the measure (Andrews, 1980).[2] The WABIS was completed by the senior wilderness instructor who rated the typical behaviors of each participant in his/her group on Day 5 (pretest) and then again on Day 30 (post-test). Similarly, each advocate used the WABIS to rate the typical behaviors of their clients on two occasions, 25 days apart. All raters received the same basic instructions for using the WABIS.

The Means-Ends Problem-Solving Procedure (MEPS) is a standardized instrument designed to measure an individual's interpersonal problem-solving orientation and ability. The MEPS procedure involved presenting each young person with the initial situation and the ending for a series of stories describing interpersonal problems. The subject fills in the middle part of the story, describing the means needed to solve the problem and reach the end of the story. Participant responses were written down verbatim and scored using the total number of Relevant Means (RM) generated by each subject.

Validity and reliability information provided by numerous studies cited in the MEPS Manual (Platt & Spivack, 1983) indicate that this instrument accurately and reliably measures means-end problem-solving skills in maladjusted populations.

The MEPS was administered to the experimental subjects on Day 10 of the wilderness course by the author. By this time in the course, subjects were heavily involved in interpersonal problem-solving via the Circle.

The Instructor Checklist of Expectations for Youth at Risk was developed through a survey of directors and senior instructors of therapeutic wilderness programs throughout North America (Wichmann, 1976). This checklist consists of the 20 items upon which there was a consensus among the 58 programs who responded to the survey. In other words, these seasoned practitioners said that it is realistic to expect youths at-risk to demonstrate these attitudes and behaviors while participating in a therapeutic wilderness program. Each staff person completed an Instructor Checklist of Expectations for Youth at Risk prior to the wilderness course they worked.

Instructor Experience. The instructors in the study had worked an average of nine 30-day courses. Individuals ranged from a low of 5 to a high of 15 courses worked. This roughly represents from one to 4 years of experience in the program.

RESULTS

Pre- and post-treatment WABIS scores for the wilderness group and the control group were used to determine whether the wilderness program reduced asocial behavior. Data were analyzed using analysis of covariance to adjust for any differences between groups in their level of asocial behavior at the time of the first WABIS rating. The post-course behavior of the wilderness program participants improved significantly in comparison to that of the control subjects when the effects of pre-intervention, asocial behavior were statistically controlled ($F = 17.22$; $df = 1,69$; $p < .01$). For the wilderness program graduates, their mean post-test score on the WABIS was 15 points higher than their mean pretest score which represents a highly significant reduction in asocial behavior. The control group did not change their level of asocial behavior. The therapeutic wilderness program reduced the asocial behavior of those who graduated.

Multiple regression was used to explore how some of the factors at work in the wilderness program related to the asocial behavior of students at the end of the wilderness course. The following variables were selected based on the Therapeutic Wilderness Model as possible predictors of the asocial behavior of students at the end of the course as measured by the WABIS: student age and pre-course asocial behavior, instructor experience and expectations for students, and the process variable of interpersonal problem solving.

Multiple regression empirically shows how much of the variance in the criterion variable, post-treatment asocial behavior, is predicted by knowing the values of the other variables. In other words, are any of the person and program variables related to why some subjects demonstrate lower asocial behavior while others demonstrate relatively higher asocial behavior at the end of a wilderness course? The perfect model would account for 100% of the criterion variance (i.e., if the exact value was known for all predictor variables, then the analysis could predict the person's exact level of post-treatment asocial behavior). The combination of variables in this analysis which best predicts asocial behavior is shown in Table 1 on the following page. "Partial R Square" represents the percentage of variance accounted for by each individual predictor variable (the extent to which it individually predicts asocial behavior), while "Model R Square" shows the cumulative percentage accounted for in the criterion of post-treatment asocial behavior. Thus, pre-asocial

Table 1

Summary of the Forward Multiple Regression Selection Procedure for the Criterion Variable of Post Asocial Behavior

Step	Variable	Partial R Square	Model R Square	Partial F	Significance Level
1	Pre Asocial Behavior	.34	.34	13.38	.001
2	Interpersonal Problem-Solving	.14	.48	11.66	.002
3	Instructor Experience	.07	.54	6.88	.01
4	Instructor Experience	.07	.61	5.56	.02

behavior accounts for 34% of criterion variance; interpersonal problem solving accounts for 14%, while instructor experience and instructor role expectations each account for 7%. The age of students was not a significant predictor. The total model accounts for 61% of the variance in post-course asocial behavior. This means that 39% of post-course asocial behavior was not predicted by this model due to measurement error and the omission of other important predictors.

As might be expected, the asocial behavior that students demonstrate at the beginning of the program accounts for most of the post-asocial behavior variance. A 30-day program cannot totally negate 15 years of asocial behavior. This variable can only be manipulated by the program through student selection. However, the other three predictors in the Table each significantly increase the predictive value of the total model and can be controlled in many ways by the program. Furthermore, interpersonal problem solving was predictive of post-course asocial behavior "over and above" all other variables ($F = 10.99$; $df = 1,30$; $p < .01$). The reader is referred to McNeil, Kelly, and McNeil (1975) for an explanation of "over and above" hypothesis testing using multiple regression.

DISCUSSION

These results empirically describe some key aspects of Level II of the Therapeutic Wilderness Model. The program significantly reduced asocial behavior. Instructor characteristics and the participants' interpersonal problem-solving skills were important in predicting asocial behavior. In other words, more instructor experience, more realistic instructor expectations, and better interpersonal problem solving by students were related to a reduction in asocial behavior. It cannot be concluded that the program taught students interpersonal problem solving and that this caused a reduction in asocial behavior because the study did not measure and compare students' precourse and post-course levels of interpersonal problem solving. However, the results do show that asocial behavior was reduced and that there is a relationship between this change and the interpersonal problem-solving skills of students.

The results of this study suggest the following areas for future practice and research:

1. An attempt should be made to decrease the rate of staff turnover within therapeutic wilderness programs. This would increase the overall level of instructor experience. Such factors as salaries and benefits, time off, and professional development should be improved.

2. Staff training and new staff orientation should include the development by instructors of appropriate role expectations for youths at-risk. Instructors often expect too little of youths at-risk. High expectations result in higher performance.

3. More emphasis should be placed upon teaching students interpersonal problem-solving skills. The Circle is a solid approach, but in practice is often limited to solving the immediate problem, setting consequences, and "getting on with the course" as preconceived by staff. More emphasis should be placed upon having students understand the process and practice the skills in solving interpersonal problems via the Circle. This could be done through more reflection, debriefing the Circle, and by gradually empowering students to take more responsibility for, and control over, it. Structured experiences designed to teach interpersonal problem solving could be used. Guided reflection upon interpersonal problem solving should be a daily routine.

4. An attempt should be made to measure changes in the interpersonal problem-solving ability of subjects over the course of the therapeutic wilderness program. This would evaluate the effectiveness of efforts to teach these skills. If the MEPS is used, the same stories should not be given on multiple occasions.

5. The theory should be refined by accounting for more of the variance in post-treatment asocial behavior in the predictor model. There are other student and instructor variables which might be important predictors. Other process variables from Level II of the Therapeutic Wilderness Model that could account

for significant criterion variance include the level of interpersonal stress, types of individual consequences, and the degree of group cohesiveness developed during the course.

Although there is much research and development to be done, it is no longer appropriate to criticize therapeutic wilderness programs for having no theoretical or research basis. The theory discussed in this paper is based upon widely accepted practices and is supported by a growing body of descriptive research. Therapeutic wilderness programs increase self-esteem and reduce asocial behavior, and we are beginning to understand how and why. The ultimate test of the value of this theory and research will be made by those enlightened helpers who lead others on the healing path of wilderness and circles.

Ted Wichmann received his Ph. D. in Educational Psychology from Southern Illinois University in 1990. He started the Spectrum program at the Touch of Nature Center at Southern Illinois University in 1976 and is currently the Associate Director for the Touch of Nature Center. He was elected to the Board of Directors in 1990 and is currently the chair for the Task Force on Accreditation. He is one of the original founders of the Adventure Alternatives Professional Group in the Association for Experiential Education.

Footnotes

[1] This article was first published in the 1991 Journal of Experiential Education, 14(2), 43-48.

[2] The WABIS scale was validated using 290 delinquent youths who participated in one of nine therapeutic wilderness programs. Andrew (1980) reported inter-rater reliability and test-retest reliability of over .95. Construct validity was determined by a 97% correct classification of delinquents from a diverse sample in a discriminate analysis procedure. The criteria for "delinquent" was adjudication by the courts.

Southern Illinois University, Carbondale, IL.

31

THREE APPROACHES TO EVALUATION: A ROPES COURSE ILLUSTRATION[1]

MARC BRAVERMAN, JAMES BRENNER, PHELAN FRETZ, & DANIEL DESMOND

Many people involved with outdoor adventure education programs strongly believe that these programs can promote psychological growth in their participants. As these programs grow in popularity, staff members and other interested persons feel a growing need to learn more about them in a systematic way. For example, staff may wish to understand more fully the variety of experiences that many participants enthusiastically report. Program designers may desire some clear outcome data that can confirm their intuitive beliefs to funding agencies or local supervisors. Likewise, school districts, corporations, and other potential client groups may wish to see convincing evaluation results before committing valuable time and resources. Moses (1990) describes the growing role of outdoor activities, particularly ropes courses, in employee-motivation programs, but also reports that skepticism exists about whether these courses have a lasting effect.

In designing evaluations of outdoor adventure programs, program staff and evaluators need to be clear about the purposes of their investigations and should take advantage of the full range of available evaluation tools. This article describes three distinct approaches to evaluating outdoor adventure programs: program monitoring, experimental studies, and naturalistic evaluation. These approaches are illustrated through their application to a case example, an adventure ropes course that is part of the 4-H program in California.

EVALUATION APPROACHES

In this article we will adopt Patton's (1986) view of evaluation, which "focuses on gathering data that are meant to be, and actually are,

357

used for program improvement and decision making" (p. 14). Using this broad view, each of our approaches is capable of providing important evaluation information, and yet the contributions that each can make are fundamentally different. The decision to use one approach or some combination of them depends on the expected use of the information and other issues pertinent to the program situation. The approaches are:

Program Monitoring

This involves the systematic collection of routine data necessary to maintain high-quality program functioning. Generally the program staff, with input from other people involved in the program, will decide what forms of information are needed on a regular, ongoing basis, and set up a system to collect and review that information. The kinds of data collected are usually straightforward: participation counts, demographics on people served, budget information, scheduling information, and so on. Some of these data can be obtained through surveys of program participants, community members, or staff members. Other kinds of information may already exist in the program files, and the monitoring activity consists of periodically summarizing and reviewing it to make sure that the program is "on course."

In setting up a monitoring system, program staff need to decide not only whether a particular form of information might be useful, but also whether it is worth the time, energy, and money needed to collect it. They must also decide how often the information should be reviewed. While it may surprise some people to think of monitoring as a form of evaluation, it fits squarely within our conception of evaluation as described above. The information gained from monitoring activities can be extremely useful for fine-tuning the program on a day-to-day operating basis, and for describing its operations to important outside parties.

Experimental Studies

These are used to answer specific, focused questions that have importance to program staff or other people with a stake in the program. Important identifying characteristics of the experimental approach are the following: 1) the evaluation question is framed in terms of specified variables that are usually defined quantitatively (e.g., scores on self-esteem scales); 2) the evaluation design is set up to see how particular variables interrelate, and should control or neutralize other factors as much as possible; and 3), value is placed on being able to generalize

358   *ADVENTURE THERAPY*

the findings to a wider group of people than those who participated in the study.

The experimental approach is most often associated with concerns about program outcomes, that is, the ways in which participants have changed and the stability of these changes. These studies usually involve comparisons, such as between one group that experiences the program and another that does not. Statistical tests are often used to clarify these comparisons. However, in our conception of this approach, we also include studies of how different variables relate within a single group. An example is the study by Drebing, Willis, and Genet (1987), which looked at how anxiety relates to satisfaction, understanding, and other program outcomes for a group of college students experiencing an Outward Bound program.

Naturalistic Evaluations

This form of evaluation attempts to describe the program from the vantage point of those who experience it directly, rather than from the vantage point of predetermined questions. As Lincoln and Guba (1985) describe, the naturalistic approach assumes that multiple realities exist in any program setting, that the process of evaluating a program is intertwined with any findings that may emerge, and that the context of the specific program studied is an essential component of any conclusions that are reached. The data in naturalistic studies tend to be qualitative, consisting of interviews and field observations. Value is placed on preserving the perspective of individuals in the group rather than describing the group as a whole through summary quantitative measures.

What we call the experimental and naturalistic approaches are often referred to as "quantitative" and "qualitative," respectively. Enormous differences exist in the meanings that are given to these various terms (e.g., Lincoln, 1989). We use the first two terms to describe ways of thinking about evaluation, and the last two terms to describe methods that can be used. These designations are similar to those used by Stecher and Davis (1987). Quantitative methods are those that use numerical data for making interpretations and arriving at conclusions, whereas qualitative methods are those that use descriptive, verbal data. Either type of method can be used in any of the three approaches described above. For example, experimental comparisons can (and often should) be based at least in part on observers' verbally rendered judgments, while interviews used in naturalistic evaluations occasionally include items that ask participants to rate their subjective opinions on a numerical scale.

THE 4-H ADVENTURE ROPES COURSE

In 1978, University of California Cooperative Extension staff started the first 4-H Adventure Ropes Course (4HARC) in San Francisco. By 1989, this course had provided the model for developing similar 4-H programs in nine other California counties. The course is a one-day experience that provides participants with a series of outdoor physical challenges, including climbing, balancing, jumping, and physical problem solving. Some of the activity stations are set as high as 60 feet in the air, producing a psychological experience of exhilaration, physical risk, and daring. This is the basis for much of the program's considerable emotional impact, even though participants are fully protected by a belay system. The activities are specifically designed to call into play the qualities of courage, creativity, athletic ability, composure, and trust in one's peers.

School groups are the most frequent users of the ropes course, with an emphasis being placed on students identified as "at-risk." Other frequently participating groups include special youth programs, corporate management teams, men's and women's self-help groups, and professional development centers. Anywhere from 500 to 1900 individuals go through the 4HARC experience each year.

To conduct their programs the staff require the assistance of trained volunteer leaders who guide participants through the experiential program with an emphasis on openness, acceptance, and discovery. A comprehensive, 50-hour 4HARC Leader Training course, which includes both technical and psycho-social aspects of leading a session, is usually held annually at each ropes course site. These training courses provide 10-30 new volunteers each year.

A Day on the Ropes Course

The experience consists of a sequence of activities divided into low and high stations, or "elements." In the morning the group works on the ground-level or low elements. These include both group-centered activities such as the "Mohawk Walk," where the group must move along a stretch of suspended cable using only each other and their collective balance for support, and individually focused activities such as the "Mantle," where participants climb a 7'-high, 1'-wide post and stand on the top. In the afternoon the group moves to the high elements. Participants walk across a rope bridge, or balance on a tiny platform and leap to a trapeze suspended from nearby trees. The final activity is the

"Wall," a group challenge in which the team must devise a way to get everyone over a 12-foot wall. The day ends with a debriefing circle where participants and leaders share their insights and feelings about the day's experience.

Levels of Intended Impact

The 4-H Adventure Ropes Course program is intended to benefit individual participants by increasing self-esteem and awareness of one's physical capabilities. A further aim is to increase problem-solving skills by having participants work through planned problems associated with particular elements. For pre-existing groups such as classes or business teams that go through the 4HARC as a unit, the program's intended impacts (in addition to the above individual-level aims) are team building and the development of mutual support. Growth in group cohesiveness is believed to derive from a variety of programmatic experiences such as communication, group decision making, group trust building, identification of group diversity, and shared interpretations on risk taking.

APPLICATION OF EVALUATION APPROACHES

The three evaluation approaches will now be illustrated by their applicability to the 4HARC. The program-monitoring activities have been ongoing for years. The experimental study was conducted last year. The naturalistic study is currently under consideration by program staff but has not yet been implemented. Following these descriptions, we will examine the relative contributions of each of the three approaches in the final section of this article.

PROGRAM MONITORING

Safety Information

The physical safety of participants must take priority over all other considerations of program impact. Program staff have instituted an "Accident/Close Call Report" that leaders complete for any incident that in their judgment reflected a threat to the safety of individuals or groups. These are reviewed regularly. The staff search for any recurrent patterns that may indicate the need to change the course elements or the techniques used to experience them. A "Construction Request Form" is also available for leaders to indicate physical areas requiring site maintenance or improvement. At the end of each program day, all leaders meet for 10-30 minutes. A debriefing discussion is held, with accompanying notes, on what worked well, what could be better, comments and concerns, special issues, and actions needed. In addition, team leader meetings are held each month to review and discuss common concerns regarding safety and operations.

Leader Effectiveness

Since the leaders of the Ropes Course are volunteers, the professional program staff need to closely monitor the systems of leader training and supervision. This is accomplished through several feedback mechanisms. "Leader Training Evaluation Forms" are written evaluation sheets that all trainees complete at the end of their training period. A "Leader Objective Check-Off List" allows the trainer to review specific competencies for each leader trainee, each of which the trainer initials upon demonstration of competency. The areas included on this sheet pertain to key safety, technical, and facilitation skill areas. Interpersonal feedback is provided by having the leaders in the team for each program-day meet after the program's completion. They are encouraged to provide each other with clear, objective, verbal feedback on each other's performance. This not only helps each leader to improve performance, but also allows an explicit opportunity for positive "strokes" and recognition.

Enrollment Statistics

Routine enrollment counts are kept for participants and leaders on demographic dimensions such as age, gender, and ethnicity. These figures are used in planning for each coming year, planning affirmative action targets, and assessing success in meeting those targets.

Feedback from Participants

At the end of each program day, participants sit down with the team of leaders in a relaxed atmosphere to reflect on their experiences. They are encouraged to verbally share their insights and feelings with the assembled group. In addition, a straightforward, one-page "Reaction Sheet" is distributed to participants, in which they are asked to describe their reactions to the day. Although it would be an error to attach too much formal significance to these immediate post-program reactions, they do serve to provide an overall sense of the day. Program staff have also found these information channels to be a good grass-roots source of ideas and suggestions.

EXPERIMENTAL EVALUATION

In 1988, the impact of the Sonoma County 4HARC experience on pre-adolescents was evaluated using an experimental, quantitative approach. The aim of the investigation was to determine how the ropes course affects personality factors such as independence, extroversion, and anxiety. Only selected points of the evaluation will be described here. A more detailed description is provided by Fretz (1989).

Study Description and Selected Results

The sample included 118 sixth-grade students from four elementary school classes in Sonoma County, California. The study employed a quasi-experimental design (Cook and Campbell, 1979), with three of the classes participating in the Ropes Course and the fourth serving as a non-equivalent comparison group. For all classes, pre- and post-testing occurred about one week apart, with the program classes completing the Ropes Course in their intact groups about 3 days after the pre-test.

The test instrument was the Children's Personality Questionnaire (CPQ). This is a commercially available, self-report inventory for elementary and early adolescent students, and measures 14 primary personality characteristics, expressed as dimensional polarities. Examples are reserved-warmhearted, phlegmatic-excitable, obedient-dominant, and shy-bold. Factor analysis has shown that these 14 variables load on four second-order factors: extroversion, anxiety, "tough poise," and independence. The reliability and validity of the CPQ have been extensively tested and are both strong. Further information is provided in the test handbook (Porter and Cattell, 1975).

An immediate post-treatment questionnaire was also administered to all students in the program classes. Information from this less formal measure was used to add explanatory perspective to the personality score results.

In general, the results showed no differences between the groups at pre-test, but significant differences at post-test (at $p < .05$) for several of the primary scales as well as two second-order factors, anxiety and independence. On the basis of the make-up of these scales, the increase in independence suggests that students gained in their abilities relating to selective perception, critical judgment, and creativity, as well as increasing in aggressiveness. The increase in anxiety suggests that students became more excitable, less emotionally stable, and more fretful following the experience. The overall pattern of results suggests that the ropes course experience has a potentially strong effect on participants of this age, offering students a mixed combination of blessings.

Interpretation

The experience seemed to produce both positive and negative impacts on these students. In contrast, a related study by Fretz (1989) reports a more uniformly positive impact on older youths. The results suggest that younger participants may not yet have acquired the life skills necessary to adequately deal with the impact of the experience. The gains in independence must be viewed in light of the concomitant increases in anxiety. Recommendations pointed to the debriefing process as a possible way to strengthen the impact of the course for these youngsters. Alternatively, it may be that use of the entire course must be reconsidered for students in this age range; perhaps they would benefit more from participating only in the low elements or some other subset of the components. A further possibility is that some criteria could be developed to help determine which youngsters are developmentally ready to participate in the course. At present, all of these possible directions for program change are being weighed and considered by the program staff.

NATURALISTIC EVALUATION

Despite the high value of studies on selected personality components, one might argue that the Ropes Course experience cannot be fully understood without understanding the total effect of the program from a personal, individual point of view. This stands in contrast to the process of deriving information from summary levels of variables measured across groups of individuals. A naturalistic approach would use qualitative methods to get at the phenomenological aspects of the experience, that is, what it feels like to go through it.

Purposes

The participants in whom we are particularly interested are, as in the study above, pre-adolescents. One main purpose of the evaluation would be to illuminate the growth process (to the degree that it may exist) in rich detail, and to get an idea of the variety of forms the process can take. Another purpose would be to explore how the experience is perceived by program staff and the volunteer course leaders. We would not be able to follow as many participants as is possible using an experimental approach, but this would be compensated for by the depth of information provided by the individual cases (see, e.g., Patton, 1987).

Information would be gained through in-depth interviewing and participant observation. An evaluation team of at least two trained evaluators would be used, to share perceptions and to allow for multiple points of focus during the operation of the program.

Sample

Naturalistic evaluation usually involves, among other things, a good deal of observation of the program in action, often with a single group of program participants. However, the Ropes Course experience for any given participant is relatively short—one day. Therefore, we would plan to observe the Course in operation over different days with a number of groups within the age range of interest. We would try to observe a range of groups with respect to factors such as their everyday relationships (e.g., both classes and other youth groups) and the degree to which they are considered "at-risk" (though a single kind of group could be focused on if that was desirable).

Data Collection

If possible, the evaluators would visit each group several days before their planned visit to the Ropes Course. They would explain that their purpose was to learn about the Ropes Course and ask for the youths' help in sharing their thoughts and feelings. It would be important to establish an atmosphere of openness and self-awareness. The evaluators would conduct semi-structured group interviews to ascertain the youths' pre-existing expectations for what will happen on the course, what they hope to gain, and how important the experience is for them at that time. They would ask what concerns the youths have in general, and how they regard the role of risk and challenge in their lives. They would also observe group interactions and try to get to know them both as individuals and as group members.

During the day on the course, the young people would be joined by the evaluation team, who would participate on the course with them to a limited degree. The evaluators would attempt to deepen the rapport and speak with the group members throughout the day to discern how the experience was progressing. They would break periodically and ask the group to express their perceptions. They would also talk individually to the youngsters when the time arose at natural points during the day. However, they would take care not to intervene directly in the interactions of the youths. They would speak to program staff and volunteer leaders as well. After the day was over, they would lead a semi-structured group interview to have the youths reflect on the experience and how they may have changed.

In addition to this focus on the youths, the evaluators would also maintain a continuing dialogue with the program staff and volunteer course leaders, meeting frequently to share their interpretations and receive feedback on ideas.

The observations of the evaluators would be guided by several wide-ranging questions, examples of which might be:

1. Which parts of the day provide the most meaning from individual participants' points of view?
2. What are the variations in the sense of risk and challenge experienced by the participants? What are the various ways in which they respond to those risks?
3. How and when do they seek support from others? How and when is this support given?
4. By what processes does trust develop between participants? What factors facilitate or hinder that development?

Design Considerations

An important consideration would be how much the evaluators participate on the course along with the youths. Although in naturalistic evaluations it is important for the evaluators to understand the experiences in a personal, subjective way (Lincoln & Guba, 1985), full participation would sharply impair the evaluators' information-gathering functions of observing and interviewing. Therefore, our solution would be to have the evaluators go through the course on an earlier day, when they could focus fully on their internal experiences. During the course day with youths, the evaluators would participate on only a small number of elements, to establish an atmosphere of belonging with the group.

All interviews would be tape-recorded, with notes being used as little as possible. This would allow the evaluators to concentrate on events going on instead of on the data-recording process. The recording of observations could be done either through taking notes or using a tape recorder, depending on which method allows greatest attention to the events in progress and which method is best accepted by the participants.

366

Some early trials could determine this decision. At times during the day it might be necessary for an evaluator to leave the scene to record an observation privately. This would be done unobtrusively and as infrequently as possible. More extensive observations would be recorded at the end of the day, after participants have left.

With evaluators serving as participant-observers, it is clear that they are not "unobtrusive." However, the naturalistic paradigm holds that the evaluator should not seek to be "invisible," that his/her presence must be noted and interpreted along with other components of the program context. Therefore, one must seek to understand rather than to remove the "effect" of the evaluator. In this case, it would be hard to imagine how one could explore participants' perceptions without a fairly strong presence encouraging them to reflect and describe their internal states. The team would strive to maximize their effort on questioning and bringing ideas into awareness. They would minimize the provision of information or opinions.

It is true that the experience as constructed here would be different from most days on the Ropes Course (as described earlier in this paper) in that there would necessarily be much more reflection and self-examination by the youths. If it was felt to be necessary, the evaluators could aim for a lower profile on a succeeding "evaluation day" and observe how this might change the information gained. Indeed, the staff might decide to incorporate some of the intense reflection into the course's typical functioning. As is often the case with the naturalistic paradigm, both the evaluation and the program may be changed in important ways while the data collection is progressing.

REFLECTIONS ON THE EVALUATION APPROACHES

All of the evaluation approaches described here have significant potential for increasing our understanding of the ropes course. However, they do reflect different ways of thinking about evaluation. In this section, we try to illustrate those differences by comparing the approaches on a number of different dimensions.

SPECIFICITY OF QUESTIONS

One important way in which the approaches differ is in the specificity of information that each approach is able to examine. For example, the program-monitoring data concern such areas as possible safety problems and assessments of the volunteer leaders. These areas are highly specific and can lead to quick and clear decisions: making the equipment more secure, identifying leaders who need more training, and so on.

The experimental approach also involves fairly specific questions which are tied closely to the measures that are used. The data help program staff to answer those questions that guided the design of the study. The quantitative measures place clear limits on the kinds of knowledge that can be gained. For example, we will not know the program's effect on problem solving unless we specifically include a problem-solving test.

The naturalistic approach allows for more comprehensive questions and allows more topic areas to be touched on by the data. This stems from the evaluators' freedom to explore questions as they arise during the course of the interviews or observations. This freedom comes at the cost of more ambiguity in the resulting answers to the questions.

ASSUMPTIONS AND AMBIGUITIES IN THE DATA

All types of data carry underlying assumptions that we use in interpreting them. These assumptions take different forms within each evaluation approach. For example, to interpret the quantitative data resulting from the CPQ, we have to know and accept the constructs underlying the test scores. The trait of "shyness-boldness" is theoretically defined in a certain way by the test developers, and that definition is reflected in the actual items making up the test. This operationalization of theory is necessary for any quantitative measurement to take place. As another example, some self-esteem scales include numerous items that relate to school achievement, while others focus more on peer relationships. For an experimental evaluation to be meaningful, the evaluator, program staff, and other stakeholders must all agree on the appropriateness of the measures used to assess important variables. The selection of these measures should be a shared process.

The assumptions underlying the meaning of qualitative data are perhaps even more critical because they are less explicit. For example, an interview question such as "Which elements gave you the strongest feelings of anxiety?" might be answered succinctly, without the interviewer and respondent ever knowing that they have different conceptions about the meaning of the term "anxiety." A reader of the evaluation report may have yet a third interpretation. A good evaluator will be on the look-out for such ambiguities, and will strive to clarify terms whenever necessary. In addition, good question construction,

368

careful listening, and good interview rapport can also help to reduce this problem.

Program-monitoring data usually contain fewer ambiguous concepts. However, much variation might still exist in what different respondents consider to be a safety-related "close call" or in judgments about what constitutes attainment of a leader-training objective. It sometimes helps to instruct respondents to err in a particular direction; for example, to label an incident as a "close call" if any doubt exists about what the appropriate judgment might be.

IMPLICATIONS FOR FOLLOW-UP

Of the approaches considered here, the naturalistic evaluation can produce the broadest possibilities for follow-up and program revision. Since the investigation is not restricted by the prior selection of instruments or topics, the interviewer's questions, the respondent's answers, and the observers' notations can all range across many aspects of the ropes course experience. Information can certainly be gained about the program's effect on affective and cognitive growth, on leader effectiveness, on operational suggestions, and on other areas touched by quantitative evaluations and monitoring activities. However, the qualitative data can also include processes of interpersonal interaction, ideas for new elements, suggestions for methods of debriefing participants, the kinds of risk to which the experience can transfer, individual differences in specific problem-solving strategies, strategies for interpreting the experience, and any other area of potential interest. The wide range of program implications that can be gained from a naturalistic approach is particularly valuable. On the other hand, such implications may take the form of ideas or hypotheses, and probably will not be as convincing as some of the conclusions coming from carefully conducted experimental studies.

QUESTIONS CREATED

One of the valuable functions of evaluation lies in its capacity to create new questions as previous ones become addressed. Naturalistic evaluations are probably the most provocative approaches for this purpose. Each interview, if it comprehensively explores the interpretations of a single individual, can give rise to a variety of hunches and hypotheses to explore. Furthermore, the nature of these hypotheses frequently involves the interplay of factors within the individual, such as the causes of anxiety, ways in which the participant interprets and expresses it, and how he/she responds to it through subsequent action. The next participant studied may have a completely different set of responses.

Experimental evaluations can create further questions too, of course, as is demonstrated in the discussion of the sixth-grade results given above. These questions will more frequently involve specific issues on how particular variables might be related; for example, whether stronger anxiety while on the course leads to stronger feelings of accomplishment later on.

CONCLUSION

We have attempted to show the contributions that can be made by each of the different evaluation approaches considered. Rather than viewing some approaches as better than others, evaluators and stakeholders should examine the possibilities offered by each approach and strive to develop a good match between the information they need and the approach they choose. The Adventure Ropes Course provides a good illustration of the need for a variety of perspectives, and the program has already benefited from this flexibility.

Marc Braverman is 4-H Youth Development Specialist for the University of California (UC) Cooperative Extension and Adjunct Lecturer in Human Development at UC Davis.

James Brenner is Youth and Human Resource Development Advisor at the Sonoma County Office of UC Cooperative Extension.

Daniel Desmond is Director of UC Cooperative Extension in Sonoma County.

Phelan Fritz is a Ph. D. student in Education at UC Davis and Director of Education and Exhibits at the Davis Science Center.

Footnote

[1] This article was first published in the 1990 Journal of Experiential Education, 13(1), 23-30.

32

ANNOTATED BIBLIOGRAPHY FOR THE THERAPEUTIC USES OF ADVENTURE-CHALLENGE- OUTDOOR-WILDERNESS: THEORY AND RESEARCH

Annotated bibliography of actual abstracts from ERIC, PsychLit, and UMI *Dissertation Abstracts International* DIALOG search compiled by H. L. (Lee) Gillis, Ph.D. These sources were initially compiled for a presentation on the therapeutic uses of adventure-challenge-outdoor-wilderness research at the Coalition for Education in the Outdoors Research Symposium, January 17-19, 1992, Bradford Woods, Martinsville, IN.

THEORY ARTICLES

Bacon, S. (1983). The conscious use of metaphor in Outward Bound. Greenwich, CT: Outward Bound USA. (ERIC Document Reproduction Service No. ED296848)

Learning is a metaphoric function in which the individual confirms or reorders his/her sense of reality by relating previous experiences with present ones. Outward Bound, an experiential learning approach, incorporates this insight in its theoretical foundations. The effectiveness of the metaphor is dependent on the extent to which the experience is isomorphic of, that is, similar in structure to, the normal life situation of the student. The validity of an attitude to human existence can be judged by the accuracy with which it reflects the characteristics of the natural world as encountered in wilderness experiences. Various chapters of this book, which is intended as an instructor's manual for Outward Bound staff, discuss the techniques involved in 1) assessing which experiences will be isomorphic with the needs of students; 2) reframing the experience so that its value will be more accessible; 3) understanding the archetypal value of the wilderness setting of Outward Bound (archetypes specifically discussed include growth, space, justice, fate, The Mother, Community, The Leader, The Hermit, and The Hero); and 4) circumventing metaphor failures. Two appendices provide outlines of the Outward Bound process and objectives. (SKW)

Bacon, S. B. (1987). The evolution of the Outward Bound process. Greenwich, CT: Outward Bound USA. (ERIC Document Reproduction Service No. ED295780)

The evolution of the Outward Bound curriculum in the United States with emphasis on how it has changed to ensure greater transfer of course learning from the Outward Bound wilderness experience to experiences in daily life is examined. A typology of curriculum models is developed consisting of 1) a first generation "Mountains Speak for Themselves" model which focuses on experience alone and which dominated Outward Bound programming from the 1960s to the early 1970s; 2) a second-generation "Outward Bound Plus" model, which emphasizes discussion, group process, and imported techniques currently in use; and 3) a third generation "Metaphoric" model, which stresses experiential metaphors and provides a direction for future curriculum evolution. An analysis of the three models contrasts their various strengths and weaknesses. Discussion, however, focuses on the four main parts of the metaphoric model applied to alcoholics as an example. This analysis suggests that the three models do not form a discrete typology, but are different, progressively more sophisticated forms of the same process. Twenty-one bibliographic references are provided. (CS)

Bacon, S. (1988). Paradox and double binds in adventure-based education. Greenwich, CT: Outward Bound USA.

Paradox and therapeutic double-bind techniques are used to overcome resistance in students with a history of success avoidance. Predictions of failure, restraining comments, and the use of paradox in

372

the midst of an activity are defended theoretically by presenting historical roots and a rationale of effectiveness. A skill-building approach focuses on examples, practitioner concerns, and common mistakes. Examples include a delinquent adolescent, a recovering alcoholic, and a female with sex-role confusion. While more traditional direct approaches will remain the standard for instructors, the integration of paradoxical techniques into adventure-based education to overcome anticipated or actual resistance can enhance effectiveness. Assumptions underlying paradoxical learning contradict the medical model with its deterministic nature of genes and biochemistry by suggesting that human growth and learning can determine behavior. Those who choose to use the paradoxical approach are doing more than adding techniques to their repertoire, they are embracing a new set of assumptions about the nature and scope of human learning. (SKW)

Berman, D. S., & Davis-Berman, J. L. (1989). Wilderness therapy: A therapeutic adventure for adolescents. Journal of Independent Social Work, 3(3), 65-77.

Outlines the development and growth of a therapeutic adventure program as a component of a private practice. After reviewing the relevant literature, consideration is given to program development. The topics of program design, staffing, patient selection, program sites, evaluation, funding, and marketing are discussed. The Wilderness Therapy Program is then presented in terms of social-work values. Wilderness Therapy incorporates a systemic view of the person in the environment and aims to enhance self-esteem. This program is compared to traditional, office-based private practice. (PsycLIT Database, Copyright 1989, American Psychological Assn., all rights reserved.)

Busby, D. R. (1984). A combination that worked for us. Federal Probation, 48(1), 53-57.

Describes an Adventure Based Learning Experience, which follows the design of the North Carolina Outward Bound Program, implemented for drug aftercare clients. The program is under the control of the Northern District of Alabama probation program. Features of the program and nonstatistical evidence of its effectiveness are described. (0 ref)

Chase, N. K. (1981). Outward Bound as an adjunct to therapy. (ERIC Document Reproduction Service No. ED241204)

The Colorado Outward Bound School (COBS) provides successful adjunct programs for special populations undergoing therapy at the Adventure Home (Boulder, CO), the Juvenile Justice Program and the St. Luke's Hospital Alcoholism Recovery Unit (Denver, CO), and the Dartmouth Hitchcock Medical Center Department of Psychiatry (Hanover, NH). The goals of the COBS therapeutic approach include increasing self-esteem, cooperation, compassion, and interdependence; resolving issues of locus of control; increasing a sense of responsibility for self and others; and learning the inherent value of risk taking. The COBS programs include three integral elements: a natural physical environment, a small social environment, and the challenges of coping with both the physical and social environments. The natural setting evokes and reinforces coping rather than defensive behaviors. The environment becomes the therapist because consequences are direct, immediate, and impartial. In small living and learning groups of 9-12, clients learn to communicate, cooperate, depend on, and trust each other in structured group discussions and in facing the common challenges of the outdoors. The challenges include natural living skills as well as frightening, risk-filled activities such as rock climbing, peak ascents, and rappelling. Successfully met challenges lead to self-confidence and a creative use of fear. (SB)

Clagett, A. F. (1989). Effective therapeutic wilderness camp programs for rehabilitating emotionally disturbed, problem teenagers and delinquents. Journal of Offender Counseling, Services and Rehabilitation, 14(1), 79-96.

Discusses the development, structure, and functions of a wilderness camp for emotionally disturbed, but not mentally retarded, adolescents and teens, ages 12-17. Criteria for inclusion in the camp are nature of offenses, varying from truancy to murder; ability to pay; and an IQ of at least 70. Topics discussed include therapeutic programs and social organizational structure of the camp. Evidence from studies taken of participants 6 months after release indicates that most did not recidivate during this period. Principle factors are presented that facilitate the rehabilitation of participants. (PsycLIT Database, Copyright 1990, American Psychological Assn., all rights reserved.)

374

Dillenschneider, C. A. (1983). Wilderness adventure programming for the mentally retarded: A rationale and therapeutic basis for program development. (ERIC Document Reproduction Service No. ED238216)

The paper explores basic concepts of mental retardation and proposes wilderness adventure programming as an approach that offers mentally retarded persons the dignity of taking a reasonable risk. Benefits of such programming are cited for affective, cognitive, and psychomotor domains. Processes involved in the therapeutic bases for program development are traced from needs assessment, component analysis (covering physical, social, task, perceived risk, and leadership components), and evaluation. An example is provided of designing a therapeutic program to increase risk-taking behavior and self-esteem. The distinction between a therapeutic and a recreational model for wilderness adventure programming is stressed. Among appended materials is a list of common program activities and the corresponding needs addressed. (CL)

Gillis, H. L., & Bonney, W. C. (1986). Group counseling with couples or families: Adding adventure activities. Journal for Specialists in Group Work, 11(4), 213-220.

Presents a rationale for using adventure activities (AAs) in group counseling (GC), which could be used as an adjunct to traditional GC processes or as the primary mode of treatment. AAs may be perceived as involving some amount of physical and/or psychological risk, especially when activities require that group members trust or depend on each other. The focus is on AAs involving physical challenge or adventure through leader-designed, structured exercises. Such activities may serve several functions (e.g., generating data for discussion after the activity). The role of the group leader in AAs is discussed. Two case examples are used to describe the adaptation of the activities in GC with couples and single parent/adolescent families.

Goodwin, J. M., & Talwar, N. (1989). Group psychotherapy for victims of incest. Psychiatric Clinics of North America, 12(2), 279-293.

Describes group treatment models for child incest victims in three age categories: preschool, latency, and adolescence. Group structures useful for male victims, the integration of family therapy with group treatment, and the need for community involvement and cultural sensitivity are emphasized. Group treatment for adult incest survivors is discussed, and special techniques used in groups for incest victims, including art and play therapy, psychodrama, bibliotherapy, wilderness encounters, and educational techniques, are outlined. (PsycLIT Database, Copyright 1990, American Psychological Assn., all rights reserved.)

Kimball, R. O. (1983). The wilderness as therapy. Journal of Experiential Education, 5(3), 6-9.

Describes the wilderness adventure experience for offenders at Santa Fe Mountain Center. The experience can reveal a composite picture of a client's global personality in the way he/she responds to tasks, demands, and stimuli. An example of a client evaluation is provided. (ERB)

Marx, J. D. (1988). An outdoor adventure counseling program for adolescents. Social Work, 33(6), 517-20.

Describes an "integrative outreach" program designed to meet the developmental needs of adolescents in the Maine state child-welfare system. Claims the program activities mirror and promote the adolescent transition from acting-out behavior to emotional verbalization and may therefore provide an intermediate step between traditional recreation and traditional clinical treatment. (Author/ABL)

Mason, M. J. (1987). Wilderness family therapy: Experiential dimensions. Special Issue: Contemporary family therapy. Contemporary Family Therapy: An International Journal, 9(1-2), 90-105.

Describes the process in which families participate in a wilderness experience (e.g., trekking, rafting). Metaphors such as climbing or paddling a canoe are translated into daily living patterns to deepen individual and family self-knowledge, self-esteem, and intimacy. Premises on which wilderness therapy are based include immediate feedback, trust, and eustress. It is suggested that by weaving various threads into a tapestry of family adventure, a family's unconscious can be unlocked. Through this process, family members can discover new and deeper parts of themselves and increase congruency. This shared experience of risk taking in a safe, supportive environment results in shared mutual vulnerabilities, increasing the intimacy in family relationships.

376

Obermeier, G. E., & Henry, P. B. (1989). Adolescent inpatient treatment. Special Issue: Practical approaches in treating adolescent chemical dependency: A guide to clinical assessment and intervention. Journal of Chemical Dependency Treatment, 2(1), 163-182.

Describes how the components of inpatient treatment help the chemically dependent adolescent to take responsibility for abstaining from alcohol and other chemicals. These components include family therapy, continuing care, group and individual counseling, medical detoxification services, and education. Research on the physical recovery of adolescents from substance abuse is cited, and a wilderness adventure program is described that exposes individuals to endeavors that foster group dynamics and "natural highs." (PsycLIT Database, Copyright 1989, American Psychological Assn., all rights reserved.)

Stich, T. F. (1983). Experiential therapy. Journal of Experiential Education, 5(3), 23-30.

Provides theoretical and practical information on the use of Outward Bound activities in a mental health setting. The first section traces the development of physical activity as an adjunctive psychiatric treatment; the second section describes a model treatment program for psychiatric patients. (ERB)

Stich, T. F., & Gaylor, M. S. (1983). Outward Bound: An innovative patient education program. (ERIC Document Reproduction Service No. ED247047)

A 1975 Outward Bound Mental Health Project, begun with a pilot project for disturbed adolescents, has evolved into an ongoing treatment option in three separate clinical settings for psychiatric patients and recovering alcoholics. Outward Bound consists of a series of prescribed physical and social tasks where the presence of stress, uncertainty, and the need for problem solving, communications, and immediate judgment provide situational analogues for problematic areas in the patient's daily life. The Outward Bound session consists of traditional activities such as individual and group problem-solving activities, ropes course, rock climbing, hiking, orienteering, canoeing, and cross-country skiing. Patients in the diagnostic categories of schizophrenia, mood disorders, neurotic and personality disorders, alcohol and drug abuse, and adjustment disorders have participated in the program conducted by a treatment team consisting of an attending physician, resident physician, nursing staff, social service, and activity therapy staff. Follow-up studies of participating patients indicate that Outward Bound was a positive experience that increased patients' self-esteem. These studies support the postulates that performance accomplishments are an influential source of information and that, when perceived to be of great magnitude, these accomplishments tend to be generalized to other situations in which performance had formerly been inhibited due to feelings of personal inadequacy. (NEC)

Stich, T. F., & Senior, N. (1984). Adventure therapy: An innovative treatment for psychiatric patients. New Directions for Mental Health Services, 21, 103-108. (ERIC Document Reproduction Service No. ED292928)

Describes an experiential therapeutic program delivered in the context of the Outward Bound model. Outward Bound is a nonprofit education institution that promotes self-growth through wilderness challenges. The Outward Bound Mental Health Project (OBMHP) differs significantly from the traditional Outward Bound experience in length. The OBMHP focuses on individual and group initiatives and on mini-expeditions in discrete units of time. The program has been used with a broad spectrum of patients whose diagnoses have included schizophrenia, mood disorders, neurotic and personality disorders, alcohol and drug abuse, and adjustment disorders. The clinical staff review patients to determine who can benefit from Outward Bound. Those invited to participate review the program and establish personal goals, which tend to vary from the concrete to the abstract depending on the patient's degree of illness, insight, and capacity to generalize. Many patients attend several day-long experiences. With repeated participation, it becomes easier for them to see the relevance of Outward Bound as a therapeutic experience and thus to establish realistic goals for themselves. Processing the experience with patients generally occurs either as a focused discussion after each activity or as a group discussion held at the end of the day. Reporting on the field experience includes staff observations, the patient's understanding of his/her psychological difficulties, and the patient's ability to generalize from the field experience to other relevant therapeutic issues. (4 ref)

EMPIRICAL ARTICLES

Banaka, W. H., & Young, D. W. (1985). Community coping skills enhanced by an adventure camp for adult chronic psychiatric patients. Hospital and Community Psychiatry, 36(7) 746-748.

Assessed the effect of a 2-week wilderness camp on 10 skill areas related to community survival of the chronically mentally ill. Forty-eight chronic psychiatric patients (mean age: 30 years) who participated in the program and 30 age-matched, nontreatment controls were evaluated before, during, and immediately and 2-3 weeks after the camp. Results show that, compared with controls, the participants improved in 7 of the 10 areas by the end of camp and maintained their improvements in four of the seven areas for several weeks following their return to the hospital. At a 6-month follow-up of discharged patients, significantly more participants than controls were in the community. (14 ref) (PsycLIT Database, Copyright 1986, American Psychological Assn., all rights reserved.)

Berman, D. S., & Anton, M. T. (1988). A wilderness therapy program as an alternative to adolescent psychiatric hospitalization. Residential Treatment for Children and Youth, 5(3), 41-53.

In two pilot backpacking trips, 14 adolescent inpatients (ages 13-17) were taken from acute psychiatric hospitals into the wilderness. Those selected were either withdrawn or acting out, except for four adolescents diagnosed with attention deficit disorder or conduct disorder. The former group showed greater change than the latter on a variety of measures, including treatment plan objectives, behavioral symptomatology, and locus of control. In general, change during the wilderness therapy program (WTP) was more rapid than during other phases of hospitalization. It is concluded that WTP appears to be a promising alternative to traditional programs. (PsycLIT Database, Copyright 1989, American Psychological Assn., all rights reserved.)

Davis-Berman, J., & Berman, D. S. (1989). The wilderness therapy program: An empirical study of its effects with adolescents in an outpatient setting. Journal of Contemporary Psychotherapy, 19(4), 271-281.

Evaluated a wilderness therapy program for twenty-three 13- to 18-year-olds in outpatient counseling. Data were collected before and after four camping trips using Rotter's Internal-External Locus-of-Control Scale, the Brief Symptom Inventory, Piers Harris Children's Self-Concept Scale, the M. Sherer et al. (1982) measure of self-efficacy, and several measures designed for this program. Following a backpacking trip that included daily therapy, a decrease in self-reported symptoms and increases in self-efficacy and self-esteem were found. (PsycLIT Database, Copyright 1990, American Psychological Assn., all rights reserved.)

Freeman, R. W., Anderson, C., Kairey, I., & Hunt, P. F. (1982). Evaluation of Camp Tortuga, a 2-week children's therapeutic day camp via Goal Attainment Scaling and locus of control. Children and Youth Services Review, 4(4), 375-388.

Evaluated the effectiveness of a 2-week, therapeutic, day camping experience in facilitating change in children, ages 8-12, with adjustment or behavioral problems. For each of the 42 Ss attending camp, three Goal Attainment Scales (GAS) were administered before camp separately to the children, parents, and counselors. These scales specified individualized behavioral goals for problem areas relating to self, family, children, and group, which could be realistically attained within 2 weeks. Postcamp GAS follow-up showed that children, parent, and counselor groups each perceived the children as achieving significant positive change in regard to specified goals. Children were also administered The Nowicki Strickland Locus-of-Control Scale for Children. The hypothesis that internals would be perceived as achieving significantly more positive behavioral change on the GAS than externals was confirmed. Discussion centers on the viability of therapeutic camping, the merits of using the GAS and the multi-informant approach, and specific therapeutic strategies indicated by the present findings. (30 ref) (PsycLIT Database, Copyright 1983, American Psychological Assn., all rights reserved.)

Gaus, C. (1981). Experiential education as an integral part of day treatment for adjudicated delinquent youth. (ERIC Document Reproduction Service No. ED269210)

The role of experiential education is the focus of this paper describing the treatment program at De La Salle Vocational, a day vocational high school for adjudicated delinquent youths. The paper begins by discussing the characteristics and needs of the students and describing the Off Campus Program, a 3-year research model designed to address the students' need for life skills. Four off-campus, experience-based learning modules are explained: 1) stress/challenge courses adapted from Outward Bound; 2) service-learning courses based on the work of the National Commission of Resources for Youth and the National Student Volunteer Program; 3) adventure-learning courses combining active experiences with traditional subject areas; and 4) community-based learning that combines intensive study of one topic area while interacting in the community. The overall treatment program is illustrated through the example of a fictitious student named Rich whose experiences are used to demonstrate the integration of academic and vocational skills with experiential learning. The final part of the paper reports preliminary findings of the project evaluation, which show significant changes in both drug use and legal involvement following the treatment program. Pre- and post-treatment results are discussed for frequency of drug use, number of arrests, interpersonal maturity, family roles, self-esteem, and school problems. A list of selected references is provided. (JHZ)

Stich, T. F., & Sussman, L. R. (1981). Outward Bound: An adjunctive psychiatric therapy: Preliminary research findings. (ERIC Document Reproduction Service No. ED239791)

According to a small study, Outward Bound can enhance the treatment of hospitalized psychiatric patients. Researchers measured the effect of a therapeutic Outward Bound program of prescribed physical and social tasks on the contentment and self-esteem of 7 patients undergoing short-term treatment at the Veterans Administration Hospital in White River Junction, Vermont. After selection by the medical staff, the 7 male patients, all between the ages of 25 and 50, participated in three weekly, 4-hour Outward Bound sessions that included a ropes course, rock climbs, and a rappel. Pre- and post-test results indicated a statistically significant effect of Outward Bound on contentment and a positive but statistically insignificant effect on self-esteem. Results of a comparison to a control group were insignificant. Effects of the Outward Bound program did not dissipate during treatment and the Outward Bound patients had a shorter mean stay in the hospital. A questionnaire and self-rating scale completed by 45% of the test group after 4 months confirmed the findings at the time of hospitalization. Further research is suggested. (SB)

DISSERTATIONS

Boudette, R. D. (1989). The therapeutic effects of Outward Bound with juvenile offenders. <u>Dissertation Abstracts International</u>, <u>50</u>/11-B, 5306. (University Microfilms No. AAD89-26357132)

The purpose of this study was to investigate the effects of an Outward Bound course as a supplemental component of a traditional probation program. Further, an attempt was made to examine two premises put forth in a theory explaining the Outward Bound process: 1) participants must be motivationally ready in order to experience the therapeutic benefits of an Outward Bound course; and 2) participation in Outward Bound leads to increased self-esteem, self-awareness, and sense of belonging.

The subjects of this study were 69 juvenile offenders who were referred to the Project Way Outward Bound program by their court counselors or probation officers. Subjects were randomly assigned to experimental and control groups. All subjects participated in a one-day ropes course. Following the ropes course, the subjects assigned to the experimental group attended a 24-day Outward Bound program, and subjects assigned to the control group proceeded with their probation plans as designated by their court counselor.

To evaluate the impact of the 24-day Outward Bound program, the Jesness Inventory and the Global Self-Esteem Scale were administered to both groups of subjects at three intervals. Both groups of subjects completed self-report measures prior to participation in the ropes course and then 1 and 4 months after this date. Recidivism data were collected at the follow-up date.

Self-report data were analyzed with a two-way repeated measures analysis of variance. Results showed significant differences between the experimental and control group only in the area of self-esteem. Both groups improved significantly on 9 of the 10 Jesness scales over time. A trend analysis indicated that the changes for the experimental group were consistently more pronounced than those for the control group. This finding was true for 9 of the 11 scales. Although this finding is the result of an exploratory trend analysis, it is strongly suggestive and supports reason for further investigation in this area.

Behavioral data were analyzed with a chi-square test. There were five categories of recidivism: no allegations, runaways, probation violations, robbery charge, or assault charge. The chi-square indicated no significant differences between the experimental and control group.

In order to study the impact of motivational readiness on Outward Bound participants, the Student Attitude Questionnaire, a self-report scale, the Instructor Rating Scale, a behavioral measure, and the Achievement Motivation scale, from the Personality Research Form, were administered at the pretest. Scores from these measures were combined and subjects were divided into high- and low-motivational readiness groups. Changes from pretest to post-test and follow-up were analyzed with a two-way analysis of variance. No significant differences were observed between high- and low- motivation groups. Implications of the findings were discussed and suggestions for future research were offered.

Callahan, R. C. (1989). Academic and therapeutic potential of the Sierra II process: An evaluation of an adapted Outward Bound diversion program for adjudicated juvenile delinquents. Dissertation Abstracts International, 51/03-A, 724. (University Microfilms No. AAD90-07084)

The primary purpose of this study was to evaluate the effects of the Sierra II program on adjudicated juvenile delinquents. Specifically, this research measured the program's effect on self-esteem, self-efficacy, locus of control, problem-solving skills, school behavior, and follow-on academic achievement. All study variables, except school behavior and follow-up academic achievement, received pre- and post-treatment assessments. Both school behavior and academic achievement received pre-, post-, 6-month, and 12-month follow-up assessments. Individuals were assigned (by the court services staff) to an experimental group and a control group.

The Tennessee Self-Concept Scale, modified Internal-External Scale, and the Generalized Expectancy of Success Scale were administered to both groups as a pre-test and post-test. The Means-Ends Problem-Solving Procedure was administered to the experimental group at the pre-test and post-test. Demographic, biographic, offense-related, and school-related data were collected on each study participant through use of Youth and School Data Forms.

Data were analyzed primarily through the use of an ANOVA with repeated measures. Where appropriate, matched t-tests were performed in order to ascertain significance between paired data samples. The variable, self-esteem, showed a significant increase over the assessment periods. The variable, self-empowerment (defined as union between locus of control and self-efficacy), showed a significant increase in the measure of locus of control, but did not show a statistically significant difference in self-efficacy. Therefore, this variable can only be partially supported. The results of the variable, problem-solving skills, showed a significant increase over the assessment periods. The results indicate that for the component variables related to school behavior and follow-up academic achievement, (negative comments, grade point average, absences/truancy, and discipline comments), only negative comments showed a significant change during the assessment periods. The research indicates that over time the Sierra II process was more effective in improving school behavior and grade point average, but that these changes did not meet study significance.

The findings of this research indicate that the Sierra II program had the theorized effect upon participants. However, further study should be undertaken to discriminate between the Sierra II components affecting behavior and achievement and those related to individual participant maturation. (Abstract shortened with permission of author.)

Duhaime, D. E. (1982). The effects of an outdoor affective education program on the self-concept, social adjustment, classroom behavior, and affective behavior of learning-disabled children. Dissertation Abstracts International, 43/03-A, 728. (University Microfilms No. AAD82-17111)

Problem: The literature indicates that the affective needs of learning-disabled children are particularly acute. Many schools have instituted programs of affective education, but research on the effectiveness of such programs is meager and inconclusive.

Several survival training and therapeutic camping programs have been reported to produce improvements in self-esteem, social development, and behavior. Since these are areas of particular difficulty for many learning-disabled children, a program of outdoor affective education was developed and implemented to determine its effects on a sample of learning-disabled students. Specifically, this research was conducted in an attempt to answer the following question: Does participation in a carefully structured, outdoor, affective education program for learning-disabled students affect self-esteem, social adjustment, classroom behavior, and affective behavior?

384

Procedure and Methods: Thirty-three boys and 15 girls, ages 10-13, were randomly selected from the population of a school for learning-disabled children in eastern Pennsylvania. From this number, 9 boys and 3 girls were then randomly assigned to each of the following groups: 1) Outward Bound, 2) Recreation, and 3) No Treatment. The remaining 12 students were designated as alternates.

Subjects were pretested on measures of self-concept, social adjustment, and classroom behavior. The Outward Bound and Recreation programs commenced and continued for 7 weeks, each according to a prearranged format and under the direction of the investigator. Observers were present during all sessions of both groups, keeping notes on group and individual behavior.

Upon completion of these programs, post-test data were collected from all three groups.

Results and Conclusions: Analyses of covariance indicated no statistically significant post-test differences in self-concept or social adjustment. In addition, there were no statistically significant post-test differences in Maladaptive Classroom Behavior among the three groups. (Author's abstract exceeds stipulated maximum length. Discontinued here with permission of school.) (UMI)

Freed, D. F. (1991). Participation in an adventure-challenge program and behavior change in emotionally impaired students. Dissertation Abstracts International, 52/02-A 428. (University Microfilms No. AAD91-20661)

This study examined the role of an adventure education program in influencing the behavior of emotionally impaired students in the Traverse Bay Area Intermediate School District's New Campus and Center Programs.

In the fall of 1987, New Campus contracted with the Traverse City (Michigan) Area Public Schools' Bay Area Adventure School to provide outdoor adventure programs for its students. This program consisted of one day of initiatives and one day of high ropes activities, as well as 2- and 3-day fall, winter, and spring overnight sessions. There was a significant difference (at the .05 level) between Behavior Evaluation Scale (BES) scores in the years after the outdoor program was implemented (N = 21 and 22), when compared to the year when there was no outdoor program (N = 16).

In order to gain a clearer understanding as to what extent behavioral changes might be attributed to the outdoor adventure program, BES subscale measures were taken before and after the winter (N = 35) and spring (N = 29) outings in 1990. Data indicated a significant difference in pre- and post-activity measures at the .01 level for New Campus and Center Program students. It is clear that these 2- and 3-day sessions can greatly influence BES subscale Interpersonal Difficulties scores on a short-term basis; however, there is not adequate evidence to suggest that numerous short outings provide positive, long-lasting change.

Open-ended interviews were conducted with New Campus staff (N = 6) and students (N = 20). Recurring themes were categorized and totaled. Students and staff unanimously agreed that the outdoor program was of benefit and should continue to be a part of the school's curriculum. The primary benefits of the outdoor program were felt to be development of outdoor skills, social skills, environmental awareness, and personal growth.

Questionnaires completed by teachers (N = 6) and students (N = 23) in the spring of 1990 indicate that participants perceive the primary benefits of the outdoor program to include increased self-concepts, the development of outdoor skills, and enhanced group interactions.

Gibson, P. M. (1981). The effects of, and the correlates of success in, a wilderness therapy program for problem youth. Dissertation Abstracts International, 42/01-A, 140. (University Microfilms No. AAD81-13511)

The purpose of this study was to investigate empirically the effectiveness of short-term wilderness therapy programs as an alternative, mental-health treatment modality. Further, an attempt was made to determine for which individuals a wilderness experience is most and least likely to be effective, in order to better understand both the potential and limits of such programs and to make more appropriate referrals to them. The subjects of this study were 89 students, 66 boys and 23 girls, who were referred to the Connecticut Wilderness School for a wide variety of problems by social service, school, and corrections agencies. Each subject participated in a 21-day Outward Bound-type course that included a variety of rigorous, challenging, and stressful wilderness activities.

Two types of dependent variables were chosen for evaluation because they are central to psychological adjustment: self-concept (which included self-esteem, self-regard, self-acceptance, and discrepancy between perceived and ideal self) and interpersonal competence (which was rated by both the wilderness school instructors and the referral agency counselors). Thirteen independent or predictor variables were examined for their possible relationship to success in a wilderness program: previous camping experience, institutionalization, self-esteem, academic achievement, motivation to change, understanding of the benefits to be derived from a wilderness program, intactness of family, parental support for participation in the program, age, race, sex, work experience, and primary referral problem. Four hypotheses were formulated, two pertaining to the changes expected from pretest to post-test on the self-concept and interpersonal competence variables, and two pertaining to the predictor variables, some of which were expected to be related and others to be unrelated to success in the program.

As predicted, comparison of pretest and post-test scores by means of paired-sample t-tests showed significant positive changes on the four self-concept measures and the two measures of interpersonal competence. Examination of the subjects' responses on the self-regard measure showed that at the end of the program subjects saw themselves as having increased in integrity, competence, and amiability. The relationship between the predictor variables and success in the program, defined operationally as the amount of change that took place from pretest to post-test on the outcome variables, was examined by means of multiple regression analyses. These analyses revealed no consistent relationship between any of the predictor variables and success in the program. A discriminant analysis of 16 students who dropped out of the program prior to its completion revealed that boys, those referred for delinquency and those with less understanding of how they might benefit from the program, are more likely than other participants to drop out of a wilderness program.

The Connecticut Wilderness School and other similar, short-term, wilderness therapy programs are effective in bringing about positive changes in the self-concept and interpersonal competence of problem youths. The lack of a consistent relationship between benefit derived from the program and background and personal characteristics suggests that the benefits are not limited to certain classes of individuals and that such programs may be more widely applicable than might have been supposed. As a possible explanation of the wide success of wilderness therapy programs, such programs can be viewed as a form of milieu therapy, in which treatment is provided by one's total environment and which has influence on many different areas of an individual's concept of self.

Gillis, H. L. (1986). An exploratory study comparing the strategic use of metaphorical introductions with traditional introductions in a one-day, adventure workshop for couples enrichment. <u>Dissertation Abstracts International</u>, <u>47</u>/09-A 3312. (University Microfilms No. AAD86-28877)

This research compared and contrasted the metaphorical introduction of physical adventure activities (group initiatives and ropes courses activities) with traditional introductions to the same activities. Two groups received metaphorical presentations (N = 20) and two groups received traditional presentations (N = 13) while each participated in one 8-hour, outdoor enrichment experience. Participants were compared on 1) relationship satisfaction, 2) couples' communication, 3) personality characteristics, 4) amount of trust and support received, and 5) the effectiveness of activities for enrichment. Results of the univariate analyses of covariance showed no differences on any of the measures between groups immediately following the activities. The metaphorical group means were consistently higher than the traditional group 6 weeks following the experience, but on only one measure were significant differences found between groups. A personality characteristic, dominance, demonstrated a significant group times measure, within group interaction $F(1, 39) = 137.27$, $p < .0042$. Most significant was the metaphorical group's rating of the enrichment activities (when compared to the traditional group's rating) as more effective for couples enrichment experiences $F(1, 35) = 7.44$, $p < .01$.

There was statistical evidence that a metaphorical approach is at least as effective as a traditional approach in introducing adventure activities. There was minimal support to indicate that the metaphorical approach has effects upon participants that are not measurable until sometime after completing the adventure experience. The metaphorical introduction of adventure activities did not prove to have a robust effect on normal, nondistressed, couples immediately after the one-day enrichment experience. Males and females participating in the experience did not differ in the present investigation with regard to trust or support received. Gender-linked cultural stereotypes found elsewhere were not supported by this investigation. Suggestions for further research were discussed as was the need for research in adventure programming to investigate more diverse populations and newer therapeutic techniques which might lead to more effective use of this powerful medium.

Gugino, H. A. S. (1987). A qualitative case study of delinquent adolescent males in a youth development center short-term treatment program. <u>Dissertation Abstracts International</u>, <u>48</u>/11-A, 2985. (University Microfilms No. AAD88-00269)

The purpose of this study was to describe the response of a group of juvenile offenders to a state-mandated, short-term treatment program emphasizing outdoor adventure activities. The specific objective was to document the degree of congruence between the perceptions of the program participants, the perceptions of the staff, and the perceptions of the investigator regarding treatment response.

A descriptive classification of eight juvenile offender profiles was developed during data collection and related to response and outcome patterns. The match between the observed needs of the 15 selected juveniles and the treatment approach was examined by assessing the relative impact of four mediating variables affecting responsiveness: 1) the age and developmental level/stage of the juvenile, 2) the extent of socialization, 3) past history of aggressive behavior, and 4) the intellectual capacities of the youth. Two developmental stages with unique needs, task requirements, and response patterns were discriminated in the treatment population based on chronological age. Three antecedent variables (socialization, history of aggressive behavior, and intellectual capacity) were categorized according to four DSM IIIR Conduct Disorders categories and five WISC-R classifications and systematically arranged in a trait-by-trait matrix. A selection effect was identified and related to treatment response and outcome.

Four areas of discrepancy related to frequency of outdoor adventure activities, the process of selection, length of stay, and program evaluation were discovered. Administrator/counselor role ambiguity and role overload were identified as partial explanations for the incongruencies. The theoretical implications of role conflict, role strain, and the considerations of determinate versus indeterminate sentencing in the juvenile justice system were discussed and applied to the findings of this study. Recommendations for future research addressed maximizing therapeutic response in juvenile offenders by investigating matching of treatment interventions to offender characteristics through more discriminating typological classification and outcome studies.

Haussmann, S. E. (1984). A qualitative study of year-round outdoor therapeutic camping programs. <u>Dissertation Abstracts International</u>, <u>45</u>/09-A, 2835. (University Microfilms No. AAD84-27540)

Year-round outdoor therapeutic camping is an emerging alternative to institutional and restrictive placement of emotionally disturbed and troubled youths. Research reports and journal articles indicate that therapeutic camping programs are an effective treatment approach though there are few reports on year-round therapeutic camping programs in the literature.

In order to establish an information base on year-round therapeutic programs, a national telephone survey was conducted. A survey instrument was developed and administered over the telephone to the directors of 27 year-round programs who agreed to participate in the study. The survey instrument was designed to secure qualitative and quantitative information to answer seven research questions in five areas: general or demographic information, camp program content, school program, camper graduation policies and procedures, and program evaluation.

Research questions, developed to determine the current status of year-round therapeutic camping programs in the United States, were: 1) What long-term residential camp programs presently exist?, 2) What populations do the programs serve?, 3) What are common elements of the camp program content?, 4) What kind of educational programming is provided in camping programs?, 5) What policies, practices, and procedures are utilized to determine when a camper is ready to graduate?, 6) What evaluation studies have been conducted to determine the efficacy of therapeutic camping?, and 7) To what extent have long-term therapeutic camping programs been influenced by the Loughmiller model?

Results of the study indicated a total of 32 year-round therapeutic camping programs all utilizing the principles developed by Campbell Loughmiller beginning in 1946 at the Dallas Salesmanship Club Boys' Camp. Although some changes have taken place over time, most notably the addition of an academic component to what was originally an experientially-based program, the basic constructs of the Loughmiller model remain dominant in all of the surveyed programs.

Other results include a directory of year-round therapeutic camping programs and a directory of foundations and organizations that operate such programs.

Kuhn, D. C. (1982). Kinetic learning methods in residential treatment. Dissertation Abstracts International, 43/02-A, 403. (University Microfilms No. AAD82-15841)

Kinetic Learning Methods (KLM) are a series of experiential ways of learning through doing and group processing which utilize an active and adventure-based approach developed from New Games, centering and balancing, group learning exercises, outdoor group problem solving, and Kinetic Psychotherapy. KLM is described, tested, evaluated, and the dynamics discussed through a case study of its use with boys in a residential treatment center for adolescents with behavior disorders.

The study develops a list of behaviors important to the boys' treatment; identifies which behaviors seem to be most affected (i.e., self-concept); provides ratings of behavior, progress, and Kirlian print change during this period; outlines the agenda and activities used and explains how they were utilized; discusses observations made of the dynamics and issues engaged in during KLM and makes recommendations for improvement; and collects evaluative ratings of the sessions from participants and staff.

Both qualitative and quantitative data are collected with emphasis on the former. No control groups exist, limiting conclusions about causal relations and generalizing to other populations. The discussions provide largely descriptive information. The evaluations by staff and participants are very favorable. Areas of behavior most commonly focused upon are positive self-concept, personal responsibility, risk taking, involvement with others, identifying feelings, considering alternatives, communication, cooperation, and expression of feelings, especially aggression.

KLM seems to work best when used with these boys in a group of six to eight, when House staff are involved in the sessions, when the boys are older, willing to talk about themselves, and open to activity, and when a connection is made between situations in the House and what is learned in KLM.

The study demonstrates how a method combining counseling and educational goals with games, exercises, and adventure activities is used in residential treatment. Further study is necessary to discover causal relationships, to verify information here, and to explore the use of KLM in other settings. A bibliography and appendix outlining the activities used is included.

Maizell, R. S. (1988). Adventure-based counseling as a therapeutic intervention with court-involved adolescents. <u>Dissertation Abstracts International</u>, <u>50</u>/06-B, 2628. (University Microfilms No. AAD89-21901)

This study explored the application of Adventure Based Counseling (ABC) (Schoel, Radcliffe, & Prouty, 1988) as a model to enhance court-adjudicated adolescents' self-concept and self-esteem, using outcome measures of school grades, disciplinary referral rate, attendance, self-concept and self-esteem inventories, participant self-report, and group progress notes. Thirty-one court-adjudicated adolescents (23 males and 8 females) were selected based upon current probation status, school attended, and age. Three groups were created, including two intervention groups (G1 and G2) and one nonintervention group (NG). Quantitative assessment of results included the Battle Culture-Free Self-Esteem Inventory (Battle, 1982), the Tennessee Self-Concept Scale (Fitts, 1965), analysis of grade point averages, disciplinary referral rates, and daily attendance. Qualitative assessment included student self-report through Experiential Rating Sheets (ERS), verbal self-report, and group and individual progress notes. The major findings of this study were that participants in ABC significantly improved Physical, Moral, and Social Self-Concept, as well as Self-Satisfaction and Total Self-Concept, as measured by the TSCS, when compared with a nonintervention group. Qualitative measures indicated a concordance with standardized measures. For G1, one-year follow-up on school-related measures indicated significant improvement in grades and a significant reduction in disciplinary referrals. Additionally, significant improvement was also noted for grades and disciplinary referrals between post- and follow-up measures. One-year follow-up on self-concept measures indicated significant improvement in Family, Social, and Total Self-Concept, as well as Self-Identity and Self-Satisfaction, as measured by the TSCS. Additionally, significant improvement was also noted for Social Self-Concept and Self-Identity between post- and follow-up measures. Significant improvement in Total Self-Esteem was also noted, as measured by the SEI. Qualitative measures for G1 indicated a concordance with standardized measures.

Mason, M. J. (1980). Relationship enrichment: Evaluating the effects of a couples wilderness program. <u>Dissertation Abstracts International</u>, <u>42</u>/01-B 161. (University Microfilms No. AAD81-09468)

The major goal of this study was to explore the effects of a wilderness Outward Bound-type experience where eustress was employed to assist couples in relationship wilderness enrichment. This was accomplished by integrating an outdoor rock-climbing program with an Outward Bound-type program in a 4-day, wilderness, couples enrichment program. The second goal was to incorporate the use of the physical self in the traditional cognitive-affective enrichment program formats using a group structure in order to discern the difference between verbal trust and the nonverbal enactment of trust. This goal is especially significant because trust has been considered the basis of all human relationships. The third goal has been to utilize eustress (the positive use of stress) in a planned way so that it can be the catalyst for change. The fourth goal was to determine what results from this experience can be applied to the knowledge base about bonded relationships.

The data analyzed here came from 20 individuals, or 10 couples, married 18 years or less. The couples were volunteer subjects from participants in a couples wilderness enrichment program. The couples were asked to participate in this study by a therapist and Outward Bound trainer who had an information session for possible participants.

All couples first filled out self-report questionnaires which focused on: 1) background information; 2) Lifestyle Assessment Inventory (LAQ); 3) Personal Assessment of Intimacy in Relationships (PAIR); 4) Family Adaptability and Cohesion Evaluation Scales (FACES); 5) Family Inventory of Life Events and Changes; 6) Self-Esteem (Tennessee Self-Concept); 7) Fundamental Relationship Orientation—Behavior (FIRO-B); and 8) Couples Climbing Questionnaire (CCQ).

The couples completed these questionnaires when they arrived at "The Edge," a large retreat home on the North Shore of Lake Superior. They had 4 days of living together, climbing, and talking together in evening discussions.

Individual (male and female) scores were separated and couples' scores were recorded on all the instruments. After the post-testing, 6 weeks after the climbing weekend experience, data were analyzed and mean scores were examined on all variables, some within the framework of the Circumplex Model (FIRO-B, FACES, and PAIR). T-tests were run to determine significance of change after the climbing weekend.

The study resulted in validation of some assumptions about relationships and enrichment. The sample consisted of nine of the couples falling within the "normal" or open range on the Circumplex model; couples had increased self-esteem at post-testing time. Trust findings were significant: women's self-trust increased at twice the rate of men's; and as women's self-trust increased, so did their "perceived intellectual intimacy." Women also reflected less need for inclusion at post-testing. Men showed higher scores on "perceived emotional intimacy" at pre- and post-testing. Although couples did show increase in life changes (stress) at post-testing, they reported less family strain.

The study reflected many of the gender-linked cultural stereotypes—that women had less trust in themselves, that males trusted equipment more than women, that women's overall wellness, including physical health, was higher than men's, and that women's perception of their partner's trust in them was less than that of men's.

The main goal of the study was to explore the relationship between the variables linked with enrichment programs for paired relationships. From this study a group of hypotheses can be generated for further research.

What we have learned here is that when couples experience an enrichment program, including nonverbal communication through the metaphor of rock climbing, we can integrate qualitative and quantitative findings to learn what dimensions of enrichment programs might have further in-depth study.

McClung, S. B. (1984). A rock-climbing program as therapy for the chronically mentally ill. Dissertation Abstracts International, 45/04-B, 1292. (University Microfilms No. AAD84-16170)

The purpose of this study was to assess the value of adventure-based programs as a therapeutic technique with the chronically mentally ill and to explore simultaneously the validity of six assessment procedures employed to gather information across a wide spectrum of personality variables. Assessment consisted of pre- and post-testing with the MMPI, the Tennessee Self-Concept Scale, and an Interview Assessment and Questionnaire devised by the researcher and measuring behavioral, self-efficacy, and phenomenological characteristics; self-reported behavioral data recorded daily for 14 weeks; monitoring group counseling goals; and a case study of each participant to identify additional relevant variables.

Research was completed on 6 outpatients at a psychiatric facility in Arizona. All participants had been diagnosed as "schizophrenic" or having "schizotypal personality disorder." The study consisted of three phases: 4 weeks of baseline data-gathering during which pretests were administered; 6 days of rock-climbing and 6 days of group counseling, each component occurring one day per week for 6 consecutive weeks; and 4 weeks of post-rock-climbing data-gathering during which pretests were administered and goal implementation was assessed. Case study information was accumulated throughout the study.

The results yielded evidence that the rock-climbing program produced positive changes in all 6 participants, primarily in how they perceived themselves and their abilities. The most valuable tools in this determination were the case studies, the Tennessee Self-Concept Scale, the interviews, and the goal implementation technique. The least valuable was the MMPI which proved to be an inadequate measure of change. Behavioral assessment is indicated to be one of the most valid of the available tools when proper implementation is feasible.

In the opinion of the researcher, maximum benefit from adventure-based programs with the chronically mentally ill can be derived and adequately assessed if the program design allows for sufficient exposure to the intervention strategy, comprehensive assessment of a wide spectrum of personality traits, and meticulous research of the appropriate assessment methods. A final indication for this population is that a supportive and caring staff is a critical variable in maximizing positive effects.

Minor, K. I. (1988). An evaluation of an intervention program for juvenile probationers. Dissertation Abstracts International, 49/10-A, 3166. (University Microfilms No. AAD88-27331)

Although the efficacy of correctional rehabilitation was questioned during the early 1970s, recent research has demonstrated that certain intervention programs, when implemented under appropriate conditions, are effective in reducing illegal behavior. The objective of this research was to evaluate the effectiveness of a court-based intervention for juvenile probationers.

The program was developed on the basis of caseworkers' assessments of youths' problems and needs. The theoretical perspective underlying the intervention consisted of a joint combination of critical, social control, and differential association theories. A major implication of theory is that the juvenile court's capacity to facilitate informal social control should be given priority over its role as an agent of formal control. Hence, the goals of the intervention were to augment social integration across conventional social institutions and, therefore, to reduce illegal activity among probationers. The program had three main components including job preparation workshops, an outdoor adventure experience, and family relationship counseling.

Forty-five youths participated in the research, with 22 of them taking part in the program and the remainder serving as controls. Effects were evaluated using a two-factor, partially randomized groups design.

Pretest and post-test data were obtained on a variety of self-report measures as well as on several measures of official delinquency. The attendance and participation of the 22 experimental subjects were monitored throughout the intervention.

The data were analyzed using analysis of covariance. Despite prior research support for each of the intervention components, few positive findings were obtained. The self-reports of the experimental and control groups were not substantially different. Likewise, few differences emerged on the official measures, which spanned an 18-month follow-up period. However, significant differences were discovered for the offense activity of those youths with lengthy histories of criminal involvement.

The attendance and participation of experimental subjects were less than satisfactory, and these are described as one explanation for the disappointing outcomes. The methodological adequacy of the research is examined, and the findings are discussed with reference to theory. Implications for further program development and research are presented.

Nunley, G. L. (1983). The effects of a therapeutic outdoor program on the locus of control and self-concept of troubled youth. Dissertation Abstracts International, 44/07-B, 2230. (University Microfilms No. AAD83-25833)

Scope and Method of Study: This study examines the effects of a therapeutic outdoor program called Project B.O.L.D. on the locus of control and self-concepts of those troubled youths participating in the program. The sample for this study consisted of 56 troubled youths selected and referred to the program from a state treatment facility, private children's homes, or community Youth Services agencies from across the state of Oklahoma. This sample was randomly assigned into two groups, a treatment group and a control group. The 56 subjects consisted of both males and females between the ages of 12 and 16. The 28 adolescents in the treatment group participated in a 5-day program called Project B.O.L.D. which consisted of a series of structured, low-to-moderate stress, adventure activities, trust exercises, and other experiential learning activities. The 28 subjects in the control remained at their place of residence. Within 3 days before Project B.O.L.D. began, each subject in both groups was administered the Nowicki-Strickland Locus-of-Control Scale for Children and the Coopersmith Self-Esteem Inventory. These same tests were administered again to each subject in both groups within 3 days after Project B.O.L.D. The split-plot analysis of variance and the dependent t-test with correlated means were used for analysis of the data.

Findings and Conclusions: The analysis indicated that there was no significant difference in the scores of these two groups on the locus-of-control measure or the self-concept measure. The results suggest that a 5-day treatment program may not be long enough to significantly impact the self-concept or locus of control, although it might well begin such a change. Additional studies are needed to corroborate the findings of this study.

Nurenberg, S. J. G. (1985). Psychological development of borderline adolescents in wilderness therapy (Outward Bound, delinquent). Dissertation Abstracts International, 46/11-A 3488. (University Microfilms No. AAD85-25967)

This study explored selected changes in borderline adolescents expected to be associated with their participation in a wilderness therapy group. Evidence of psychological growth was sought in test/retest comparisons of the subjects' ego functioning, self-reports of anxiety and depression, ability to separate from parents, and locus of control.

The theoretical works of Mahler, Winnicott, and Masterson provided the major theoretical background for the study. A naturalistic panel design was employed using a sample of convenience. The sample consisted of 13 adolescents, between the ages of 14 and 19, who were involved in wilderness group therapy. The adolescents were interviewed at two times separated by a 10-month interval. The measurements used were the Ego Strength Scale, the Nowicki-Strickland Scale of Externality, two modified Thematic Apperception Test cards (focused on separation issues), and the Costello-Connery Scale of Depression and anxiety. A semi-structured interview served to corroborate quantitative findings.

The findings suggested that the adolescents felt greater impulse control, autonomy, relatedness, and self-esteem. Scores on a subtest for greater frustration tolerance were not statistically significant. The subjects perceived themselves as more separated from parents, less depressed and anxious, and more internally oriented. The interviews reflected similar findings.

Certain aspects of wilderness group therapy such as the stress factor, the leader as good rapprochement mother, and the holding environment of the group, appeared to encourage the adolescents' renegotiation of earlier developmental issues as they tackled age-appropriate tasks. The leaders and the group, as transitional phenomena, might also have enabled the adolescents to internalize their therapeutic experience.

Pfirman, E. S. M. (1988). The effects of a wilderness challenge course on victims of rape in locus of control, self-concept, and fear. _Dissertation Abstracts International, 49_/07-B, 2870. (University Microfilms No. AAD88-18574)

This study examined the effects of a 3-day wilderness course, Wilderness Challenge, as an adjunctive treatment for victims of rape with respect to fear, locus of control, and self-esteem. The participants were evaluated by the Modified Fear Survey, the Tennessee Self-Concept, and the Levenson Locus of Control. Outward Bound and EVE in Colorado, and the Santa Fe Mountain Center in New Mexico, conducted the wilderness courses. Subjects of this study were 16 women, ages 18 and over, who were victims of rape and in therapy, and who were referred by their therapists. The research was conducted during the summer of 1987.

A repeated time-series design was utilized. Data was collected at four times, 2 weeks before the course, one week before the course, the last day of the course, and 4 to 6 weeks following the course. Analysis of variance was used to examine the data. Thirteen hypotheses representing three areas (fear, self-esteem, and locus of control) were tested.

Results indicate that after the Wilderness Challenge course and at the .10 level of significance, there was a significant decrease in participants' overall level of fear, fear of rape, and fear of failure. In addition, the participants reported increased self-esteem, including positive feelings toward their body, identity, and interactions with others. Results also showed that the victims saw other people and chance events as having less control over their lives.

One hypothesis that was retained indicated that even though the women saw others and chance events as having less control over their lives, they had not yet internalized their perceptions of having more internal control, although there was a trend in that direction. The second hypothesis that was retained indicated that the participants' perceptions did not significantly change in relation to seeing themselves as "good" or "bad" persons.

The statistical data from this study indicate that a 3-day wilderness program containing specific activities in a structured sequence may be effective as an adjunctive treatment in ameliorating long-term symptoms in victims with rape trauma. It may be specifically effective with increasing locus of control, reducing fear, and increasing self-esteem.

Rice, S. (1988). A study of the impact of long-term therapeutic camping on self-concept development among troubled youth. Dissertation Abstracts International, 49/07-A, 1706. (University Microfilms No. AAD88-19365)

Long-term, residential, wilderness therapeutic camping is an approach for treating troubled youths which substitutes an existing environment for one which is situationally demanding, yet physically and emotionally secure. The study was an ex post facto investigation of the relationship between long-term therapeutic wilderness camping and self-concept development among behaviorally and emotionally troubled youths from the Eckerd Family Youth Alternative, Inc.'s 11 therapeutic camping programs. Specific research questions resulting from the overall analysis of the impact of the treatment on self-concept development examined linear combinations of client characteristics as predictors of change in self-concept following treatment.

The overall treatment effect was analyzed by utilizing paired-differences t-tests for each of 11 dependent measures on the Jesness Inventory. Client factors of gender, race, age, IQ, legal status, family status, and socioeconomic status were further investigated as to their relationship with change in self-concept induced by treatment. Multiple regressions and ANOVAs were performed to investigate these relationships.

The data revealed that, on nine Jesness subscales, t-values were significant at the .01 alpha level. On the subscales measuring Immaturity and Social Anxiety, difference values were not significant at the .05 alpha level. Analysis of regression and ANOVA results revealed IQ to be a statistically significant predictor in relation to change on five subscales of the Jesness (i.e., Value Orientation, Immaturity, Manifest Aggression, Repression, and Denial). All were significant at the .05 alpha level. Family status was predictive of change on the measures of Social Maladjustment and Autism (.05 alpha level). Variables of race and socioeconomic status were each determined to be statistically significant predictors of change on the Withdrawal-Depression measure (.05 alpha level). Legal status was related to change on the Asocial Index at the .05 alpha level. None of the independent variables seemed to be systematically related to change on Alienation.

Results of this study offer research implications for further study regarding therapeutic camping and self-concept development. They suggest that the program should direct its attention toward youths with the intellectual capacity to conceptualize the program elements. Parental involvement should be emphasized.

Schwartz, P. D. (1983). Rainbow: A therapeutic residential summer camp milieu and its effects on 6- to 12-year-old emotionally disturbed children. Dissertation Abstracts International, 44/11-A, 3356. (University Microfilms No. AAD84-03281)

Despite the long history enjoyed by therapeutic camping for emotionally disturbed children and the enthusiasm it has received from professionals over the years, there is little empirical evidence demonstrating its effectiveness as a clinical intervention. This study determined the effects of participation in an 8-week, psychodynamically oriented, therapeutic summer camping program on 6- to 12-year-old emotionally disturbed boys and girls. The study was also designed to determine whether this model of therapeutic camping was equally effective across some of the subclassifications and behavioral categories characterizing emotionally disturbed children.

Two hundred fifty-eight 6- to 12-year-old emotionally disturbed children were the subjects for this study. Seventy-two of these children enrolled in the Camp Rainbow therapeutic summer camp program and served as the experimental sample, while the remaining 186 children, not enrolled in any structured camping or recreation program, served as controls. The groups were pretested in June, prior to the beginning of the Rainbow program, and post-tested 8 weeks after the program ended. Children were pre- and post-tested in their educational environments utilizing the Tannenbaum and Levine Classroom Participation Scale, a two-part behavior-rating scale. The scores for both groups on the Classroom Participation Scale were subjected to factor analysis yielding four strong factors for Part I of the scale (Interpersonal Conduct, Self-Sufficiency, Use of Materials, and Peer Relations) and three strong factors for Part II (Aggressive/Disruptive, Anxious/Withdrawn, and Inattentive/Immature).

The results suggested that 8 weeks after the end of the therapeutic camping program, the experimental sample as a group improved on both Part I and Part II of the scale and on all seven factors indicative of a decrease in maladaptive behavior patterns. Although the results of this study suggest that this model of therapeutic camping is an effective clinical intervention, the program, although somewhat more successful with Anxious/Withdrawn children than with either Aggressive/Disruptive or Inattentive/Immature children, doesn't appear to be singularly effective with any one typology of emotionally disturbed child.

Walton, R. A. (1985). Therapeutic camping with inpatient adolescents: A modality for training in interpersonal cognitive problem-solving skills (self-esteem, residential treatment). <u>Dissertation Abstracts International</u>, <u>47</u>/08-B, 3549. (University Microfilms No. AAD86-28822)

This investigation examined the effect a therapeutic camping program would have on the scores of adolescent psychiatric inpatients on the Means-Ends Problem-Solving Procedure, the Nowicki-Strickland Locus-of-Control Scale for Children, and the Tennessee Self-Concept Scale.

Subjects from a residential treatment program were matched for age, sex, and reading level and then randomly assigned to one of two conditions. Subjects in the experimental condition received exposure to a treatment program that was in addition to treatment already being provided. The control condition received no additional treatment other than two recreational camping trips.

The treatment program consisted of 6 one-hour-per-week group sessions, and weekend camping trips following the third and sixth group session. Camping skills were used as a medium to teach problem-solving skills. The camping trips provided an opportunity to use these new skills. A 6-week follow-up period completed the program. The control condition consisted of 6 weeks of no treatment followed by 6 weeks of partial treatment (two recreational camping trips.)

Results indicated a significant increase in problem-solving skills and internality for the treatment group. No significant differences were found for self-esteem. It was concluded that therapeutic camping did serve as a useful adjunct to more traditional therapies when treating adolescents in an inpatient setting.

Limitations of the study were addressed. Small sample size, subject attrition, and scheduling conflicts may have served to limit the treatment effect. Subject selection, application of consequences, and investigator involvement may decrease external validity. Recommendations for future research included a larger sample, greater communication between research and residential staff, a greater variety of dependent measures, and the systematic inclusion of related treatment conditions to determine their singular and combined effects on outcome.

Weeks, S. Z. (1985). The effects of Sierra II, an adventure probation program, upon selected behavioral variables of adolescent juvenile delinquents. <u>Dissertation Abstracts International</u>, 46/12-A, 3607. (University Microfilms No. AAD85-26895)

The purpose of this investigation was to compare the Sierra II group, a wilderness adventure program, to a control group receiving a traditional probation program on recidivism and school behavior pre- and post-program and 6 months following the program. The second part of the study was to analyze the effects of Sierra II, serving as a probation alternative on selected behavioral variables (self-esteem and interpersonal effectiveness) in a group of juvenile delinquents. Pre-, post-, and 3-month follow-up tests were given to the experimental group. The subjects for this study (N = 18), with ages ranging from 13 to 17 years, were adjudicated through the Virginia Beach Juvenile Court System and referred to the Sierra II Program from the field units. The control group (N = 18), with ages ranging from 13 to 17 years, was randomly selected from a pool of adjudicated delinquents from the Virginia Beach Juvenile Court System.

Data relative to recidivism, school behavior, self-esteem, and interpersonal effectiveness were analyzed by an ANOVA with repeated measures. The results of the variable, recidivism, showed a significant decline in crimes for both groups over the three time periods (pre-, post-, and follow-up; $p < .001$). There was also a significant interaction between the Sierra II and the control group over the pre- to post-time period on recidivism ($p < .001$). The results indicated that for the four variables of school behavior (number of teachers' negative remarks, grades, absences, and number of discipline remarks), absences was the only variable which showed a significant interaction effect over the pre- to post-time period between the Sierra II and the control groups ($p < .05$). The 6-month treatment phase of the Sierra II Program was more effective than the 6-month treatment phase of the control group in reducing absences. The Sierra II participants showed a significant improvement on the behavioral variables of self-esteem and interpersonal effectiveness over the three time periods ($p < .001$). Further research needs to be implemented to evaluate the successful program components that distinguish the Sierra II Probation Program from the traditional probation programs.

West, F. W. (1989). An evaluation of the effects of a systematic short-term therapeutic camping program on the behavior and problem-solving skills of socially and emotionally disturbed children. Dissertation Abstracts International, 50/02-A, 351. (University Microfilms No. AAD89-0940110)

The purpose of this study was to evaluate the effects of a series of short-term, overnight, therapeutic camping trips on the behavior and problem-solving skills of socially and emotionally disturbed (SED) children. The subjects of this study were 22 SED boys, ages 10 to 13, who were assigned to Centennial School, a university-affiliated, private, special education school. The subjects were divided between two self-contained classes.

The experimental group participated in eight 2- to 3-night therapeutic camping trips. The therapeutic activities that were conducted during the camping trips included activities designed to promote self-confidence, such as ropes courses, and activities designed to promote group process, where all the boys had to cooperate in order to accomplish a difficult task, such as climbing over a high wall.

There were two dependent variables. Weekly averages of the Centennial School Point System, a truncated frequency count, were used to measure changes in behavior. These changes were analyzed using visual analysis techniques within subject, across subjects, and across groups. A descriptive analysis was done on the Problem-Solving Meeting Questionnaire, a rating tool developed to measure the quality of group process which was completed by the teachers immediately following each problem-solving meeting.

The results indicated that, for 10 of the 12 boys in the experimental group, a series of therapeutic camping trips had some or much effect on improving the boys' behavior during the camping trips. For 8 of the 10 children whose behavior improved during camping, the camping trips resulted in an increase in the level of inappropriate behavior immediately following some of the camping trips. Procedural integrity measures were utilized to substantiate the findings.

Therapeutic camping promoted group process as measured by the Problem-Solving Meeting Questionnaire. The experimental group participated in six problem-solving meetings, while the comparison group did not have any problem-solving meetings for the entire year of the study.

Limitations of the study were addressed. Implications of the findings for professionals interested in using therapeutic camping as a treatment intervention for socially and emotionally disturbed children were discussed.

Wichmann, T. F. (1990). Interpersonal problem-solving and asocial behavior in a therapeutic wilderness program (adventure programs). Dissertation Abstracts International, 52/05-A. (University Microfilms No. AAD91-29891)

The asocial behaviors of 36 male youths at-risk who participated in a 30-day therapeutic wilderness course were studied. Asocial behavior was measured with the Wichmann-Andrew Behavior Intervention Scale (WABIS), a 40-item, Likert-type behavior rating scale. A quasi-experimental, nonequivalent control-group design was used. Data were analyzed using analysis of covariance to adjust for pretest differences between groups. It was found that experimental subjects differed significantly from control subjects on post-treatment asocial behavior when the effects of pre-intervention asocial behavior were statistically controlled.

This study also examined several multiple linear regression models. It was discovered that interpersonal problem solving, as measured by the Means-End Problem-Solving (MEPS) Procedure, accounted for 24% of the variance in post-treatment asocial behavior. Furthermore, interpersonal problem solving is predictive of post-asocial behavior over and above age, pre-asocial behavior, instructor experience, and instructor role expectations. A forward selection, stepwise regression analysis was used to form the best predictor model for the criterion, post-treatment asocial behavior. The best predictor model included the variables of pre-asocial behavior, interpersonal problem solving, instructor experience, and instructor role expectations. This model accounted for 61% of the variance in post-treatment asocial behavior.

Witman, J. P. (1989). Outcomes of adventure program participation by adolescents involved in psychiatric treatment. Dissertation Abstracts International, 50/01-B, 121. (University Microfilms No. AAD89-07355)

This study investigated the outcomes of adventure program participation by adolescents involved with psychiatric treatment. The proliferation of such programs has raised questions regarding their efficacy.

Subjects of the study included 11 experts in the field of adventure programming, 207 participants in adventure programs at 12 adolescent treatment programs, and the 24 leaders of the programs in which participants were involved. The experts, through a modified Delphi process, identified skill/attitude outcomes and valued program characteristics. Program participants indicated their level of agreement with those items through a questionnaire administered at the conclusion of their program involvement. They also cited perceived differences between adventure and other treatment. A week after their participation, a random sample (N = 42) of participants responded to interview questions regarding their discussion and application of the program experience. Program leaders added the perspective of diagnostic/evaluative information gained.

Findings indicated that the majority of participants gained personal skills/attitudes relevant to treatment, particularly with regard to self-concept and interpersonal relatedness. "Process" characteristics of the adventure experience were valued more than "content" characteristics. Additionally, participants perceived the adventure program as different from other treatment, talked about the program with others, and applied skills and attitudes gained in the program in situations beyond the program itself. These situations included applications in other treatment, with peers, and with families. The program was also cited by many participants as being an enjoyable/"fun" social and interactive experience. Program leaders reported gaining a variety of diagnostic/evaluative information regarding participants. Among the independent variables which were analyzed, "site" had the most influence on reported outcomes.

Implications of the study for practice include the need to develop family, pre-adolescent, more "process" oriented, and outpatient adventure programs. Additionally, programs need to be of longer duration (20 or more hours) and have a variety of activities in order to maximize benefits. Research that further specifies outcomes and identifies longitudinal impacts of participation is also indicated.

Wright, A. N. (1982). Therapeutic potential of the Outward Bound process: An evaluation of a treatment program for juvenile delinquents. Dissertation Abstracts International, 43/03-A, 923. (University Microfilms No. AAD82-18950)

An evaluation was conducted of the effects of an adapted Outward Bound program on delinquent youths. Specifically, the study measured the program's effects on the self-esteem, self-efficacy, locus of control, cardiovascular fitness, and problem-solving skills of the participants. Individuals were assigned to an experimental group and a control group through a random process existent within the referral system of the agency. Experimental subjects participated in the 26-day wilderness treatment program. The control-group subjects were waiting for placement in the program.

The Tennessee Self-Concept Scale, modified Internal-External Scale, Generalized Expectancy for Success Scale, and modified Harvard Step Test were administered to both groups as a pretest and a post-test. The Means-Ends Problem-Solving Procedure recording simple demographic information and offense history from agency case files was given to the experimental group at the pretest and post-test. A background information sheet was also completed on each subject .

The data analysis used the analysis of covariance, matched t-tests, and product-moment correlation techniques. The analysis revealed that there was a significant difference between the experimental and control group in self-esteem ($p < .01$), internality ($p < .01$), and fitness ($p < .05$) at the end of the wilderness program. The experimental subjects were found to show a significant increase in self-esteem ($p < .001$), self-efficacy ($p < .01$), internality ($p < .001$), and fitness ($p < .001$) between the beginning and the end of the program. The experimental group however showed no gain at all in problem-solving skills. The analysis also demonstrated that neither the seriousness of offense history nor the demographic variable of age was strongly related to having a more positive experience in the adapted Outward Bound program.

The major conclusions of the study were that the program made a significant impact on the participant's physical fitness and self-orientation (i.e., self-esteem, self-efficacy, and locus of control). In contrast to those positive program effects, the study demonstrated that participants failed to show an increase in problem-solving skills as a result of the program.

Ziven, H. S. (1988). The effects of the challenge group treatment program on psychiatrically hospitalized adolescents. Dissertation Abstracts International, 49/10-B, 4567. (University Microfilms No. AAD88-17729)

The purpose of this study was to evaluate the effectiveness of the Challenge Group treatment program, a challenging, physical, group problem-solving treatment technique, applied as part of an acute-care, adolescent psychiatric inpatient program. Previous research on related programs—Outward Bound and Project Adventure—has suggested, but not concluded, that this type of treatment might be an effective adjunct to psychiatric treatment. Eighty-four hospitalized adolescents, diagnosed with conduct disorder or affective disorder, were divided into two groups, an experimental group which received the Challenge Group within the occupational therapy program and a comparison group which received the occupational therapy program alone. All other psychiatric treatment was comparable between groups. Groups were compared for differences in their improvement in psychological health, as defined by self-esteem, locus of control, interpersonal relatedness, psychiatric symptoms, and social adjustment. The experimental group, and certain of its gender-diagnosis sub-groups, improved more than the comparison group in self-esteem, locus of control, and interpersonal relatedness. Poor outcome was examined through case study. Ramifications of the findings for future psychiatric applications were discussed.

Zwart, T. J. (1988). The effects of a wilderness/adventure program on the self-concept, locus-of-control orientation, and interpersonal behavior of delinquent adolescents. Dissertation Abstracts International, 49/07-A, 1709. (University Microfilms No. AAD88-16827)

The purpose of this study was to examine the effects of a 26-day therapeutic wilderness program for delinquent adolescent males on three conceptually distinct but closely related constructs: self-concept, locus-of- control orientation, and interpersonal behavior. Justification for the study was derived from the limitations of past wilderness/adventure research which suggested that there was a need for additional research on the effects of this type of alternative program for delinquent adolescents.

It was hypothesized that following participation in this program, the youths would exhibit increased self-concept and more internal locus-of-control orientation, would express higher needs for inclusion and affection and a lower need for control, and would display more socially adaptive interpersonal behaviors.

In order to examine the research questions, three self-report inventories were administered to 43 adjudicated delinquent male adolescents participating in this program which serves as an alternative to traditional detention treatment. A sample of 45 male delinquents in a traditional detention program served as a comparison group. In addition to the pretest, post-test, and follow-up self-report data, behavioral observations were obtained from the instructors of the wilderness courses.

The results of this study failed to show a significant treatment effect on any of the primary dependent variables. The lack of a significant effect on the self-concept and locus-of-control variables was attributed primarily to apparent exaggeration and inaccurate self-report by the subjects in both samples. While there was no statistically significant effect on the three measures of interpersonal need, the results of the behavioral observations by the group leaders indicated that the participants learned more socially appropriate behaviors as a result of the experience (they were observed to communicate more effectively, to be more responsible and sociable, and to possess higher self-esteem). It was suggested that future researchers might continue to study these variables, especially the interpersonal effects of participation. It was also suggested that qualitative research methods and research on specific program variables would be appropriate.

H. L. (Lee) Gillis, Ph.D. is an Associate Professor in Psychology at Georgia College in Milledgeville, Georgia, and a licensed psychologist in part-time private practice. He has been associated with the field of adventure therapy since 1976 and has attempted to accurately document and disseminate the many therapeutic uses of adventure found in the literature in hopes of moving the field forward.

SECTION 6

THE FUTURE OF
ADVENTURE THERAPY

Craig Dobkin

33

THE FUTURE OF THE PROFESSION OF ADVENTURE THERAPY

MICHAEL A. GASS, Ph.D.

Throughout this book, the rationale and demonstrated effectiveness of the field of adventure therapy have been outlined through theoretical models, sample programs, and research studies. For a field with such a short history, there have been some exciting and rapid advancements. Some of these advances include the effective applications of adventure therapy to a variety of therapeutic populations, the development of specific prescriptive techniques particular to adventure therapy as well as methods that successfully interact with other disciplines, and the ability of outcome studies to provide evidence of achievements in working with populations where other approaches have experienced limited success.

However, there have also been some shortcomings that limit the current applications of adventure therapy as well as the future development of the field. One major difficulty has been the lack of professional material to advance the credibility of adventure therapy as a profession. It is hoped that this book, as well as other recent publications (e.g, Schoel, Prouty, & Radcliffe, 1988), are beginning to rectify this situation. This lack of printed material to educate professionals and adequately portray to others the strengths of the field, often combined with a lack of understanding of the medium used to achieve the objectives of adventure therapy (e.g., initiative games, ropes course elements), can openly invite skepticism from closed-minded colleagues. The spontaneity of the experiences in adventure therapy that are so valuable in allowing clients to release inappropriate defenses can also contribute this initial short-sighted perspective.

Another shortcoming of the field is that, in being so new, the field has no established system of determining who is and is not qualified as an adventure therapist, let alone what the qualities are that separate "good" adventure therapists from "not so good" ones. Years of experience in the profession often is not a valid indicator of quality in the field, for one year of doing things "correctly" seems to be much more healthy for the advancement of the profession than 20 years of misusing the practices of the field. It has often been the case that in order to receive internal and external professional recognition for using therapeutic techniques with adventure programming, individuals interested in using this type of therapy have had to excel not only in the therapeutic elements of their colleagues (e.g., psychotherapy, social work, family therapy, recreational therapy), but also in the professional elements of adventure programming. Gillis et al. (1991) have advanced the need for achieving this type of "cross training" between professions, but they have also pointed out that there seems to be a lack of training in professional programs (e.g., academic settings, institutional settings) that truly advances the intersection of these concepts and the resulting methods that occur when these two disciplines are combined.

The purpose of this section of the text is to examine the evolutionary process of adventure therapy as a profession, forecast where current trends in the field may take this emerging profession, and introduce critical pieces from the articles that follow this introduction. Of all of the chapters of the text, some of the chapters included in this section probably represent some of the more controversial ideas in the field. The thoughts in this introduction should be included in such controversy.

THE EVOLUTION OF ADVENTURE THERAPY AS A PROFESSION

Looking at the present condition of the field often raises the question: "Where is adventure therapy in its development as a profession?" In looking at the qualities that constitute the body of a profession, Millerson (1964; in Kultgen, 1988, p. 60) conducted a survey of 21 sources that described the sociological characteristics of a profession. The following characteristics were placed in the following rank order (with the number of sources that identified this quality listed in parentheses):

1. Integrity is maintained by adherence to a code of conduct (13).
2. The profession is organized and represented by associations of distinct character (13).
3. A profession involves a skill based on theoretical knowledge (12).
4. The skill requires extensive and intensive training and education (9).
5. Professional service is altruistic (8).
6. The professional must demonstrate competence by passing a test (8).

7. The profession assumes responsibility for the affairs of others (5).
8. Professional service is indispensable for the public good (2).
9. Professionals are licensed, so their work is sanctioned by the community (2).
10. Professionals are independent practitioners, serving individual clients (2).
11. Professionals have a fiduciary relationship toward their clients (2).
12. Professionals do their best to serve their clients impartially without regard to any special relationship (2).
13. They are compensated by fee or fixed charge (2).
14. Professionals are highly loyal to their colleagues (1).
15. They regularly contribute to professional development (1).
16. Their prestige is based on guaranteed service (1).
17. They use individual judgment in applying principles to concrete problems (1).
18. The work is not manual (1).
19. Profits do not depend on capital (1).
20. Professional status is widely recognized (1).

While this is a loose collection of characteristics, with many of which most adventure therapists would disagree (e.g., the work not being manual?), it does point to areas where the field of adventure therapy needs development in order to further establish itself. Efforts contained in this section of the book (e.g., the establishment of a series of ethical principles for adventure therapy within the Association of Experiential Education) are steps in the correct direction if the field of adventure therapy is to be taken more seriously as a profession in a traditional sense.

One manner of looking at the potential professional evolution of adventure therapy is to view it on a developmental continuum similar to the evolution of some other professional fields. Such a developmental continuum might look something like this:

```
◄─────────── X? ───────────────────────────►
```

| Application used by other professionals | Separate field with shared yet common elements possessed by other professionals | Separate field possessing entirely separate elements |

This continuum represents the evolutionary processes of some applied professions. Some professions begin as applications that are used by professionals in other disciplines. These professionals initially use such techniques because it makes "practical sense" to use them to reach the objectives of their own profession. As these techniques evolve and advance, they begin to foster the development of theoretical constructs that remain valid across more than several isolated applications. As this occurs, they begin to produce a body of knowledge that is separate from the initial sources of their evolution. As these constructs differentiate from one another, they begin to be perceived differently internally by those professionals using them as well as by those professionals external to the use of these constructs. The disciplines share common elements, but their implementation of these elements is separate and distinct. As the new area emerges and is refined, it begins to develop its own body of knowledge, practices, and applications to the point to where it becomes a separate entity from the original allied profession.

The question of such a process becomes: "Where is the development of adventure therapy as a profession at this point?" If one views the elements outlined by Millerson, there are several concepts that are well on their way to being established (e.g., professional service is altruistic, professional service is indispensable for the public good). Other elements remain far from being implemented (e.g., the profession assumes responsibility for the affairs of others, integrity is maintained by adherence to a code of conduct) or questionable as to whether they should be implemented (e.g., the professional must demonstrate competence by passing a test; professionals are licensed, so their work is sanctioned by the community).

The "X?" placed on the continuum seems to be a current "best-guess estimate" on where the "average" evolution of the field's practices stands at this point. As evidenced throughout this book, the field has strong applications to a number of professions (e.g., psychotherapy, social work, family therapy, recreational therapy) and has begun to emerge with several elements that form a unique body of knowledge, supported by other allied professions but separate from the practices found in these professions.

It is interesting to note that in the excellent article included in this section of the book by Martha Matthews (1991), staff attorney at the National Center for Youth Law (NCYL), she compared a potential collaboration between the Association for Experiential Education (AEE) and Council on the Accreditation of Service for Families and Children (COA) on the possibility of professional self-regulation of adventure therapy programs. In this article, she felt that the COA possessed the expertise to cover the "therapeutic, client-care aspects" of wilderness programs while the AEE possessed "more expertise in setting standards for technical safety aspects in adventure activities" (p. 15). Note that while many individuals may strongly disagree with such perspectives (like those being advanced in this section of this book), it does point to the manner in which the field is currently being surveyed and seen as a collection of elements from multiple sources.

How far will the profession of adventure therapy advance? Will adventure therapy remain or return to being an application of other therapies, or will it emerge as a profession unto itself? The answer to these questions will be provided in the future, but the trends of the next 10 years will provide insight into how the field will develop as a profession.

ELEMENTS OF THE ADVENTURE THERAPY PROFESSION

As highlighted by Millerson earlier, there are several critical pieces that point to a field's emergence as a profession. One of these is how professionals in the field are treated in their career efforts. The first article by Michael Gass is an adaptation from a 1988 presentation delivered at a conference on "Careers in the Outdoors." In this article, he identifies areas that serve as both strengths and weaknesses in our profession (i.e, commitment, independence, investment, experience base, process orientation, and dreams for better situations). He also discusses areas that will lead to the positive development of the profession in adventure therapy (i.e., security, successes, financial support, and balance).

In his article on career development, Gass addresses the sometimes inappropriate manner in which emerging professionals are treated in the field. Stephen Morse provides a representative biography of his experiences as an emerging practitioner, outlining the process many professionals go through as a developing professional. It reinforces the need for training programs to provide staff with the abilities and resources to meet these challenges in a successful manner.

As one can recognize from Morse's article, staff development is critical for the growth of adventure therapists, the improvement of adventure therapy programs, and the advancement of the profession of adventure therapy. Joe Stehno provides one model that portrays staff development as a critical feature in the ongoing professional development of an adventure therapist throughout his/her professional work in a program. Stehno points to staff recruitment, orientation, communication, support services, instructional clinics, and evaluation as all playing a role in reaching the objective of advancing adventure therapy through individuals and programs.

How is the field perceived by external professionals? As mentioned earlier in this section, an article that gives great insight into this phenomenon is the piece compiled by Martha Matthews of the NYLC. In her article, she points to the adventure therapy field as providing some of the best and worst of societal responses to troubled adolescents. Her updated report of the current status of the role of regulating wilderness therapy programs should be "required reading" for those professionals wishing to reflect on how the field is systemically affected by other programs and desiring to know external trends that will possibly shape each program's internal practices in the near future.

Kultgen (1988) stated that "professional societies must support individuals by providing effective codes of ethics and by contriving some means of protecting a person's reputation, career, livelihood if he/she confronts an organizational complex" (p. 9). Regardless of whether one agrees with Kultgen, it is difficult to demonstrate that the profession of adventure therapy has advanced to this point. The establishment, in 1991, of ethical principles by the Adventure Therapy Professional Group of the Association for Experiential Education is an exciting indication that the field of adventure therapy is moving in this direction. The current ethical principles of this professional group and their background are presented in this section. These should also be critical reading for all professionals working in the field of adventure therapy. Although established, it is important to remember that they remain a "working document," and professionals are encouraged to stay updated on future revisions and developments.

Discussing ethical guidelines is one matter; practicing them can obviously lead to resulting dilemmas. Robert Creal and Nancy Florio do an excellent job of reflecting on the effects of certain practices in adventure therapy and how programs should constantly be assessing themselves and their client practices. Ethical practices, as with all areas of professional development, must be seen as areas in need of continual development and revision to have true application to the field of adventure therapy.

34

ENHANCING CAREER DEVELOPMENT IN ADVENTURE PROGRAMS[1]

MICHAEL A. GASS, Ph.D.

The purpose of this presentation is to challenge all of us to look critically at the state of our profession. In order to enhance professional and career development in adventure programs, we must face several challenges and initiate a healthy and growing educational process. In order to be effective, this process should require that we look at the future of the profession with a new vision, which is somewhat exciting and threatening at the same time.

THE CURRENT STATUS OF OUR PROFESSION

Can we enhance our profession to accomplish our goals in an improved and healthier manner? Where are we now? Who are we? Compared to other professions, we're still pretty young. Some of our "elder" colleagues recently celebrated their 25th anniversary, which obviously points to the comparatively recent development of our field. In being "young" in our development, our field possesses a wide range of opportunities without many restrictive boundaries. This adds to the uncertainty of our lifestyles, but most of us have accepted this risk in order to reach perceived needs in a way that can help others.

What does it mean to work in the outdoors or to use "alternative" settings, like conducting therapy on ropes courses for instance? When you introduce yourself to others and describe what you do, what kind of response do you get? Do people think that you are a valued and respected professional, or that you're just "dropping out" for a while but pretty soon, you'll get your act together and come back to being a responsible person? Does working in the outdoors mean that we're looking for an escape from things such as "real problems," "big business," or "traditional practices"? For some adventure therapists this may be the case, and I would state that if this is so, we are destroying not only the foundations of positive

417

change that our field is trying to bring about, but also the field of adventure therapy itself.

Probably the best way to look at how we might have acquired such external perceptions and internal perspectives is to look at the strengths and weaknesses that our field possesses. These are the qualities that we often count as our strengths:

STRENGTHS OF OUTDOOR PROGRAM PROFESSIONALS

- Strong commitment
- Independent
- Lifestyle investment
- Experience based
- Process oriented
- Dream for better situations

1) Commitment. In some ways, our field is comprised of highly committed individuals. We not only help people to help themselves, we try to make the world a better place. This makes us feel good and it should. To these ends, we're willing to work long hours, usually until exhaustion sets in. We have a hard time saying "no," but that means we can say "yes" a lot. To coin a phrase from a common joke, "How many adventure therapists does it take to change a light bulb? Just one, but they'll be upset if you don't allow them to change more." We go that extra mile for people to really help them make a difference. As a field, we have capitalized on our energy. We take people out to the woods and stay with them for 30 days straight, 24 hours a day. Not many other professionals can, or even want to, make this claim.

2) Independence. We are independent; we pride ourselves in being self-sufficient. We use terms like "solo experience" and "being one in harmony with nature." Living on your own in nature is often seen as a plus in our profession. Most other professionals would see this as detrimental and frightening.

It's amazing how many cards we carry to show how independent we are. Open up your wallet and they will all drop down and hit the floor. Speaking just of the As, we have all the American Red Cross cards, from whitewater canoeing and sailing to Advanced First Aid and CPR. We also have the AEE, the AAHPERD, the AMPG...and those are just the As. Our independence makes us flexible enough to cover a great number of needs. We're often multifunctional within the populations with which we work and that makes us feel good.

418

3) Lifestyle investment. Robert Frost said: "My vocation and avocation together." What a nice harmony! This is often what pushes many professionals forward. Our lifestyle matches our work and we become more motivated because of the intrinsically rewarding nature of our work. Vacations? We work on our vacations. Some professions revolve work around vacations; others revolve vacations around work. We go on vacation to save the whales, participate in Earth First rallies, or do service projects.

4) Experience based. "Learn by direct experience," "Experience is the best teacher," "Learn by doing"—these are great things. I was on a program once where I had talked about Maslow's thoughts on self-actualization experiences. I shared with the group Maslow's belief that people generally experience approximately eight peak experiences in their lifetime. One of the clients with whom I was working turned to me and said, "Well, I've already had two this morning so I better slow down or I'm going to use them all up in one day." We enable people to reach new heights with the way that we work.

5) Process oriented.   Quite often we are more process-oriented than product-oriented. We like phrases like, "We don't teach people to be better rock climbers, we use rock climbing to make better people." We give our clients the ability to exercise responsibility and also to be held accountable for their actions. It's incredible that we can do both of those things at the same time; we are probably one of the few professions to achieve this.

6) Dream of better situations. Our focus often leads us to make the best of difficult situations. We focus on change and in so doing, empower participants through the environments in which we work.

Those are our strengths, yet they are our also some of our greatest weaknesses.

STRENGTHS AND WEAKNESSES OF OUTDOOR PROGRAM PROFESSIONALS

Strengths	Weaknesses
Strong commitment	Strong commitment
Independent	Independent
Lifestyle investment	Lifestyle investment
Experience based	Experience based
Process oriented	Process oriented
Dream for better situations	Feet off the ground

1) **Strong commitment.** We are so committed that we have great difficulty with self-care. We usually treat others better than ourselves, and we expect to have the energy to accomplish tasks that we would never dream of asking our participants to consider. However, our level of commitment is often misread. I was on a panel at a mental health workshop a week ago where a person said to me, "If I could just find a responsible outdoor leader, I would hire that person. I've had two before, paid them an adequate salary, $25,000-$30,000 a year, but they weren't responsible."

"What do you mean?" I asked. "Outdoor leaders are some of the most responsible people I've ever known." He said, "Well, when we had meetings to attend, they would get so wrapped up in washing sleeping bags that they wouldn't make it to the meeting. When we had to present a budget, the outdoor leader would be off doing the equipment checks at a ropes course." As this example illustrates, our commitment needs to be congruent with the vision and the value system of other professionals in the organizations in which we are members.

2) **Independence.** We are so independent that we run the risk of overlooking the strength and necessity of interrelatedness. We miss valuable opportunities to interact with others. Our flexibility and independence sometimes cloud our sense of direction and the intent of the message we wish to send to other people. Bob MacArthur (1986) uses the term "Mainstream Fringe." I think that term does a wonderful job of describing how too many of us conduct our professional endeavors. We're not going to get sucked into the mainstream, we're going to stay out on the fringe. Unfortunately, when we do enter the mainstream, we are sometimes too transient in our lifestyles to commit to a community and make a difference. We are too concerned about our own freedom to invest in other people for too long. We need to change this if we wish to create lasting change in the systems where we work and with our clients.

3) **Lifestyle investment.** It's obviously draining. The types of interpersonal dynamics that happen in outdoor education and the boundaries that we cross when we say "yes" to requests instead of saying "no" obviously affect our lifestyle. We would probably be alarmed to see the results of a research study that examined the effects of our profession on the destruction of interpersonal relationships.

4) **Experience based.** We focus so intently on being experiential that we sometimes lose track of our theoretical base or what we can dictate to others through written material. The small amount of material that does exist tends to be more of a "how to" than a "why." How can we justify the "how to" if we don't communicate the "why" to people? If we choose to live just by our own experiences, then the extent of our field becomes

the length of one person's lifetime. Our professional experiences need to pyramid on each other or we are destined to keep reinventing problems when we could be solving them and expanding our horizons.

5) Process oriented. As I said previously, we are process-oriented instead of product-oriented. This often makes it difficult to explain and demonstrate to others what we do. Many times we say, "But if you could just go with us, you would understand what we do and then you would support our ideas." We must realize that we can't always take everybody with us to help them understand. We need to come up with additional ways to communicate to others about our programs.

I had a student in a class who came back to me after a wonderful experience leading some high-school youths up Mt. Adams in New Hampshire. I asked him about the trip and he said, "I did this fantastic thing this weekend, a great educational experience for these high-school students." In an attempt to further his learning, I asked, "Did they learn anything?" He forcefully replied, "Of course they learned something being up on Mt. Adams! We saw the sun rise and the frost fall off the trees. It was beautiful." I asked, "What was it that they learned?" He got so upset that he walked away. He came back, and we have been working on it ever since. The top of Mt. Adams was a fantastic experience, but we must be able to better describe the product of such an experience if we plan to maintain our wonderful processes. How can people help and support us if they don't understand what they are helping and supporting?

6) Dream for better situations/Feet off the ground. We dream for better situations but when we dream, our feet come off the ground. With our eyes on the clouds, we have little time for investment in things such as "politics," "administration," "ethics," "peer review," and "research"; however, these are critical for growth and change in any profession.

ENHANCING CAREER DEVELOPMENT

If we're going to change these problems and make things more healthy for ourselves and our field, how do we go about doing so? Here are some of the factors that will help us:

1) Security. Security begins from within. We need to feel secure in what we do to have a chance to flourish. We need to be able to place people in program positions where they can grow, receive constructive feedback, and not burn out. Too many programs take their burned-out staff and throw their carcasses away after they have become numb, only to replace them with new, fresh bodies until they also burn out. If a staff member burns out in a program, it's partly our fault as a profession. We need to change the field to ensure that people feel secure as outdoor professionals and as human beings. Those two entities must blend together.

2) Success. I truly enjoy what Willi Unsoeld said: "Success is not a destination, it is the quality of what you do." We need boundaries where we can say, "I *will not* say 'yes' on the other side of this boundary." The first place to start is with some easy, non-negotiable values. Just think of the message you send to someone if you say, "This is a four-man tent." Shouldn't you have said "four-person tent?" Small adaptation, yes, but think of the successful attitude and message that it sends. Where does *quality* programming end and too much *quantity* programming take over? That's another good boundary for us. We're not going to step over that line. We're going to retain high quality in what we do.

And ethics? There are currently two adventure programs in the United States that I know of that train Central Intelligence Agency members. I spoke with one program on the phone 2 weeks ago; they wanted some assistance with program planning. Should I feel that there is a difference between sharing information with this person and sharing information with a program for unwed mothers trying to break the destructive cycle of welfare? This is something we should work on. Jasper Hunt (1990) and the Adventure Alternatives Professional Group of the AEE are doing some critical things for us as far as developing a revision of ethical issues in experiential education and developing ethical standards in the field of adventure therapy. We need to push ourselves in a proactive manner toward successively higher levels of "quality" in order to keep our goals in sight and to feel successful and good about ourselves.

3) Financial Support. How much is enough? We're not talking about the "Lifestyles of the Rich and Famous," but we need to be paid as other professionals. If we're educating, we need to be paid as educators. If we're providing therapy, we need to be paid as therapists. If we're doing recreational programming, we need to be paid as recreational programmers. This will not happen overnight, but a commitment to heading in this direction needs to be made. I talked with a program on the phone yesterday and one statement they're making is to *refuse* to put an instructor in the field unless they can pay that instructor $100 a day.[2] Maybe we're not all there yet and maybe this is not the answer, but it's the type of commitment to staff we should be making. People must have the resources to achieve their life-care goals and maintain perspective.

Another challenge I would like to mention is that of internship opportunities. Some of these can be enriching and sustaining, but some programs seem to want "cheap labor" under the guise of internships. We need to change these practices. We should view the internship as an apprenticeship, the process of continuing to develop our craft or art. We are artists and this is the way we should perceive our profession: caring for one another and developing our craft to the highest degree possible. We're not doing this if we are abusing the entry-level members and future leaders of our field.

4) **Balance.** We need balance for perspective and growth. We need compensation time to balance our efforts for healthy restoration. I worked with a hospital this summer and one of the programming difficulties in adventure therapy that they experienced was that you can't always do outdoor activities in 45-minute blocks of time or 8 hours. Their resolution was to have staff work 4 days a week, 10 to 12 hours a day, with 3 days off. Other therapists work 40 hours a week, why should they demand more from the adventure therapists? We need to give ourselves time for regeneration, self-care, and introspection.

CONCLUSION

How do we achieve positive career development? The first step is to look at how similar we are instead of looking at how different we are. We need to seek out our similarities. One quality existent in healthy adventure therapy programs is the ability to work well within larger systems. A healthier perspective is achieved because the program supports and recognizes that it is part of a larger system. Another beneficial perspective is to realize that adventure therapy programming serves as the medium, and our role is to meet the specific needs of the people through the means that we provide. A third point is the education of co-workers. One person I spoke with said that the most important thing that she does in her job is to touch base with her administration. How many of us rate this quality as being one of the most important things that we do in our programs? We need to educate others more on what we do. We need to advance beyond the stage of "if you don't do it, you won't understand it." We must get beyond that without losing the special talents that we possess.

We also need to focus on the message that we are providing great things for people and they're keeping those things. A great metaphor that I like to use when I'm speaking to people is this: When we come back from an experience we're all dirty and grimy. When we go into the showers, the dirt will wash off, but the special ways in which we've changed don't go down the drain. They stay with us. We must conduct adventure therapy in this manner: don't let the good things that we do go down the drain. With teaching, therapy, or programming, we need to focus on the integration of what we're doing. In punctuating this, I'd like to use a Willi Unsoeld (1970) quote:

Therefore, it provides you with a final test. Why don't you stay in the wilderness? Because that isn't where it's at; it's back in the city, back in downtown St. Louis, back in Los Angeles. The final test is whether your experience of the sacred in nature enables you to cope more effectively with problems—and sometimes it doesn't, sometimes it just sucks you right out into the wilderness and you stay there the rest of your life—then when that happens, by my scale of value, it's failed.

You go to nature for an experience of the sacred; and I point out to you that it is not the only place that one can go, but in outdoor programs and in my own experience it's the one that tends to be emphasized. You go there to re-establish your contact with the core of things, where it's really at, in order to enable you to come back into the world of people and operate more effectively. So I finish with the principle: Seek ye first the kingdom of nature that the kingdom of all people might be realized.

We need to focus on achieving this message in our programs and making sure that it comes back home with our clients.

Finally, we must increase our connectedness with one another. We have two excellent activities that illustrate concepts that we don't live by enough. One is the "Trust Circle" and the other is the "Web of Life." When I do the circle Trust Fall, I ask clients to stand in the middle while the rest of the group stands and spots on the outside. If the spotters fail in their task, the person in the middle will fall and hit the ground. Is this a metaphor of what is happening too often in our field? And what happens with the "Web of Life" when we remove one entity from the circle or that entity isn't working? The rest of the system needs to take up the slack and often the whole system fails. These outcomes of activities seem all too analogous to what happens in our field all too often.

We need be aware that if one of our programs is having difficulty, it affects each and every one of us. I've received a number of calls from programs wanting to change their marketing strategies after hearing that another program was running an outdoor programming/adventure therapy scam. Instead of changing the public's perception of adventure therapy, they wanted to know how to distance themselves from the image that the program was presenting. One program contacted me and said that after 10 years of trying to build their program, they had lost one of their funding sources when its director read a newspaper article about the ineffectiveness of outdoor programming.

One way to increase our connectedness is to view ourselves in terms of "wholeness." I like this concept because it emphasizes the fact that our field is comprised not only of specific and separate programs, but also of the interactions between our programs. We cannot overlook these interactions for in them lies the strength of our field. Our work begins today. Let us not stay out on the fringe of isolation, let us join the fray of interdependence. Let us build one another up and, by so doing, stop the deterioration of professionals and the destruction of our field. Let us concentrate on our interactions and place our differences in positions where they can be truly valued. This is what we must accomplish to enhance our careers of "doing."

Footnotes

[1] This chapter is from the transcript of a keynote speech entitled "Enhancing Career Development in Outdoor Programs and Services" delivered by Michael Gass at the "Careers in Outdoor Programs" Conference in Greenfield, Massachusetts, on December 10, 1988.

[2] This program has raised its level of funding staff to a minimum of $150 in 1992.

35

SURVIVING AN OUTDOOR ADVENTURE GROUP[1]

STEVEN MORSE, M.A.

As the title indicates, this is not a treatise dealing strictly with the pleasures of outdoor adventure. Instead, it is a portrayal of outdoor adventure through the eyes of a newcomer to the field, both as a participant and as a leader. My experiences up until now have been at both extremes and at all stops in between. I feel it worthwhile to write of these experiences because I see them as being typical of novice leaders. I also feel that my recent personal struggles with an outdoor program that I organized and ran, reflect the essence of why outdoor programs and experiential education are effective.

In the summer of 1986, I was initiated into the field when I worked as a recreation counselor in a residential school for boys in Boston. Students participated in a modified Outward Bound program that involved a variety of outdoor activities, including pull-boating, sailing, canoeing, environmental service, wilderness camping, and backpacking. The delinquent clients and my own lack of experience with the activities combined for an unpromising beginning for my career as a youth worker. I was often intimidated by the clients themselves, by their intense anger, by their inability to control their behavior, and by their unwillingness to follow instructions.

Mostly, though, I was intimidated by the fact that I was expected to serve as a co-leader on trips where I was not sure if I could manage myself. On the flat-water canoe trip, the waters were unusually high—five out of eight canoes overturned and the majority of the clothes and sleeping bags were soaked. On that same trip I contracted a case of poison ivy so severe that it surprised even the dermatologist. On the final and most challenging trip, an attempted ascent of Mt. Washington in New Hampshire, it seemed as though the majority of our time was spent trying to convince the group members to put their packs on instead of throwing them into the woods in frustration.

The summer seemed to consist of one struggle after another. "Ropes course is stupid.... Sailing is boring, I'd rather be playing basketball.... I'm not gonna be in this canoe.... My pack is too heavy.... I hate tuna casserole! Can't we have hamburgers or something.... Don't tell me what to do. Get out of my face."

Because of these struggles and the difficulties I had with the job, I began to have doubts about myself as a youth worker and about the program as a whole. The struggles with the group members overwhelmed me to the point to where I lost sight of the program's goals. Our intention was to expose this group of teenagers to risk-taking activities, to activities that would stress them and scare them, to activities that were so far removed from their urban upbringing that they would at times feel overwhelmed. Most importantly, our goal was to bring them into contact with a part of themselves that they felt good about.

I still cannot say exactly what made me start to feel positive about the experience. It was partially the obvious pride that the group took in their efforts on all the trips, but particularly on the final expedition. It was partially the genuine delight that the group took in seeing the slide show at the end of the program. The subtle changes that some of the students had experienced showed me that this program could be effective. A further contribution was my personal growth as I mastered outdoor skills and behavior management.

When the summer program began, my main goal was to simply survive each day. My work-day was dominated by my fears of not being able to work with delinquent youths. I was extremely uncomfortable with setting limits and was as ill at ease in the woods as the clients were. These concerns persisted for most of the summer. When it came time for the final trip, these concerns were only heightened. After 10 weeks of working with the group, I did not feel any more confident than I did when the program first started. During this last trip, the program started to come together for me. I was able to see the point to all the things we had done in preparation for this trip: the group challenges, the shorter overnights, and the emphasis on team-work. I also found that I had more limit-setting skills than I had previously acknowledged. When I felt safer and more comfortable with these teenagers, I realized that I liked them more than I had previously acknowledged. Most striking is that while I swore to myself during Week 6 of the program that "I would never see these kids again once the summer is over," 3 weeks after the completion of the program I found myself visiting the school to see how they were doing.

My initial experience was clearly a pivotal one. Had I not taken the position as a recreation counselor, I might not have been exposed to outdoor experiential education. Had the job been any more difficult, I probably would have never even considered continuing in the field. If the program had not been so well designed, I might not have seen changes in some of the participants. The lesson I learned from my initial experience is that the process was at times difficult and painful, both for staff and clients, but out of that pain came the pride, delight, and growth of self-esteem.

To bring events up to the present, I was inspired enough by my initial experience to participate in an Outward Bound course. Later I participated in an Appalachian Mountain Club training program for youth workers interested in experiential education. This past summer I ran an outdoor adventure program through my position as a youth outreach counselor. What I found when I attempted to organize a program on my own is that I had to contend with a whole new set of struggles that were in many ways analogous to those that I had had to deal with as a recreation couselor, and also analogous to those struggles that face the participants of outdoor adventure programs.

Initially, the prospect of organizing a program was an overwhelming task. To begin with, the youth outreach position was primarily that of a clinician/advocate for the adolescents of the community. Outdoor adventure fit into the philosophy of the program because it is viewed as an alternative approach to therapy. However, because this approach was new, I had to start from scratch. Contacts had to be initiated to organize service projects; funding had to be arranged; transportation had to be secured; and, most importantly, I had to find clients.

After the essentials were attained, a new set of tasks presented themselves: menu planning, route planning, trip planning, grocery shopping, phone calls, continued meetings with other agencies, meetings with prospective clients, and meetings with their parents. At times I found myself lying awake at night trying to remember all the details I had to take care of the next day lest the whole program fall to pieces.

While managing the details seemed monumental, organizing this program was intrinsically satisfying. It was gratifying for me to provide the local parks service with volunteers for projects that were underfunded and understaffed (trail building, trail maintenance, and river clean-up). Similarly, it was gratifying to provide senior citizens at a nursing home the opportunity to spend time and share personal experiences with young people. Lastly, there was satisfaction in organizing the program and watching it get off the ground successfully.

At the risk of depicting this program as being a smooth-running, well-oiled machine, some of the main obstacles should be noted. One of the most difficult tasks was obtaining clients. Within the community, there was a large pool of teenage boys who could be categorized as "at-risk." The challenge was to get them to commit to the program. I arranged with the high-school administration to provide physical education credit to all participants who successfully completed the course. Even with the incentive of gym credit, it took prodding and convincing. Two weeks before the program was to begin, I had put together a group of eight boys who "assured" me that they were interested. One week before the program, five of them dropped out.

This was an especially difficult time for me. I felt frustration and anger, having put so much effort into the organization of the program only to have the majority of the participants drop out. I interpreted their withdrawal as a personal rejection. My first reaction was to cancel the program, but fortunately I did not. Ironically, the remaining participants responded by recruiting some friends to participate.

After the program began, the group and its dynamics provided yet another set of challenges. Foremost were the ceaseless power struggles that I encountered with the group. These struggles were clearly emanating from the individuals' lack of trust, abundance of anxiety, and difficulty in relinquishing any control. I recognized many of the struggles because I had seen them while working as a recreation counselor. I also recognized them from my personal Outward Bound experience; my group had directed them at our leader. What was unfamiliar was that now I, the leader, became the focus of the group's struggles. All of their insecurities, distrust, and control issues were tested on me. Fears about safety were manifested through the group members' initial refusal to enter the woods without hunting knives. Similarly, the group's consensus was that a transistor radio was necessary "just in case something important happened." Distrust showed itself through the difficulties on the ropes course and on the rock-climbing trip. Anxiety emerged through one member's panic as he tried to flee from our campsite during our first night in the woods.

While not an easy task for the group or for me, trust did slowly develop. I passed enough of their "tests" so that they felt that they would be safe with me. Enough limits were set to provide structure, and enough time and understanding were provided so that each individual felt that he was being understood. Specifically, the group demonstrated that they felt safe by finally agreeing to do the backpacking trip minus the buck knife and radio. They demonstrated trust by everyone's participation in the ropes course. They demonstrated that they could deal with their anxieties by pulling together around one member as he cried and said he could not stand being so alone in the woods.

As I processed my experience as a leader, I realized that I had been through much of it before—I had utilized my past experiences in designing this summer's program. I recognized the subtle changes in the group members, and I was all too familiar with the struggles we had had with each other.

Most significantly, though, I recognized the difficulties that both the group and I endured as the program progressed. To me, this mutual struggle reflects the essence of experiential education. It was not merely the group that was being challenged by the experience of being in an outdoor adventure program; I too, as a leader, was challenged. The group struggled to cope with rigors of a summer outdoor program; I struggled with the rigors of running a summer outdoor program. The group wanted to quit when they could not have their way; I was tempted to quit when I did not get my way. And as the group felt overwhelmed by the challenges presented to them, I, too, at times, felt overwhelmed.

My initial experience could best be summed up by a quote from one of the participants while hiking on the backpacking trip. "God, I hate this! These packs are heavy.... I have no water.... I hate the food you've been feeding us.... We are never gonna make it back to the van. Are you going to do this next summer?"

Steven Morse, M.A., has since left his position as Youth Outreach Counselor for the city of Newton, Massachusetts, and is presently enrolled as a doctoral student in School Psychology at the State University of New York at Albany. After surviving the last outdoor adventure, he hopes to lead another soon.

Footnote

[1] This article was originally published in the 1990 Journal of Experiential Education, 1(13), 20-22.

36

A STAFF DEVELOPMENT MODEL[1]

JOSEPH J. STEHNO

In the past, staff development in many adventure programs has consisted of an occasional workshop on medical, wilderness, or technical topics. Staff development, however, is more than a scattered collection of theoretical, practical, or technical activities. Literature from other professions (e.g., higher education) documents the need for well-integrated staff development programs that attend to the systematic enhancement of personal interests, instructional abilities, and an understanding of the organization's missions, objectives, and procedures (e.g., Dowling, 1982; Verma, 1984). Staff development should be individualized enough to provide technical assistance and interpersonal skills training for each staff member, as well as provide opportunities for organizational development and change.

A number of models have been suggested in recent years to attend to the growth and development needs of individual staff and the entire organization. Many of these models are based on research in adult learning and incorporate concepts and principles derived from adult development theories (e.g., Duncan, 1982; Houle, 1972). Other models generally follow a sequence of identifiable stages, beginning with problem or need identification and proceeding to stages of implementation, evaluation, and feedback (e.g., Fuller & Evans, 1985; Vogler, 1980).

Most of these models exhibit a "cyclical" design, with the evaluation stage of one sequence forming the assessment stage of the next series of training events. The models assume and expect participants to be actively engaged in and responsible for the planning and implementation of training and development activities. Many of the models stress the importance of holistic development, with training attending to motivation as well as technical competence. These models also recognize that an organization's development program be mutually beneficial, addressing the specific needs of staff while providing a means for the organization to attain its goals.

PARSON'S DEVELOPMENT MODEL

One model that has provided an effective structure for staff development in community colleges and has also proved equally effective in a wilderness program setting is the model suggested by Parsons (1980). Parson's model consists of the following six components:

1. Recruitment: Locating high-quality instructional staff is the responsibility of a search committee and all full-time staff. A variety of sources are used, but primary emphasis stresses personal contact and referral. Selection and hiring is not left to chance, but is a shared endeavor.

2. Orientation: Introducing new staff to veteran staff and to the program is essential. Orientation activities include a "buddy" system, handbooks, tours, technical and topical workshops, and informal communication sessions. The primary objective of this component is to quickly and thoroughly incorporate and familiarize new staff with program personnel and procedures.

3. Communication: Keeping staff informed of upcoming events, policy changes, and important information cannot be neglected, especially when staff are working diverse and varied schedules. In addition to information dissemination, communication increases a sense of identity and involvement within the organization.

4. Support Services: Providing the necessary equipment and resources so that high-quality programs can be conducted is evidence of the organization's commitment to both staff and participants. Such items as professional literature, consultants, instructional materials, and secretarial assistance allow staff the freedom to concentrate on their primary concerns of instruction and supervision.

5. Instructional Clinics: Commonly known as pre- and in-service workshops, clinics provide the necessary skills instruction to keep staff competently informed and proficient in their areas of expertise. Clinics may include problem-solving simulations, discussions, and other experiential or didactic sessions focusing on technical, interpersonal, or organizational issues.

6. Evaluation: Assessing the impact and effectiveness of part of all of the development program provides data and input that can be recycled into other components of the model, thus keeping the process fresh and stimulating. Frequent staff performance evaluations can lead to remedial activities or system-wide improvements, as long as the intention is directed toward positive growth.

Parson's model is obviously not unique in its content, since many of the other models contain similar components and activities. However, two distinctive features of this model should be noted. First, the design is logical and progressive, initially addressing the needs of staff as they join the organization, followed by systematically attending to their involvement and improvement as they mature. Second, the model is comprehensive enough to be flexible and adaptable to many situations.

APPLICATIONS TO A WILDERNESS PROGRAM SETTING

Positive results have been noted since the Touch of Nature Wilderness Programs (TONWP) at Southern Illinois University adapted Parson's model as its basic training and development format in 1986. Because the Wilderness Programs operate on a year-round basis, conducting activities in a variety of wilderness areas from Canada to Colorado, and serving a wide range of clients, a comprehensive and flexible model was needed to train and nurture the 40-50 staff who work with the TONWP during any given year. Like other large adventure programs, the TONWP required a staff development model that was responsive to the concerns and issues involved in effectively orienting 20-30 part-time staff who work for periods averaging 3 to 5 months before moving on. Many new staff members need extensive training to become familiar with the Program's philosophy, objectives, and operational policies, while the training needs of experienced staff in this area are minimal. Technical, medical, and instructional competencies obviously vary, and the maturity and experience levels, along with judgment abilities, differ significantly among this group.

At the same time, the training and development of 15-20 relatively permanent, full-time staff needed to be addressed. While there were differences in their experience and skill levels, as a group they were familiar with the theoretical foundations and the day-to-day procedures of the Program. All possessed the technical competencies to lead and supervise the various outdoor activities conducted by the Program, and most of this experienced group had worked in all of the wilderness areas used for trips and courses. Their tenure at Touch of Nature ranged from one to 7 years, and most had worked in at least two other outdoor programs. The majority held appropriate medical and aquatic certifications, and all possessed and demonstrated solid individual and group counseling/ facilitation skills. Since the full-time staff were so qualified, their training needs were not immediately evident. An occasional rockcraft or medical inservice was usually enough to keep them up-to-date on technical skills, while periodic crisis intervention or role- playing sessions, topical seminars, or local workshops maintained their interpersonal and processing abilities.

The major problem experienced by this group was the redundancy of issues and the repetitiveness of outdoor activities and groups. After working in the same course areas, instructing the same events, and working with the same populations, there was little personal or professional challenge and limited opportunities for growth. It was obvious that a development program was necessary for the veteran staff, and the Parson's model provided the design which formed the basis for the creation and implementation of such a program.

RECRUITMENT

Parson's model was initially implemented in the fall of 1986, when preliminary efforts were being made to recruit staff for the following summer. The recruitment component of the model needed little modification from strategies conducted in previous years, since time lines and procedures were fairly well established and deemed effective. The major change was primarily in attitude. The recruitment phase, instead of being viewed as an annual administrative processes, was now seen as the formative stage of staff development. Considered in this light, resume reviews, interviews, and other informational processes provided the Program with assessment data on individual as well as staff needs, abilities, and desires. This information eventually became part of the agenda for summer staff training in May 1987, and the center of individual staff development plans throughout the summer and fall. Another major shift in the recruitment process brought increased opportunities for full-time staff to be involved in recruiting and interviewing. Their experience with people and their familiarity with the Wilderness Programs made them effective recruiters and interviewers while providing them with stimulation and novelty following field instructional responsibilities.

ORIENTATION

As a result of including the Parson's staff development model, orientation efforts were significantly modified. A "New Staff Orientation Manual" was compiled and distributed to staff approximately one month before they arrived at Touch of Nature. This manual served to answer a number of frequently asked questions, gave new staff a composite "picture" of what to expect, and provided them with an understanding of what was expected of them. Another change was that full-time staff volunteered and were then randomly assigned to serve as "mentors" for incoming summer staff. Mentors were responsible for making daily contact with their new staff member, arranging tours of the Center and the

436

immediate course area, and involving them in the social and professional activities of the Program. As a result, new staff quickly became identified as members of the community and became familiar with many of the staff with whom they would work throughout the summer months.

COMMUNICATIONS

Initiating and maintaining vertical and horizontal communication within a large, complex organization may be one of the most difficult aspects of any development program. The problem can be exacerbated in outdoor programs where staff may work on different schedules and be spread over different course areas. The communications component of staff development included notices on bulletin boards, newsletters, course briefings and debriefings, and weekly, monthly, and annual meetings. Social events were also considered opportunities for the exchange of ideas and information. Most importantly, program leaders established a tone and format conducive to frequent and regular communications. Attention to communications involved "MBWA — Management by Wandering Around" (Peters & Waterman, 1982), with course directors and program directors visibly present when and where staff were conducting activities.

SUPPORT SERVICE

For several years, the Wilderness Programs attempted to reduce expenditures by operating with part-time logistical and secretarial support. In the short run, this effort accomplished its objective; in the long run, the Program suffered severe consequences. For example, despite commendable efforts on the part of the staff, the lack of a full-time logistics coordinator resulted in equipment that was lost, misplaced, or left in a state of disrepair. A "bare bones" equipment budget resulted in the eventual accumulation of worn-out, inoperable, or unusable gear. Instructional staff spent time and energy finding or fixing equipment that led to complaints and general dissatisfaction with logistical aspects of the Program.

Similarly, a part-time secretary was simply not able to handle all of the clerical demands placed upon her. It became apparent that full-time, professional personnel were necessary. Based on this observation, both positions were filled in 1986 and the overall quality and efficiency of the Program has markedly improved. Instructional staff were freed to devote more time to participants while the external image and internal organization of the Program were greatly enhanced and conducted in a more professional manner. Attention to detail, in the form of professional literature, community resources, assistance with housing, training subsidies, insurance, and a myriad of other services, became part of the foundation for the development and growth of staff.

INSTRUCTIONAL CLINICS

No experiential outdoor program can function without relevant and purposeful training sessions. Such instructional opportunities were indispensable for seasonal or part-time personnel. Pre- and in-service training, focusing on technical and interpersonal skills, were well designed and based on real or expected needs of the program and staff.

Senior staff were assigned training responsibilities in the form of group instruction and/or one-on-one work with novice staff. The expertise and experience of veteran staff were used by involving them in the production of instructional materials, field manuals, and training programs. At the same time, the talents and skills of newer staff, identified during the recruitment process, were incorporated into training activities. Expecting all staff to function as "trainers" for other staff created an atmosphere of interdependent support and respect for the diverse abilities that each person possessed. Involving staff in the planning and implementation of training increased interest and investment in the outcomes, while communicating an attitude of professionalism and pride.

Workshops on topics of staff interest were arranged with local social service agency personnel and private consultants on a "trade-for-services" basis. In addition, Advanced Lifesaving, Advanced First Aid, and CPR classes were offered on a regular basis at the Center. The Wilderness Programs conducted at least two all-staff training trips per year to wilderness areas used for Program activities. Besides familiarizing staff with the course area, these trips significantly aided in the building of teamwork and camaraderie in the group. The Program subsidized most training activities; however, staff were occasionally asked to contribute a small amount, which they frequently generated from self-initiated fundraising ventures.

EVALUATION

For staff, evaluation was seen as a combination of formal and informal methods and events. Formal performance evaluations were conducted on a regular basis with individual staff (as required by University regulations).

These sessions served to provide structure and regularity to the assessment process because they involved the completion of Civil Service evaluation forms by staff and supervisory personnel. Informal evaluations occurred on a continuous basis at a number of "contact" points. Pre-course briefing and post-course debriefing sessions had built-in opportunities for evaluation and goal-setting discussions. Bi-weekly staff meetings were occasions for two-way dialogue on common concerns and individual initiatives. Casual discussions and feedback sessions among staff were also fairly common.

On the organizational level, evaluations were conducted periodically as a way of assessing and redirecting Program priorities. All staff were encouraged to provide input and involve themselves in the problem-solving and planning processes that resulted from these meetings. Incident and accident reports were compiled, regularly reviewed, and frequently lead to changes in operational procedures. Solicited and unsolicited feedback from participants and referral agency personnel was monitored, considered, and incorporated into Program planning activities. Information from all of these and other sources was essential and pertinent to the creation or reformation of Program objectives and as content for the ongoing training and development of staff.

CONCLUSIONS

There is obviously much more that has been written on this topic, not only in the realm of higher education, but in most professional fields. As organizations and instructional fields become increasingly more technical and complex, staff development assumes a more essential role in the tasks of addressing the needs of staff and promoting their growth, while keeping them informed and involved in organizational concerns. Although there are a number of models that can be selectively adapted and modified to meet the requirements of an experiential program, it is important that the process and structure of the staff development program be cautiously planned and thoughtfully implemented. Development involves the systematic and progressive cultivation of individual and collective skills, attitudes, and values while concurrently attending to the enhancement of the organization's mission and goals. And since experiential programs strive to develop the potential of participants, it is equally imperative that the purpose of staff development becomes "...helping staff move beyond present competencies toward perceived ideals." (Teschner & Walter, 1984).

Joe Stehno is the Special Needs Counselor and Coordinator of Experiential Education programs at Pembroke Academy in Pembroke, New Hampshire. He is also on the faculty at Franklin Pierce College in Concord, New Hampshire, and a partner of Impact Training, an experiential management training firm. Joe was the Director of the Wilderness Programs at the Touch of Nature Center in Carbondale, Illinois, and is a doctoral candidate in Educational Administration and Higher Education at Southern Illinois University.

Footnote

[1] This article was originally published in the 1988 <u>Journal of Experiential Education</u>, <u>1</u>(11), 33-37.

37

WILDERNESS PROGRAMS OFFER PROMISING ALTERNATIVES FOR SOME YOUTH: MORE REGULATION LIKELY[1]

MARTHA MATTHEWS, J. D., Ph.D.
NATIONAL CENTER FOR YOUTH LAW

Introduction

The past few years have brought a resurgence of interest in, and controversy over, programs that use outdoor adventure activities, such as hiking, mountaineering, canoeing, etc., as part of a therapeutic approach to adolescents' behavior problems. There is a wide variety of wilderness programs, from state-run programs for adjudicated delinquents, to private agencies that serve delinquents, status offenders, and/or court dependents under contract with state agencies, to entirely private non-profit and for-profit organizations whose clients are referred by parents or therapists. VisionQuest, Outward Bound, Associated Marine Institutes, and Wilderness Conquest are some of the well-known programs.

Wilderness youth programs are important because they may represent the "best and the worst" of societal responses to troubled adolescents. At one extreme, they may be a vital alternative to traditional juvenile correctional institutions. Some reputable and long-standing programs have shown remarkable success in working with adolescents who would otherwise be institutionalized. At the other extreme, there have been instances of physical and emotional abuse, unsafe practices, and—in a few tragic cases—deaths of adolescents in private wilderness programs.

Two related recent developments have occurred. First, in 1990, Utah responded to the deaths of two adolescents in wilderness programs by drafting new licensing standards applicable to all such programs operating in Utah. Because many wilderness programs are mobile and operate in several states, the Utah licensing agency sponsored a conference of regulators in other western states to coordinate policies regarding wilderness programs. Thus, there has been considerable new state regulation of wilderness programs from 1990 to the present time. At the same time, private providers' associations have become concerned about unsafe and abusive programs and have taken steps toward accreditation and peer-review processes.

RESEARCH AND POLICY STUDIES

Social science researchers have described the general characteristics and principles of wilderness programs, and have documented the positive effects of some programs on adolescents' self-esteem, social skills, and behavior. The literature, however, consistently stresses the need for further research, especially process studies examining how these programs work and follow-up studies examining the programs' long-term effects, if any, on adolescents' behavior.

The origins of contemporary wilderness programs have been traced back to several sources, including: the "forestry camp" model for juvenile corrections, first popularized in the 1930s, in which adjudicated youths participated in outdoor work projects in addition to counseling and education programs; and the Outward Bound program, first developed in the 1940s to train seamen to work together in rigorous conditions (Roberts, 1989).

In the 1970s, wilderness programs received a wave of attention in the social-science literature as a promising rehabilitative alternative to traditional juvenile institutions (e.g., Krajick, 1978; Nold & Wilpers, 1975). Several early studies (e.g., Behar & Stephens, 1978; Kelly & Baer, 1971) indicated that these programs could improve adolescents' self-esteem and reduce future antisocial behavior. Since that time, wilderness programs have became more widespread and better-known in the fields of juvenile corrections and social services.

Recent studies (e.g., Roberts, 1989) generally describe wilderness youth programs in terms of a sustained course of outdoor activities involving physical challenge and perceived risk, in which adolescents and staff are required to work together, and which provide a fertile setting for counseling and education to address the adolescents' emotional and behavioral problems. There is, however, wide variation among wilderness programs, in program length (programs last anywhere between 3 weeks and 2 years); population served (adjudicated delinquents, status offenders, "at-risk" youths, court dependents, youths with substance-abuse problems, emotionally disturbed adolescents, or some combination of these categories); types of activities (backpacking, rock climbing, canoeing, sailing, cave exploring, etc.); type and frequency of counseling and education offered; family involvement; and follow-up or aftercare (Roberts, 1989). In addition, some more traditional residential facilities, such as group homes and residential treatment facilities, offer wilderness activities or expeditions as part of their educational or therapeutic programming.

The characteristics of wilderness programs that may make them more humane and effective than traditional youth corrections programs include low youth-to-staff ratios, intensive involvement of staff in daily activities, frequent informal counseling and conflict resolution, and, of course, a physical setting that engages the adolescents' interest and gives them a sense of challenge and achievement (Greenwood, Lipson, Abrahamsen, & Zimring, 1983; Roberts, 1989).

The basic rationale for wilderness programs is that adolescents will overcome patterns of antisocial behavior when confronted with an environment that cannot be manipulated, in which real obstacles must be overcome by hard work and cooperation with others, in which adolescents' actions have real-world positive or negative consequences, and in which initiative and responsible behavior lead to positive results (Greenwood et al., 1983; Kraft & Sakofs, 1984; Marx, 1988; Roberts, 1989; Wichman, 1991) For example, in most programs the adolescents are responsible for preparing their own meals. Unless all of them perform their tasks—gathering firewood, hauling water, cooking, etc.—nobody will eat. In this context, rules, rewards, and punishments do not appear as arbitrarily imposed by staff. Instead, rules have a clear relation to the adolescents' safety and well-being, and they enjoy or suffer the natural consequences of their own actions, instead of rewards and punishments meted out by staff.

There is, however, very little empirical data to confirm or refute this theory. A few studies have examined the short- and long-term effects of wilderness programs in terms of psychological and/or behavioral measures. Their results, while generally favorable, are tentative and inconclusive (e.g., Marx, 1988; Roberts, 1989; Sakofs, 1991; Wichman, 1983; Winterdyk & Griffiths, 1984). The need for further research is generally acknowledged (e.g., Roberts, 1989; Winterdyk & Griffiths, 1984; Wichman, 1991).

Two areas in which researchers often find wilderness programs lacking are "transfer of learning" and follow-up (Gass, 1985; Winterdyk & Griffiths, 1984; Wichman, 1991). Unless program staff help the adolescents to see the relevance of their experiences to their own lives, the social and problem-solving skills learned will be "put away in the equipment room along with the ropes and backpacks" at the end of the program (Gass, 1985, p. 24). Moreover, unless adolescents receive help with the transition back to their family and home environment, any gains they make may be negated by a return to poverty, lack of educational and job opportunities, and/or family dysfunction. Another problem frequently cited is the scarcity of staff who are experienced both in outdoor skills and in counseling skills (Wichman, 1991).

In general, the studies indicate that potential benefits of wilderness programs may justify their use as an alternative to traditional juvenile corrections approaches, but only if staff are well trained, adequate safety practices are in place, and the programs include a follow-up component and otherwise foster the transfer of learning into the adolescent's home environment.

STATE REGULATORS' RESPONSE TO SAFETY CONCERNS

In the summer of 1990, two incidents occurred involving deaths of adolescents in private wilderness programs, which spurred regulatory activity in Utah and other western states. On May 9, 1990, 15-year-old Michelle Sutton died of dehydration and exposure while hiking in the Summit Quest program. The program was based in Utah, but the death occurred on a program expedition in Arizona. On June 27, 1990, 16-year-old Kristin Chase died of heat stroke while hiking in the Challenger program in Utah. Both incidents led to criminal investigations, and the founder of the Challenger program now faces criminal charges. The parents of both adolescents, who placed their children in the programs because of behavior problems, have brought wrongful death actions.[2]

Both Summit Quest and Challenger are funded primarily from tuition paid by parents (or parents' health insurance policies). Decisions to accept adolescents into these programs were generally made by parents on the basis of information provided by program staff, without governmental involvement. Both programs accepted adolescents who did not consent to attend the program. (Other, more reputable wilderness programs generally accept adolescents only if they consent to participate.)

Even before the Challenger and Summit Quest incidents, Utah's child protective agency had removed several children from the Challenger program due to allegations of maltreatment. The deaths, however, prompted the Utah legislature to enact legislation enabling the state's Department of Human Services to adopt and enforce licensing standards for wilderness programs. The new standards were developed and implemented in the fall of 1990 (Utah Code, 1990). In addition to general standards applicable to all residential facilities, the standards governing staffing, equipment, admission and screening, nutrition, First Aid and general safety, transportation, and environmental precautions were developed. They do not, however, include safety rules for specific outdoor activities. Since that time, Utah's Office of Licensing has granted licenses to 13 wilderness programs, suspended the licenses of two programs, and denied licenses to two new applicants (Kreher, 1991).

In May of 1991, the Utah Office of Licensing sponsored a conference of agency officials and attorneys general in other western states to discuss policy concerning wilderness programs. (Because many wilderness programs are mobile, there was concern among state officials that tightening regulations in one state might merely cause less reputable programs to move to other states.) After the Utah conference, the National Center for Youth Law (NCYL) conducted an informal survey of the western states that sent representatives to the conference. Of these states:

- three (Utah, Arizona, and Nevada) have licensing standards specifically developed for wilderness programs (Utah, 1990; Arizona; 1985; Nevada; 1991);
- one (Colorado) applies regulations developed for recreational camps to wilderness youth programs (Andrews, 1991);
- three (California, Washington, and Hawaii) apply licensing standards developed for other types of residential facilities, such as foster homes and group homes, thus effectively preventing the operation of any wilderness programs in those states (Dodds, 1991; McCartan, 1991; Farrell, 1991);
- three (Hawaii, Idaho, and North Dakota) are contemplating development of licensing standards specifically for wilderness programs (Farrell, 1991; Ackerman, 1991; Doll, 1991).

The regulations, specifically tailored to wilderness programs in Utah, Arizona, and Nevada, are fairly similar in structure and scope, focusing mainly on program administration and staffing, admission and screening, and ensuring the health, safety, and proper treatment of clients. Arizona, however, has the most detailed and specific standards, while Nevada's are the most broad and general.

In addition to these recent developments in western states, there are several other important examples of state regulation of wilderness programs. New Jersey, in 1989, received federal grant funding to study several innovative youth programs, including wilderness programs. That state developed and implemented a "regulatory module" for wilderness programs, including a general policy statement, administrative and program requirements, and health and safety requirements. New Jersey's standards, unlike those developed in the western states, also include safety rules covering various specific outdoor activities, such as hiking, rock climbing, canoeing, skiing, etc. (New Jersey, 1991).

In addition, Florida has had longstanding contracts with several wilderness programs, including Outward Bound, Eckerd Family Youth Alternatives, and the Florida Sheriffs' Youth Ranches, both for dependent minors at-risk of delinquency and for adjudicated youths. Florida has licensing standards that cover "short-term wilderness programs" as well as other types of residential care for dependent minors (Florida, 1987). Wilderness programs serving adjudicated youths, however, are not covered by these standards, but instead are subject to general and health and safety regulations (Muley, 1991). Similarly, South Carolina's Department of Youth Services contracts with an Associated Marine Institute program for adjudicated youths (Wilson, 1991). Finally, the Massachusetts Department of Youth Services has, since 1970, operated its own wilderness program, Homeward Bound, for adjudicated youths. This appears to be the only instance of a state-run wilderness program.

Thus, there are a variety of available models for state regulation of wilderness programs. If a state agency does not take the unusual step of running its own wilderness program, it can enact regulations tailored to the special purposes, conditions, and potential dangers of wilderness programs, such as those developed in New Jersey, Utah, Arizona, and Nevada. Such regulations serve both to avoid the potential dangers of unregulated, unsafe programs such as Challenger and Summit Quest, and to permit the operation of the well-run programs that have received praise in the social science literature.

PROFESSIONAL SELF-REGULATION

Concurrently with the western states' recent regulatory activity, private service providers have shown increased interest in self-regulation. Voluntary professional accreditation with peer review has been proposed as a way to prevent abusive and unsafe practices, enhance the professionalism of wilderness programs, and assist state agencies and parents in selecting appropriate placements.

The Council on Accreditation of Services for Families and Children is an independent accreditation service sponsored by several major children's service organizations.[3] COA publishes standards for a wide range of social services agencies and mental health programs, including group homes and residential treatment centers, and offers accreditation review to any program, public or private, that requests it.

COA is currently planning to add therapeutic wilderness programs for youths with emotional or behavioral problems to the types of residential facilities it accredits, and is in the process of developing standards that can be applied both to full-time wilderness programs and to residential facilities that offer a wilderness component. COA plans to publish these standards by the end of 1992. COA accreditation, however, is entirely voluntary and is an expensive and labor-intensive process. For this reason, social service and mental health agencies already accredited by COA (especially member programs of COA's sponsoring organizations) may be more likely to seek accreditation of wilderness components of their programming than might free-standing, independent wilderness programs.

There is, however, another proposal for professional accreditation that may reach more wilderness programs. The Association for Experiential Education is a private professional association to which many wilderness programs and other outdoor recreational and adventure programs belong.[4] The AEE is currently developing accreditation standards and a peer review process for wilderness programs.[5] Because many wilderness programs already belong to the AEE, small, independent wilderness programs may be more likely to seek AEE accreditation than COA accreditation. There is also a possibility of collaboration between these two organizations, since the COA's area of expertise mainly concerns the therapeutic, client-care aspects of wilderness programs, while the AEE has more expertise in setting standards for technical safety in adventure activities.

Both accreditation systems, however, are only in the planning stages. Even when in place, they will remain voluntary and self-selected. Professional accreditation cannot fully address the problems created by "maverick" programs unless it becomes so widely accepted and sanctioned that a program could not remain in business without it. Accreditation is, however, a promising development toward uniform and accepted professional standards. As these standards are further articulated by providers' associations, it is possible that future state regulation will be coordinated with, or will incorporate by reference, such professional standards.

THE ROLE OF CHILD ADVOCATES

Children's advocates may become involved in issues regarding wilderness programs in various ways. A public defender may propose a wilderness program as an alternative to commitment to a locked facility. A dependent child's counsel may advocate placement of a troubled adolescent in a wilderness program, instead of yet another group home. On the other hand, an advocate may be called upon to get a youth released from a harsh or unsafe program, or to protect a child against involuntary commitment to a wilderness program.

Advocates can encourage state agencies to consider wilderness programs as part of an array of community-based services for youths at-risk. At the same time, children's advocates can help to ensure that such programs do not operate without some adequate system of accountability, whether through government regulation or professional accreditation and peer review, or both.

Because wilderness programs are often small, mobile operations operating in remote areas, they may fall between the cracks of state, tribal, and federal jurisdiction. If these programs continue to proliferate, and regulation to ensure quality and prevent abuse continues to be an issue, there may be a need for uniform national standards, either through federal legislation or through coordination among states (and, in some western areas, tribal authorities).

Children's advocates have an important role to play in exploring constructive alternatives to traditional—often inhumane and ineffective— responses to at-risk youths. Wilderness programs offer a promising alternative, but only if they are physically and emotionally safe and nonabusive, and only if they provide transition or follow-up services that ensure that the wilderness experience will translate into a real change in adolescents' lives when they return to their families and communities.

Martha Matthews is a staff attorney at the National Center for Youth Law. She received her J. D. and Ph.D. from the University of California at Berkeley's Jurisprudence and Social Policy Program. She is a veteran of clerkships at all levels of the federal courts, including a stint clerking for Justice Harry Blackmun of the U. S. Supreme Court.

Footnotes

¹ This article originally appeared in the November-December 1991 issue of the <u>Youth Law News</u>. For subscription information, please contact the National Center for Youth Law, 114 Sansome St., Suite 900, San Francisco, CA 94104-3820. (415) 543-3307.

² Following the Sutton incident, the Summit Quest program moved its operations to Nevada. That state's child protective agency removed eight children from the program in early 1991. In July 1991, in litigation between Summit Quest and the state agency, the agency was granted an injunction barring Summit Quest from operating until Nevada's new licensing standards for wilderness programs went into effect. See Summit Quest v State of Nevada, Department of Human Resources, # CC-1940791 (7th Judicial District, July 25, 1991).

³ The sponsoring organizations are: The Child Welfare League of America, National Association of Homes and Services for Children, Catholic Charities of America, the Association of Jewish Family and Children's Agencies, the Lutheran Ministry system, and the National Committee for Adoption.

⁴ The AEE publishes a widely-recognized manual, <u>Safety Practices in Adventure Programming</u>, Priest, S. and Dixon, T., (1990), which covers general health and safety, staff qualification, environmental impact, and ethical concerns as well as safety practices specific to various outdoor activities.

⁵ In addition to these efforts, several individual programs, including Outward Bound, Wilderness Conquest, and Wilderness Encounter, have developed their own formal manuals or standards of practice.

38

ETHICAL PRINCIPLES FOR THE THERAPEUTIC ADVENTURE PROFESSIONAL GROUP [1,2]

STATEMENT OF PURPOSE

Since therapeutic adventure programs profoundly affect individual lives, it is the purpose of these principles to advocate for the education, empowerment, and safety of those who participate in these programs by establishing a minimum standard of ethical care and operation. Individuals who adhere to these principles will be considered as upholding, contributing to, and promoting a high standard of operation and service by the Therapeutic Adventure Professional Group of the Association for Experiential Education.

A. DEFINITION OF PROFESSIONALS

The term "professional" that is used in these ethical principles represents individuals who are members of the AEE Therapeutic Adventure Professional Group. These principles may have application to other members of the AEE, but the items contained in these ethical principles only pertain to Therapeutic Adventure Professional Group members of the AEE.

B. APPLICABILITY

The activity of professionals subject to these Ethics Principles may be reviewed under these Ethical Principles only if the professional is identified as a member of the Therapeutic Adventure Professional Group of the Association for Experiential Education. Purely personal activities having no connection to or effect on these professional roles are not subject to the Ethical Principles.

C. RELATED ETHICAL PRINCIPLES

Professionals subscribing to these ethical principles must be aware of other ethical codes and laws that intersect with the statements in Ethical Principles.

D. ETHICAL PRINCIPLES OF THE THERAPEUTIC ADVENTURE PROFESSIONAL GROUP OF THE ASSOCIATION FOR EXPERIENTIAL EDUCATION

1. Competence[2]

Professionals strive to maintain high standards of competence in their work. They recognize the boundaries of their particular competencies and understand the potential limitations of adventure activities. Professionals exercise reasonable judgment and take appropriate precautions to promote the welfare of participants. They maintain knowledge of relevant professional information related to the use of adventure experiences and they recognize their need for ongoing education. Professionals make appropriate use of professional, technical, and administrative resources that serve the best interests of participants in their program.

1.1 Boundaries of Competence

(1) Professionals provide services only within the boundaries of their competence, based on their education, training, supervision, experience, and practice.

(2) Professionals provide services involving specific practices after first undertaking appropriate study, training, supervision, and/or consultation from persons who are competent in those areas or practices.

(3) In those areas where generally recognized standards for preparatory training do not yet exist, professionals take reasonable steps to ensure the competence of their work and to promote the welfare of participants.

(4) Professionals seek appropriate assistance for their personal problems or conflicts that may impair their work performance or judgment.

1.2 Continuing Training

Professionals are aware of current information in their fields of activity and undertake ongoing professional efforts to maintain the knowledge, practice, and skills they use at a competent level.

2. Integrity

Professionals seek to promote integrity in the practice of adventure programming. In these experiences, they are honest, fair, and respectful of others. In describing or reporting their qualifications, services, products, fees, and research, professionals do not make statements that are false, misleading, or deceptive. Professionals strive to be aware of their own belief systems, values, needs, and limitations and the effect of these on their work.

2.1 Interaction with other Professionals

In deciding whether to offer or provide services to those already receiving services elsewhere, professionals carefully consider the potential participant's welfare. Professionals discuss these issues with participants in order to minimize the risk of confusion and conflict, consult with other professionals when appropriate, and proceed with caution and sensitivity.

Professionals do not engage, directly or through agents, in uninvited solicitation of services from actual or potential participants or others who, because of particular circumstances, are vulnerable to undue influences (e.g., respecting client relationships).

2.2 Supervision

Professionals delegate to their employees, supervisees, or students only those professional responsibilities that such persons can perform competently. Within the limitations of their institution or other roles, professionals provide proper training or supervision to employees or supervisees. Professionals also take reasonable steps to see that such persons perform these services responsibly, competently, and ethically.

3. Professional Responsibility

Professionals uphold ethical principles of conduct, clarify their roles and obligations, accept responsibility for their behavior and decisions, and adapt their methods to the needs of different populations. Professionals consult with, refer to, and cooperate with other professionals and institutions to the full extent needed to serve the best interests of participants. Professionals are concerned about the ethical professional conduct of their colleagues. When appropriate, they consult with colleagues in order to avoid unethical conduct. Because of its direct negative influence on participants as well as on the field, professionals are strongly urged to report alleged unethical behavior to appropriate and prescribed channels. Professionals are ethically bound to cooperate with professional associations' inquiries concerning ethical misconduct.

3.1 Basis for Professional Judgments
Professionals have an adequate basis for their professional judgments and actions that are derived from professional knowledge.

3.2 Initiation and Length of Services
Professionals do not begin services for individuals where the constraints of limited contact will not benefit the participant. Professionals continue services only as long as it is reasonably clear that participants are benefiting from that service.

3.3 Concern for the Environment
Professionals conduct adventure experiences in a manner that has minimal impact on the environment. Professionals do not conduct adventure experiences where permanent damage to wilderness environments will occur as a result of programming.

4. Respect for People's Rights and Dignity

Professionals respect the fundamental rights, dignity, and worth of all people. They respect the rights of individuals to privacy, confidentiality, and self-determination. Professionals strive to be sensitive to cultural and individual differences, including those due to age, gender, race, ethnicity, national origin, religion, sexual orientation, disability, or socioeconomic status. Professionals do not engage in sexual or other harassment or exploitation of participants, students, trainees, supervisees, employees, colleagues, research subjects, or actual or potential witnesses or complainants in investigations and ethical proceedings.

4.1 Policy Against Discrimination
Professionals do not discriminate against or refuse professional services to anyone on the basis of age, gender, race, ethnicity, national origin, religion, sexual orientation, disability, or socioeconomic status.

4.2 Ethic of Empowerment
Professionals respect the rights of participants to make decisions and help them to understand the consequences of their choices. Professionals assist participants in charting the course of their own lives. They respect the rights of participants to make decisions affecting their lives that also demonstrate an equal concern for the rights of others.

4.3 Describing the Nature and Results of Adventure Programming
When professionals provide services to individuals, groups, or organizations, they first provide the consumer of services with appropriate information about the nature of such services and their rights, risks, and responsibilities. Professionals also provide an opportunity to discuss the results, interpretations, and conclusions with participants.

4.4 Informed Consent
Professionals respect participants' rights to refuse or consent to services and activities. Participants must be well informed of the fees, confidentiality, benefits, risks, and responsibilities associated with these services and activities prior to participation. Professionals make reasonable efforts to answer participants' questions, avoid apparent misunderstanding about the service, and avoid creating unrealistic expectations in participants. Professionals inform participants of the relevant limitations of confidentiality as early as possible and the foreseeable uses of the information generated through their services. In the case of participants who are minors, parents and/or legal guardians must also give informed consent for participation. Professionals obtain informed consent from participants, parents, or guardians before videotaping, audio recording, or permitting third-party observation.

4.5 Fees
Professionals charge appropriate fees for services. Fees are disclosed to participants at the beginning of services and are truthfully represented to participants and third-party payers. Professionals are not guided solely by a desire for monetary reimbursement. They are encouraged to contribute a portion of their professional time for little or no personal advantage.

4.6 Advertisement

Professionals accurately represent their competence, training, education, and experience relevant to their practices. This practice includes using:

(1) Titles that inform participants and the public about the true and accurate identity, responsibility, source, and status of those practicing under that title.
(2) Professional identification (e.g., business card, office sign, letterhead, or listing) that does not include statements that are false, fraudulent, deceptive, or misleading.

4.7 Distortion of Information by Others

Professionals make efforts to prevent the distortion or misuse of their clinical materials and research findings. Professionals correct, whenever possible, false, inaccurate, or misleading information and representations made by others concerning their qualifications, services, or products.

4.8 Public Opinions and Recommendations

Professionals, because of their ability to influence and alter the lives of others and the field, exercise special care when making public their professional recommendations and opinions (e.g., public statements and testimony).

5. Concern for Welfare

Professionals are sensitive to real and ascribed differences in power between themselves and their participants, and they avoid exploiting or misleading other people during or after professional relationships.

5.1 Professional Relationships

Professionals provide services only in the context of a defined professional relationship or role.

5.2 Dual Relationships

Professionals are aware of their influential position with respect to participants and avoid exploiting the trust and dependency of such persons. Because of this, professionals make every effort to avoid dual relationships with participants that could impair professional judgment (e.g., business or close personal relationships with participants). When dual relationships exist, professionals take appropriate professional precautions to ensure that judgment is not impaired and no exploitation occurs.

5.3 Sexual Relationships
Sexual intimacy with participants is prohibited during the time of the professional relationship. Professionals engaging in sexual intimacy with past participants bear the burden of proving that there is no form of exploitation occurring.

5.4 Physical Contact/Non-Sexual Contact
Adventure activities often include various forms of physical contact between professionals and participants or among participants (e.g., spotting, checking climbing harnesses, holding hands). Professionals are sensitive and respectful of the fact that participants experience varying degrees of comfort with physical contact, even when it is offered for safety, encouragement, or support. Whenever possible, professionals inform, explain, and gain consent for usual and customary forms of physical contact. Professionals are aware of individual needs when initiating physical contact, especially if the contact is meant to communicate support (e.g., hugs, pats) and is otherwise not required for a particular activity. Except when safety is a factor, participants have the right to limit or   refuse physical contact with professionals and participants.

5.5 Behavior Management
Each program and professional will approach the topic of managing behavior with a concern for dignity and safety for both participants and professionals. Definitions of appropriate and inappropriate behaviors of participants should be made clear to participants before any adventure programming commences.

Professional responses to inappropriate behaviors should be clearly understood by both professionals and participants and carried out in an appropriate manner. There should be clear documentation of staff training and awareness about program policies concerning the management of unsafe behavior. Policies should never advocate the use of restraint unless participant(s) impose a threat to themselves or others. Restraint should never be used as a punishment or as a means to frighten, humiliate, or threaten a participant. Whenever possible, restraint should be avoided and as passive as possible. All behavior management should be accurately documented.

5.6 Physical Needs of Participants

Participants will be provided with the necessary water, nutrition, clothing, shelter, or other essential needs they require for the environment they are living in, unless there is a prior mutual consent between participants and professionals and it is recognized that this will serve a valid purpose (e.g., solo). At no time during any program will the withholding of these needs be used as a punitive measure.

5.7 Physical Treatment of Participants

At no time will participants be asked to perform excessive physical activity as a means of punishment. There should be a direct relationship between the participants' physical activity levels and the objective of the experience.

5.8 Appropriate Use of Risk

The amount of actual emotional and physical risk participants experience in adventure activities will be appropriate for the objectives and competence level of participants. Professionals use appropriate judgment when choosing activities that expose participants to actual or perceived physical and emotional risks.

5.9 Assisting Participants in Obtaining Alternative Services

Professionals assist participants in obtaining other services if they are unwilling or unable, for appropriate reasons, to provide professional help. Professionals will not unilaterally terminate services to participants without making reasonable attempts to arrange for the continuation of such services (e.g., referral). Experiences are planned with the intent that decisions made during and after the experience are in accordance with the best interest of participants.

5.10 Confidentiality

Professionals respect the right of participants to decide the extent to which confidential material is made public. Professionals may not disclose participant confidences except: (a) as mandated by law; (b) to prevent a clear and immediate danger to a person or persons; (c) where the professional is a defendant in civil, criminal, or disciplinary action arising from services (in which case participant confidences may be disclosed only in the course of that action); or (d) if there is a waiver previously obtained in writing, and then such information may be revealed only in accordance with the terms of the waiver.

Unless it is contraindicated or not feasible, the discussion of confidentiality occurs at the onset of the professional relationship.

5.11 Use of Case Materials with Teaching or Professional Presentations

Professionals only use participant or clinical materials in teaching, writing, and public presentations if a written waiver has been obtained in accordance with Principle 5.10 or when appropriate steps have been taken to disguise participant identity and assure confidentiality.

5.12 Storage and Disposal of Participant Materials

Professionals store and dispose of participant records in ways that maintain confidentiality. Records should be maintained for a minimum of   seven (7) years.

6. Social Responsibility

Professionals are aware of their professional responsibilities to the community and society in which they work and live. Within the limitations of their roles, professionals avoid the misuse of their work. Professionals comply with the standards stated in the *AEE Safety Practices in Adventure Programs* book as well as with the particular laws in their particular geographical and professional area. Professionals also encourage the development of standards and policies that serve the interests of participants and the public.

Footnotes

[1] Background of Ethical Guidelines

At the 19th Annual Conference for the Association for Experiential Education in St. Paul, Minnesota, one of the critical needs identified by the Therapeutic Adventure Professional Group was the establishment of a set of ethical principles for adventure therapy. At that time, a committee was formed to: 1) examine the feasibility of such a development, 2) help to research ethical principles used by other professionals, and 3) serve as a "conduit" to help synthesize the input of others.

Input for the initial creation of these documents was from a number of sources, which included: 1) the 1991 draft of the American Psychological Association (APA) ethics code, 2) the 1991 revised code of ethics of the American Association of Marriage and Family Therapy (AAMFT), 3) the 1986 ethics code for therapeutic recreation specialists, 4) Jasper Hunt's work in the second edition of "Ethical Issues in Experiential

Education" (1990), and 5) Tim Marshall's work on these principles from the Aspen Achievement Academy guidelines (1991), which have become part of the licensing standards for the State of Utah under the "Outdoor Youth Programs" section.

The work of this committee was presented at a Pre-Conference session of the Therapeutic Adventure Professional Group at the 1991 AEE Conference at Lake Junaluska. During this session, these principles were revised by a group of 27 invested professionals. During the Conference, the Therapeutic Adventure Professional Group voted to accept these principles given that it notifies organizations like the APA and AAMFT that it was using portions of their ethical codes and that it would recognize their input into its work. The AAMFT, after consultation with their legal counsel, has given the Therapeutic Adventure Professional Group permission to use portions of their ethical code. The APA is still in the process of responding to the Association's request. The legal consequences of such codes are also being investigated.

Since their approval at the Conference, the principles have been reviewed and commented on by more professionals. Most of these comments have been extremely positive, a number of individuals thinking that the entire Association should establish such principles. Some of the perplexing issues (i.e., areas where we could make these principles even better) that have been brought up include:

1) A. Definition of Professionals—"This raises interesting issues. Does paying $35 to the AEE make one a professional?" "Who is going to police programs that are unethical? Is this 'policing' part of being a professional?"
2) C. Related Ethical Codes—"This section is too vague to be useful. What do I have to know about the Islamic Fundamentalist codes? It would be better if it was more explicit."
3) 3.3 Concern for the Environment—Some people felt that this section was unclear. "Do you mean 'legal wilderness only?'" "How about bolts in rocks?"
4) 4.1 Policy against Discrimination—(Note: this section has drawn the most attention.) Some people challenged this statement as an effort to be "politically correct" and it was "troublesome." Specific questions in this policy were: (a) with gender, does this imply that women- or men-only groups would be discriminatory?, (b) with ethnicity, does this mean that not choosing to provide services for a Ku Klux Klan group would be discrimination?, (c) with religion, does this mean that Christian programs must include satanists? Some of these arguments may be for exceptional

circumstances, but they do raise attention to areas that need to be addressed.

5) 4.4 - Clarify the "limitations of confidentiality"—one person thought that this should be more clear.

6) 6 - Social responsibility—One person stated that something needs to be said about a professional's primary responsibility being the welfare of the client before the institution.

Other ideas that have been raised include:

- the need for specific negative rights that clients possess
- something about the importance of empirical research to undergrid the practice and implications for scanty or non-existent research for practice
- something about marketing materials accurately reflecting the practice (e.g., the pictures used to show only smiling faces—rarely crying, hurt, or enraged faces).
- something about separation of powers (i.e., some form of court of appeals for clients to turn to for aid against an organization or specific practitioner).

Ideas like these will serve to further the evolution of these principles. Other areas of future development include a clearer definition of particular principles, the establishment of a collection of ethical dilemmas and scenarios in adventure therapy that help to further define these practices, and a decision on how such principles will be regulated and monitored.

² The Therapeutic Adventure Professional Group appreciates the permission to use portions of the ethical principles from the American Psychological Association (APA) and the American Association of Marriage and Family Therapy (AAMFT). Note that the six main ethical principles used here follow the standards set by the APA. It also greatly appreciates the support of the APA and the AAMFT in the development of these ethical standards and their current evolutionary process.

39

THE FAMILY WILDERNESS PROGRAM: A DESCRIPTION OF THE PROJECT AND ITS ETHICAL CONCERNS[1]

ROBERT S. CREAL, Ph.D.
NANCY FLORIO

The development of any program requires that there be consideration of the impact of the program's ethical issues. The purpose of this article is to describe the development of the Family Wilderness Program (FWP) and to discuss the ethical questions that were raised during its development. The dilemmas and ethical concerns presented here are specific to the FWP, but can be viewed as questions confronting all therapeutic programs that choose to utilize wilderness/adventure mediums.

JUSTIFICATION FOR THE FAMILY WILDERNESS PROGRAM

The FWP represents a marriage of two disciplines with different roots: psychotherapy stemming from psychology and adaptive programming stemming from experiential education. The connections between therapy and adaptive programming have already been well documented by Chase (1981), Kimball (1983), and Kirkpatrick (1983). In brief, wilderness approaches elicit a wide range of human emotions and experiences in situations where an individual's typical defense mechanisms are no longer useful. Consequently, the individual is forced to be creative and adaptive in developing new, constructive coping skills. The penalties for not building new coping skills are immediate and direct, and act as an ongoing impetus for learning and behavior change. In addition to this emphasis on the individual, wilderness approaches require facing challenges in small groups.

This often leads to the development of an interdependency among the participants in the group which fosters communication, cooperation, trust, and social learning. Speculation suggests that families in the wilderness are not only affected by the pressures on the individual members, but also by the characteristics of the small group process.

The theory behind the FWP relies heavily on the statements made by Kimball (1983) when he incorporated the wilderness approach with the projective theory of psychology. The projective theory states that the more ambiguous a situation (in terms of stimulus, expectations, and types of responses), the more the individual will attempt to place structure and interpretation on that situation. This structure and interpretation are not dictated by the characteristics of the situation, but rather by the individual's personality. Because of this, the projective theory states that an understanding of a person can be obtained by examining how the person responds to ambiguous situations. Similarly, in the wilderness, structure and interpretation are dictated by the individual's personality. Kimball (1983) stated the following: "...demands of the wilderness are capricious and require adaptability. Although expectations are made clear during the wilderness expedition, a whole range of responses is possible. Personal characteristics and behaviors emerge in sharp focus" (p. 7).

It is believed that the capricious nature of the wilderness is as effective a projective technique with families as it is with individuals. The characteristics of the family system are forthcoming and on display in the wilderness, and thus allow therapeutic intervention in a here-and-now manner. In addition, such an open display of a family system provides ongoing material with which a therapist will be able to work in future weeks (Kirkpatrick, 1983).

DESCRIPTION OF THE FAMILY WILDERNESS PROGRAM

In order to understand the ethical questions to be considered, it is necessary to have more complete information about the program and the types of people who are the participants. The FWP is part of Housatonic Adolescent Hospital (a psychiatric hospital within the Department of Children and Youth Services in Connecticut). The hospital treats youngsters, ages 14 to 17, who are experiencing such severe emotional/behavioral difficulties that they cannot be treated within the context of other less restrictive settings. The target population of the FWP is the families of those adolescents at Housatonic Adolescent Hospital who have been adjudicated delinquent.

The adolescents have been pulled from their home, adjudicated delinquent, and placed in the hospital. By the time of hospitalization, the family has often exhausted all of its resources in an effort to change the situation, and generally gives the appearance of being unable to do any more. Neither the family nor the youngster is satisfied with what has happened to their lifestyle. The relationship between parents and children during this crisis has frequently become circular and circumscribed. It is circular in that the youngster acts out, the parents respond by punishment or showing dissatisfaction, and the youngster counters with rebellion and again acts out. It is circumscribed in that there is minimal basis for interactions other than this negative circular one. The respective family members find it difficult to remember past positive interactions within the family and find it equally hard to appreciate positive qualities in each other. Although the parents and the youngster may be looking for answers, they maintain little or no respect for each other and consequently are unable to listen to one another.

Despite these problems, the family approach is seen as one of the most beneficial therapy modalities available in working with adolescents. The family seems to maintain a strong influence on the adolescent and consequently, family involvement in treatment increases the likelihood of successful resolution. Because of the strong therapeutic effectiveness, the Housatonic Adolescent Hospital expects that all families will be involved in therapy.

The family in the FWP participates in a series of graduated wilderness challenges throughout the course of treatment. The order, frequency, and difficulty of activities are determined on an ongoing basis and are designed to meet the specific rehabilitation needs of the family. The family usually attends a one- to 2-hour session once a week. Occasionally, an extended session of 4 to 8 hours is provided for specific activities. This is an adaptation of the typical wilderness program that uses longer outdoor excursions as an adjunct to other therapy programs (Chase, 1981; Kimball, 1983; Kirkpatrick, 1983). The FWP attempts to be an integral part of the treatment by involving the family in weekly sessions on a long-term basis. Thus, all activities in which the families are involved must fit into a restrictive time frame. Examples of the activities include initiatives, group and individual problem-solving activities, canoeing, and rock climbing.

The initiatives present the family with challenges that seem impossible when first encountered, but that can be resolved. The resolution requires cooperation, thought, and creative problem solving on the part of the family members. The participants discover the satisfaction gained from working with others, the fulfillment that results from confronting and overcoming problems, and the knowledge that there is more than one acceptable point of view within the family. More powerful challenges are presented as the family develops better communication skills, greater respect for one another, and a more supportive method of interaction. The purpose of increasing the challenges is specifically to increase the level of stress on the family. Families of delinquent adolescents frequently become dysfunctional at times of high stress. The FWP uses the stronger challenges to teach the family the process of coping constructively and effectively during these high-stress times. The family learns to take risks, to assess its strengths and weaknesses, and to make decisions concerning the most effective distribution of its assets. This process disturbs the equilibrium of the family system. Material that the family has worked hard at sealing over or avoiding is uncovered. The defenses that the family has used to keep the material hidden have failed, which requires that the family members must develop new processes and methods to define their relationships. Verbal sessions are frequently used to debrief the family and to help reinforce the learning that has taken place. The goal is to have the family apply the newly acquired coping skills from the wilderness to the more relevant problems they face. This is the long-term goal of this therapy. People often see the wilderness experience as only applying to the unique outdoor situation and feel that it has little to do with everyday life. The therapist guides and encourages the family to make this connection. The constant introduction of the wilderness approach with the ongoing verbal process reinforces the notion that the new coping skills work in a variety of situations and are an available part of the family system which can be applied to problems at home.

ETHICAL CONCERNS FOR THE FAMILY WILDERNESS PROGRAM

In this section, several ethical questions are outlined. The discussion includes the interpretation of the problem and the rationale for a solution. This is not an attempt to offer the "correct answers," but rather is provided to allow the reader an opportunity to critically review the authors' thinking processes and to agree or disagree with the solutions.

Question #1—When does problematic behavior warrant the kind of powerful, relatively untried intervention such as FWP? The wilderness orientation is a powerful and intrusive approach. Families are placed in situations that are unfamiliar, that may be physically uncomfortable, and that may disrupt the family system to the point of emotional turmoil. There are many families, therefore, that may not be appropriate for the FWP. It could be argued that one needs to have a very good reason for using this

466   *ADVENTURE THERAPY*

sort of intrusive approach. Question #1 suggests that the behavior must warrant the intervention. If the behavior is extreme, then an intrusive intervention (FWP) can be justified.

The authors resolved this question by limiting the participants in the FWP to families of adolescents who have been adjudicated delinquent. This decision was made for two reasons. First, behaviors of adolescents who have gone through the court system are extreme and have been untouched by the usual family/community resources. Second, there is documentation that a wilderness approach has been effective in working with a delinquent population (Kelly & Baer, 1968) and thus might also work well with the families of a delinquent population.

Question #2—Does the format of the FWP compromise the effectiveness of the wilderness approach? This is a complicated question that focuses on the use of weekly, 2-hour sessions as the time frames. Traditional wilderness programs usually involve expeditions several days in length. Certainly the FWP does not have the high-impact status of this type of course design. However, effectiveness is a long-term issue that may not be totally dependent on level of impact. It is the degree to which the person or the family has integrated the learnings from the wilderness experience into the personality or system, respectively. A strength of the FWP, which is not available to most programs, is the ability to work with a family over the course of 7 to 9 months. The belief is that the continuous reintroduction of a wilderness experience will be successful in terms of overall integration.

Therefore, the effectiveness of the wilderness approach is not felt to be compromised by the format of FWP. However, this question is open to research. The decision is one of program strategy that is based on sound theory and that is less disruptive to the family. This decision does not act as a resolution to program format question, but is a response that allows the project to move forward. In fact, rather than acting as a solution, this strategy has raised other ethical concerns (See questions 3 and 4).

Question #3—Does the FWP format bring emotionally laden issues to the surface too quickly? A benefit of a longer expedition is that issues that are quickly raised can usually be settled to some degree within the time frame of the experience. This is in contrast to a verbal, family therapy format in which a family may take several sessions to bring issues to the fore and in which the family members are much more in control of how quickly emotions surface. Within one session, the FWP instigates the expression of emotion for the family that may need to remain on hold for a week until the following session. This seems to be an unfortunate consequence of using an approach that perhaps is best suited for a several-day experience within the time frame of a more traditional family therapy approach.

Problems do occur from the abrupt uncovering of family issues. There is less concern for the delinquent adolescent than for the family because the adolescent has professional care constantly available to help work through whatever issues arise. The family, on the other hand, returns home with problems still unresolved and with no immediate professional help.

The format of the FWP does seem to bring issues to the surface too quickly in some instances. On occasion, it has been necessary to adapt the traditional time frames a bit by spending more time with family members after a session in an effort to debrief, and by maintaining telephone contact throughout the week to be supportive to the family during particularly stressful times. Thus far, this action has been a successful resolution of the issue.

Question #4—Is the power of the FWP too great? This question is similar to Question 3 except here we are discussing the technique and not the time frame. Many families are quite rigid and need a powerful technique, such as a wilderness approach, to achieve progressive change. The threat created by having a rigid structure manipulated, however, may be more than the family can handle and consequently, they may attempt to obstruct treatment. For example, an adolescent may express intense anger stemming from family conflict by violently acting out. The adolescent may find acting out easier than and preferable to discussing family issues in an open, honest way. If we force the issues to surface experientially through the FWP, the adolescent will likely act out or refuse to participate in treatment. In essence then, some families may become casualties to the power of the intervention by backing out of their commitment to the program.

However, stating that a therapeutic technique is too powerful is like stating that a dessert tastes too good. One must decide how powerful a technique to use, and when to use it. The choice of activities and the manner in which they are offered are critical, especially in rigid families. The therapist must carefully assess the coping ability and the flexibility of the family, and choose an intervention that has the highest likelihood of creating therapeutic progress without being overwhelming to the family system. The authors are becoming more aware of the importance of this choice as the work in the FWP may have been a contributing factor to the unsuccessful discharge of a youngster. (This will be discussed in more detail in the case history.)

Question #5—When is the most appropriate time to let the family know what it means to be in the FWP? Ethical guidelines are clear. People have the right to know in advance what the program entails. If this guideline was followed in strict measure, families would be told in the first meeting of the intention to take them up the side of a cliff, to have them do acrobatic stunts high in the trees, to take them down a raging river, etc. The FWP would also be a program with very few participants. Most of the families have relatively little exposure to the wilderness and would find high-impact activities too threatening to contemplate. Therefore, they are not initially informed of all of the details of the high-impact experiences.

The program, however, does have a procedure that is felt to safeguard the rights of the families. The action-oriented approach of the FWP is described, as is the fact that much of the therapy will be occurring outdoors. For more detailed information concerning initiatives and activities, the families must become engaged in the process of family therapy. The process is one of leading them from the easier activities to ones that are much more challenging. Prior to engaging in the activity, all participants are trained in the safety measures, and the risks and the rules of each event are explained fully.

Families learn about FWP throughout the time of their participation in the program. They are given the information as it directly affects their family work. Their rights to informed consent are further guaranteed by allowing them the freedom not to participate in a given activity. If a family refuses to be involved in an activity, a more acceptable activity or possibly a verbal mode of family therapy will be utilized. Thus far, there have been no families who have refused to cooperate.

Question #6—Does the delinquent adolescent have the right to say "no" to the FWP? The answer to this is complicated due to the unique pressures placed on the delinquent by the legal system. Most frequently, delinquents are admitted voluntarily to Housatonic Adolescent Hospital as a condition of probation. If they refuse to volunteer for treatment (which is their choice), then they are placed in a more restrictive setting. Part of accepting hospitalization is accepting the treatment that the hospital offers and following the rules the hospital provides. If the delinquent adolescent refuses to cooperate with part or all of their treatment program, consequences which entail varying degrees of severity result. The hospital could go as far as to discharge the individual and return him/her to the more restrictive setting. Of course, the adolescent always maintains the right to sign out of the hospital and go to the more restrictive setting on their own. Typically, less severe consequences are given first in an effort to persuade the youngster to cooperate with treatment. There are many times when a delinquent adolescent will not participate in one form of treatment (e.g., individual therapy, FWP) but cooperates with the rest of hospital treatment. In a situation where there is partial compliance to treatment, the hospital makes the decision concerning discharge or consequences on a case-by-case basis. If the youngster refuses to participate in the FWP (Question #6) due to objections to the orientation, the hospital will make a decision about offering a more traditional approach. The adolescent, however, is not given the right to refuse family therapy.

Ethical guidelines state that the individual has the right not to participate in treatment. They further state that when the individual is under the control of another person (e.g., the delinquent is in the hospital), there is a heightened responsibility to safeguard the individual's rights. This right is offered to the individual in an all-or-none fashion. To accept treatment is to participate in the entire hospital treatment program. Anything less is unacceptable, for then the adolescent would be dictating the process of treatment and would likely resist the more threatening and more effective approaches. The adolescent can always make the decision to leave treatment if desired, but the legal pressures still remain.

Question #7—Is the FWP a research project? All participants in a research project need to be informed in advance that they are taking part in research. The only exception to the informed consent guideline is if advanced knowledge would distort the results of the research, and if the research is sufficiently important to justify including people without their knowledge. If the FWP was a research project, signed consent forms from each member of each family would need to be obtained.

The authors have interpreted the FWP, in consultation with the administration of the hospital, as a therapeutic treatment program that has ongoing evaluation, not as a research project. The distinction here is a bit vague. A great deal of data has been collected on all members of the hospital's long-term unit in an effort to see if the FWP is an effective orientation of family therapy. In addition, the authors are writing this article and are offering a presentation on the FWP. An article, a presentation, data collection—all actions that resemble research. The distinction is based on the fact that the FWP evaluation is similar in practice to other hospital-sponsored program evaluations that are done to ensure the effectiveness of treatment. The distinction is also based on the fact that there is no solid design. Research would involve a much cleaner experimental design with a pre-determined end-point of the project. At present, the FWP is expected to be ongoing.

Question #8—When is it appropriate to disregard the treatment team? The FWP functions as one part of a treatment team, the strength and effectiveness of which is determined by the cooperativeness of its various parts. Consequently, working within the guidelines of the team is expected and is part of the agreement when accepting a family therapy assignment. Ethical standards argue that the agreement be honored by the therapists. There are times, however, when a therapist must do something different because a situation was not anticipated by the team. Such spontaneous adaptation of the treatment is a part of all of the team's components.

Disregarding the wishes of the team is an even stronger issue for the FWP. Much of the power of the FWP is in building a consistency of experience over several weeks. This is the method the FWP utilizes to compensate for not having the high-impact experience of a long expedition. If the FWP experience is interrupted too often, the effectiveness of the approach can be compromised. There may be times when the family therapist will need to decide which is more important, the needs of the team or the need for keeping consistency of experience. The issue is an ongoing one that is very important; to disregard totally either component is to sacrifice to some degree the quality of treatment.

Question #9—Is the FWP cost effective? This question cannot be answered yet. However, it must be recognized that the FWP is expensive in terms of money for equipment and additional personnel, and in terms of staff time. Traditional family therapy takes one or two therapists approximately 1½ hours per week, whereas the FWP has time and staff requirements that are much greater. Relatively few youngsters at the hospital have access to the FWP. Is the benefit for those who are in the program worth the loss of staff time available to the other youngsters? Whether the FWP is a financially viable approach will be answered in a few years.

CASE HISTORY

The following example is a case that was part of the FWP. It is offered here as a practical demonstration of Questions 3 and 4.

R. S. is a 15-year-old, single, white male who had a long history of acting-out behaviors. His parents were divorced and had established close relationships with other people. R. S. claimed he hated his father and was petrified of him due to father's previous angry episodes. In contrast, he saw his mother as a saint. Sessions were held with each parent and R. S.

In straight verbal sessions, R. S. was not responsive to either parent in that he tended to withdraw into his own thoughts. In the experiential sessions, his relationship with his father was much more genuine, warm, and spontaneous than his relationship with his mother. Despite this, he continued to downgrade his relationship with his father and continued to upgrade the relationship with his mother. It was clear that emotions were being stirred in that R. S. was attempting, with hospital staff, to understand why his father was so interested in him, when his father had never shown concern before. On one occasion, R. S. worked with staff in a variety of modalities for several days in order to build up courage to confront his father. He spoke with his father appropriately and assertively on several issues—an interaction that was new for him. Eventually, R. S. stopped cooperating with treatment and eloped on a number of occasions. He became so disruptive that the hospital decided to no longer treat him and consequently, he was returned to a more restrictive setting.

Although many factors enter into a youngster's change in behavior, the possible contributing factor of the power of the FWP cannot be overlooked. R. S. seemed to be acting out the mother's bitterness toward the father by attempting to maintain a negative relationship with him. The possibility of becoming closer to his father meant abandoning his mission for his mother. The closeness of the relationship with the father that was being developed experientially was perhaps too threatening in terms of the perceived cost of the relationship with his mother. In any event, R. S. abandoned the treatment process.

Interestingly, prior to R. S. backing out of treatment, his parents formed a much more effective parental system. They no longer undermined each other's authority with R. S. and they were much less angry with each other. In fact, they supported each other and attempted to negotiate firmness and consistency in setting limits with their son. Therefore, when R. S. began to act out in treatment, his parents became stronger and more united. The more R. S. acted out, the stronger his parents became. When he was eventually sent to the more restrictive setting, both he and his parents were told that he could reapply to the hospital if his motivation was strong.

R. S. was not interested and was hoping that one of his parents would rescue him from the restrictive setting. Together they refused to do this in an effort to place concentrated pressure on R. S. to reapply for treatment. This improvement of the parental subsystem was a significant gain in treatment.

Although R. S. is no longer in treatment, he is still being influenced by the effects of family therapy. Eventually the parents' consistency and strength may overcome the stubbornness of R. S. and may encourage him to seek treatment.

The ethical concern is that R. S. was in a treatment program and left unsuccessfully. Perhaps he was not ready for treatment or perhaps the format (Question 3) and the power (Question 4) of the FWP brought issues to the surface so quickly that he was overwhelmed. The question needs to be asked, if the issues had moved more slowly, would R. S. still be in treatment?

CONCLUSION

This article has offered a description of the ethical questions that were part of the development of the FWP and a description of the ethical questions that have been raised as the program has been operating. The issues outlined here are specific to the FWP and are meant to show the kinds of normal dilemmas that must be addressed in developing a program.

There is a temptation in setting up a program for one's creative need to be the sole determining factor. We all want to develop programs that are useful and exciting. However, it is important to raise the questions of ethics at the program's initial stages and to continue to raise these questions throughout the program's development and operation. A strong sense of ethics is an integral part of establishing the types of powerful programs that are best suited to help people in need. More and more, the programs that will be considered viable will be those that, in addition to all else, are also justified on ethical grounds.

In order for a program to work effectively, it must adhere to societal norms. If for no other reason, this point requires close attention to ethical considerations. Society expects that the rights of the individual will be maintained and that steps will be taken by the program or institution to ensure that people are treated ethically. Quite simply, if we do not raise the ethical questions for ourselves, other people will bring them to our attention. If we do not monitor our activities on an ongoing basis, somewhere a hot issue will explode; and then we will find ourselves monitored by external sources. We will begin to lose some of the freedom and flexibility that we currently enjoy.

Robert Creal is the Associate Director of Housatonic Adolescent Hospital, Newton, Connecticut, for adjudicated youths and their parents. He was the was co-director of the Family Wilderness Program. Robert has a Ph. D. in clinical psychology and is a licensed psychologist with a private practice. He has worked with a variety of populations in both general and therapeutic settings. He is on the Board of Directors of youth homes in New Haven, Connecticut.

Nancy Florio was the co-director of the Family Wilderness Program at Housatonic Adolescent Hospital, in Newtown, Connecticut, until 1987. Nancy has worked with a number of outdoor programs, including the Daryl Hall School and The Wilderness School. She is currently raising two children on a full-time basis and sees the Family Wilderness Program as some of the most valuable work she has accomplished professionally.

Footnote

[1] This article was originally published in 1986 in M. A. Gass & L. Buell (Eds.), Proceedings Journal from the 14th Annual AEE Conference, Boulder, CO: Association for Experiential Education, 47-55.

Preparation of this article was supported in part by Connecticut Office of Policy and Management, Justice Planning Division Grant 8433434054X to the authors.
We gratefully acknowledge the support of Housatonic Adolescent Hospital, Temple Lodge #127 A. F. & A. M., and specifically David McDaniel, Leonard Suchotliff, Kimberly Wills, and David Brumer for participation in the Family Wilderness Program.

REFERENCES

Craig Dobkin

References

Abarbanel, S. (1988). Conquering the mountain. Family Circle, 66-70.

Adams, S. (1975). Evaluative research in corrections: A practical guide. Washington, D.C.: U.S. Department of Justice.

Adams, W. D. (1970). Survival training: Its effects on self-concept and selective personality factors of emotionally disturbed adolescents. (Doctoral dissertation, Utah State University, 1969). Dissertation Abstracts International, 31, 388B.

Ackerman, P. (1991). Personal communication. State Licensing Coordinator, Idaho, August 6.

Agosta, C., & Loring, M. (1987). Wilderness therapy: A powerful tool for healing. NCASA News, 13-14.

Agosta, C., & Loring, M. (1988). Understanding and treating the adult retrospective victim of child sexual abuse. In S. M. Sgroi (Ed.), Vulnerable populations: Vol. I. Evaluation and treatment of sexually abused children and survivors. Lexington, MA: Lexington Books.

Ahsen, A. (1973). Eidetic behavior. Yonkers, NY: Eidetic.

Alabama Department of Youth Services. (1983). Wilderness program evaluation report. Alabama Department of Youth Services. Division of Planning, Research, and Development.

Alcoholics Anonymous. (1976). NY: Alcoholics Anonymous World Services, Inc.

Andrew, S. H. (1977). An evaluation of two stress-challenge programs for delinquent youth. Unpublished master's thesis, Southern Illinois University, Carbondale, IL.

Andrew, S. H. (1980). A validation of the Wichmann-Andrew Delinquency Intervention Scale. Unpublished doctoral dissertation, Southern Illinois University, Carbondale, IL.

Andrews, D. (1991). Personal communication. Colorado Office of Child Care Licensing, November 15.

Archer, R. P. (1987). Using the MMPI with adolescents. Hillsdale, NJ: Eribnum.

Babor, T. F., Dolinsky, Z., Rounsaville, B., & Jaffe, J. (1987). Unitary versus multidimensional models of alcoholism treatment outcomes: An empirical study. Journal of Studies on Alcohol, 49(2), 167-176.

Bacon, S. (1983). The conscious use of metaphor in Outward Bound. Denver, CO: Colorado Outward Bound School.

Bacon, S. (1988). Paradox and double binds in adventure education. Greenwich, CT: Outward Bound. (ERIC Reproduction No. 296 832)

Bacon, S. (1987). The evolution of the Outward Bound Process. Greenwich, CT: Outward Bound. (ERIC Document Reproduction Service No. ED 295 780)

Bacon, S., & Kimball, R. (1989). The wilderness challenge model. In R. D. Lyman (Ed.), Residential and inpatient treatment of children and adolescents. NY: Plenum Press.

Banaka, W., and Young, D. (1985). Community coping skills enhanced by an adventure camp for adult chronic psychiatric patients. Hospital and Community Psychiatry, 38(7), 745-748.

Banderhoff, S. (1992). Wilderness family therapy: An innovative treatment approach for problem youth. Doctoral dissertation, University of South Carolina.

Bandura, A. (1986). Social foundation of thought and action: A social cognitive theory. Englewood Cliffs, NJ: Prentice-Hall.

Bandura, A. (1977). Self-efficacy: Toward a unifying theory of behavioral change. Psychological Review, 84, 191-215.

Bass, E., and Davis, L. (1988). The courage to heal. NY: Harper & Row.

Battle, J. (1981). Culture free self-esteem inventories for children and adults. Seattle: Special Publications.

Behar, L., & Stephens, D. (1978). Wilderness Camping: An evaluation of a residential treatment program for emotionally disturbed children. American Journal of Orthopsychiatry, 48(4), 644.

Bernstein, A. (1972). Wilderness as a therapeutic behavior setting. Therapeutic Recreation Journal, 1(6).

Bernstein, S. (1973). The relationship of antecedent variables and process variables to differential outcome in a stress challenge program. Unpublished doctoral dissertation, Southern Illinois University, Carbondale, IL.

Black, C. (1986). Children of alcoholics. In R. Ackerman (Ed.), Growing in the Shadow (pp. 105-111). New York: Health Publications.

Blakely, M. (1987). After rape: The long journey back. Unpublished manuscript. Denver, CO: Colorado Outward Bound School.

Bateson, G. (1979). Mind and nature: A necessary unity. New York: Dutton.

Bloom, B. S. (1956). Taxonomy of Educational Objectives. London: Longman Group.

Blos, P. (1968). Character formation in adolescence. The psychoanalytic study of the child, 23, 245-263.

Bokey, D. (1987). Outward Bound in search of foundations. Unpublished master's thesis, Queens University, Kingston, Ontario, Canada.

Borg, W. R., & Gall, M. D. (1983). Educational research: An introduction. New York: Longman.

Browne, J. H., & Christensen, D. N. (1986). Family therapy theory and practice. Belmont, CA: Brooks/Cole.

Buell, L. (1983). The 24-hour experience: An outdoor adventure program. Greenfield, MA: Environmental Awareness Publications.

Bureau of Justice Statistics. (1990). BJS Data Report, 1989. Rockville, MD: Justice Statistics Clearinghouse.

Burton, L. M. (1981). A critical analysis and review of the research on Outward Bound and related programs. Doctoral dissertation, The State University of New Jersey, Rutgers, NJ. Dissertation Abstracts International, 51/03-A, 724. (University Microfilms #AAD90-07084)

C., P. (1989). Quote from student evaluation form of three-day course.

Campbell, D. T., & Stanley, J. C. (1963). Experimental and quasi-experimental designs for research. Chicago, IL: Rand McNally.

Canfield, J., & Wells, H. C. (1976). One hundred ways to enhance self-concept in the classroom. Englewood Cliffs, NJ: Prentice-Hall.

CARE Networker. (1990). 3(4).

Caruso, B. (1987). The impact of incest. MN: Hazelden Foundation.

Castle, M., & Eastman, J. (1985). Challenge therapy: An innovative treatment for adolescent alcoholics in a residential setting. In M. Gass (Ed.), Exploring horizons: The implications of experiential learning sourcebook. (ERIC Document Reproduction Service No. ED 241 204)

Cataldo, C. J. (1982). Wilderness Bound Experience: Testing competence in a survival setting. An unpublished doctoral dissertation. New York: Columbia University.

Cave, S. E. (1979). Evaluation of level of stress and group cohesiveness in the wilderness experience using the MMPI and sociograms. Unpublished doctoral dissertation, University of New Mexico, Albuquerque, NM.

Chase, N. (1981). Outward Bound as an adjunct to therapy. (ERIC Document Reproduction Service No. ED 241 204)

Churchard, T. (1980). Rochester alternative school; Alternative education model: A guide to implementation. Unpublished manuscript. Rochester, NH: Rochester Public Schools.

Clagett, A. F. (1989). Effective therapeutic wilderness camp programs for rehabilitating emotionally disturbed, problem teenagers and delinquents. Journal of Offender Counseling, 11(1), 79-96.

Clapp, C., & Rudolph, S. (1990). Adventure therapy with families: The family challenge program. In R. Flor (Ed.), Proceedings manual for the 18th Annual Association for Experiential Education Conference: Integrating experiential education (pp. 71-75). Boulder, CO: Association for Experiential Education.

Clowes, G. H. A., Jr., & O'Donnell, T. F., Jr. (1974). Current concepts - heat stroke. New England Journal of Medicine, 291, 564-567.

Cluster of Symptoms and Severe Pathologies Handout #5. (1988). Albuquerque, NM: Sexual Assault Treatment Services.

Collingwood, T. R. (1972). Survival camping: A therapeutic mode for rehabilitating problem youths (Technical report). Little Rock, AR: Arkansas Rehabilitation and Research Training Center.

Coleman, J. S. (1974). Youth: Transition to adulthood (Report of the Panel on Youth of the President's Science Advisory Committee). Chicago: The University of Chicago Press.

Cook, T. D., & Campbell, D. T. (1979). Quasi-experimentation: Design and analysis issues for field settings. Skokie, IL: Rand-McNally.

Cooper, M. I., Russel, M., & George, W. H. (1988). Coping, expectancies, and alcohol abuse: A test of social learning foundations. Journal of Abnormal Psychology, 97(2), 218-230.

Corey, G. (1990). Theory and practice of group counseling (3rd ed.). Pacific Grove, CA: Brooks/Cole.

Creal, R. S., & Florio, N. (1986). The family wilderness program: A description of the project and its ethical concerns. In M. Gass & L. Buell (Eds.), Proceedings Journal for the 14th Annual AEE Conference: The season of ingenuity: Ethics in Experiential Education. Boulder, CO: Association for Experiential Education.

Csikszentmihalyi, M. (n. d.). Flow: Studies in Enjoyment. (PHS Grant Report N. RO1HM 22883-02)

Curtis, R. C., & Sticker, G. (Eds.) (1991). How people change inside and outside of therapy. New York: Plenum Press.

Cytrynbaum, S., & Ken, K. (1975). The Connecticut Wilderness Program: A preliminary evaluation report (Report submitted to the State of Connecticut Council on Human Services). Hartford, CT.

Dahaime, D. E. (1982). The effects of an outdoor affective education program on the self-concept, social adjustment, classroom behavior and affective behavior of learning disabled children. (Doctoral dissertation, University of Pennsylvania, 1982). Dissertation Abstracts International, 43, 728A.

Davis, M., & Wallbridge, D. (1981). Boundary and space: An introduction to the work of D. W. Winnicott. New York: Brunner/Mazel.

Denton, W. (1986). Introduction to marriage and family enrichment: A shift in the paradigm. Journal of Psychotherapy and the Family, 2(1), 3-6.

DePaul, A. From victim...to victor. Washington Post, date and page unknown. Available through the Colorado Outward Bound School.

DeSantis, R., & Manley, J. (1988). Suspended Adolescence. Dublin, NH: Beech Hill.

de Shazer, S. (1982). Patterns of brief family therapy. New York: Guilford Press.

Desmond, E. W. (1987). Out in the open. Time, 130(22), 80-90.

Dewey, J. (1938). Experience and education. New York: Macmillan.

Dodds, D. (1991). Personal communication. California Community Care Licensing Bureau, August 2.

Doll, J. (1991). Personal communication. North Dakota Office of Foster Care Administration and Licensing, July 3.

Dowling, N. G., & Roland, H. (1982). Institutional and faculty life cycle changes. Community College Review, 10(2), 36-40.

Drebing, C. E., Willis, S. C., & Genet, B. (1987). Anxiety and the Outward Bound process. Journal of Experiential Education, 10, 17-21.

Drengson, A. R. (1980). Wilderness travel as an art and as a paradigm for outdoor education. Quest, 32(116), 117.

Duncan, M. E., & McCombs, C. (1982). Adult life phases: Blueprint for staff development planning. Community College Review, 10(2), 26-35.

Durgin, C. H., & McEwen, D. (1990). Troubled young people after the adventure program: A case study. Journal of Experiential Education, 14(1), 31-35.

Emerick, C. D., & Hansen, J. (1983). Assertions regarding effectiveness of treatment for alcoholism. American Psychologist, 38, 1078-1088.

Epstein, N., Baldwin, L., & Bishop, D. (1983). The McMaster family assessment device. Journal of Marital and Family Therapy, 9(2), 171-180.

Eriskson, E. (1980). Identity and the life cycle. New York: W. W. Norton.

Evenson, M. (1980). An Adlerian activity approach to family enrichment (Doctoral dissertation, University of Arizona). Dissertation Abstracts International, 41, 4264A.

Evenson, T., Evenson, M., & Fish, D. (1986). Family enrichment: A rehabilitation opportunity. Rehabilitation Literature, 47(11-12), 274-280.

Ewert, A. (1987). Research in outdoor adventure: Overview and analysis. In G. Robb (Ed.), The Bradford Papers Annual, Volume II. Bloomington, IN: Indiana University.

Ewert, A. (1990). Research update: Revisiting the concept of self-esteem through outdoor experiential activities. Journal of Experiential Education, 13(2), 56.

Ewert, A. (1989). Research in experiential education: An overview. Journal of Experiential Education, 10(2), 4-7.

Exton-Smith, A. N. (1972). Phenothiazines in cold weather. British Journal of Medicine, 1, 441.

Farrell, T. (1991). Personal communication. Deputy Attorney General of Hawaii, August 13.

Fergusen, D. (1983). The wilderness experience: A cost effective treatment modality for psychiatric patients. In G. Robb (Ed.), The Bradford Papers, Volume III. Bloomington, IN: Indiana University.

Festinger, L. (1957). A theory of cognitive dissonance. Evanston, IL: Row, Petersen.

Fish, L. S., & Piercy, F. P. (1987). The theory and practice of structural and strategic family therapies: A Delphi study. Journal of Marital and Family Therapy, 13(2), 113-125.

Fisch, R., Weakland, J., & Segal, L. (1983). The tactics of change: Doing therapy briefly. San Francisco: Jossey-Bass.

Frazer, J. S. (1982). Structural and strategic family therapy: A basis for marriage or grounds for divorce? Journal of Marital and Family Therapy, 8, 13-22.

Freed, A. (1980). The borderline personality. Social Casework, 61(9), 548-558.

Freeman, G. W., Spilka, B., & Mason, R. C. (1968). Delinquency and the Outward Bound program: An empirical evaluation of a radical approach to delinquency. Paper presented at the Convention of the Rocky Mountain Psychological Association, Denver, CO.

Fretz, P. R. (1989). Challenge and its impacts: Assessment of the Challenge Sonoma 4-H Adventure Ropes Course. Unpublished master's thesis, University of California, Davis.

Fuller, J. A., & Evans, F. J. (1985). Recharging intellectual batteries: The challenge of faculty development. Educational Record, 66(2), 30-34.

Fuoco, F. (1983). Outward Bound: Adjunctive therapy for the treatment of alcoholism. Greenwich, CT: Outward Bound.

Garland, J. A., Jones, H. E., and Kolodny, R. L. (1973). A model for stages of development in social work groups. In S. Bernstein (Ed.), Explorations in group work. Boston, MA: Milford House.

Gass, M. A. (1992). Adventure therapy: Therapeutic applications of adventure programming. Boulder, CO: Association for Experiential Education.

Gass, M. A. (1985). Programming the transfer of learning in adventure education. Journal of Experiential Education, 8(3), 24-32.

Gass, M. A., & Dobkin, C. H. (1991). A book of metaphors. Durham, NH: University of New Hampshire. Available through the authors.

Gass, M., & McPhee, P. (1990). Emerging for recovery: A descriptive analysis of adventure therapy for substance abusers. Journal of Experiential Education, 13(2), 29-35.

Gaston, D. K. (1978). An evaluation of the Connecticut Wilderness School: A wilderness challenge program for delinquent teenagers (Doctoral dissertation, University of Conneticut, 1978). Dissertation Abstracts International, 40, 914B.

Geba, B. H. (1973). Breathe away your tension. New York: Random House.

Gendlin, E. T. (1972). Ground rules for group sessions. Unpublished paper, University of Chicago Department of Psychology, Chicago, IL.

Gibbons, D. C. (1981). Delinquent behavior (3rd ed.). Englewood Cliffs, NJ: Prentice-Hall.

Giblin, P. (1986). Research and assessment in marriage and family enrichment: A meta-analysis study. Journal of Psychotherapy and the Family, 2(1), 79-96.

Giblin, P., Sprenkle, D., & Sheehan, R. (1985). Enrichment outcome research: A meta-analysis of premarital, marital and family interventions. Journal of Marital and Family Therapy, 11(3), 257-271.

Gibson, M. L. (1984). The Outward Bound experience: A new and unique humanistic approach for the treatment of alcoholism. In T. F. Stich (Ed.), Outward Bound in alcohol treatment and mental health (pp. 77-98). Greenwich, CT: Outward Bound.

Gibson, P. (1981). The effects of and the correlates of success in a wilderness therapy program for problem youths (Doctoral dissertation, Columbia University, 1981). Dissertation Abstracts International, 42, 140A.

Gibson, P. H. (1979). Therapeutic aspects of wilderness programs: A comprehensive literature review. Therapeutic Recreation Journal, 13(2), 30.

Gilligan, S. G. (1989). Therapeutic trances. NY: Brunner/Mazel.

Gillis, H. L., & Bonney, W. C. (1989). Utilizing adventure activities with intact groups: A sociodramatic systems approach to consultation. Journal of Mental Health Counseling, 11(4), 345-358.

Gillis, H. L., & Bonney, W. C. (1986). Group counseling with couples or families: Adding adventure activities. Journal for Specialists in Group Work, 11(4), 213-220.

Gillis, H. L., & Gass, M. A. (in press). An overview of adventure experiences in marriage and family therapy. Journal of Marriage and Family Therapy.

Gillis, H. L., & Simpson, C. (1992). Project Choices: Adventure-based residential drug treatment for court referred youth. Journal of Addictions and Offender Counseling, 12, 12-27.

Gillis, H. L., Gass, M. A., Clapp, C., Rudolph, S., Nadler, R., & Banderhoff, S. (1992). Family adventure questionnaire: Results and discussion. In C. Birmingham (Ed.), Association for Experiential Education: 1991 Conference Proceedings and Workshop Summaries Book (pp. 29-39). Boulder, CO: Association for Experiential Education.

Glasser, P. H., Sarri, R., & Vinter, R. (1974). Individual change through small groups. New York: The Free Press.

Glasser, W. (1965). Reality therapy, a new approach to psychology. New York: Harper & Row.

Glenn, S., & Nelson, J. (1987). Raising children for success. Fair Oaks, CA: Sunrise Press.

Goldstein, E. (1983). Clinical and ecological approaches to the borderline client. Social Casework, 64(6), 353-362.

Golins, G. (1978). How delinquents succeed through adventure-based education. Journal of Experiential Education, 1(2), 26-30.

Golins, G. L. (1980). Utilizing adventure education to rehabilitate juvenile delinquents. Las Cruces, NM: New Mexico State University, Clearing House on Rural Education and Small Schools. (ERIC Document Reproduction Service No. 187 501)

Gove, R. B. (Ed.). (1981). Webster's third new international dictionary. Springfield, MA: G & C Merriam.

Greenwood, P., & Zimring, F. E. (1985). One more chance: The pursuit of promising intervention strategies for chronic juvenile offenders. Santa Monica, CA: Rand Corporation Press.

Greenwood, P., Lipson, A., Abrahamsen, A., & Zimring, F. (1983). Youth crime and juvenile justice in California. Rand Corporation, 84-89.

Guidubaldi, J., & Cleminshaw, H. (1985). Divorce, family health, and child adjustment. Family Relations, 34(1), 35-41.

Haddock, B. D. (1990). Substance abuse counseling in community corrections: A primer. Journal of Addictions and Offender Counseling, 11, 2-12.

Hale, A. (1988). 1988 National Safety Network Report. Bellefontaine, OH: National Safety Network.

Haley, J. (1988). Problem-solving therapy. San Francisco: Jossey-Bass.

Haley, J. (1973). Uncommon therapy: The psychiatric techniques of Milton H. Erickson. New York: Norton.

Haley, J. (1963). Strategies of psychotherapy. New York: Grune and Stratton.

Harmon, P., & Templin, G. (1978). Conceptualizing experiential education. Unpublished manuscript. Denver, CO: Colorado Outward Bound School.

Harris, C. (1982). Wilderness program for adolescents with cancer. Unpublished manuscript, Breckenridge Outdoor Education Center.

Hathaway, S. R., & McKinley, J. C. (1982). Minnesota Multiphasic Personality Inventory: Group form. Minneapolis, MN: National Computer Systems.

Hauser, J. (1987, October). Adventure programming in the hospital setting. Paper presented at the New York State Outdoor Education Conference, Cortland, NY.

Havens, M. (1985). Ethical challenges in the outdoor setting. Therapeutic Recreation Journal, 19(2), 75-80.

Havens, M., & Fain, G. (1986, October). Learning from ethical dilemmas. Paper presented at the Association for Experiential Education Conference, Moodus, CT.

Hayes, R. L., & Hayes, B. A. (1986). Remarriage families: Counseling parents, stepparents and their children. Counseling and Human Development, 18(7), 1-8.

Heath, D. B. (1986). Social and cultural factors in families with alcohol-related problems. In D. Lewis & C. Williams (Eds.), Providing Care for Children of Alcoholics (pp. 1-7). Deerfield Beach, FL: Health Communications.

Hendricks, G., & Willis, R. (1975). The centering book. Englewood Cliffs, NJ: Prentice-Hall.

Hendy, M. H. (1975). Outward Bound and personality. Unpublished doctoral dissertation, University of Oregon, Eugene, OR.

Herr, E. (1989). Counseling in a dynamic society: Opportunities and challenges. Alexandria, VA: American Association for Counseling and Development.

Hillman, B., & Evenson, M. (1981). Family enrichment: An activity group process for multiple families. Journal for Specialists in Group Work, 6(1), 22-28.

Hofstadter, D. (1979). Godel, Escher, Bach: An eternal golden braid. New York: Basic Books.

Holmes, S., et al. (1976). Working with the parent in child abuse cases. In F. Turner (Ed.), Differential Diagnosis and Treatment in Social Work (pp. 637-650). New York: The Free Press.

Houle, C. O. (1972). The design of education. San Francisco: Jossey-Bass.

Hudson, F. (1991). The self-renewing adult, the self-renewing society. San Francisco: Jossey-Bass.

Hunt, J. (1990). Ethical issues in experiential education. Boulder, CO: Association for Experiential Education.

Hunter, M. (1986). Teach for transfer. El Segundo, CA: TIP Publications.

Hunter, I. R. (1984). The psychological impact of high adventure programs: A review of therapeutic potential. Corrective and Social Psychiatry and Journal of Behavior Technology Methods and Therapy, 30(1), 1-9.

Hunter, I. R. (1987). A generic outdoor rehabilitation program evaluation proposal. Corrective and Social Psychiatry and Journal of Behavior Technology Methods and Therapy, 33(3), 221-225.

Hutton, C. (1988). The effects of wilderness and follow-up advocacy programs on the behavior of juvenile delinquents. Unpublished master's thesis, Department of Recreation, Southern Illinois University, Carbondale, IL.

Instructor Field Manual. (1980). North Carolina Outward Bound School: Morganton, NC.

Israel, E. (1989). Treatment intervention with battered women. Unpublished doctoral dissertation. Greeley, CO: University of Northern Colorado.

Jacobsen, E. (1929). Progressive relaxation. Chicago: University of Chicago Press.

James, T. (1980). Can the mountains speak for themselves? Unpublished manuscript. Denver, CO: Colorado Outward Bound School.

Jensen, M. (1979). Application of small group theory to adventure programs. Journal of Experiential Education, 2(2), 39-42.

Kalisch, K. (1979). The role of the instructor in the Outward Bound process. Three Lakes, WI: Honey Lakes Camp.

Kaplan, L. (1979). Outward Bound: A treatment modality unexplored by the social worker profession. Child Welfare, 58(1), 37-47.

Kaplan, S. & Talbot, J. F. (1983). Psychological benefits of wilderness experience. In I. Altman & J. F. Wohwill (Eds.), Behavior and the Environment (p. 166). New York: Plenum Press.

Kazdin, A. E. (1991). Effectiveness of psychotherapy with children and adolescents. Journal of Consulting and Clinical Psychology, 59(6), 785-798.

Kelly, F. J., & Baer, D. J. (1968). Outward Bound schools as an alternative to institutionalization for adolescent delinquent boys. Boston, MA: Fandel Press.

Kelly, F. J. (1974). Outward Bound and delinquency: A ten-year experience. Paper presented at the AEE Conference on Experiential Education, Estes Park, CO.

Kelly, F., & Baer, D. (1971). Physical challenge as a treatment for delinquency. Crime and Delinquency, 17, 437.

Kernburg, O. (1975). Borderline conditions and pathological narcissism. New York: Jason Aronson.

Kernberg, O. (1976). Object relations theory and clinical psychoanalysis. New York: Jason Aronson.

Kerr, P. J., & Gass, M. A. (1987). Group development in adventure education. Journal of Experiential Education, 10(3), 26-32.

Kidder, P. (1988). Challenge programming in the mental health field: Brattleboro Retreat. Brattleboro, VT. The Roland Report, 2(2), 10. (Available from Roland & Associates, Inc., 41 Avon St., Keene, NH 03431).

Kimball, R. (1983). The wilderness as therapy. Journal of Experiential Education, 5(3), 6-9.

Kimball, R. O. (1979). Wilderness experience program: Final evaluation report. Santa Fe, NM: State of New Mexico Forensic System, Health and Environment Department.

Kimball, R. O. (1980). Wilderness adventure programs for juvenile offenders. (Grant No. 79 JN-AX-0018). Chicago: University of Chicago, National Center for the Assessment of Alternatives to Juvenile Justice Processing, The School of Social Service Administration.

King, K. (1988). The role of adventure in the experiential learning process. Journal of Experiential Education, 11(2), 4-8.

King, D., & Harmon, P. (1981). Evaluation of the Colorado Outward Bound School's career development course offered in collaboration with the training, education, and employee development department of Martin-Marietta Aerospace. (Available from Harmon Associates, 3732 Sixteenth St., San Francisco, CA 94114.)

Kirkpatrick, T. (1984). Outward Bound as adjunct to family therapy in the treatment of alcoholism. In T. F. Stich (Ed.), Outward Bound in alcohol treatment and mental health (pp. 21-34). Greenwich, CT: Outward Bound.

Kirkpatrick, T. (1983). Outward Bound as an adjunct to family therapy in alcoholism. Greenwich, CT: Outward Bound.

Kjol, R., & Weber, J. (1990). The 4th fire: Adventure-based counseling with juvenile sex offenders. Journal of Experiential Education, 13(3), 18-22.

Krajick, K. (June , 1978). Working our way home. Corrections, 32.

Kreher, P. (1991). Personal communication. Office of Licensing, June 14.

Kolb, D. (1991). When is a metaphor not a metaphor? Journal of Experiential Education, 14(3), 53-54.

Kraft, R., & Sakofs, M. (1985). The theory of experiential education. Boulder, CO: Association for Experiential Education.

Kultgen, J. (1988). Ethics and professionalism. Philadelphia, PA: University of Pennsylvania Press.

L., R. (1989). Quote from student evaluation form of a three-day course.

Lankton, S., & Lankton, C. (1983). The answer within: A clinical framework of Ericksonian hypnotherapy. New York: Brunner/Mazel.

Landry, P. (1986). The instructor's handbook. Thunder Bay, Ontario: Canadian Outward Bound Wilderness School.

Lazarus, R., & Launier, R. (1978). Stress-related transactions between person and environment. In L. Pervin and M. Lewis (Eds.), Perspectives in interactional psychology. New York: Plenum.

Lebow, J. L. (1987). Developing a personal integration in family therapy: Principles for model construction and practice. Journal of Marital and Family Therapy, 13, 1-14.

Leroy, E. (1983). Adventure and education. Journal of Experiential Education, 6, 18-22.

Levitt, L. (1982). How effective is wilderness therapy: A critical review. In F. E. Bolteler (Ed.), Proceedings: Wilderness Psychology Group Third Annual Conference (pp. 81-89).

Lincoln, Y. S. (1989). Qualitative research: A response to Atkinson, Delamont, and Hammersley. Review of Educational Research, 59, 237-239.

Lincoln, Y. S., & Guba, E. G. (1985). Naturalistic inquiry. Newbury Park, CA: Sage.

Loughmiller, C. (1965). Wilderness Road. University of Texas: Hogg Foundation.

Lord, L. J. (1987). Coming to grips with alcoholism. US News and World Report, 56-63.

Luckner, J. (1989). Effects of participation in an outdoor adventure education course on the self-concept of hearing-impaired individuals. American Annals of the Deaf, 134(1), 45-49.

MacArthur, R. (1987). Habits of the heart. Journal of Experiential Education, 10(1), 5-11.

Mace, D. (1979). Marriage and family enrichment: A new field? The Family Coordinator, 28(3), 409-419.

Mace, D., & Mace, V. (1986). The history and present status of the marriage and family enrichment movement. Journal of Psychotherapy and the Family, 2(1), 7-18.

Madanes, C. (1989). Strategic family therapy. San Francisco: Jossey-Bass.

Mahler, M. (1979). The selected papers of Margaret S. Mahler: Vol. II. Separation-Individuation. New York: Jason Aronson.

Mahler, M., Pine, F., & Bergman, A. (1975). The psychological birth of the human infant. New York: Basic Books.

Mahoney, M. J. (1986). Human change process. Seminar at the University of California at Santa Barbara.

Maluccio, A. (1979). Promoting competence through life experiences. In C. Germain (Ed.), Social work practice: People and environments. New York: Columbia University.

Marsh, H., & Richards, G. (1985). The Outward Bound bridging course for low-achieving high school males: Effect on academic achievement and multidimensional self-concepts. Unpublished manuscript. Department of Education, The University of Sydney, Australia.

Marx, J. D. (1988). An outdoor adventure counseling program for adolescents. Social Work, 33(6), 517-520.

Mason, M. (1987). Wilderness family therapy: Experiential dimensions. Contemporary Family Therapy, 9(1-2), 90-105.

Masterson, J. (1972). Treatment of the borderline adolescent: A developmental approach. New York: John Wiley.

McCartan, R. D. (1991). Personal communication. Assistant Attorney General of Washington, July 12.

McLellan, A. T., Luborsky, L., Woody, G. E., & O'Brien, C. P. (1980). An improved diagnostic evaluation instrument for substance abuse patients. Journal of Nervous and Mental Disease, 168(1), 26-33.

McNeil, K. A., Kelly, F. J., & McNeil, J. T. (1975). Testing research hypotheses using multiple linear regression. Carbondale, IL: Southern Illinois University Press.

Millerson, G. (1964). The qualifying associations. London: Routledge and Kegan Paul.

Miner, J. L., & Boldt, J. (1981). Outward Bound U.S.A.: Learning through experience in adventure-based education. New York: William Morrow.

Minuchin, S. (1974). Families and family therapy. Cambridge, MA: Harvard University Press.

Minuchin, S., & Fishman, H. C. (1981). Family therapy techniques. Cambridge, MA: Harvard University Press.

Mishe, J. (1985). The borderline adolescent. In C. B. Germain (Ed.), Advances in clinical social work. Silver Springs, MD: National Association of Social Workers.

Mitchell, R. G. (1983). Mountain experience: The psychology and sociology of adventure. Chicago: The University of Chicago Press, p. 178.

Moses, S. (1990, January). Morale programs face effectiveness questions. APA Monitor, p. 20.

Moustakas, C. (1959). Psychotherapy with children: The living relationship. New York: Ballantine.

Muley, M. (1991). Personal communication. Hurricane Outward Bound School, Florida, October 17.

Naches, A. M., & Roberts, J. A. (1967). An evaluation of several effects of the three ESEA "Dare to care" programs on evolved students, faculty, parents, and community members. Unpublished manuscript. Adams County School District #12, Denver, CO.

Nadler, R. S., & Luckner, J. L. (1992). Processing the adventure experience: Theory and practice. Iowa: Kendall/Hunt Publishing Company.

Napier, R. W., & Gershenfeld, M. K. (1983). Making groups work: A guide for group leaders. Boston: Houghton Mifflin.

Naranjo, C., & Ornstein, R. E. (1971). On the psychology of meditation. New York: Viking Press.

Newcomb, M. D., & Bentler, P. M. (1989). Substance use and abuse among children and teenagers. American Psychologist, 44, 242-248.

Nold, J., & Wilpers, M. (1975). Wilderness training as an alternative to incarceration. In C. R. Dodge (Ed.), A nation without prisons (pp. 155-170). Lexington, MA: Lexington Books.

Novak, M. (1976). The family out of favor. Harpers, 252, 42-45.

Nurenburg, S. (1985). Psychological development of borderline adolescents in wilderness therapy. An unpublished doctoral dissertation, Smith College School for Social Work.

O'Hanlon, W. H. (1990). A grand unified theory for brief therapy: putting problems in context. In J. K. Zeig & S. G. Gilligan (Eds.), Brief therapy: Myths, methods, and metaphors. New York: Brunner/Mazel.

O'Hanlon, W. H. (1988). Taproots. New York: Norton.

Oliver, J. (1988). An evaluation of the Colorado Outward Bound School's Survivor of Violence Recovery Program. Unpublished manuscript. Denver, CO: Colorado Outward Bound School.

Olson, D., & McCubbin, H. (1985). Family inventories: Inventories used in a national survey of families across the life cycle. St. Paul, MN: University of Minnesota Family Social Science.

Otto, H. A. (1975). Marriage and family enrichment programs in North America: Report and analysis. The Family Coordinator, 24(2), 137-142.

Otto, H. A. (1972). Fantasy encounter games. Los Angeles: Nash Publishing.

Outward Bound Brochure. (1979). Greenwich, CT.

Outward Bound alcohol and drug programs. (1983). Denver, CO: Colorado Outward Bound School.

Papp, P. (1983). The process of change. New York: The Guilford Press.

Papp, P. (1980). The Greek chorus and other techniques of family therapy. Family Process, 19, 45-57.

Parsons, M. H. (1980). Realizing part-time faculty potential: New directions for community colleges. San Francisco: Jossey-Bass.

Patton, M. Q. (1986). Utilization-focused evaluation. Newbury Park, CA: Sage.

Patton, M. Q. (1987). How to use qualitative methods in evaluation. Newbury Park, CA: Sage.

Perls, F. S. (1969). Gestalt therapy verbatim. Moab, UT: Real People Press.

Peters, T. J., & Waterman, R. H. (1982). In search of excellence. New York: Time Warner Books.

Pfirman, E. S. (1988). The effects of a wilderness challenge course on victims of rape in locus of control, self-concept, and fear. Unpublished manuscript. Greeley: University of Northern Colorado.

Piaget, J. (1977). Equilibration processes in the psychological development of the child. In H. E. Gruber and J. J. Voneche (Eds.), The Essential Piaget. New York: Basic Books.

Pill, C. J. (1990). Stepfamilies: Redefining the family. Family Relations, 39(2), 186-193.

Platt, J. J., & Spivack, G. (1983). Manual for the Means-Ends Problem-Solving Procedure (MEPS): A measure of interpersonal cognitive problem-solving skill. Philadelphia, PA: Hahnemann University School of Medicine.

Polez, D., & Rubitz, F. (1977). Staff perceptions of the effects of therapeutic camping upon psychiatric patients' attitudes. Therapeutic Recreation Journal, 1(2), 70-73.

Porter, W. (1975). The development and evaluation of a therapeutic wilderness program for problem youth. Unpublished master's thesis. Denver, CO: University of Denver.

Porter, R., & Cattell, R. (1975). Children's personality questionnaire handbook. Champaign, IL: Institute of Personality and Ability Testing.

Price, R. H., Cowen, E. L., Lorion, R. P., & Ramos-McKay, J. (1989). The search for effective programs: What we learned along the way. American Journal of Orthopsychiatry, 59, 49-58.

Priest, S. (1992). Questions about research in adventure education for the 1990s. In K. Henderson (Ed.), Proceedings Manual for the Research Symposium for the Coalition in the Outdoors.

Prigogine, I., & Stengers, I. (1984). Order out of chaos! Man's new dialogue with nature. New York: Bantam.

Project Apollo. (1976). A stress challenge approach to experiential learning: Accumulative results for September 1973 through December 1975 (Research Report). Murray, KY: Murray State University.

Quay, H. C., & Peterson, D. R. (1987). Revised behavior problem checklist. Odessa, FL: Psychological Assessment Resource.

Quinsland, L., & Van Ginkel, A. (1984). How to process experience. Journal of Experiential Education, 7(2).

Raths, L. E., Harmin, M., & Simon, S. B. (1966). Values and teaching: Working with values in the classroom. Columbus, OH: Charles E. Merrill.

Redl, F., & Wineman, D. (1965). Children Who Hate. New York: The Free Press.

Richards, A. (1981). Kurt Hahn: The midwife of educational ideas. Unpublished doctoral dissertation. Boulder, CO: University of Colorado.

Robb, G., Havens, M., & Witman, J. (1983). Special education, naturally. Bloomington, IN: Indiana University.

Roberts, A. (1989). Wilderness experiences: Camps and outdoor programs. In A. Roberts (Ed.), Juvenile Justice: Policies, Programs, and Services.

Rohnke, K. E. (1988). The bottomless bag. Hamilton, MA: K. E. Rohnke (available from the author).

Rohnke, K. E. (1989). Cowstails and cobras II. Hamilton, MA: Project Adventure.

Rogers, C. (1970). On encounter groups. New York: Harper and Row.

Rogers, C. R. (1961). On becoming a person. Boston: Houghton Mifflin.

Roland, C. (1985). The need for sequencing. The Roland Report, 1(3), 5-6. (Available from Roland & Associates, Inc., 41 Avon St., eene, NH 03431).

Roland, C. (1983). Outdoor managerial training programs: Do they "work"? In G. Robb (Ed.), The Bradford Papers, Volume III. Bloomington, IN: Indiana University.

Roland, C. (1982). Adventure education with people who are disabled. In G. Robb (Ed.), The Bradford Papers, Volume II, 39-51. Bloomington, IN: Indiana University.

Roland, C., & Havens, M. (1981). An introduction to adventure: A sequential approach to challenging activities with persons who are disabled. Loretto, MN: Vinland National Center.

Roland, C., Summers, S., Friedman, M., Barton, G., & McCarthy, K. (1987). Creation of an experiential challenge program. Therapeutic Recreation Journal, 21(2), 54-63.

Roland, C., Keene, T., Dubois, M., & Lentini, J. (1989). Experiential challenge program development in the mental health setting. The Bradford Papers Annual, Volume III. Martinsville, IN: Bradford Woods Outdoor Center.

Rosenthal, D. (1977). Genetic theory and abnormal behavior. New York: Academic Press.

Rosenthal, L. E. (1981). Risk exercise (RE) and the youth of today. Stress, Autumn, 9-14.

Rossi, E. L. (Ed.). (1980). The collected papers of Milton H. Erickson on hypnosis. New York: Irvington.

Sakofs, M. (1991). Assessing the impact of an Outward Bound program for adjudicated youth. Journal of Experiential Education, 14(2), 49.

Sattler, J. (1982). Assessment of children's intelligence and special abilities. New York: Allyn & Bacon.

Sawin, M. M. (1979). Family enrichment with family clusters. Valley Forge, PA: Judson Press.

Schoel, J., Prouty, D., & Radcliffe, P. (1988). Islands of healing: A guide to adventure-based counseling. Hamilton, MA: Project Adventure.

Selye, H. (1978). On the real benefits of eustress. Psychology Today, pp. 60-70.

Shader, R. I. (Ed.). (1975). Manual of psychiatric therapeutics: Practical psychopharmacology and psychiatry. Boston: Little, Brown.

Shader, R. I., DiMascio, A., et al. (1975). Psychotropic drug side effects. Baltimore, MD: Williams and Wilkins.

Shapiro, S. (1976). "Human Relations in Education" course taught at University of California at Santa Barbara.

Shroeder, H. M., & Leigh, R. E. (1967). Effects of Outward Bound training on urban youths. Unpublished manuscript. Princeton, NJ: Princeton University.

Shore, A. (1977). Outward Bound: A reference volume. NY: Lopp Litho.

Siegal, A. (1969). The effects of media violence on social learning. Violence and the media: A staff report to the National Commission on the Causes and Prevention of Violence. Washington, D.C.: U.S. Government Printing Office.

Simmel, G. (1973). On group size and quality of interaction. In E. H. Mizruchi (Ed.), Substance of sociology: Codes, conducts and consequences (2nd ed.) (pp. 161-166). New York: Meredith Corporation.

Simon, S., Howe, L., & Kirschbaum, H. (1972). Values Clarification. New York: Hart.

Smith, R., Schoffner, S., & Scott, J. (1979). Marriage and family enrichment: A new professional area. The Family Coordinator, 28(1), 87-93.

Smith, T. (1985). Real versus perceived risk. In G. Robb (Ed.), Issues in Challenge Education and Adventure Programming. Bloomington, IN: Indiana University.

Smith, T. (1982). Self-concept, special population and outdoor therapy. In G. Robb (Ed.), The Bradford Papers, Volume II. Bloomington, IN: Indiana University.

Smith, T. (1980). The sunrise model for outdoor education and outdoor therapy. In G. Robb (Ed.), The Bradford Papers, Volume I. Bloomington, IN: Indiana University.

Smith, T. E. (1981). Wilderness beyond...wilderness within. McHenry, IL.

Soreff, S., & Olsen, P. (1975). Emotional emergency. Emergency Medicine, 224-234.

Stanton, M. D. (1981). An integrated structural/strategic approach. Journal of Marital and Family Therapy, 7(4), 427-438.

State of Arizona. (1985). Article 73. Arizona Department of Economic Security, Mobile Program Agency Licensing Standards.

State of Florida. (1987). Chapter 10M-9.

State of Nevada. (1991). Nevada Assembly Bill 546, amending Nevada revised statutes, Chapter 432A (effective October 1, 1991).

State of New Jersey. (1991). New Jersey Administrative Code Chapter 128, Subchapter 9.

State of Utah. (1990). Utah Code 62A-2-1(18) & Utah Administration Code 804-8.

Stecher, B. M., & Davis, W. A. (1987). How to focus an evaluation. Newbury Park, CA: Sage.

Stevens, J. P. (1971). Awareness. Moab, UT: Real People Press.

Stich, T. F. (1983). Experiential Therapy. Journal of Experiential Education, 5(3), 24.

Stich, T., & Sussman, L. (1981). Outward Bound—An adjunctive psychiatric therapy: Preliminary research findings. Greenwich, CT: Outward Bound.

Stich T., & Senior, N. (1981). Adventure therapy: An innovative treatment for psychiatric patients. New Directions for Mental Health Services, 3(21), 103-108.

Stich, T. (Ed.). (1984). Outward Bound in alcohol treatment and mental health: a compilation of literature. Greenwich, CT: Outward Bound.

Stich, T., & Gaylord, M. (1983). Outward Bound: an innovative patient education program. Greenwich, CT: Outward Bound.

Stich, T., & Senior, N. (1984). Adventure therapy: An innovative treatment for psychiatric patients. In B. Pepper & E. Ryglewicz (Eds.), Advances in treating the young adult chronic patient: New directions for mental health services. San Francisco: Jossey-Bass.

Stich, T. F., & Gaylord, M. S. (1984). Risk management in adventure programs with special populations: Two hidden dangers. In T. F. Stich (Ed.), Outward Bound in alcohol treatment and mental health (pp. 161-173). Greenwich, CT: Outward Bound.

Strasburg, P. A. (1978). Violent delinquents: A report to the Ford Foundation from the Vera Institute of Justice. New York: Monarch.

Svobodny, L. (1979). Increasing self-concept through Outward Bound. Paper presented at the Annual International Convention, The Council For Exceptional Children, Dallas, TX.

Swain, M. (1986). The family cluster approach to enrichment. Journal of Psychotherapy and the Family, 2(1).

Teale, E. W. (Ed.). (1954). The wilderness world of John Muir (p. 319). Boston: Houghton Mifflin.

Teschner, D. P., & Walter, J. J. (1984). How to improve the hiring, training, and professional development of the staff. Journal of Experiential Education, 7(2), 14-22.

The core of learning is experience. (1991). Boulder, CO: Association for Experiential Education brochure.

Thompson, S. C. (1981). Will it hurt less if I can control it? A complex answer to a simple question. Psychological Bulletin, 96, 84-101.

Tobler, N. S. (1986). Meta-analysis of 143 drug prevention programs: Quantitative outcome results of program participants compared to a control or comparison group. Journal of Drug Issues, 56, 537-568.

Twelve steps and twelve traditions. (1981). New York: Alcoholics Anonymous World Services, Inc.

Unsoeld, W. (1974). Spiritual values of the wilderness. A presentation given at the 3rd Annual Convention of the Association for Experiential Education. Denver, CO: Colorado Outward Bound School.

Verma, S. (1984). Staff development: A systematic approach. Education Canada, 24(3), 9-13.

Vogler, D. E. (1980). In-service: Developing faculty strength. Community College Review, 8(4), 22-27.

Walker, L. (1984). The battered woman syndrome. NY: Harper & Row.

Walsh, V., & Golins, G. (1976). The exploration of the Outward Bound process. Denver, CO: Colorado Outward Bound School.

Wartik, N. (1986). Learning to dare again. MS Magazine.

Watzlawick, P., Weakland, J., & Fisch, R. (1974). Change: Principles of problem formation and problem resolution. New York: W. W. Norton.

Webster, S. (1989). Safety Standards for ropes course elements and initiatives. Hamilton, MA: Project Adventure.

Webster, S. (1989). Safety standards for ropes course elements and initiatives. Hamilton, MA: Project Adventure, p. 34.

Webster's third new international dictionary of the English language—unabridged. (1971). Chicago: Encyclopedia Britannica.

Wechsler, D. (1974). Manual for the Wechsler Intelligence Scale for Children—revised. New York: Psychological Corporation.

Weeks, G., & L'Abate, L. (1982). Paradoxical psychotherapy: Theory and practice with individuals, couples and families. New York: Brunner/Mazel.

Weeks, S. (1985). The effects of Sierra II, an adventure probation program, upon selected behavioral variables of adolescent juvenile delinquents. Dissertation Abstracts International, 46, 3607A.

Weinstein, M., & Goodman, J. (1980). Everybody's Guide to Noncompetitive Play: Playfair. San Luis Obispo, CA: Impact.

Wichmann, T. (1992). Of wilderness and circles: Evaluating a therapeutic model for wilderness adventure programs. Journal of Experiential Education, 14(2), 43-48.

Wichmann, T. F. (1990). Interpersonal problem solving and asocial behavior in a therapeutic wilderness program. Unpublished doctoral dissertation, Southern Illinois University, Carbondale, IL.

Wichmann, T. F. (1976). Affective role expectations for delinquent youth in environmental stress-challenge programs. Unpublished master's thesis, Southern Illinois University, Carbondale, IL.

Will, O. (1959). Human relatedness and the schizophrenic reaction. Psychiatry, 22(3), 205-223.

Wills, T. A., & Vaughn, R. (1989). Social support and substance use in early adolescence. Journal of Behavioral Medicine, 12(1), 321-339.

Wilson, R. (1991). Personal communication. Midlands Marine Institute, October 18.

William, H. C., & Chun, F. Y. (1973). Homeward Bound: An alternative to the institutionalization of adjudicated juvenile offenders. Federal Probation, 37, 52-57.

Winn, W. (1982). Physical challenge approaches to psychotherapy. In G. T. Nickerson & K. S. O'Laughlin (Eds.), Helping through action: Action oriented therapies (pp.163-168). Amherst, MA: Human Resource Development Press.

Winnicott, D. (1965). The maturational process and the facilitating environment. London: Hogarth.

Winterdyk, J., & Griffiths, C. (1984). Wilderness experience programs: Reforming delinquents or beating around the bush? Juvenile & Family Court Journal, 35, 36-38.

Witman, J. (1987). The efficacy of adventure programming in the development of cooperation and trust with adolescents in treatment. Therapeutic Recreation Journal, 21(3), 23-29.

Whitaker, C. A., & Malone, T. P. (1981). The roots of psychotherapy. New York: Brunner/Mazel.

White, H., & Fadiman, J. (1976). Relax. The Confucian Press.

White, M., and Epston, D. (1990). Narrative means to therapeutic ends. New York: W. W. Norton.

White, R. (1959). Motivation reconsidered: The concept of competence. The Psychological Review, 66, 297-333.

Woodside, M. (1986). Familial patterns of alcoholism. In D. Lewis and C. Williams (Eds.), Providing Care for Children of Alcoholics (pp. 31-37). Deerfield Beach, FL: Health Communications.

Wright, A. (1982). Therapeutic potential of the Outward Bound process: An evaluation of a treatment program for juvenile delinquents (Doctoral dissertation, Pennsylvania State University, 1982). Dissertation Abstracts International, 43, 923A.

Yalom, I. D. (1975). The theory and practice of group psychotherapy. New York: Basic Books.

Zeig, J. (1980). A teaching seminar with Milton Erickson. New York: Brunner/Mazel.

Zelman, S., and Guillan, R. (1970). Heat stroke in phenothiazine-treated patients: A report of three fatalities. American Journal of Psychiatry, 126, 1787-1790.

Zuckermann, M. (1979). Sensation seeking: Beyond the optimal level of arousal. Hillsdale, NJ: Eribaum.

Index

A

B

D

E

F

ADVENTURE THERAPY

J

Jesness Inventory   382
Julia Dyckman Andrus Memorial   179

K

Kaplan, Stephen   44
Kimball, Richard   153, 323
Kinetic learning methods   391

L

Leadership issues   184, 241, 362
Leadership styles   184
Learning
  consequential learning   190
  Interpersonal problem solving skills   355
  stages   232
Legal issues   441
Levenson Locus of Control   398
Limit setting   88
Listening   241, 294
Locus of control   380, 398

M

Marketing   205
Maslow, Abraham   191
Means-Ends Problem Solving (MEPS) Proce-
    dure   352, 383, 401, 404, 406
Medication
  contraindications   161
Metaphor
  processing   220, 224, 249
  use   50
Minnesota Multiphasic Personality Inventory (MMPI)   343, 395
Models   199, 255
Modified Fear Survey   398
"Mountains Speak for Themselves" processing
    mode   220, 221, 224, 226
Muir, John   43

N

Narcotics Anonymous 336, 338
Nashua Brookside Hospital 196
Natural consequences 25
Naturalistic evaluation 359, 364, 396
New York State Division for Youth (DFY) 189
Novelty of setting 63
Nowicki Strickland Locus-of-Control Scale for Children 380, 401

O

Outpatient programs 331
Outward Bound 12, 95, 150, 201, 215, 324
"Outward Bound Plus" processing model 220, 222, 226, 249

P

Paradox 131, 259
Parson's staff development model 434
Personal Assessment of Intimacy in Relationships (PAIR) 393
Physical fitness 37, 52
Piers Harris Children's Self-Concept Scale 380
Play 109
Policy studies 442
Problem-Solving Meeting Questionnaire 403
Processing/Debriefing 105, 199, 212, 219, 336
   alternative 289
   circle-up 349
   considerations 237
   definition 219
   designing 231
   emergency procedures 165, 288
   focusing 234
   non-verbal techniques 295
   purposes of 219
   sample questions 239
   traditional processing problems 285
Professional relationships 454
Professional responsibility 453
Professionalism 411

T

U

W

ADDITIONAL BOOKS FROM
THE ASSOCIATION FOR EXPERIENTIAL EDUCATION
PUBLISHED BY KENDALL/HUNT

THE THEORY OF EXPERIENTIAL EDUCATION, THIRD EDITION
Karen Warren, Mitchell Sakofs, and Jasper S. Hunt, Jr., editors
ISBN #0-7872-0262-2
The third edition of this groundbreaking book looks at the theoretical foundations of experiential education from a philosophical, historical, psychological, spiritual, and international perspective.
AEE Member price $30.00/Non-member $38.95

EXPERIENTIAL LEARNING IN SCHOOLS AND HIGHER EDUCATION
Richard Kraft and Jim Kielsmeier, editors
ISBN #0-7872-0183-9
This expanded anthology contains some of the best articles published in the *Journal of Experiential Education* to address the role of experiential education at all levels of schooling. General theory, service-learning, research and evaluation, cultural journalism, the environment, and practical ideas are just some of the subjects covered.
AEE Member price $30.00/Non-member $38.95

ETHICAL ISSUES IN EXPERIENTIAL EDUCATION, SECOND EDITION
by Jasper S. Hunt, Jr.
ISBN #0-8403-9038-6
An examination of the current ethical issues in the field of adventure programming and experiential education. Examples of topics include: ethical theory, informed consent, sexual issues, student rights, environmental concerns, and programming practices.
Member price $16.00/Non-member $23.00

BOOK OF METAPHORS, VOLUME II
by Michael Gass, Ph.D.
ISBN #0-7872-0306-8
A compilation of presentations, many of them therapeutic or corporate in nature, designed to enhance learning for clients participating in experience-based programs. The presentations cover topics such as assessment and ethics, steps for framing experiences, logistics, verbal introductions, and debriefing.
Price TBA

To order a title call Kendall/Hunt Publishing Company at (800) 228-0810.